Strategies for
Joint Ventures

Other Books

by

Kathryn Rudie Harrigan

Strategies for Declining Businesses
(1980)

Strategies for Vertical Integration
(1983)

Strategic Flexibility:
A Management Guide for Changing Times
(1985)

Managing for JointVenture Success
(1986)

These titles are published by
Lexington Books

Strategies for
Joint Ventures

Kathryn Rudie Harrigan
Columbia University

Lexington Books
D.C. Heath and Company/Lexington, Massachusetts/Toronto

Library of Congress Cataloging in Publication Data

Harrigan, Kathryn Rudie.
    Strategies for joint ventures.

    Includes index.
    1. Joint ventures—United States. I. Title.
HD62.47.H37   1985   338.8′ 8973   85-40110
ISBN 0-669-10448-5 (alk. paper)

Second printing, February 1987
Published simultaneously in Canada
Printed in the United States of America
International Standard Book Number: 0-669-10448-5
Library of Congress Catalog Card Number: 85-40110

The paper used in this publication meets the minimum requirements of American National
Standard for Information Sciences—Permanence of Paper for Printed Library Materials,
ANSI Z39.48-1984.
∞ TM

Contents

Figures

Tables

Foreword

Our enterprise system is on trial. Companies are now expected to provide sustained growth in the face of global competition and social constraints. And this pressure has fomented a search for creative ways to improve our adaptability in managing business firms.

Joint ventures provide one of the hopes. By combining strengths from two or three companies perhaps we can find new benefits from cooperation and improve productivity. The pooling of complementary strengths in a separate, new venture is the key. Through such a device it may be possible to achieve more effective use of resources, to adjust more quickly to new technology, or to gain access to large-scale economies. Indeed, during the last few years the number of domestic joint ventures has increased sharply.

This book is the first in-depth analysis of *domestic* joint ventures. It moves far beyond a listing of situations where joint ventures might be productive—and the usual antitrust strictures on where not to step. Instead, the main focus is on where and how companies can build cooperative arrangements that enable them to make advances which they *could not make alone*.

The evidence shows, however, that a joint venture is a delicate undertaking. Tender, loving care is frequently required if the potential benefits are to be realized.

This study includes the following distinctive contributions.

1. An *analytical framework* provides prospective cooperating firms with a guide to the possible benefits and pitfalls of using joint ventures. The framework indicates important considerations for each stage from first contemplating cooperation to dissolving the partnership after it ceases to serve both parties well.

2. The viability of the joint venture itself—the *newly created entity*—is of critical importance. The cooperating companies, the "parents," each have their own distinct objectives; but these objectives will be served only if the new venture, the "child," is provided with enough resources and enough independence to become a sound operating unit. A joint venture must be considered as a *troika*—the child as well as its parents.

3. Problems of operating a joint venture, after it is established, require continuing involvement. The study shows that the *interactions between the child and each parent* are sensitive. What to share, what to protect, what is fair for each parent—such questions as these are never fully answered. Who really governs is more important than the distribution of stock ownership.

4. The *passage of time* is likely to modify what each parent wants from a specific joint venture. Partly this reflects the degree of success of the child. However, changes in the interests, the available resources, and the relative bargaining power of each parent often sharply alter what a parent seeks. Because of this inevitable shift in the viewpoints of members of the troika, the analytical framework includes change over time as a critical feature of joint venture management.

5. The analysis shows that joint ventures typically are an *unstable form of organization*. Even when the child prospers, one parent is likely to buy out the interests of the other. New alignments are fashioned. Such instability does not mean that establishing the joint venture was unwise. During its life it may have served a very useful purpose. But, at least in the domestic arena, joint ventures usually are transitional arrangements.

The exploratory nature of the study flushed out many other concepts and insights. After developing the analytical framework, Harrigan tested the framework in different industries. She examined background and success of 492 specific joint ventures and 392 other cooperative arrangements, and summarizes this experience in chapters 13 through 15. No other study has analyzed the individual characteristics of such a wide array of joint ventures. Moreover, much of the existing literature focuses on foreign joint ventures, whereas this investigation concentrates on U.S. domestic ventures.

The research approach is similar to Harrigan's study of *Strategies for Vertical Integration*. The data base is much broader than a few case studies. Indeed, it invites comparison of experience in industries with varying characteristics. However, each joint venture received individual attention. There is a depth of analysis that is not possible in studies that rely on remote, abstracted statistical figures.

Because it is exploratory, the study raises more questions than it answers. Ideas for possible action abound, but no simple formulas are presented. Rather, the book is a gold mine of information and insights; managers dealing with joint venture problems must do their own digging and sorting for guidance on their specific situation.

With this book we have a quantum increase in the available knowledge about designing and managing joint ventures.

William H. Newman
Chairman, Strategy Research Center
Graduate School of Business
Columbia University

Preface

My study of domestic joint-venture strategies offers a normative framework to analyze a chaotic topic. It explains, in part, why certain patterns of cooperative strategies have been more prevalent within some U.S. industries than within others. It also suggests which joint-venture strategies are inappropriate within certain corporate and competitive contexts. My "tool kit" is the literature of strategic management and, particularly, of industrial organization economics. It draws upon the case research tradition of industrial economists, such as Markham, MacKie, and Tennant—who used industry studies to test theories concerning competition. It follows the tradition of Chandler, Caves, Porter, Rumelt, and others in synthesizing theoretical constructs from industrial economics with those of corporate strategy in order to develop frameworks of industry and competitor dynamics.

A framework for using joint ventures is posited. It contrasts which cooperative strategies work best in various competitive environments: (1) capital-intensive versus labor-intensive industries; (2) those where products can be differentiated effectively versus those where products are treated like commodities; (3) industries characterized by rapid technological change versus those where technologies change slowly; (4) industries where competitors offer services versus manufactured products; (5) embryonic industries versus those where relationships between buyers and suppliers, product standards, and other norms of competition have been better established; and (6) industries characterized by local versus international versus global competition. The chapters that examine differences in joint-venture practice by industry conform to these key structural traits. Thus this study follows the traditions of industrial organization economics research.

Issues of integration and the creation of corporate synergies are also examined in this study, and their consideration follows traditions of research in strategic management. In my study of joint ventures, I have encountered two kinds of U.S. firms—those that have used joint ventures successfully and those that have not. One benefit of a hybrid study, such as mine, is the ability to compare common issues of joint-venture formulation, operation, and termination across and within industries in order to unearth patterns of success. Specifically, this study notes recurring patterns of behaviors concerning (1) which types of firms formed alliances; (2) for which purposes; and with (3) what provisions for raw materials, supplies of components, or other ways to obtain necessary inputs as well as provisions for selling the joint venture's outputs. It assesses whether these terms made any difference in joint-venture success. Comparisons across industries provided insights concerning (1) which types of firms coordinated their joint ventures closely with their ongoing business activities, (2) which types of firms duplicated facilities in their joint ventures that paralleled those of wholly owned business units, and (3) which types of firms placed all assets for some activities within their joint ventures to avoid internecine conflicts. It suggests which parent–child arrangements were more prevalent (and appropriate) within which types of industries.

My research is presented in a uniform and straightforward format that allows readers to skim those industry chapters of lesser interest and concentrate on the competitive issues of greatest interest to them. The history of U.S. joint ventures is sketched in chapter 1, and the uses of joint ventures (which motivated the 884 alliances of this study) are enumerated in chapter 2. The three perspectives of the joint-venture strategy model—(1) partner-to-partner; (2) parent-to-child; and (3) child as competitor in a specific industry context— are presented in chapters 3 through 5, and their robustness is assessed in the summaries contained in chapters 13 through 16. Business practitioners may wish to jump immediately to the summary chapters and to digest the strategy model of chapters 3, 4, and 5 for greater understanding later.

Academicians will note in chapter 6 that the industry chapters follow a structure that parallels the three perspectives of the joint-venture strategy model. The industry chapters present both data and evaluations of the model. The joint ventures and other forms of cooperative strategy reported in the industry chapters are reported chronologically, by parent firms, in order (1) to show which firms were most likely to use cooperation as a strategy option and (2) to illustrate the *oligopolistic response* aspect of competitive behavior. Briefly, firms copied their competitors' behaviors under conditions of great demand or structural uncertainty. When customer characteristics were better understood, technology had been proven, product standards were well established, or other uncertainties concerning how to satisfy customer demand most effectively had been resolved, firms were more individualistic in their uses of joint-venture strategies.

Finally, as chapter 2 notes (and chapter 16 reemphasizes) government policies motivate some joint ventures and discourage other combinations. A clearer understanding of how U.S. firms have used this strategy option to cope with the risks, costs, and other uncertainties of doing business should suggest more enlightened policies of economic regulation for (1) firms' uses of joint ventures within the United States and (2) for the competitive conditions that motivated firms' uses of joint ventures to cope with adversity.

Acknowledgments

F unding for travel, telephone interviews, research assistants, and typing was made possible by grants from the Strategy Research Center and the Committee on Faculty Research, Columbia Business School. Thanks to Dean John C. Burton for this generous assistance. I am especially grateful to the corporations that support the Strategy Research Center; their funding greatly facilitates our scholarly investigations of strategic management issues.

Enthusiastic research assistants at Columbia Business School collected photocopies and background materials for each industry. They include Holly Wallace, M.B.A. 1983 (of Merrill, Lynch), Elizabeth J. Gordon, M.B.A. 1983 (of Time, Inc. Video Group), John Richardson Thomas, M.B.A. 1983 (of Topaz, Inc.), Mary Ellen Waller (M.B.A. 1982), and Stanley Seth (M.B.A. 1983). Chapters 11 and 12 draw on materials from an earlier study where Stanley W. Herman (M.B.A. 1982) and Paul A. Gelburd, M.B.A. 1982 (of Morgan Stanley) were of great assistance. Special thanks are due to Harold Hamman Martin, J.D.-M.B.A. 1982 (of Shearman & Sterling), for legal research assistance and to Carlos Garcia, M.B.A. 1984 (of Pfizer, Inc.) for computer programming and other valuable assistance.

Nida T. Backaitis and John G. Michel, doctoral candidates at Columbia University, deserve extraordinary recognition as research assistants, for they carried the burden of exhausting hours of photocopying, assembling industry briefing papers, and providing helpful summaries of these materials to supplement my field interviews. The quality of chapters 7 through 12 was improved greatly because John's and Nida's skills and efforts far exceeded that normally found in research assistants. John Michel went the "extra mile" by providing internal memoranda concerning his analyses of joint-venture patterns in the petrochemicals, pharmaceuticals, medical products, genetic engineering, steel, and electronic components industries. Schooled as they are in industrial organization economics as well as strategic management, I have no doubt that Nida Backaitis and John Michel will each make extraordinary scholarly contributions to the field of management. John and Nida are also much appreciated for their labors as my teaching assistants, for they ensured (along with Christopher Hanson, Ph.D. candidate, of Pappas, Carter, Evans & Koop Pty Ltd., Melbourne) that I was well prepared to teach my M.B.A.-level business policy classes, as well as my M.B.A.-level and doctoral-level seminars on competitive strategy.

Many colleagues helped me by providing materials, suggestions, and comments on the manuscript at various stages of its development. At the risk of slighting helpful questions and other academic assistance received, I thank in particular William H. Newman, Samuel Bronfman Professor of Democratic Business Enterprise and chairman of the Strategy Research Center, for his valuable ideas and encouraging comments all through this research program, and Donald C. Hambrick, director of the Strategy Research Center. I thank my colleagues at Columbia, Robert Drazin, James W. Fredrickson, Leonard Sayles, Michael Tushman, E. Kirby Warren, Samuel Bronfman Professor of Democratic Business Enterprise, and Bob Yavitz, Paul Garrett Professor of Public Policy and Business Responsibility, for their comments on my manuscripts. I thank Richard E. Caves and Michael E. Porter of Harvard University, Sanford Berg of the University of Florida, Jerome Duncan of the University of Manitoba, Barry Haimes (Kidder, Peabody), Richard Rumelt, William Ouchi, Mitchell P. Koza, and Srinivasan "Cheenu" Balakrishnan of the University of California at Los Angeles, Henry Mintzberg of McGill University, John R. Schermerhorn, Jr., of Southern Illinois University, Cynthia Spanhel of the University of Texas, Ram Charan, and Milton Handler of Kaye Scholer, Fierman, Hays & Handler for their contributions of materials and suggestions.

Dr. Mary Anne Devanna, the administrator of the Strategy Research Center's funds, and Gayle Lane managed the financial details of this study. Maxine Braiterman, Marta Torres, and especially Lisa Lowell and Maureen Gelber typed endless versions of this manuscript under great time pressures while maintaining their sense of humor. Jeff Jullich ("the fastest ten fingers on earth") provided extraordinary typing assistance with interview tapes (to create source files) and industry studies. I am grateful that Viviane Bennaroch helped stuff envelopes and pitched in on the typing quagmire when the work load grew immense. She gave new meaning to the word *vivacious*. Lydia Fatjo-Santiago remained composed and efficient as she managed the spider's web of telephone messages we created. Carol Landes and Linda Brodzinski in the Office of Support Services provided extra helpers—additional typing, transcribing, and telephone assistance for which I am grateful. Most notably, I am grateful to have the help of Joy Glazener, the superstar who typed original manuscripts, transcribed tapes, input industry studies into my personal computer, coordinated the mailings, synchronized the photocopying with my eleventh-hour demands, immersed herself in the word processing challenge, and performed other herculean tasks to ensure the manuscript's timely completion. With this book, Joy moves from beatification to canonization because her enthusiasm and willingness to help in every way and at all times to move this manuscript to completion were truly selfless.

This study could not have been completed without the assistance and information provided by many executives (who must remain anonymous). They completed my questionnaires, answered my telephone questions, unearthed archival data, commented on several versions of background papers, chapter drafts, and other materials, and granted me their precious time for personal interviews and for other tasks associated with the Delphi study. Their feedback has been extremely useful in clarifying points about the use of joint-venture strategies. I commend their enthusiasm in responding to each iteration and their willingness to help academic researchers to study complex and sensitive topics in strategic management. Relevant academic research concerning strategic management requires that managers will bring their firms into our laboratory and let us dissect their decisions. For this help, I am truly grateful.

Don Hambrick was extraordinarily helpful in reading chapter drafts and giving me timely and constructive criticism. I commend his willingness to help junior researchers, for Don's example sets the tone for colleagial behavior that makes the Columbia Business School a leading forum for research in management.

Again I acknowledge the enormous intellectual debt owed to William H. Newman, a paragon and pioneer in the field of strategic management. As director of the Strategy Research Center, he funded my research. As a colleague, Bill always found time to give me great ideas and thoughtful, detailed comments on chapter drafts (even under impossible timetables), as he crisscrossed the nation by plane. His unabashed enthusiasm for this research effort and for the idea of doing research is inspiring to young faculty. His candor in giving feedback concerning findings and their presentation greatly accelerated the progress of this study. Bill's zeal in finding a clear way to explain a complex model has been both encouraging and awe-inspiring.

The Columbia Business School and its Management of Organizations faculty are uniquely positioned to support empirical research in strategic management. I have benefited greatly from exposure to its culture. Flaws in this manuscript are mine alone; excellence is due to the splendid colleagues, the generous support, and the many other virtures of Columbia University.

1
Domestic Joint Ventures

As business risks soar and competition becomes more volatile, firms have embraced joint ventures with increasing frequency. This pattern should not be surprising. Joint ventures have long been used by entrepreneurial firms to expand into new businesses and tap new markets, particularly within newly industrializing nations. What is surprising, however, is a pattern that indicates that joint ventures are now being used voluntarily as a strategy option within mature economies, such as the U.S. economy.

This new use of joint ventures is a change in corporate practice that has not been chronicled adequately. This shortfall in the strategic management literature reflects a serious weakness in what managers know about cooperative strategies. Investigations into the efficacy of joint ventures (and other forms of cooperative strategies) are especially timely now because some governments, like that of the United States, have recently taken a friendlier attitude toward the use of joint ventures.[1] Moreover, cooperative strategies can change industry structures in a manner that could lead to significant changes in competitive behavior. Their widespread use could exacerbate competition or stabilize profit levels, depending on how domestic joint ventures are lawfully used.

This chapter sketches how the use of joint ventures (and other cooperative strategies that are sketched in its appendix) has changed over time and why this strategy is now of increasing interest in firms' home markets. It presents an overview of the theory that is developed in chapters 3, 4, and 5 and tested in subsequent chapters, using industry examples.

Joint Ventures in Mature Economies

Previous discussions of joint ventures have often considered cooperative strategies from the perspective of firms that were expanding their domains overseas.[2] Entry by U.S. firms, for example, into overseas markets often required them to take local firms as partners. Asymmetries in partners' resources, technologies, managerial systems, and experiences frequently translated into asymmetrical managerial control over joint ventures in these studies, although proceeds were split in proportion to equity shares. Decision making was not truly shared because one partner took a passive role. (In earlier studies, passive partners were often considered to be the *best* joint-venture partners; they caused fewer hassles.)

When joint ventures are entered into voluntarily and are meant to be more than risk-sharing or financing arrangements, however, strategists must leave behind the old view of them as inadequate; a different set of issues becomes germane when joint ventures are a strategic option. Past studies, for example, have devoted little attention to the use of joint ventures as a competitive weapon within mature economies. They have overlooked the use of joint ventures as a new approach to global competition, technology transfer, or other strategic challenges. There has been no discussion, for example, of whether different competitive circumstances or environmental conditions make the use of joint ventures more (or less) appropriate as a strategy option. Little thought has been given to the question of how domestic firms in mature economies might best respond to the plethora of new alliances they may face as competitors if the use of joint ventures becomes widespread. The issue of child-firm viability has received scant attention.[3]

These questions are of interest because analyses of different competitive practices (like those of Japanese firms, for example) have revealed different attitudes regarding interfirm cooperation than those traditionally harbored by Western competitors. There is curiosity regarding whether such cooperative strategies are in any way superior to how firms usually approach competitive strategy formulation. The media make the recent burst of joint-venture announcements look like a stampede. Consequently, novice firms are now plunging into cooperative strategies without seeing the pitfalls those strategies may entail. These problems arise because few firms based in countries with mature economies used domestic joint ventures prior to the 1980s (particularly in the United States). Firms forging alliances in such economies for the first time now are often unaware of the strategic issues surrounding joint ventures.

Joint Ventures Defined

In this study, joint ventures are separate entities with two or more active businesses as parents. Examples include TriStar Pictures (Columbia Pictures, CBS, and Home Box Office), Satellite Business Systems (IBM and Aetna Life & Casualty) and Genecor (Corning Glass Works and Genentech), among others.

"Operating Joint Ventures." This study emphasizes "operating joint ventures," those partnerships by which two or more firms create an entity to carry out a productive economic activity and take an active role in decision making, if not also in operations. (The joint ventures studied herein do *not* include passive financial investments made by parties that are not involved in the new entity's strategic business decisions. Thus, most real estate partnerships where one or more partners are passive investors are excluded. Limited partnerships undertaken to drill for oil or make movies are also excluded, where financing partners are passive.)

The scope of the joint ventures examined herein could include manufacturing arrangements (for example, the 1976 agreement among McDonnell-Douglas, Boeing, the French firm Dessault-Bereguet Aerospace, and the Japanese firms Mitsubishi, Kawasaki, and Fuji to make jets), and distribution arrangements (for example, the creation of Siemens-Allis in 1977 to sell electric utility products such as switchgear), as well as research and development arrangements (such as the Microelectronics and Computer Technology Corp.). Because they are *operating* joint ventures, each parent makes a substantial equity contribution in the form of capital and technology, marketing experience, personnel, or physical assets. But most important, actively involved parents contribute their access to distribution networks. (If neither partner controls such access, the likelihood of success for the joint venture will be reduced, as is explained in chapters 3, 4, and 5.) Access to local markets is a necessary ingredient for success.

"Spider's Web" Joint Ventures. "Spider's web" joint ventures link many firms to one pivotal partner. Depending on the needs of each partner and the sensitivity of information and resources to be exchanged, a domestic firm could forge a variety of patterns for cooperation that keep outsiders at bay while strengthening its own position. In this manner, a smaller firm might establish joint ventures with different large competitors to form a counterbalancing pattern of agreements. Thus, a player might hedge its bets concerning which firms will eventually attain dominance in a particular industry. The spider's web is the opposite of a strategy whereby firms pick the future industry champion early and bet all resources on it to get an exclusive joint venture. Powerful firms can form spider's webs of joint ventures with themselves at the hub of the web while holding their partners to exclusive partnerships with them alone. Chapters 3, 4, and 5 suggest when firms can and should practice polygamy.

An Emphasis on the "Child." The primary emphasis of this analysis is on the viability of the "child," the entity created by partners for a specific activity. This is an area that needs investigation because insufficient thought was given to making the child capable of standing on its own in many joint ventures that failed (or never came to fruition). Parent firms' relationships with their child are crucial to joint-venture success. But parents must make certain adjustments to their strategies to make their child a viable competitor. Thus the dynamics of parent–child relationships dominate joint-venture success. The logic of competitive strategy must be reworked to recognize the interdependencies that may exist (and be exploited) between parents and child when joint ventures are embraced.

Other Forms of Cooperative Strategy

Other forms of cooperative strategy range from acquisitions (where one firm absorbs another) to informal agreements to work together where firms pool their resources and knowledge. As table 1–1 indicates, the cooperative strategy alternatives differ in their proportions of ownership equity and control over joint activities.

Some firms can attain their objectives through *wholly owned* business units that have been obtained (or developed) through mergers, acquisitions, or programs for internal venture development. These arrangements give firms *full equity ownership* of assets and skills, as well as full responsibility for the risks they will face when diversifying.

At the other extreme, in table 1–1, are nonequity arrangements such as cooperative agreements, R&D partnerships, cross-licensing (or cross-distribution agreements), and other joint activities. These do not create a separate entity, and they involve no equity ownership. Consequently, they provide the least control over the very assets and skills firms may seek. Between these extremes are minority investments (and operating joint ventures), options that give firms partial equity control of the resources needed to diversify. These arrangements may provide for contractual controls as well, but only *operating* joint ventures will create new entities with shared ownership and shared managerial controls. The benefits and costs of these strategies are contrasted with joint ventures in appendix 1A.

Table 1–1
Cooperative Strategy Alternatives

Full Ownership Control	Partial Ownership and Contractual Control	Contractual Control Only
Mergers (or acquisitions)	Operating joint ventures	Cooperative agreements
Internal ventures (and spin-offs to full business unit status)	Minority investments	R&D partnerships
		Cross-licensing or cross-distribution arrangements
		Joint activities

Joint Venture as a Key Strategic Decision

The joint venture (and other forms of cooperative strategies) is one of the firm's key corporate strategy decisions—along with entry, exit, capacity expansion, and diversification—but despite its importance, the cooperative strategy decision has not been well understood. Firms need a framework for coping with joint ventures, or they cannot expect to use this strategy effectively. They need a calculus to help them make the cost–benefit tradeoffs that confront them when evaluating joint-venture proposals. They need to understand the forces that increase the value of a joint venture (or accelerate its dissolution) so that they may manage these forces to their best advantage. They must realize how their parochial concerns prevent joint ventures from being viable. These, and other issues concerning joint-venture strategies, are explored in this study.

A New Look at Joint Ventures

To set the stage for the framework presented in chapters 3, 4, and 5, the historical view of domestic joint ventures is contrasted with how firms use joint ventures in mature economies like the United States in the 1980s. Briefly, firms now use joint ventures differently than they have in the past because they have found that joint ventures offer better ways to cope with the competitive challenges of rapid technological change, increasing interdependencies between industries and global competition rather than go it alone.

A Brief History

In the past, *joint ventures* were defined in law as partnerships. (Many early studies of joint ventures did not distinguish between active and passive parents; few were interested specifically in *operating* joint ventures.) Some joint ventures were corporations whose stocks were owned by at least two other corporations and that engaged in a business different from that of the parents (even if the difference was merely geographical). Some incorporated joint ventures issued their own securities. But the *partnership* form of joint venture offered parents the greatest *flexibility*, if it was well structured.

Joint ventures originated as commercial or maritime enterprises used for trading purposes. They were one of the oldest ways of transacting business and were originally used as a commercial device by the merchants of ancient Egypt, Babylonia, Phoenicia, and Syria to conduct sizable commercial and trading operations, often overseas. Subsequently joint ventures were used by the merchants of Great Britain in the fifteenth and sixteenth centuries, and companies of leisure class adventurers were organized through joint ventures to carry on trade and to exploit the resources of various far corners of the globe, such as America and India.[4]

Use of joint ventures in the United States dates back at least to 1880 when railroads used joint ventures for large-scale projects. Partnerships for mining may be even older. Early in the twentieth century joint ventures were formed in the United States to pool risks in shipping, gold exploration, and other undertakings. One of the largest projects ever to be conducted as a joint venture involved the apportionment and development of crude oil reserves in the Middle East by four American oil companies in ARAMCO.[5] During the 1950s joint ventures became more popular as vehicles for U.S. business enterprise, and by 1959 at least 345 domestic joint ventures were operated by the 1,000 largest corporations.[6] These early joint ventures were often vertical arrangements undertaken by two or more competitors, such as the joint venture between Pechiney Ugine Kuhlman's Howmet and Alumax (itself a joint venture between AMAX and Mitsui) to share primary aluminum reduction plants for a supplying facility. Firms like these shared their supplier's capacity because the minimum efficient scale of an upstream plant was often so large that no firm could utilize its full output alone. Moreover, there were substantial scale *diseconomies* in running these plants below their engineered capacities.

Joint ventures have become a way of life for some industries, such as offshore oil exploration or jet engines. Joint ventures of all types abounded in entertainment in the 1960s, such as co-production in motion pictures and television, joint production of phonograph records, joint holdings of theaters, and so on. When the Federal Trade Commission (FTC) examined U.S. joint ventures during the 1960s, it found that 66 percent of them were in the manufacturing sectors, with 72 percent of that subset in four industry groups: paper products (for example, Washington Post, Inc., and Dow, Jones Co., or Coastal Lumber and James River Corp.) (SIC 26); chemicals (for example, American Cyanamid and Pittsburgh Plate Glass) (SIC 28); stone, clay, and glass (for example, Lafarge (the leading French firm) and Lone Star Industries) (SIC 32); and primary metals (including, for example, several ocean mining ventures, such as (1) Kennecott Copper, Rio Tinto-Zinc Corp., Consolidated Gold Fields, Ltd., British Petroleum, Mitsubishi, and Noranda Mines, Ltd.; (2) U.S. Steel, Sun Co., and Union (Belgium) Miniere; (3) Lockheed Missiles & Space, Billiton International Metals (of Royal Dutch/Shell), Amoco Minerals Co., and Bos Kalis Westminster Group; and (4) a venture comprised of Inco, Ltd., Sedco, Inc., a group of German companies, and six Japanese companies, respectively) (SIC 33). Over half of the FTC's list was comprised of chemical joint ventures (like Owens Corning Fiberglas Co., Dow Corning Corp., Koppers Pittsburgh Co., and Mobay Chemical Co., for example), and 90 percent of them were engaged primarily in the production of fibers, plastics, and rubbers (SIC 282), basic chemicals (SIC 281), or drugs and medicines (SIC 283).[7] During the years

1960 to 1968, the FTC reported that at least 1,131 U.S. firms were involved in the formation of over 520 domestic joint ventures and that these were primarily in the manufacturing sector.

Duncan's 1980 empirical study of U.S. domestic joint ventures reinforced this old picture of how firms used this strategy option. Table 1–2 illustrates the distribution of domestic joint-venture announcements, using Duncan's 1980 database, which terminated with 1975 announcements of joint ventures. The experiences of U.S. firms in forming and managing domestic cooperative strategies shown in table 1–2 does not seem large when compared with that of firms based on the European Economic Community (EEC), however. (It is difficult to compare the experiences of U.S. firms with those of European firms because records of the exact number of domestic EEC joint ventures are not highly reliable; one effort to register such arrangements flooded regulators' offices with between 60,000 and 120,000 notifications of joint-venture activity.)[8] U.S. firms are just now beginning to consider the evidence concerning the attractiveness of joint-venture strategies. This study emphasizes U.S. domestic joint-venture experiences *after* 1975, the period Duncan's 1980 study did not address.

An Explosion in Joint-Venture Activity

Since 1978 the use of joint ventures within mature economies like the United States has blossomed due to the many technological and economic changes that precipitated deregulation, globalization, and increasing emphasis on the need for product innovation. In 1983 alone the number of cooperative strategies announced in some industries, like communications systems and services, exceeded the sum of all previously announced U.S. joint ventures in that sector, as table 1–3 illustrates. By 1985 domestic joint ventures had become an important means of supplementing strengths and covering weaknesses within the United States and other mature economies. The willingness of firms to contemplate cooperative strategies where previously they would not do so represented a watershed in their way of thinking about business strategy. It also raised a warning flag for firms that had not yet considered the implications of this strategy option. (The other new trend in domestic joint-venture practice was the unwillingness of partners to take passive roles.) More joint ventures and other forms of cooperative strategy will undoubtedly be launched in the wake of increasingly rapid rates of technological change, deregulation, and globalization. Moreover, boundaries are blurring between industries as the capabilities of information processing and data transmission technologies link together formerly disparate products.[9] Managers need to understand how changes like these affect their need for joint ventures.

Given that interfirm cooperation has suddenly become prevalent within certain types of industries (detailed in chapter 7 and thereafter), it would seem

Table 1–2
Duncan's 1980 Database of Announced Joint Ventures per Year, 1964–75

Industry	1964	1965	1966	1967	1968
Coal extraction	—	—	—	—	—
Oil extraction	—	2	5	1	3
Alternative energy (includes synthetic fuels)	—	—	—	—	—
Other mining activities	1	—	5	6	3
Food processing	—	—	2	1	1
Textile products	—	2	—	—	—
Pulp and paper	1	2	1	1	2
Printing, publishing	—	2	2	—	1
Chemicals	2	10	13	4	4
Pharmaceuticals	—	—	—	—	1
Medical products	—	—	1	1	—
Glass, stone, clay, and concrete	1	3	3	1	2
Metals processing	1	1	1	—	—
Steel	—	—	—	—	—
Metals fabrication	1	—	4	3	3
Light machinery	—	1	1	—	—
Heavy machinery	—	2	2	2	5
Engines	—	—	1	—	—
Automotive	—	—	—	—	1
Aerospace	1	—	1	—	—
Electronic components	—	—	1	—	2
Electronic equipment	—	—	—	—	—
Precision controls	—	—	—	2	1
Robotics	—	—	—	—	—
Software	—	—	—	—	—
Computers and peripherals	—	—	1	2	—
Electronic consumer products	—	—	2	—	—
Videotape and videodisc	—	—	—	—	—
Photocopy and office equipment	—	2	—	—	1
Electrical equipment	—	—	2	—	2
Communications equipment	—	2	2	—	3
Motion pictures	—	—	1	—	—
Programming, cable communications	—	—	—	—	—
Cable communications services	—	—	—	—	—
Communications systems and services	—	—	—	—	—
Financial services	—	1	—	—	1
Advertising services	—	—	—	—	—
Pipelines	—	—	—	—	—
Timesharing services (includes databases)	—	—	—	—	2
Leasing services	—	—	—	—	—
Wholesaling, retailing, and distribution	—	1	4	1	1
Other services[a]	—	—	4	8	7
Total	8	31	59	33	46

[a]Primarily real estate and contract R&D enterprises.

1969	1970	1971	1972	1973	1974	1975	Total
—	—	1	—	—	1	1	3
2	1	6	2	4	2	—	28
—	—	—	3	—	2	1	6
5	4	4	1	2	—	1	32
2	3	1	3	6	3	2	24
1	—	4	1	4	1	—	18
—	4	3	1	1	2	—	18
3	—	2	—	—	—	—	10
10	7	7	3	7	3	5	75
—	—	1	1	2	—	1	6
—	—	—	—	—	1	1	4
1	1	—	—	—	3	1	16
—	—	—	—	—	—	—	3
1	2	1	—	3	—	2	9
1	3	—	5	5	—	—	25
1	—	1	1	—	1	—	6
1	1	4	3	2	3	1	26
1	1	1	—	—	1	—	5
2	1	1	1	1	—	—	7
2	—	1	—	—	—	1	6
2	—	—	2	1	—	—	8
—	—	—	—	—	—	—	0
1	1	1	—	—	—	2	8
—	—	—	—	—	—	—	0
—	—	—	—	—	—	—	0
1	2	1	3	—	—	2	12
—	—	—	—	—	—	—	2
—	—	—	—	—	—	—	0
—	—	—	—	—	—	1	4
—	1	1	1	—	1	2	10
2	4	1	1	2	1	—	18
—	1	—	1	—	—	1	4
—	—	—	1	1	—	—	2
—	—	—	—	1	—	—	1
—	—	—	1	—	—	1	2
—	1	—	2	1	2	—	8
—	—	1	—	—	—	—	1
—	—	—	—	—	—	—	0
8	—	5	1	—	—	—	16
—	1	—	—	—	—	2	3
4	6	6	3	3	3	4	36
13	16	17	7	5	3	4	84
64	61	71	48	51	33	36	541

Table 1–3
Announced Joint Ventures per Year

Industry	Pre-1969	1970	1971	1972	1973	1974	1975	1976
Coal extraction	—	—	1	1	—	3	1	7
Oil extraction	2	1	—	2	2	4	2	5
Alternative energy (includes synthetic fuels)	2	1	—	1	—	4	2	4
Other mining activities	2	—	2	1	1	—	—	6
Food processing	1	1	1	1	—	1	2	2
Pulp and paper	—	—	—	—	1	1	1	1
Printing, publishing	—	—	—	1	—	—	1	1
Chemicals	1	2	1	1	1	3	3	10
Pharmaceuticals and cosmetics	1	1	—	—	—	—	1	1
Medical products	1	—	—	1	1	—	1	1
Metals processing	1	1	—	1	—	2	—	2
Steel	—	—	—	—	—	1	2	1
Metals fabrication	2	—	—	—	—	—	—	2
Light machinery	—	—	—	—	—	—	—	—
Heavy machinery	—	—	1	1	—	—	—	5
Engines	1	—	—	—	—	2	—	—
Automotive	—	—	1	—	—	—	—	1
Aerospace	—	—	—	1	—	—	1	—
Electronic components	1	—	—	2	—	—	—	1
Electronic equipment	—	1	—	—	1	—	—	3
Precision controls	—	—	—	—	—	—	—	—
Robotics	—	—	—	—	—	—	—	—
Software	—	1	—	1	—	1	—	1
Computers and peripherals	—	—	—	—	—	—	1	1
Electronic consumer products	—	—	—	—	—	—	—	—
Videotape and videodisc	—	—	—	—	—	—	—	—
Photocopy and office equipment	—	1	—	—	—	—	1	1
Electrical equipment	—	—	1	—	—	—	—	1
Communications equipment	—	—	1	—	2	1	1	2
Motion pictures	—	—	—	2	—	—	—	—
Programming, cable communications	1	1	2	1	—	—	—	2
Cable communications services	—	—	—	2	—	—	—	—
Communications systems and services	—	—	—	—	—	—	—	—
Financial services	—	1	2	—	4	9	2	4
Advertising services	—	—	—	—	—	—	—	—
Pipelines	2	—	—	—	—	—	2	—
Database services	—	—	—	—	—	—	—	—
Leasing services	—	—	—	—	—	—	—	—
Wholesaling, retailing, distribution	—	—	—	—	—	—	—	—
Other services	—	—	—	—	—	—	—	—
Totals	18	14	13	20	13	31	23	65

1977	1978	1979	1980	1981	1982	1983	1984	Totals
2	1	1	3	3	na	na	na	23
3	4	1	3	1	na	na	na	30
3	3	—	5	5	na	na	na	30
4	1	—	1	1	1	—	—	20
1	—	1	3	na	na	na	na	14
4	2	—	3	na	na	na	na	13
—	2	—	3	1	na	na	na	9
5	7	4	6	3	4	27	1	79
3	1	1	—	8	1	3	5	26
1	3	1	1	3	—	4	5	23
2	1	2	1	—	1	1	—	15
—	1	1	—	—	1	1	7	15
2	3	3	2	1	—	4	—	19
—	—	—	2	—	—	7	—	9
4	2	2	1	2	—	7	—	25
1	—	1	2	1	—	4	7	19
1	1	2	2	2	—	6	1	17
1	—	1	1	—	1	6	—	12
1	—	1	—	—	2	5	9	22
—	2	1	1	—	—	2	na	11
—	1	3	—	1	1	1	1	8
—	—	—	—	2	2	2	4	10
2	1	—	3	5	—	8	4	27
—	2	2	2	—	—	3	8	19
—	—	—	—	—	—	4	—	4
—	—	1	4	1	5	—	1	12
—	1	2	—	2	—	2	1	11
1	3	1	1	1	1	1	—	11
2	—	1	2	—	3	20	17	52
—	1	—	2	—	1	4	—	10
1	1	—	—	3	7	10	3	32
1	1	1	6	4	9	7	3	34
—	—	—	—	1	10	53	3	67
3	7	1	2	2	2	36	18	93
—	—	—	—	—	1	4	na	5
1	2	—	—	—	1	na	na	8
—	—	—	—	—	—	10	1	11
—	1	—	—	1	—	2	na	4
—	—	—	1	—	—	10	na	11
1	3	1	—	—	—	15	na	20
50	58	36	63	54	54	269	99	880

that managers need a way to consider what effect this structural change will have on their industries, on their firms, and on the new ways in which they must compete. For example, it is doubtful that military aircraft will be made or sold without the assistance of partners in the future. Cooperation is becoming mandatory within the automotive industry. Risky ventures, like satellite communications, coal gasification, or other undertakings involving costly and untried technologies, are the inevitable forums in which joint ventures will occur. In light of this, firms need a new way of thinking about the joint venture as a strategy option. As economic growth slows, as markets shrink or become crowded, as industries become global, and as technological change accelerates to speeds at which individual firms cannot recover their initial investments alone, a new language of cooperation (not warfare) is mandatory. Otherwise, firms may encounter difficulties in delivering adequate value to their customers, in replenishing their base of skills, and in safeguarding their abilities to increase long-term shareholder value.

A Paradox

This study is motivated by the observation of a paradox. Joint ventures (and other forms of economic cooperation) have been formed in settings where firms chose to cooperate *without* duress from sovereign governments. Where regulations prevented joint activities previously, some managers have even lobbied for relaxation of these constraints. Despite their apparent eagerness for the freedom to cooperate, however, many managers seem to pursue a knee-jerk approach to such strategies; they jump in without thinking through their motivations or how the child will fit into their scheme for strategy implementation. Integration has rarely occurred (or has occurred badly). An adversarial attitude among partners (as well as between parent and child business units) has replaced the zeal of a true entrepreneurial effort. These tensions show little sign of abating because U.S. managers are not inclined to accept a passive role in siring and rearing joint ventures that will operate within the United States. Managers must find a way to sort through the tensions of shared decisionmaking if this strategy option is to succeed.

A Global Challenge

For some applications, joint ventures must have more of the feverish intensity of underdogs trying to break into closed markets and less of the opportunistic coupling (and uncoupling) behavior that has characterized recent joint-venture arrangements. Deregulation, the electronics and communications revolution, and blurring national industry boundaries make all firms vulnerable again. As they evaluate whether to cooperate in forming joint ventures (or not) in such settings, firms must make tradeoffs among gaining new skills, entering new industries, helping their nations' domestic economies (by creating or saving jobs), creating new competitors, or risking the atrophy of in-house capabilities. Since joint-venture partners could include domestic competitors, local firms who are new to the child's industry, or foreign firms (who may already be competitors in the child's industry), the tradeoffs involved in choosing joint-venture partners should be evaluated in the context of global competition as well as in simple competitive terms.

As national champions within the maturing markets of Japan, the EEC and the United States seek new markets to conquer, and the challenge of domestic joint ventures becomes even more acute—for these competitors see the greatest payoff in invading each others' markets. As chapter 12 will explain, one of the most important new uses firms can make of joint ventures is in forging global strategies within mature economies. (*Global strategies* are those that recognize that competition can no longer be confined to a single nation's boundaries.)[10]

Most U.S. joint ventures were previously regarded as a means to enter *foreign* markets; they were not considered to be part of the network of business units firms used to cope with world-scale competition. Now firms must consider this additional use for joint ventures. *This is a novel way for U.S. firms to consider their use of joint ventures.* Although firms will often think of production scale economies, technological innovation, and new sourcing arrangements as a means of meeting the oncoming global challenge, fewer managers may recognize the potential advantages of joint ventures. This myopia may be due, in part, to the way joint ventures have been used historically. It may also be due, in part, to a recognition of the difficulties inherent in coordinating the activities of the joint ventures with those of the global system if the child is to stand alone as a viable economic entity. The problems associated with making joint ventures work most effectively within a global strategy are significant strategic and managerial challenges.

Questions Regarding Joint-Venture Strategies

If managers are to use joint ventures effectively, they need a way to assess who would make the best partners for their firms and how to manage relationships with their child. Relationships will be most effective if managers can spark (and sustain) some chemistry between these parties. Because making joint ventures work is largely a matter of managing the chemistry among partners, their child, and the industry in which the venture will compete, managers must discover how they could best enhance the benefits of these relationships within their joint ventures. They must develop a way to tell in advance whether joint-venture chemistries will succeed and when that chemistry is failing.

Strategic Symmetry—Resource Asymmetries

Symmetry occurs where partners possess strategic missions, resource capabilities, managerial capabilities, and other attributes that are evenly matched. Symmetry of need to be engaged in joint ventures is a stabilizing force, as is agreement among partners in their vision for the joint venture.

Asymmetry develops when attributes are unevenly matched. Resource asymmetries among partners are a *stabilizing* force, but asymmetries in the speed with which parents want to exploit an opportunity, the direction in which they want to move, or in other strategic matters are *destabilizing* to joint ventures. If managers are to use joint ventures effectively, all parties—managers within the parents and their child—must understand how asymmetries in parents' skills, resources, and objectives will affect the joint venture's ability to thrive or languish. Moreover, they must develop ways to nurture good relationships among partners and between parent and child.

Reasonable Expectations

Domestic experience in using joint ventures within the United States has been limited, and it is not clear which objectives managers can reasonably expect to achieve through them. But it has been estimated that over half of the joint ventures ended recently were ill-conceived at birth because the objectives of the joint venture were unclear, because their parents' capabilities were poorly matched, or because they aspired to achieve more than was possible in the industries where they competed. Managers recognize that their joint ventures must compete in hostile industries in the 1980s, but they need to understand why some industry conditions will make the use of joint ventures more risky than others. They need to understand why joint ventures can achieve better performances within some environments than within others. Managers must also be able to recognize whether their particular joint venture was well conceived and whether its implementation is well timed.

Timing

Timing is an important part of effective joint-strategy formulation in situations where environments change rapidly because firms that move first can often gain access to better partners, which in turn could give them a competitive advantage that late entrants could not capture as easily. Moreover, managers need to understand how the evolution of industries' structural conditions (and competitive conduct) can make joint ventures seem more (or less) attractive within certain industries, as in the example of Control Data Corporation and NCR, Inc.'s joint venture to manufacture computer peripherals (Computer Peripherals Inc.). Managers must be able to recognize whether there will be penalties for entering joint ventures in firms' home markets too late (as in the example of the automobile industry, where the best partners may already have been taken) and whether there will be penalties for holding on to joint ventures too long (as in the example of Skagg-Albertson's combination of food and drug stores). Managers must consider *whether* moving early through joint ventures will offer their firms opportunities to create synergies, as in the example of the nationwide legal clinics of Hyatt Legal Services housed with H&R Block's tax preparation offices, just as they would do when contemplating the timing of any other type of diversification. Finally, managers must consider *when* they could best leverage their relationships between joint venture and parent to strengthen parent firms' competitive advantages, as in the example of Burson-Marsteller Inc. (a U.S. public relations house), which formed a joint venture with Fuji Ad Systems Corp. some time ago, or Young & Rubicam, which recently formed a joint venture in advertising with Dentsu.

In summary, managers need to understand how joint ventures can help their firms supplement internal resources and capabilities, in order to help them build strengths and bargaining power by responding faster to competitive challenges. They need to realize whether joint ventures can create synergies—through vertical relationships or by sharing resources—and what limitations on synergies the child's needs for operating autonomy will create. If joint ventures and other forms of cooperative strategies are helpful in solving technological problems and increasing value-added margins, managers need to realize how they can best protect these sources of competitive advantage while learning about state-of-the-art products and processes within their child's industries. Managers must understand how to use the inevitable technological bleedthrough that occurs in joint ventures to their firms' best advantage, as well as how to overcome the not-invented-here syndrome of in-house business units when they attempt to transfer technology between parent and child. Finally, managers must be able to find the right partners for diverse competitive environments and to manage their relationships with their partners as carefully as they would manage other treasured resources. They need a touchstone in order to assess whether their joint venture is working to the best of this strategy option's potential or whether something is awry. The effective use of joint-venture strategies requires managers to consider these and other questions about cooperative strategies that have been unanswered until now. Many forces (that previous empirical studies have never addressed) contribute to the differences between well-formulated joint ventures and those that failed. Chapters 3, 4, and 5 detail those forces in a framework that is tested in the industry studies of chapters 7 through 12.

Overview

Joint ventures will be increasingly important in the development of new industries, the revitalization of mature industries, the rationalization of firms' portfolios, and the enhancement of firms' competitive advantages. Given the accelerating pace of industry evolution and the increasing interdependencies among players within industries like electronics, software, communications, office equipment, precision controls, and machine tools, managers must consider all of their firms' options carefully, including cooperative strategies.

Given the importance of joint ventures and the many unanswered questions remaining, there is a need for a rigorous inquiry that distinguishes among environments where joint ventures might be undertaken with varying expectations for success. It is important to recognize that firms have different strategic objectives, asymmetric strengths, and other important differences that will temper their choices concerning joint-venture partners, industries to enter, and other dimensions concerning cooperative strategies. It is important also to recognize the nature of those differences that push partners apart and divide their child's loyalties at times when firms should be working together for mutual gain. A framework is needed that incorporates these differences into patterns that suggest which arrangements are most likely to prosper.

Such frameworks and patterns are offered and tested in this study. It is structured in the following manner. Chapter 2 reviews the costs and benefits of cooperative strategies. Chapters 3, 4, and 5 (representing the relationships between partners, between parent and child, and between the child and its environment, respectively) develop a theory of joint-venture formulation, operation, and termination. The chapters construct a framework of the dynamics of parents' motives, strengths, and behaviors in working with each other (and their child) as these must be tempered by the success requirements of the child's competitive environment. Chapter 3 examines issues such as *whether* to form joint ventures and *what form* they will take from the perspective of parent firms. Chapter 4 presents a framework describing the tradeoffs between coordination (to exploit synergies) and autonomy (to maximize the child's performance), which characterize parent–child relationships. Chapter 5 takes the child's perspective concerning the success requirements of the diverse competitive industries where it competes and how these needs must temper the relationship that its parents may have envisioned.

Three levels of analysis are presented: the linkages of parents to the joint venture, the linkages of parents to each other, and the special attributes endowed on the joint-venture entity in its own right as an industry competitor. This analytical approach is appropriate because it incorporates the capabilities that each parent brings to competition within a potentially alien industry as well as the synergies that may be created by joining with partners in a joint venture.

Chapter 6 describes the research methodology used to test the adequacy of the framework. It explains the data sources, mode of presentation, data processing, and a summary of how the data were used. Chapters 7 through 12 present the data in a series of industry chapters that contrast the use of joint ventures within industries of varying capital intensity (and asset inflexibility), varying product differentiability, and varying rates of technological change. The industry chapters also examine joint ventures as sales growth slows, industry structures evolve, and industries become global. The usefulness of the frameworks is reviewed in each type of industry setting. Chapters 13 and 14 summarize findings concerning parent–child relationships and focus on the use of joint ventures as a means of adapting to change and as technological change agents, respectively. Summary chapter 15 is devoted to guidelines for creating and managing joint venture relationships, while chapter 16 discusses public policy issues concerning joint ventures.

This inquiry concerning the effective use of domestic joint ventures coincides with a decrease in the expected life of technological innovations and an increased blurring of industry boundaries. The insights it offers should be of interest to strategists, students of corporate strategy, and public policy makers.

Notes

1. Taylor, Robert E., 1984, "Joint Ventures Likely to Be Encouraged by Friendlier Attitude of U.S. Officials," *Wall Street Journal,* November 5:8; "Joint Ventures: Justice Becomes a Cheerleader," 1984, *Business Week,* November 19:48–49.

2. Ballon, Robert J., ed., 1967, *Joint Ventures and Japan* (Tokyo: Sophia University); Beamish, Paul, and Lane, Henry W., 1982, "Need, Commitment and the Performance of Joint Ventures in Developing Countries," working paper (Toronto: University of Western Ontario); Business Inter-national, 1965, *Ownership Policies at Work Abroad* (New York: Business International); Business International, 1971, *European Business Strategies in the United States: Meeting the Challenge of the World's Largest Markets* (Geneva: Business International); Business International, 1972, *Recent Opportunities in Establishing Joint Ventures* (New York: Business International).

3. See Boyle, S.E., 1968, "An Estimate of the Number and Size Distribution of Domestic Joint Subsidiaries," *Antitrust Law and Economics Review* (1):81–92; Pate, J.L., 1969, "Joint Venture Activity, 1960–1968," *Economic Review* (Cleveland: Federal Reserve Bank of Cleveland) 16–23; Pfeffer, J., and Nowak, P., 1976, "Joint Venture and Interorganizational Interdependence," *Administrative Science Quarterly* 21(3):398–418; Duncan, Jerome L., Jr., 198, "The Causes and Effects of Domestic Joint Venture Activity," Ph.D. diss., University of Florida; Ferguson, Roger W., Jr., 1981, "The Nature of Joint Venture in the American Manufacturing Sector," Ph.D. diss., Harvard University; Berg, Sanford V., Duncan, Jerome, Jr., and Friedman, Philip, 1982, *Joint Venture Strategies and Corporate Innovation* (Cambridge, Mass.: Oelgeschlager, Gunn & Hain), for patterns of parent linkages to progeny and relationships of parents to each other.

4. Nichols, Henry W., 1950, "Joint Ventures," *Virginia Law Review* 36: 425–459; Eaton, Frederick M., 1952, "Joint Ventures," *Antitrust Law Symposium*

1952—Proceedings of the Fourth Annual Meeting, Section on Antitrust Law, New York State Bar Association 135–144; Jaeger, Walter H.E., 1960, "Joint Ventures: Membership, Types, and Termination," *American University Law Review* (9)2:111–129.

5. Hale, G.E., 1956, "Joint Ventures: Collaborative Subsidiaries and the Antitrust Laws," *Virginia Law Review* 42:927–938; Bergman, Michael, 1962, "The Corporate Joint Venture under the Antitrust Laws," *New York University Law Review* 37: 712–734; Dixon, Paul Rand, 1962, "Joint Ventures: What Is Their Impact on Competition?," *Antitrust Bulletin* 7(3):397–410.

6. Boyle, Stanley E., 1960, "The Joint Subsidiary: An Economic Appraisal," *Antitrust Bulletin* 5(3):303–318; "Joint Ventures and Section 7 of the Clayton Act," 1962, *Stanford Law Review* 14:777–799.

7. Boyle, S.E., 1968, "An Estimate of the Number and Size Distribution of Domestic Joint Subsidiaries," *Antitrust Law and Economics Review* 1:81–92.

8. Baden Fuller, Charles, and Hill, R., 1984, "Industry Strategies for Alleviating Excess Capacity: The Case of the Lazard Scheme for UK Steel Castings," working paper, London School of Business; Baden Fuller, Charles, 1984, "The Economics of Closure and Industry Dynamics," working paper, London School of Business.

9. Harrigan, Kathryn Rudie, 1976, "Antitrust Implications of the Data Communications Industry," M.B.A. thesis, University of Texas at Austin.

10. Porter, Michael E., 1980, *Competitive Strategy: Techniques for Analyzing Industries and Competitors* (New York: Free Press); Hout, Thomas, Porter, Michael E., and Rudden, Eileen, 1982, "How Global Companies Win Out," *Harvard Business Review* 60(5):98–108.

Appendix 1A:
Cooperative Strategy Alternatives

The strategy alternatives sketched in table 1–1 are discussed herein with respect to their benefits and costs. Key issues that managers must distinguish in choosing a cooperative strategy include: (1) parents' abilities to cope with diverse management controls and integrating mechanisms, (2) time required to complete strategic mission, (3) autonomy required for the child to compete effectively, and (4) whether synergies, technology transfers, exposure to innovative practices, or other activities requiring numerous, multilevel parent–child contacts are intended. In brief, managers should be realistic in assessing their firms' motives for cooperating and how they intend to manage their relationship with the child.

Joint ventures are no panacea; if managers cannot stimulate innovative behaviors using the full-equity ownership alternatives (developed below), they will do *no better* in joint ventures, especially if they expect to rule them also with an iron hand. Distasteful as it may be for them, some firms would do well to accept a passive managerial role in exchange for their skills, patents, and personnel contributions and let another team run their joint venture.

Alternatives Involving Full Equity Ownership

Mergers or Acquisitions

This category is included to offer a robust treatment of alternatives. Some firms will *not* cooperate with others in developing new skills, penetrating new markets, or attaining other objectives. They will purchase the resources and knowledge that they desire (or will develop them in-house), assuming they are available, as in the example of IBM's purchase of Rolm. Unfortunately for these firms, some assets and skills are not for sale. Some risks are too large to shoulder alone. Even if firms devoted their full energies to achieving some tasks, they would need the assistance of outsiders to succeed.

What explains firms' preferences for fully owned ventures? Perhaps their managers enjoy being in charge of large and complex projects. Or perhaps they consider shared ownership (and authority) too cumbersome to be effective. Many managers believe that wholly owned ventures are less likely to fail than partially owned ones, and they expect wholly owned ventures to provide them with maximum returns (as well as the highest degrees of secrecy). If a venture is fully owned, they reason, their firms need not share their unique competitive edge with outsiders. If they cannot buy the skills they seek from outsiders, the managers of such firms are undaunted. Their preferences for full ownership lead them to believe that they can develop the needed skills in-house themselves, as in the example of IBM's development of the Personal Computer.

Internal Venturing

Use of internal venturing also assumes that managers prefer to control their firms' expansions, innovations, diversifications, or other strategic investments *alone* for reasons sketched above. But this option recognizes that the dominant cultures of their firms are poor incubators for entrepreneurial ideas. In this strategy option, managers who recognize that their employees' good ideas are not getting to the marketplace create internal venturing units, as in the example of Allied Corporation. They hope that by supporting these ideas and keeping these business units small enough to respond to competitive stimuli quickly, their personnel will be able to create a regular menu of innovations, as in the example of the Bell Laboratories. Unfortunately for these firms, entrepreneurial employees often want equity in the ideas they develop. Soon firms find they must create equity-sharing programs to keep such employees from starting their own firms. Before they recognize what has happened, managers find their firms have entered into joint ventures with their employees in order to keep these innovations in-house.

Internal venturing is like venture-capital activities by outside investors in the sense that capital (sometimes managerial assistance and advice as well) are entrusted to the start-up businesses. Investors could adopt a "hands-off" attitude regarding the start-up venture, or they could foster its development, as in the example of sponsors that actively intervene in their start-up firms' decisions.

As the venture develops, somebody must pay the piper, of course. Corporate parents will expect their internal ventures to generate cash and other internal, competitive, and strategic benefits for the firm. Venture capitalists will expect their payoffs. Impatience from either financing source compounds the venture's difficulties in developing a position of long-term competitive advantage. Integrating internal ventures with corporate parents successfully will be as problematic as it would be with other shared-equity arrangements. (Recalling that strategic business units (SBUs) develop identities that make them seek autonomy from corporate systems, provisions will be needed to ease start-up ventures into the corporate family. Unless corporate management sends strong signals to the contrary, the attitude of sister SBUs concerning the new venture will be adversarial.)

Internal joint ventures have been used successfully by international firms to mediate between strong-willed managers in sister SBUs. For example, when General Electric sought to integrate electric iron manufacturing on a worldwide basis, it created internal joint ventures within its international sector to permit SBUs to share the benefits of a new technology as well as its risks and costs. Formal arrangements to mediate between conflicting viewpoints, like the matrix form of organization, are other ways of attaining the benefits of internal venturing.

Alternatives Involving Partial Ownership

Joint Ventures

Joint ventures (the focus of this analysis) offer shared-equity control and shared returns, with lower risks to bear than if firms pursued their strategic objectives alone. Managers within joint ventures where one parent is *passive* allow the strong partner to lead; they mediate between viewpoints within operating joint ventures where parents are *actively* involved in the child's activities. Because, as chapter 4 explains, joint ventures can be unwieldy to govern, they will *not* be appropriate strategic responses within all settings.

A robust analysis of joint ventures considers parents' perspectives; and their concerns include: (1) *whether* they should cooperate (or not) and *when*; (2) *what type of partner* they want; (3) *who contributes what resources* and expects *what outputs* or other benefits in exchange; (4) how each partner's *contributions* (and receipts) *are valued*; and (5) how the *balance of power* is revalued when asymmetries develop. It also considers the child's perspective, and its concerns reflect the success requirements of its industry. These include: (1) how to obtain or develop the *crucial resources,* skills, or other factors needed to become an effective competitor and (2) how to gain the *autonomy* needed to compete effectively. Finally, a robust analysis of joint-venture strategies considers the dynamics of relationships between the players—partners, parents, and child—in their protean triangle (or quadrangle). In theory, the child should be a superior competitor: It can draw on the strengths of two or more parents; synergies (not to mention eugenics) arise from such mutually beneficial contacts. In fact, the synergies and other benefits that chapter 2 enumerates must be consciously managed by all players if they are to be realized.

Minority Investments

Minority investments do not create a new entity; investors share the equity of the ongoing firm, instead. These are investments in ongoing firms who may possess skills or resources that investing firms wish to understand better, as in the example of Kellogg's investment in Agrigenetics. Minority investments can be a means of fortifying a fledgling supplier or other pioneering firm without acquiring them outright, as in the example of IBM's investment in Intel. Again, these arrangements could be a form of venture capital, used where entrepreneurs have little interest in being acquired but need infusions of capital, as in the example of Biogen N.V.'s pattern of minority investments. (If larger firms tried to buy their firms, the founders and key personnel might resign, as in the example of many small, Silicon Valley types of firms.)

A minority investment by a larger firm may be the only way for the investing firms' managers to obtain the knowledge or access desired from smaller firms, as in the example of the genetic engineering firms. Like the internal venturing option (described above), issues concerning what level of *parent intervention* will be appropriate in operating decisions, how to manage *intrafirm relationships*, what capabilities (other than cash) investing firms might provide, and other issues must be resolved in order to make minority investment strategies effective.

Alternatives Involving No Ownership Control

Cooperative Agreements

Cooperative agreements refer to *nonequity* forms of cooperative strategies. The term will be used throughout this study to provide a generic alternative to those activities where partners share equity or create a child or where one partner acquires the other. Cooperative agreements can be a variety of arrangements between two or more separate firms for the exchange of performances; they do not provide for jointly owned entities, nor do they generally provide for future joint decision making beyond the life of their performances as equity joint ventures do.

In cooperative agreements, tasks are performed by cooperating firms within their respective facilities, as in the example of a contract to act as second source for a well-specified product. Partners control the cooperative agreement through contracts that may specify product configurations, delivery schedules, price, or other terms. It is not clear whether skills and knowhow are transferred from one partner to another in cooperative agreements, since the most efficient way to perform tasks may be to do them in the proficient partner's facilities, as in the example of Cetus's agreements with its many partners. If knowledge or skills transfer *is* desired, another arrangement (such as *licensing*) may be more appropriate than cooperative agreements, especially where technology is central to a venture's well-being.

Research and Development Partnerships

Research and development partnerships are agreements to fund research. Technological cooperation through research consortia offer firms an opportunity to accelerate their industries' rates of innovation, as in the example of the Microelectronics & Computer Technology Corp.

U.S. firms traditionally avoided such arrangements before their technological leadership was challenged; but relaxed federal antitrust guidelines concerning R&D partnerships (and concerns about being noncompetitive global players) now encourage greater use of joint licensing consortia in the future, even among horizontal competitors (to form a horizontally related child). Federal research support is not unusual. What is novel is the recent willingness among antitrust agencies to allow the formation of jointly owned entities that presumably will have a life of their own and hold property rights.

Under the terms of some of the new R&D partnerships, a general partner contracts with the user group (the consortium) to take or pay for a certain volume of the product in question (such as megabyte semiconductor chips), contingent only on meeting predetermined cost and performance specifications. The general partner contracts with appropriate laboratories to do the work that is necessary, using arm's-length contractual arrangements to avoid antitrust problems. Funding is obtained by syndicating venture capital money from the private sector. (The investment is relatively low in risk, since commercial success is guaranteed in advance and since the best partners' laboratories are doing the research.)

When the product is developed, the general partner either licenses the technology back to the individual companies (the consortium) or manufactures the product for the consortium to exploit scale economies and surge far down the experience curve. (The general partner also may hire an individual firm to do the manufacturing for the benefit of the group.) The consortium partners can obtain proprietary rights to the new technology without putting in any money because they are bound by take-or-pay contracts. Often the consortium's members' laboratories perform the development work that they wanted to do while being paid to do so by investors. Finally, if the general partner in the R&D partnership is a nonprofit organization, then the cash flow that accrues to it after paying off the limited partners will be available to fund second- and third-generation projects.[1]

Prior to late 1984 the principal constraints on the widespread use of R&D partnerships in the United States had been those of antitrust policies. In general it had been feared that joint research ventures could harm competitive vigor and prevent independently conceived inventions from ever competing in the marketplace (a concern that could be overcome by running parallel research projects). Critics of these arrangements have argued that the patents granted to research consortia could constitute bottlenecks that might convey substantial bargaining power to the partners. Thus provisions for access to patents by nonmembers through licensing agreements may become necessary if joint R&D partnerships are to become widespread.[2] But such licensing provisions may instead retard the use of R&D partnerships, given the preferences of many managers for control over their operations and over the technologies that give them competitive advantages. (Given this preference for secrecy regarding technological agreements and given other reasons explained in chapters 3, 4, and 5, some firms prefer the greater technological and managerial control provided for by joint ventures.)

Cross-Licensing and Cross-Distribution Agreements

Cross-licensing arrangements cover technology developed independently by separate firms for the same (or similar) products or processes. Firms trade licenses to gain knowlege about processes that other firms may have developed, as in the example of Eli Lilly and Genentech. *Cross-distribution* arrangements permit one firm to market the products of another in a specified geographic region, as in the example of SmithKline Beckman, and Fujisawa Pharmaceutical. Firms trade product lines to offer each respective customer group a wider array of products. Cross-distribution agreements can be a way of forestalling entry into firms' home markets. Their use suggests that local firms possess sufficient bargaining power to control the autonomy of newcomers that seek market penetration (a point that is developed at length in chapters 3, 4, and 5).

The geographic limitations imposed by these swaps of technology, brand names, and other resources look like divisions of markets, to some antitrust authorities. Accordingly, partners that form cross-licensing or cross-distribution agreements must be sensitive to local antitrust policies and accommodate them in their agreements as well as their implementation.

Joint Bidding Activities

A consortium can be a loose association of contractors bidding together for a job that they may subdivide (so that each firm has a separate contract with the customer for a portion of the work) or delegate to one member to operate for the welfare of all consortium members. Offshore drilling activities are an example of a consortium. Although many joint bidding activities include some sort of binding agreement in the event that the bid is accepted, the duration of the venture could be quite brief. By contrast, other bidding consortiums do not provide for any ongoing commercial relationships after tasks have been subcontracted. (Customary agreements, friendships, and historical precedent sometimes supersede the need for binding agreements, especially in regions where managers are quite homogeneous in their outlooks.)

Joint bidding activities have become a structural characteristic of the off-shore oil exploration industry, where firms' joint activities include not only joint bidding arrangements but also unitization agreements, jointly owned pipelines (or production properties), crude oil exchanges, and joint process-ing agreements. The rules underlying such agreements provide for the protec-tion of pioneers' risk-taking investments when new firms join the group. Latecomers cannot obtain access to the fruits of the joint bidding activity without paying some premium to compensate the original venturers.

Oil firms have so many joint activities that the terms of a typical contract are well-understood (and accepted) by all players as being a standard that protects their interests fairly. Accordingly, oil firms have learned how to move in and out of joint ventures with minimum disruptions to their ongoing activities. Some oil firms have learned to maximize the advantages of joint ventures so well that when these firms invested heavily in the petrochemicals industry they used their knowledge of joint ventures to gain competitive ad-vantage in that industry as well. (This change is described in chapter 11.)

Notes to Appendix 1A

1. Merrifield, D. Bruce, 1983, "Forces of Change Affecting High Technology In-dustries," *National Journal,* January 29:253–256; "High Tech Companies Team Up in R&D Race," 1983, *Business Week,* August 15:94–95; Krosin, Kenneth E., 1971, "Joint Research Ventures under the Antitrust Laws," *George Washington Law Review* 39(5):1112–1140. The U.S. Department of Justice has challenged only three research coalitions in the last two decades—and each involved significant collateral restraints that retarded innovation. These were suits against an automobile manufacturers' association that was accused of deliberately delaying development and installation of emission control devices, against the Wisconsin Alumni Research Fund, which was charged with using grant-back licensing arrangements to acquire exclusive control over patents involving the Wurster process for coating pharmaceutical products, and a suit against the Aircraft Association and twenty major aircraft firms, who were attacked due to their long-standing patent pooling and cross-licensing agreements. See Ewing, Ky P., Jr., 1981, "Joint Research, Antitrust, and Innovation," *Research Management* 24(2):25–29.

2. Krosin, Kenneth E., 1971, "Joint Research Ventures under the Antitrust Laws," *George Washington Law Review* 39(5):1112–1140; Ewing, Ky P., Jr., 1981, "Joint Research, Antitrust, and Innovation," *Research Management* 24(2):25–29.

2
Motives for Joint-Venture Formation (and Termination)

Much has been written about the use of joint ventures (and other cooperative strategies) as risk-sharing arrangements, but it has been largely descriptive, not analytical. It has not addressed questions concerning *what makes for an effective domestic joint-venture strategy*: such as why managers should consider using them, what advantages can be captured through cooperation, and why domestic joint ventures have been avoided until recently in many U.S. industries. Much has been written about why joint ventures seem unattractive (even when legal barriers do not prohibit their use), but little has been written about *how these drawbacks might be overcome* while still maximizing the benefits of joint ventures.

In order to understand why domestic joint ventures have not worked well in the past, it is necessary to review what managers hoped to attain by their use. This is done in this chapter in the form of a literature review. The chapter's primary purpose is to consolidate and summarize joint-venture concepts used in earlier studies. Some of the earlier uses researchers found for joint ventures are summarized in table 2–1. But new uses for joint ventures are also suggested in table 2–1, and these competitive and strategic uses anticipate the new materials contained in chapters 3, 4, and 5, which deal with vital aspects of joint ventures that have yet received scant attention. These issues provide the basis for the analytical model that is developed in the next three chapters. Thus, chapter 2 anticipates questions (which are covered in chapter 3) concerning how firms should combine their one or more strengths with the reciprocal strengths of their *partners*. It anticipates questions (which are covered in chapter 4) concerning how *parents* should maximize the synergistic benefits of their newly strengthened child in relationships with their wholly owned business units. And table 2–1 anticipates questions (which are covered in chapter 5) concerning how the *child*—as the embodiment of its parents' joint-venture strategy—should compete within diverse industry environments. These new uses of joint ventures are illustrated in the field studies of chapters 7 through 12.

Table 2-1
Motivations for Joint-Venture Formation

A. Internal uses
   1. Cost and risk sharing (uncertainty reduction)
   2. Obtain resources where there is no market
   3. Obtain financing to supplement firm's debt capacity
   4. Share outputs of large minimum efficient scale plants
      a. Avoid wasteful duplication of facilities
      b. Utilize by-products, processes
      c. Shared brands, distribution channels, wide product lines, and so forth
   5. Intelligence: obtain window on new technologies and customers
      a. Superior information exchange
      b. Technological personnel interactions
   6. Innovative managerial practices
      a. Superior management systems
      b. Improved communications among SBUs
   7. Retain entrepreneurial employees

B. Competitive uses (strengthen current strategic positions)
   1. Influence industry structure's evolution
      a. Pioneer development of new industries
      b. Reduce competitive volatility
      c. Rationalize mature industries
   2. Preempt competitors ("first-mover" advantages)
      a. Gain rapid access to better customers
      b. Capacity expansion or vertical integration
      c. Acquisition of advantageous terms, resources
      d. Coalition with best partners
   3. Defensive response to blurring industry boundaries and globalization
      a. Ease political tensions (overcome trade barriers)
      b. Gain access to global networks
   4. Creation of more effective competitors
      a. Hybrids possessing parents' strengths
      b. Fewer, more efficient firms
      c. Buffer dissimilar partners

C. Strategic uses (augment strategic position)
   1. Creation and exploitation of synergies
   2. Technology (or other skills) transfer
   3. Diversification
      a. Toehold entry into new markets, products, or skills
      b. Rationalization (or divestiture) of investment
      c. Leverage-related parents' skills for new uses

As table 2-1 indicates, there are many situations where joint ventures could be useful, and these have been grouped into *internal benefits* (such as risk-sharing, no markets, scale economies, better information and practices, and reduction of turnover), *competitive benefits* (such as influence over industry evolution, timing advantages, and globalization, plus the opportunity to create more effective strategic postures), and *strategic benefits* (such as synergies, technology, or other skills transfer and diversification).

Evidence concerning the benefits (and costs) of joint ventures comes primarily from a literature that has described international experiences. Many of the same problems (and successes) will be encountered when using joint ventures in firms' *home* markets if their domestic economies are mature. Except for industries like oil exploration (where U.S. firms established ways of pooling interests, operating authority, and profits long ago by necessity), Asian and European firms have accumulated more experience in using operating joint ventures successfully than U.S. firms have.[1] Because the 1980s will be an era of rapid technological innovation and challenges from imports and deregulation, U.S. firms must increase their understanding of *why* joint ventures are desirable and *how* to use joint ventures effectively, and they must do so quickly.

Uses of Joint Ventures

Previous studies (and observation of current management practices) have suggested many uses for joint ventures, but they also suggested ambivalence concerning the use of this risk-sharing strategy. If managers could overcome their inhibitions regarding joint ventures and develop systems to use them effectively, their firms could build strengths and gain knowledge by cooperating. They could even preempt competitors from forcing their marketplace to change disadvantageously, as in the example of the automotive industry.

Internal Uses

As table 2–1 suggests, joint ventures should not be seen as a way to hide weaknesses. Rather, if they are used prudently, joint ventures can be a way of *creating internal strengths*. Joint ventures can be resource-aggregating and sharing mechanisms that allow firms to concentrate their resources in those areas where they possess the greatest respective strengths, as in the examples of Merrill, Lynch's joint ventures with IBM, Western Union, and Lombard, Odier, respectively. Companies like Rolls Royce, General Electric, and Pratt & Whitney in airline engines cooperated because they were anxious to have a piece of the pie but did not care to risk financial indigestion by investing alone. Some projects, such as the Great Plains coal gasification venture, would never be undertaken without this means of spreading risks and costs. Joint ventures are particularly appropriate where projects involve great uncertainties, costly technological innovations, or high information costs, as in the energy industries. Through them, small firms gain access to larger quantities of capital than would have been available through the ordinary licensing of their technology, as with medical products or others with very long payback periods.

Technology, distribution networks, and other assets that provide internal strengths *are not always for sale*, as in the example of the mining ventures of Nord Resources Corp. As the resource dependency literature has noted, sometimes firms cannot afford to acquire the resources and competence they need.[2] Frequently, the knowledge and assets that they seek cannot be purchased, as in the example of market access within industries such as consumer electronic products, where channels of distribution are already well established. In those situations, joint ventures could be considered as a means of coping with uncertainties and building strengths. They could provide firms with resources for which there are no equally efficient substitutes, as in the example of the ventures between American Natural Resources and Petrofina (or ENI, Krupp Handel, and Occidental Petroleum Corp.) to mine coal.

Joint ventures can be a means of utilizing a new manufacturing process, a by-product, or a new capability, such as the Brokerage Transaction Services joint venture between GTE and Control Data.[3] Co-production, common procurement, and other joint activities are becoming the means for firms to attain increased efficiency, productivity, scale economies, and other benefits commonly attributed to interfirm cooperation, such as are exemplified by joint ventures in the communications industries. Improved brands or distribution networks could increase sales force productivity, and access to an economical source of low-cost, better-quality raw materials could provide both parents with better profit margins.[4]

As table 2–1 suggests, joint ventures could build internal strengths by offering firms a window on promising technologies, like robotics, genetic engineering, and solar energy. In addition to providing access to modern technological information, joint ventures could offer better opportunities for engineers to exchange technical staff (a useful feature of R&D joint ventures, as in electronics) and could save firms costly and unnecessary duplicate research and development efforts, so that partners do not both go down the same blind alley. In summary, joint ventures *could* offer parent firms many technological, financial, marketing, and managerial strengths, if managed effectively. The trick is to realize these benefits.

If managers are open to change, joint activities can be a way to build strengths through innovation, as in their managerial practices and ways of diffusing technology. Managerial practices could be modernized through contact with other firms' innovative information systems and administrative techniques, as with ventures that bring together international partners. Firms could become more flexible strategically, since joint ventures could facilitate better information exchange and could enhance communications, if they were managed effectively.

Finally, table 2–1 (and earlier studies) suggest that joint ventures could build internal strengths by reducing personnel turnover, thereby conserving firms' most valuable resources, their entrepreneurial talent. Joint ventures offer an excellent method for retaining managers who lack the capital backing needed to launch their own business ideas. If the parent can guide the activities of the child while relying on its entrepreneurial managers to act as operator, the joint venture could function like the form of venture capital that once was practiced before dispassionate financial controls were the primary form of contact entrepreneurs had with their backers.

Competitive Uses

Beyond the benefits noted by past studies, it should be clear that joint ventures have the potential to become an effective competitive weapon. Joint ventures could be used in pioneering new industries because they minimize the capital investments that firms must commit to embryonic and potentially volatile settings, such as the office equipment industry. Table 2–1, which suggests some of these competitive uses of joint ventures, indicates that a prospective strategic posture requires firms to *seize initiatives* and to *force their industries' structures to evolve* in a favorable manner.[5] It means that managers should draw on the experiences of firms within mature industries concerning cooperative strategies and apply their knowledge to emerging industries to accelerate the *pace* and control the *direction* of structural evolution.

Table 2–1 suggests that joint ventures could *create competitive strengths* like vertical linkages or consolidate firms' existing market positions, as in the example of a joint venture formed to mine Pennsylvania coal by Conoco, Ashland Coal, Saarbergwerke, and Rheinische Braunkohlenwerke. They tame potentially tough customers (such as the armed forces when purchasing armaments) or gain technological assistance from access to innovations pioneered in other industries (such as applying the knowledge of customer needs to the development of vertical software). Erratic competitors who threaten industry stability could be mollified by drawing them into arrangements that focus their efforts on longer-term objectives rather than short-term gains from price cutting.

Table 2–1 also indicates that joint ventures could *rationalize mature industries*, like metals processing. They could combine foundering partners within mature industries (to consolidate its structure and permit competitors to survive in a new form) and eliminate excess capacity (which could exacerbate industry volatility) through such coalitions.[6]

Joint ventures could be a means of preempting suppliers or customers from integrating in a manner unfavorable to the firm, as in the example of software programmers joining forces with hardware firms, and table 2–1 argues that joint ventures could blunt the abilities of ongoing firms to retaliate by binding potential enemies to the firm as allies, as in Rolls Royce's joint ventures with Pratt & Whitney and with General Electric, respectively. Thus firms could gain new competitive capabilities (or enter new markets) faster, gain market power, or stake out leadership positions in emerging industries.[7] Entry through joint venture may occur more rapidly than individual entry (since less capital is required to enter). Properly structured joint ventures could allow firms to move faster toward innovations and to improve their competitive positions within global arenas, as in the example of General Motors' joint ventures in automobiles. (Note that timing will be an important part of competitive strategy in this situation if pioneering firms could gain access to the *best* partners and gain a competitive advantage that late entrants cannot replicate.) As chapter 5 notes, parents risk creating new competitors if they do not structure their joint ventures advantageously. But if joint ventures are destined to become an inevitable structural feature within their industries, then firms must seek out the best partners available *quickly* to preempt their competitors from linking up with these firms instead. Joint ventures may also offer salvation for older global industries where the joint activities of automotive firms, for example, seem to point to a new trend—the exploitation of joint economies in order to ward off other competitors that are making inroads into key markets.[8]

The competitive benefits shown in table 2–1 that are enjoyed by firms that enter joint ventures will differ by their positions. Newcomers seeking to enter a new geographic market, such as Takeda Chemical Industries entering the U.S. ethical pharmaceuticals with Abbot Laboratories, may see joint ventures as an insurance policy against domestic trade barriers. For them, moving some operations to the target market may be a means of easing political tensions. Sometimes firms with technological complementarity may cooperate out of necessity to gain a local identity, as in the example of military aircraft ventures between British Aerospace, MBB, VFW-Fokker, and Seritalia. For firms that are already engaged in the business that the proposed joint venture will encompass (such as Control Data in the database management business), the critical competitive question is often *whether* they should trade access to their sales networks for the capabilities outsiders could offer.

Table 2–1 notes that joint ventures can defend current strategic positions against forces that are too strong for one firm to withstand, as in the example of the joint venture between General Motors and Toyota. Through the combined internal resources of diverse firms, joint ventures could create more effective competitors, like Ethyl Corp., Alumax, or Dow Corning.[9] They could provide a buffer to marry dissimilar cultures, thereby providing larger firms with access to innovations made by the types of researchers who prefer to reside in smaller organizations like the genetic engineering firms, for example, because they want no part of large firms and the "professional management" practices that characterize them. In brief, the unexplored structural and competitive potential of joint-venture strategies could be immense if managed skillfully.

Strategic Uses

Table 2–1 suggests that joint ventures could be strategic weapons, as well. Joint ventures can be a way to implement *changes* in firms' strategic positions, as in the example of Combustion Engineering and Rockwell in atomic reactors. They can increase (or decrease) firms' domains, as in the example of Mitsui's joint venture with AMAX, stabilize their existing domains, as in the example of the steel industry, or help them to achieve diverse strategy objectives, as in the example of Corning Glass Works and Siemens in fiber optics.[10] The strategic objectives that could be attained by using them are numerous, provided they are managed effectively.

If relationships are managed correctly, table 2–1 notes that joint ventures may create synergies with parent firms' activities, as in the example of Hilton Hotels, which learned how to use joint ventures overseas. (In 1975 Hilton built hotels only within the United States with joint venture partners, except for Las Vegas.) Cooperative strategies could offer a means of leveraging synergies between the skills and resources of parent and child. As an intermediate alternative between acquisition (or internal development) and dependence on outsiders, joint ventures represent a special, highly flexible means of enhancing innovation or achieving other strategic objectives which managers should not overlook.

As product lives become increasingly short and the rate of technological innovation accelerates, table 2–1 suggests that joint ventures could become increasingly important as a means of attaining "toehold" entries into new businesses that may be of long-term strategic importance to venture partners, such as cable communications for newspaper publishers. They can allow firms to diversify into attractive but unfamiliar business areas, as in the examples of Sony's joint ventures with Pepsico, Wilson Sporting Goods, and Prudential Insurance, respectively. Joint ventures could help firms to diversify from unfavorable businesses into more promising ones, as in the example of Philips's using a joint venture with M/A-Com to test demand for fiber optics.

Table 2–1 also points out that joint ventures may be a means of entering (or divesting) businesses, as in the example of the Airbus Industrie entry—composed of Aerospatiale (47.9%) of France, Messerschmitt-Bolkow-Blohm (MBB) (31.1%) of Germany, VFW-Fokker (16.8%), itself a Dutch/German joint venture, and Construcciones Aeronauticas (4.2%)—or of expanding internationally, as in the example of ALCOA, which reentered the world aluminum markets in 1959 by using a partnership. In addition to providing a less risky means of entering new markets, joint ventures could provide a nondisruptive means of divesting substantial businesses that no longer fit corporate objectives.

In summary, as table 2–1 has noted, many *internal, competitive,* and *strategic* benefits can be gained through joint ventures if managers must forge cooperative strategies. The strategic benefits of diversification and synergies with sister business units need further discussion, for these benefits attributed to joint ventures are particularly difficult to manage effectively.

Diversification Uses

When joint ventures are used as a means of diversifying from or enlarging the scope of firms' ongoing activities, the way in which the child is related to its parent determines its *pattern of diversification*. If the joint-venture child is *horizontally* related to a parent, it performs the same product, market, or technology tasks that the parent performs, albeit in a different geographic arena, as in the example of Airborne Freight's joint venture in Canada.

Vertical joint ventures create children whose activities and outputs could supply to or distribute for their parent firms, as in the example of Knight-Ridder's newsprint joint venture with Media General. *Diversifying* joint ventures (which are neither horizontal nor vertical) create entities that do not perform activities that their parents perform, as in the example of General Tire & Rubber's joint venture (with La Quinta) in motels. Nor can parents consume the products or services of diversifying joint ventures.

Since there will be at least two parents, two or more types of relationships can exist between a joint venture (child) and its parents. If partners are not competitors, then different patterns of diversification will relate each parent to the joint-venture child in this study.

Horizontal Cooperation. Parents may form joint ventures that create horizontally related competitors to expand their market scopes, expand or fill out their product lines, or rationalize excess capacity, as in the example of American Maize's corn wet milling joint venture with Amalgamated Sugar. Innovation may be their primary motive to cooperate, as in the example of General Electric's sodium-sulphur joint venture with the Electric Power Research Institute. (When horizontally related parents join forces to create a supplier or distribution channel, it is classified as *vertical cooperation* in this study because their *child* is vertically related to its parents.)

The issues associated with horizontal cooperation are those of creating new competition (a horizontally related child) versus deterring potential entrants. These are tradeoffs that U.S. firms have faced several times in the past.[11] In the 1980s the major difference is that potential partners are often foreign horizontal competitors possessing absolute cost advantages over ongoing domestic firms. These intruders need not create a joint venture to enter the domestic firm's markets successfully, as chapter 3 explains. With them, the issue for domestic firms becomes whether the cooperative advances of potential entrants should be welcomed or rebuffed.

Vertical Cooperation. Vertical joint ventures (those where the child is at a different stage of the transformation chain than its parents are) are often formed to decrease dependency on outsiders and circumvent market imperfections. They could also be used to develop young industries, as in the example of American Natural Resources' participation in the Great Plains coal gasification project.[12] Sometimes competitors will join forces to build supplying plants that are larger than either firm could use alone to exploit scale economies, or they may pioneer new distribution channels together, as in the example of Trintex's videotex shopping service venture (IBM, CBS, and Sears). If effective product differentiation could give their firms sustainable advantages (and if economies necessitate sharing a facility), managers will forge vertical joint ventures, as in the example of Merrill, Lynch's database joint venture with IBM. Most likely, parents will do so because quality control depends on good relationships between production stages, as in the example of Tracer Technologies' spectral analyzer venture. Thus, suppliers (or buyers) may form a child to improve raw material or component quality, to design new products, or to shore up local firms' positions against imports, as in the example of computer makers forming joint ventures with local electronic components firms.

Earlier studies, which regarded joint ventures primarily as a means of entering newly industrializing countries (where infrastructures often did not exist previously), found many vertical joint ventures. Vertical integration is often necessary early in the development of an economy, as in the example of the U.S. railroad firms' many activities during the nineteenth century. It is also necessary within embryonic industries if an appropriate infrastructure does not yet exist, as in the example of the early years of the personal computer industry when Texas Instruments owned computer retail stores. Vertical joint ventures are most prevalent in new industries and young economies.

Diversification and Cooperation Strategies. Diversifying joint ventures (involving parents who are not horizontally or vertically related to the child's activities) are used to gain access to knowledge, technology, or other resources that firms seek, as well as to enter new and unfamiliar businesses where entry barriers are so high that firms could not enter alone, as in the example of MCA's videodisc player joint venture with IBM. *Related* diversification joint ventures exploit some core skill or expertise of their parents—whether it is marketing, R&D, production, or managerial skills, as in the example of Volt Information Sciences' joint venture with Minnesota Mining & Manufacturing. (*Unrelated* diversifications do not.)

As with the horizontal and vertical diversifications discussed above, the true strategic benefits of joint ventures cannot be assessed until the other sides of the triangle can be assessed. In brief, the strategic benefits anticipated from diversification (and associated synergies) depend on the dynamics of relationships between parents with their child, between firms as partners, and be-tween the child and its competitive environment. Managers embrace joint ventures where they anticipate that (1) synergies with their firms' wholly owned business units can be exploited or (2) they can attain scale or inte-gration economies. But (as chapters 4 and 5 will explain), synergies and economies cannot be realized unless the appropriate managerial systems are in place and unless parents allow their child sufficient autonomy to cope with competition effectively.

Drawbacks of Joint Ventures

Despite their many potential uses and benefits, joint ventures frequently go awry and create problems. There are dangers in using joint ventures, which include antitrust problems, sovereignty conflicts, losses of autonomy and control, and a loss of competitive advantage through strategic inflexibility. Some of these drawbacks are due to the relative inexperience of firms in using joint ventures. Others are due, in part, to their governments' ignorance con-cerning this strategy option, as well as unrealistic trade policies. Finally, prob-lems are created by parent firms' *inabilities to manage* joint ventures effectively, and these are the primary concern of this study.

Antitrust Problems

Because legislators cannot foresee all technological changes that may occur when they draft a law, governments' policies regarding economic regulation must be dynamic. Some industrialized nations, like the United States, have enforced strict antitrust laws that prohibited cooperative strategies when they appeared to function as monopolies do or behaved collusively.[13] But late in 1984 U.S. antitrust officials indicated that joint ventures might be tolerated (even among competitors within highly concentrated markets) if *efficiency gains* offset the harm to competition that such arrangements had previously been assumed to create.[14]

Note that until 1984 U.S. antitrust authorities preferred to treat many forms of cooperative strategy as though the partners had merged, as in the ex-ample of Olin's joint venture with Pennsalt. (The lawsuit suggested that *all* forms of cooperation were suspect and that strategists should prepare for an-titrust challenges whenever planning corporate alliances within the United States.) When firms plan joint ventures within such environments, it is par-ticularly important to show a procompetitive design and an antitrust-sensi-tive explanation of the (1) need for the joint venture, with convincing por-trayals of the (2) inability of *either* parent to go it alone, the (3) expected gains in efficiency from cooperation, the (4) stream of new products (or technologies) that the alliance could create, and (5) what role the joint venture would play in promoting the growth and international competitiveness of the national economy. Because cooperative strategies raise questions of market division and limited freedoms to compete vigorously,[15] aspiring partners must write their joint-venture agreements carefully, with thoughtful provision for the resolution of disputes and modifications to suit local antitrust agencies. Neglect of this aspect of joint-venture planning could result in costly litigation with public agencies (or private parties), wasteful exposure of company resources on litigation, exposure of firms' innermost business secrets, and potential loss of competitive momentum.[16]

Sovereignty Conflicts

In the traditional use of joint ventures as a means of expanding internationally, firms often accepted local firms as partners because they were unwilling to license their competitive advantages but local laws prohibited majority ownership by outsiders, as in the example of Japan until recently.[17]

Often the objectives of host nations are not the same as those of the joint-venture partners, and this conflict is likely to persist even within mature, industrialized economies. For example, domestic partners frequently want to import highly advanced technologies and leading global brand names into their home markets as a sort of instant remedy that would give them overwhelming advantages over local competitors. But host governments frequently want those technologies that create jobs for the greatest number of workers. Alternatively, foreign partners may form joint ventures with local firms to use technologies that exploit the advantages of lower wages, as in the example of General Motors' Korean joint venture with Daewoo to make automobiles. But many host governments want the most modern technologies, rather than those that would make the most sense from parents' viewpoints. Thus, the state-versus-firm conflict results in different perspectives concerning the timing of exploiting innovations or transferring technology between parent and child.[18]

The result of these conflicts could be problems in day-to-day operations or in capital recovery if foreign parents are unwilling to accommodate governments' economic development plans.[19] In brief, decisions regarding whether to license technology (or brand names) or take local partners in joint ventures cannot be analyzed using traditional schemes of technology transfer if host governments exert substantial bargaining power, especially if local partners are nationalized firms.[20] If local partners exerted such bargaining power, they would be able to disrupt the schedule by which their global partners had intended to share that knowledge that gave them competitive advantages overseas, as when they enforce mandatory licensing of second-source suppliers.[21]

Loss of Autonomy and Control

In addition to problems concerning local regulation, many conflicts within joint ventures arise from the simple fact that *there is more than one parent.* Each parent wants to coordinate the child's activities with its own, and often partners have not created mechanisms to resolve day-to-day deadlocks in decision making. Poorly structured joint ventures encourage the types of political behavior problems sketched in appendix 2A. Parents often find they differ in their *long-term* objectives, time horizons, operating styles, and expectations for the venture (especially with respect to potential for synergies with the joint venture), as in the example of research-oriented partners teamed with marketing-oriented firms. Parent's fears that they will lose strategic flexibility prevent joint ventures from being effective, and such fears often exacerbate the difficulties of coordinating the child's daily operations, as in the example of ventures where technologies change rapidly.

The costs of cooperating in a joint venture will often be sizable because they involve a multitude of resources to be committed, including time, money, materials, personnel, and communications, as in the example of General Dynamics' venture to build cryogenic tankers for liquid natural gas (LNG) transportation. There will be drawbacks from opportunities forgone, and parents will often be concerned over their *perceived* loss of control over invested capital, technical resources, and proprietary information that might be disseminated to outsiders, as in the example of many electronics ventures. Commitments to ongoing partners may reduce firms' opportunities to forge alliances with other firms in the future.[22] Fears concerning firms' losses of strategic flexibility can weigh most heavily of all; thus some firms refuse even to discuss the use of joint activities as a means to supplement their ongoing strategies.

Strategic Inflexibility and Loss of
Competitive Advantages

Many internal benefits could be enjoyed if joint ventures were used effectively, but since firms seek diverse strategy objectives when forging joint ventures, there will be limits to what they should expect to achieve through them.

Past studies suggest that in their eagerness for gain, firms have often invested too little of the appropriate time or resources in their joint ventures. Most frequently, parents expected synergies to accrue without explicitly managing for their creation. Parent representatives on governing boards have devoted too little attention to the strategic direction of the joint venture, perhaps because the wrong representatives served on them. Parents have maintained too much control over the child's investment, business expansion, or other important decisions, perhaps because they were uncertain what the venture should achieve and were reluctant to trust the child's managers to make these decisions correctly.

If the reasons for forming joint ventures are poorly conceived, if partners are not selected carefully, if firms have overestimated their partners' strengths, or if the agreements and systems used to control the venture are inadequate, such that each partner believes the other is shortchanging it, firms may often be worse off than they were before entering joint ventures.

Giving half-hearted attentions to joint ventures is as bad as giving too much attention and often creates handicaps for both parents and child. Sometimes joint ventures grow up to enter markets where managers had not anticipated they would be competitors, as in the example of Pan American—which was ordered in 1963 to divest its interest in Panagra (a joint venture between Pan American and W.R. Grace) after it tried to block Panagra's request before the Civil Aeronautics Board for the award of routes that competed with Pan American's services. Worst of all, poorly structured agreements can spread the firm's expertise to third parties that are not members of the joint venture, and this inadvertently occurs where joint ventures are structured loosely in terms of policies for personnel rotation and other ways of repatriating knowledge.[23] These strategic issues are crucial for joint venture success and are covered in chapters 4 and 5.

Participation in joint ventures could have adverse effects on the corporate prestige, identity, or strategic positions of partners because the venture's activities may sap the motivation and innovative fervor of their personnel within ongoing business units, especially if the management systems that integrate parent and child do not arbitrate between their needs adequately. Some parents found that when resources and capabilities were commingled, the weaker partner often benefited the most, as in the example of small firms that team with larger, experienced firms. If joint ventures were horizontal, strong firms found that they had more to lose than to gain by cooperating, especially if the knowledge comprising their technological core was highly appropriable. If linkages were forged with specific suppliers or distribution channels, firms often increased (rather than decreased) their exposure to shortfalls and bottlenecks because doing so meant alienating vertically related outsiders that might have served as safety nets when shortages (or surpluses) occurred.

The problems that U.S. firms have encountered in managing their international joint ventures suggest the types of difficulties that could arise domestically as well. In particular, joint ventures with global partners may be tolerated only as long as the global firm is required to have local partners by law *or inexperience*, as in the example of the termination of Fujitsu's joint venture with TRW, Inc.

Previous studies have well documented that having partners means that decision making will be cumbersome.[24] Revisions to production plans are difficult, and plant closings become a frequent source of conflict in many joint ventures, especially in unionized industries. The difficulties encountered historically concerning controversies about new product designs, production scheduling (and locations), and vertical integration arrangements explain, in part, why many firms that have entered joint ventures overseas dispose of their partners as soon as was feasible, rather than perpetuate an ill-fitting alliance.[25] Joint ventures have even been considered to be impediments to the flexibility of firms' global strategies because effective competition requires manipulation of *all* parts of firms' global networks—yet consider the examples of the chemicals, oil, or other global industries where effective use of transshipments must be frictionless. Joint ventures have long played an important role in firms' global schemes in these industries. What accounts for these differences in experiences?

A Timely Managerial Challenge

Knowing merely the potential uses and drawbacks of joint ventures, as the preceding sections have sketched them, is not an adequate analysis for their managers. Literature searches describing the benefits and costs of joint ventures are fine, but they do no more than point out to managers the challenges that must be overcome. They are not enough because they do not go far enough in addressing how to manage the tensions of joint-venture relationships. *The missing link in understanding joint-venture strategies is analysis of the dynamic interactions of the three key actors.*

Joint ventures have become so prevalent within the United States that every manager needs to consider what effect this structural change will have on the way that his or her firm will compete. Joint ventures are an important structural trait of emerging industries such as alternative energy, communications services, and biotechnology industries. As such, they represent a key strategy decision that has the potential to force an industry to evolve in an unfavorable way if firms are not alert. Joint ventures bring the viewpoints of new players (parents) into the competitive arena, and they can create stronger, hybrid opponents (the children) if managers can channel the interactions between parent and child, and between partners, into an effort to make the child a formidable player within its industry. Unless managers understand these dynamics, they cannot formulate effective joint-venture strategies.

Past studies indicate that managers have often disparaged joint ventures, believing them to be too complex, too ambiguous, or too inflexible.[26] But as the challenges of competition increase, as projects grow larger and more risky, and as technologies become too expensive to afford alone, managers must learn how to use joint ventures, even in their firms' home markets.[27] Despite the reluctance of many firms to participate in them and their relatively high failure rates, joint ventures are becoming common entry strategies, even within industries that have become global, like the aerospace industries. Yet strategic tradeoffs must be made when joint ventures are employed. Compromise will be necessary. The next three chapters describe these compromises.

Notes

1. Aharoni, Yair, 1966, *The Foreign Investment Decision Process* (Boston: Division of Research, Graduate School of Business Administration, Harvard University); Dymsza, William A., 1972, *Multinational Business Strategy* (New York: McGraw-Hill); Gullander, Stefan O.O., 1975, "An Exploratory Study of Inter-Firm Cooperation of Swedish Firms," Ph.D. diss., Columbia University; Young, G. Richard, and Bradford, Standish, Jr., 1977, *Joint Ventures: Planning and Action* (New York: Arthur D. Little and the Financial Executives Research Foundation).

2. Pfeffer, Jeffrey, 1972, "Merger as a Response to Organizational Interdependence," *Administrative Science Quarterly* 17:382–394; Pfeffer, Jeffrey, and Nowak, P., 1976, "Joint Ventures and Interorganizational Interdependence," *Administrative Science Quarterly* 21(3):398–418; Williamson, Oliver, 1975, *Markets and Hierarchies: Analysis and Antitrust Implication* (New York: Free Press).

Pfeffer and Nowaks's (1976) study of the patterns of joint-venture activity hypothesized that interorganizational linkages could be used to manage both competitive and symbiotic interdependencies. (The terminology comes from Pfeffer (1972), where vertical linkages were entered into to absorb *symbiotic* interdependence, horizontal linkages absorbed *competitive* interdependence, and nonrelated linkages were a form of diversification.) Thus to the extent that firms within industry *A* were interdependent with firms within industry *B*, a higher proportion of joint ventures would be found with firms of that industry, and the higher the concentration of an upstream industry, the greater correlation between joint ventures and purchase interdependence because firms would have few alternate sources of supply. The systematic pattern they sought was tested using industry-level data, and their sample was limited only to joint ventures between domestic partners for which financial (corporate-level) data were available. Their dependent variable was the pattern of interorganizational linkage activity accomplished through joint ventures. (Specifically, Pfeffer and Nowak (1976) looked at industry-level data, such as (a) proportion of industry$_i$'s purchases made from industry$_j$, (b) proportion of industry$_i$'s sales made to industry$_j$, and (c) proportion of industry$_i$'s total transactions made with industry$_j$, including both sales and purchases.) Their results suggested that there may be several motives for coalitions but that transactions interdependence showed high correlation with joint-venture activity. Although their data were not appropriate to test hypotheses linking participants from diverse industry settings with each other, their research represents one of the first empirical tests of the motives for joint-venture formation.

3. Drucker, Peter, 1974, *Management: Tasks, Responsibilities, Promises* (New York: Harper & Row); Hlavacek, James D., and Thompson, V.A., 1976, "The Joint Venture Approach to Technology Utilization," *ILEE Transactions on Engineering*

Management EM-23(1):35–41; Yoshihara, Hideki, 1971, "The Japanese Multinational," *Long Range Planning*, pp. 41–45; Berg, Sanford V., and Friedman, P., 1980, "Corporate Courtship and Successful Joint Ventures," *California Management Review* 22(2):85–91.

4. Ballon, Robert J., ed., 1976, *Joint Ventures and Japan* (Tokyo: Sophia University); Franko, Lawrence G., 1971, *Joint Venture Survival in Multinational Corporations* (New York: Praeger; Daniels, John D., 1971, *Recent Foreign Direct Manufacturing Investment in the United States: An Interview Study of the Decision Process* (New York: Praeger).

5. Harrigan, K.R., 1984, "Joint Ventures and Global Strategies," *Columbia Journal of World Business* 19(2):7–16.

6. Killing, J. Peter, 1983, *Strategies for Joint Venture Success* (New York: Praeger).

7. Bivens, Karen Kraus, and Lovell, Enid Baird, 1966, *Joint Ventures with Foreign Partners* (New York: National Industrial Conference Board); MacMillan, I.C., 1980, "How Business Strategies Can Use Guerilla Warfare Tactics," *Journal of Business Strategy* 1(2):63–85; MacMillan, I.C., 1982, "Seizing Competitive Initiative," *Journal of Business Strategy* 2(4):43–57; MacMillan, I.C., 1983, "Preemptive Strategies," *Journal of Business Strategy* 4(2):16–26.

8. Orski, C. Kenneth, 1980, "The World Automotive Industry at a Crossroads: Cooperative Alliances," *Vital Speeches* 47(3):89–93.

9. Bachman, Jules, 1965, "Joint Ventures in the Light of Recent Antitrust Developments: Joint Ventures in the Chemical Industry," *Antitrust Bulletin* 10:7–23; Brodley, Joseph F., 1979, "Joint Ventures and the Justice Department's Antitrust Guide for International Operations," *Antitrust Bulletin* 24:337–356.

10. Edstrom, Anders, 1975, "Acquisition and Joint Venture Behavior of Swedish Manufacturing Firms," working paper, University of Gothenburg; Pfeffer, Jeffrey, and Salancik, Gerald R., 1978, *The External Control of Organizations: A Resource Dependence Perspective* (New York: Harper & Row).

11. Estimates of the patterns between partners and between parent and child business entities have varied substantially in the past. See Boyle, Stanley E., 1968, "An Estimate of the Number and Size Distribution of Domestic Joint Subsidiaries," *Antitrust Law and Economics Review* 1:81–92; Pate, J.L., 1969, "Joint Venture Activity, 1960–1968," *Economic Review* (Cleveland: Federal Reserve Bank of Cleveland), pp. 16–23; Pfeffer, Jeffrey, and Nowak, Phillip, 1976, "Patterns of Joint Venture Activity: Implications for Antitrust Policy," *Antitrust Bulletin* 21(2):315–359; Ferguson, Roger W., Jr., 1981, "The Nature of Joint Ventures in the American Manufacturing Sector," Ph.D. diss., Harvard University. Boyle (1968) found that 44 percent of the joint ventures he studied were horizontal and less than 10 percent were unrelated or conglomerate diversifications. Pate (1969) found that nearly 50 percent of the parents forming joint ventures were already horizontally related; nearly 80 percent of the parents forming JVs from 1960 through 1968 were either horizontally or vertically related. Pate also found that more than 50 percent of the relationships between parents and progeny in the JVs formed between 1960 through 1968 were vertical and more than 80 percent of the arrangements resulted in horizontal and/or vertical relationships between one or more parents and JV progeny. Pfeffer and Nowak (1976) found that 56 percent of the joint activity in their sample was undertaken between horizontally related firms.

In Ferguson's (1981) study, of the 145 JVs for which full information on SIC codes of parent and child were available, the principal outputs of only thirteen were in the same three-digit SIC industry as *both* parents; less than 10 percent of the JVs represented no diversification on the part of at least one of the parents in Ferguson's study.

12. Harrigan, K.R., 1983, *Strategies for Vertical Integration* (Lexington: Lexington Books).

13. Mead, W.J., 1967, "The Competitive Significance of Joint Ventures," *Antitrust Bulletin* 12:819–849; Davidow, Joel, 1977, "International Joint Ventures and the U.S. Antitrust Laws," *Akron Law Review* 10:161–173; Rowe, Frederick M., 1980, "Antitrust Aspects of European Acquisitions and Joint Ventures in the United States," *Law and Policy in International Business* 12(2):335–368.

14. "Joint Ventures: Justice Becomes a Cheerleader," 1984, *Business Week*, November 19:48–49; Taylor, Robert E., 1984, "Joint Ventures Likely to Be Encouraged by Friendlier Attitude of U.S. Officials," *Wall Street Journal*, November 5:8; Halverson, James T., 1984, "Transnational Joint Ventures and Mergers under U.S. Antitrust Law," in *Proceedings: Fordham Corporate Law Institute* (New York: Bender).

15. Broden, Thomas F., and Scanlon, Alfred L., 1958, "The Legal Status of Joint Ventures Corporations," *Vanderbilt Law Review* 11:689; Tractenberg, Paul, 1963, "Joint Ventures on the Domestic Front: A Study in Uncertainty," *Antitrust Bulletin* 8(4):797–841; Berghoff, John C., 1963, "Antitrust Aspects of Joint Ventures," *Antitrust Bulletin* 9(2):231–254; Turner, Donald F., 1980, "An Antitrust Analysis of Joint Ventures," unpublished manuscript, of counsel, Wilmer & Pickering, Washington, D.C.; Brodley, Joseph F., 1982, "Joint Ventures and Antitrust Policy," *Harvard Law Review* 95(7):1523–1590.

16. Turner, D.G., 1965, "Conglomerate Mergers and Section 7 of the Clayton Act," *Harvard Law Review* 78:1790; Gesell, Gerhard A., 1965, "Joint Ventures in Light of Recent Antitrust Developments: Joint Venture and the Prosecutor," *Antitrust Bulletin* 10(1 + 2):31–40; Bachman, Jules, 1965, "Joint Ventures and the Antitrust Laws," *New York University Law Review* 40:651–671; Treeck, Joachim, 1970, "Joint Research Ventures and Antitrust Law in the United States, Germany and the European Economic Community," *Journal of International Law and Politics* 3(1):18–55; Ewing, K.P., Jr., 1981, "Joint Research, Antitrust, and Innovation," *Research Management* 24(2):25–29.

17. Vernon, Raymond, 1971, *Sovereignty at Bay: The Multinational Spread of U.S. Enterprise* (New York: Basic Books); Vernon, Raymond, 1977, *Storm over the Multinationals* (Cambridge, Mass.: Harvard University Press); Wright, Richard W., and Russel, Colin S., 1975, "Joint Ventures in Developing Countries: Realities and Responses," *Columbia Journal of World Business* 10(2):74–80; Gregory, Gene, 1976, "Japan's New Multinationalism: The Canon Giessen Experience," *Columbia Journal of World Business* 11:122–126; Wright, Richard W, 1977, "Canadian Joint Ventures in Japan," *Business Quarterly*, 42–53.

18. Vernon, Raymond, and Wells, Louis T., Jr., 1976, *Manager in the International Economy* (Englewood Cliffs, N.J.: Prentice-Hall); Young, G. Richard, and Bradford, Standish, Jr., 1976, "Joint Ventures in Europe—Determinants of Entry," *International Studies of Management and Organizations* 12(6):85–111.

19. Franko, L.G., 1976, *The European Multinationals* (London: Harper & Row).

20. Vernon, Raymond, 1966, "International Investment and International Trade in the Product Cycle," *Quarterly Journal of Economics* 53(2):191–207; Gabriel, Peter P., 1967, *The International Transfer of Corporate Skills* (Boston, Mass.: Harvard Business School, Division of Research); Harrigan, Kathryn Rudie, 1984, "Innovations by Overseas Subsidiaries," *Journal of Business Strategy* 5:7–16.

21. Davis, Howard, 1977, "Technology Transfer through Commercial Transactions," *Journal of Industrial Economics* 26(2):161–175; Ray, Edward John, 1977, "Foreign Direct Investment in Manufacturing," *Journal of Political Economy* 85(2): 283–297.

22. Friedman, W., and Kalmanoff, G., 1961, *Joint International Business Ventures* (New York: Columbia University Press); Edstrom, Anders, 1975, "The Stability of Joint Ventures," working paper, University of Gothenberg; Picard, Jacques, 1977, "How European Companies Control Marketing Decisions Abroad," *Columbia Journal of Business* 8(1):113–121.

23. Krosin, Kenneth E., 1971, "Joint Research Ventures under the Antitrust Laws," *George Washington Law Review* 39(5):1112–1140; Duncan, Jerome L., Jr., 1980, "The Causes and Effects of Domestic Joint Venture Activity," Ph.D. diss., University of Florida; U.S. Department of Justice, Antitrust Division, 1981, "Antitrust Guide for Joint Research Programs," *Research Management* 24(2):30–37; Sczudlo, Raymond S., 1981, "Antitrust Aspects of Shared EFT Systems," *Journal of Retail Banking* 23–29; Brodley, Joseph F., 1982, "Joint Ventures and Antitrust Policy," *Harvard Law Review* 95(7):1523–1590.

24. Berg, Sanford, Duncan, Jerome, and Friedman, Philip, 1982, *Joint Venture Strategies and Corporate Innovation* (Cambridge, Mass.: Oelgeschlager, Gunn & Hain).

25. Marquis, Harold L., 1964, "Compatibility of Industrial Joint Research Ventures and Antitrust Policy," *Temple Law Quarterly* 38(1):1–37; Franko, Lawrence G., 1971, "Joint Venture Divorce in the Multinational Company," *Columbia Journal of World Business* 4(3):13–22.

26. Twiss, Brian, 1974, *Managing Technological Innovation* (London: Longman Group); Friedman, Philip, Berg, S., and Duncan, J., 1979, "External vs. Internal Knowledge Acquisition: An Analysis of Research and Development Intensity and Joint Ventures," *Journal of Economics and Business* 31(2):103–110; Killing, J. Peter, 1982, "How to Make a Global Joint Venture Work," *Harvard Business Review* 6(3):120–127.

27. Gullander, Steffan, 1976, "Joint Ventures and Corporate Strategy," *Columbia Journal of World Business* 11:104–114.

Appendix 2A:
Political Theories of Joint Ventures

Theories describing political behavior may be applied to analyses of joint venture strategies. This appendix sketches a literature of political behavior and provides additional references for interested readers. The creation of joint ventures is analogous to *coalition formation*, in which interest groups that are committed to achieving common goals join forces.[1] These factions cooperate when needed and compete otherwise.[2] Homogeneous management teams—those who approach problem solving similarly to potential partners—will find joint ventures easier to manage. Homogeneous parents will agree more frequently on the actions to be taken to remedy their child's performance shortfalls, as in the example of the oil industry or the entertainment industry, where spider's webs of joint ventures are commonplace.[3] Heterogeneous management teams, by contrast, will be more prone to political behavior, since their perceptions of problems (and possible solutions) are more likely to differ.[4] Such differences will materialize, for example, in the diverse commercialization paths preferred by high technology–based firms compared with lower technology–based firms, as in the example of biotechnology joint ventures, as well as in other areas where joint-venture partners must agree on strategic actions.[5] Coalition formation and political behavior may be predicted to occur in all joint activities, and managers must be aware that politics can stymie the smooth running of joint ventures,[6] as can resource asymmetries and other forces discussed below. These caveats are discussed in length in chapters 3, 4, and 5.

Notes to Appendix 2A

1. March, J.G., 1962, "The Business Firm as a Political Coalition," *Journal of Politics* 24:662–678; March, J.G., and H.S. Simon, 1958, *Organizations* (New York: Wiley); Gamson, W.A., 1961, "A Theory of Coalition Formation," *American Sociological Review* 26:372–382; Duncan, W.J., 1976, "Organizations as Political Coalitions: A Behavioral View of the Goal Formulation Process," *Journal of Behavioral Economics* 5(1):25–44; Pearce, John A., and De Nisi, Angelo S., 1983, "Attribution

Theory and Strategic Decision Making: An Application to Coalition Formation," *Academy of Management Journal* 26(1):119–128.

2. Riker, W.H., 1962, *The Theory of Political Coalition* (New Haven, Conn.: Yale University Press). Ironically, a firm with no slack resources would not be predicted to engage in coalition-building activities, since one of the strategic functions of organizational slack is to provide resources for creative and innovative experimentation. An ailing firm cannot form a joint venture that favors its interests, see Cyert, R.M., and March, J.G., 1963, *A Behavioral Theory of the Firm* (Englewood Cliffs, N.J.: Prentice-Hall); Schermerhorn, John R., Jr., 1974, "Determinants of Cooperative Interorganizational Relations: Notes toward a Working Model," in Green, T.B., and Ray, D.F., eds., *Proceedings: Academy of Management* (Boston: National Academy of Management); Schermerhorn, John R., Jr., 1975, "Determinants of Interorganizational Cooperation," *Academy of Management Journal* 18:846–956; Schermerhorn, John R., Jr., 1976, "Openness to Interorganizational Cooperation: A Study of Hospital Administrators," *Academy of Management Journal* 19:225–236. See in particular Bourgeois, L.J., III, 1981, "On the Measurement of Organizational Slack," *Academy of Management Review* 6(1):29–39. Bourgeois noted that internal slack measures can include working capital items, dividends, and administration expenditures and that external slack could include debt capacity (or borrowing power) and credit rating. Changes in the spread between interest paid on short-term loans and the prime lending rate indicate which firms might obtain cheaper funds and changes in firms' abilities to generate funds from equity sources. These are measures suggesting various firms' levels of slack resources.

Bourgeois and Singh (1983) conceptualized slack in terms of an *ease-of-recovery* dimension to provide an empirical measure of organization slack using the financial indicators suggested above. In their framework, slack is comprised of available, recoverable, and potential slack. Briefly, *available slack* consists of resources that are not yet assimilated into the technical design of the firm (such as excess liquidity), *recoverable slack* consists of resources that have already been absorbed into the system design as excess costs (such as overhead) but may be recovered during adverse times, and *potential slack* consists of the capacity of the firm to generate extra resources from the environment, as by raising additional debt or equity capital. (See Bourgeois, L.J., III, and Singh, Jitendra, 1982, "Organizational Slack and Political Behavior within Top Management Teams," working paper, Stanford University, presented at the 1983 National Academy of Management Meetings, Dallas.)

Joint-venture formation is a political activity that must serve the aspirations of the dominant coalition of managers. Since it may well *cost* firms their slack resources in order to explore, establish, and maintain a joint venture, these managers will likely reject the risk associated with joint-venture formation if their objectives are not maximized, yet their firms' are often most in need of the benefits that joint ventures could offer. See Thompson, James D,. and McEwen, William J., 1958, "Organizational Goals and Environment: Goal-Setting as an Interaction Process," *American Sociological Review* 23:23–31; West, Malcolm W., Jr., 1959, "The Jointly-Owned Subsidiary," *Harvard Business Review* 32; Litwak, Eugene, and Hylton, Lydia F., 1962, "Interorganizational Analysis: A Hypothesis on Coordinating Agencies," *Administrative Science Quarterly* 6:395–420; Reid, W., 1964, "Interagency Coordination in Delinquency Prevention and Control, *Social Service Review* 38:418–428; Guetzkow,

Harold, 1966, "Relations among Organizations," in Bowers, Raymond V., ed., *Studies on Behavior in Organization* (Athens, Ga.: University of Georgia Press), 13–44; Aiken, M., and Hage, J, 1968, "Organizational Interdependence and Intraorganizational Structure," *American Sociological Review* 63:912–930; Litwak, Eugene, and Rothman, Jack, 1970, "Towards the Theory and Practice of Coordination Between Formal Organizations," in Rosengren, William R., and Lefton, Mark, eds., *Organizations and Clients* (Columbus, Ohio: Merrill); Pennings, Johannes, 1981, "Strategically Interdependent Organizations," in Nystrom, P.C., and Starbuck, W.H., eds., *Handbook of Organizational Design, vol. 1* (New York: Oxford University Press).

    3. Hambrick, Donald C., and Mason, Phyllis A., 1982, "Upper Echelons: The Organization as a Reflection of Its Top Managers," working paper, Columbia University.

    4. Filley, A.C., House, R.J., and Kerr, S., 1976, *Managerial Process and Organizational Behaviors* (Glenview, Ill.: Scott, Foresman).

    5. Levine, Sol, and White, Paul E., 1961, "Exchange as a Conceptual Framework for the Study of Interorganizational Relationships," *Administrative Science Quarterly* 5:583–601; Levine, S., White, P., and Paul, B., 1963, "Community Interorganizational Problems in Providing Medical Care and Social Services," *American Journal of Public Health* 53:1183–1195; Evan, William M., 1965, "Toward a Theory of Inter-Organizational Relations," *Management Science* 11: B217–B230; Barren, Roland L., 1967, "The Interorganizational Field as a Focus for Investigation," *Administrative Science Quarterly* 12:396–419; Wren, D.A., 1967, "Interface and Interorganizational Coordination," *Academy of Management Journal* 10:69–81; Reid, William J., 1971, *Interorganizational Coordination: A Review and Critique of Current Theory* (Washington, D.C.: U.S. Department of Health, Education & Welfare); Warren, Roland L., 1972, *The Concerting of Decisions as a Variable in Organizational Interaction* (Chicago: Aldine-Atherton); Starkweather, David B., 1972, "Beyond the Semantics of Multihospital Aggregations," *Health Services Research* 7: 58–61; Walton, R., 1972, "Interorganizational Decision Making and Identity Conflict," in Tuite, M., Chisholm, R., and Radnor, M., eds., *Interorganizational Decision Making* (Chicago: Aldine), 9–19; Van de Ven, A.H., 1976, "On the Nature, Formation and Maintenance of Relations among Organizations," *Academy of Management Review* 1:24–36; Bacharach, Samuel B., and Lawler, Edward J., 1980, *Power and Politics in Organizations* (San Francisco: Jossey-Bass).

    6. Thompson, James D., and McEwen, William J., 1958, "Organizational Goals and Environment: Goal-Setting as an Interaction Process," *American Sociological Review* 23:23–31; West, Malcolm W., Jr., 1959, "The Jointly-Owned Subsidiary," *Harvard Business Review* 32; Litwak, Eugene, and Hylton, Lydia F., 1962, "Interorganizational Analysis: A Hypothesis on Coordinating Agencies," *Administrative Science Quarterly* 6:395–420; Aiken, M., and Hage, J., 1968, "Organizational Interdependence and Intraorganizational Structure," *American Sociological Review* 63:912–930; Litwak, Eugene, and Rothman, Jack, 1970, "Towards the Theory and Practice of Coordination between Formal Organizations," in Rosengren, William R., and Lefton, Mark, eds., *Organizations and Clients* (Columbus, Ohio: Charles E. Merrill); Schermerhorn, John R., Jr., 1974, "Determinants of Cooperative Interorganizational Relations: Notes Toward a Working Model," in Grun, T.B., and Roy, D.F., eds., *Proceedings: Academy of Management* (Boston: National Academy of Management); Schermerhorn, John R., Jr., 1975, "Determinants of Interorganizational Cooperation," *Academy of Management Journal* 18:846–956.

3
Interactions among Joint-Venture Parents: The Analytical Model

Given shorter product lives, given maturing domestic economies, given the explosive effect of technological improvements on communications, computers, biotechnology, and other arenas where industry boundaries are formerly distinct, and given that many industries have become global in their scope of competition, how does one analyze the use of joint ventures in mature economies? From parent firms' perspectives, when do joint ventures make sense? Which firms are most appropriate as partners? What should they offer the venture? How should each partner's contributions to the joint venture be valued? When are there timing advantages in forging joint ventures, and how will changes in relationships between partners affect the joint venture's fate?

These and other questions concerning cooperative strategies are addressed in the joint-venture framework presented below. It covers the dynamics of relationships between firms as partners, relationships between parent and child, and relationships between the child and its competitive environment as these affect the viability of joint-venture strategies for its parents. As the heavy arrows in figure 3–1 indicate, chapter 3 will treat the first of these relationships—that of partners coming together in an agreement to form a joint venture (or other form of cooperative strategy). Because the framework is complex, portions of it are developed in three separate chapters that correspond to its three perspectives; chapter 4 addresses parent–child relationships, and chapter 5 presents the framework that relates that child to its competitive environment. An integrated overview of the framework is presented first.

Firms go through a cost–benefit analysis when deciding whether to form joint ventures. They expect to reap attractive benefits by cooperating, but at the same time firms hesitate when evaluating whether to cooperate because they may have to make significant sacrifices in doing so. Faced with the disadvantages that can be associated with joint ventures, firms may prefer to

I am indebted to William H. Newman for his many helpful suggestions concerning this chapter.

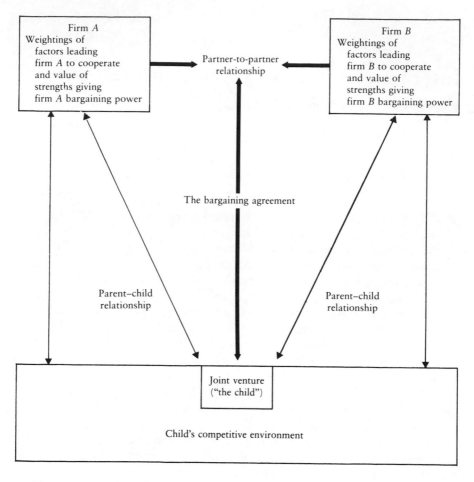

Figure 3–1. Partner-to-Partner Relationships Creating a Joint Venture

harness the advantages of cooperative strategies by using *nonequity* arrangements, such as those sketched in appendix 1A. But assuming that cooperation will be necessary in order for firms to achieve their strategic objectives, it would be helpful to have a framework that suggests which forces influence the viability and durability of joint ventures. It would be helpful to understand how firms might design and run joint ventures to be most effective.

This chapter presents a framework that describes how the joint-venture bargain might best be struck. A series of hypotheses are proposed herein concerning *whether* joint ventures will be formed and *how* they will be structured. The framework assumes that the joint-venture child requires access to certain inputs and a healthy market for its outputs in order to be viable. (Whether access to these input and distribution channels will be provided by the joint venture's parents (or not) is left open in the development of the framework because many arrangements are possible. Vertical relationships, as well as horizontal relationships, are included among the many possible links that parent firms may have with their joint ventures.) If a joint venture is not viable, it is not expected to survive for long.

An Overview of the Joint-Venture Framework

The resources and attributes parent firms will share with their child affect both their willingness to form a joint venture and each parent's relative bargaining power therein. Whether the bargain that parents strike in cooperating will take the form of a joint venture (or other cooperative arrangement) depends on the bilateral bargaining power among its parents and on other forces (discussed below). This *balance of power* evolves over time due to the effects of a variety of internal and external change forces (also explained below). Although joint ownership may endure in some ventures for decades (as in the example of Royal Dutch/Shell), parents will often resolve the tensions of shared decision-making arrangements by dissolving their joint-venture partnerships earlier rather than later. Thus, cooperative strategies are, at best, transitory organizational arrangements in many cases.

Hypotheses comprising the joint-venture framework are sketched in figure 3–2 and numbered. Arguments concerning the forces that determine parents' motivations and fears, their strengths and shortfalls, and their willingness to form joint ventures are developed here and in chapters 4 and 5. (Tests of the framework appear in chapters 7 through 12.) The framework is dynamic, and discussion of it will progress in three stages: (1) a single-firm analysis of the costs and benefits of forming a joint venture, (2) the meshing of two (or more) firms' bargaining positions to form a joint-venture agreement, and (3) changes in their initial bargain as conditions change. As was noted in figure 3–1, these three stages of analysis address but one side of the strategic triangle (or quadrangle)—the partners' side. An overview of the entire three- (or multi-) sided relationship of joint-venture strategies follows. Details of the partners' side of the argument complete this brief sketch of the joint-venture formation decision.

Summary of Single-Firm Considerations

Hypotheses concerning individual firms' positions are sketched in this section. Briefly, in figure 3–2, parent firm *A* seeks certain (1) benefits from affiliating

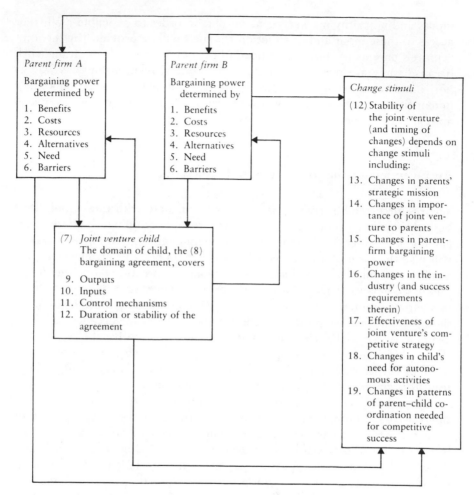

Figure 3–2. Model of Joint-Venture Activity

with firm *B*. These benefits are its reasons to cooperate with a partner. Firm *A* also faces (2) costs in using joint ventures that may be too significant for it to accept. If firm *A*'s costs exceed expected benefits, negotiations to form joint ventures with firm *A* become fruitless or will take some other form. But if firm *A* sees benefits such as synergies, scale economies, or other benefits sketched in chapter 2 that exceed costs, a bargain may be struck. Thus, the first premise of the joint-venture framework is that effective joint ventures will be formed *only* if each firm believes that there is greater advantage in cooperating than there will be costs. (Firm *B* also performs this analysis before it is ready to strike a bargain.)

Each firm in figure 3–2 possesses resources and skills that could serve as potential inputs to the joint venture. The greater the firms' (3) resources and (4) alternatives for attaining their objectives, the greater their bargaining power. But the greater their (5) need to cooperate, the less their bargaining power will be in negotiating the joint-venture agreement. The greater the magnitude of opportunity costs or other disadvantages firms perceive in cooperating, the higher will be their (6) barriers to cooperation. (It will be necessary to overcome these inertia barriers if a joint venture is to be formed initially. After the agreement is consummated, inertia barriers will impede *renegotiations* of the bargaining agreement, encumber parents' abilities to use their child effectively, and limit the child's ability to compete advantageously.)

A Summary of Bargaining Agreement Considerations

In figure 3–2, the *form* of the (7) child is the net result of the bilateral bargaining power of its parents. Its form (equity joint venture or other arrangements sketched in appendix 1A) will be defined by (8) terms of a bargaining agreement (and this framework may be applied to other forms of cooperative strategy that are beyond the scope of this study). The agreement, which defines the child's domain of activities, will specify its (9) outputs, and it may specify its customers, as well. (The purpose of the joint venture's existence is usually defined by these outputs.)

Terms of the bargaining agreement between parent firms should specify which (10) inputs are necessary for the joint venture to attain its objectives. These inputs may be provided for by the child's parents through a variety of vertical integration arrangements, or they may be obtained from outsiders. The child cannot be viable, however, if its parents do not provide for an *economic* source of (or means of attaining) these inputs.

The (8) bargaining agreement in figure 3–2 also specifies the (11) control mechanisms that parent firms will use to ensure that the benefits they desired were indeed received. The control mechanisms provide for how partners develop managerial resources, how the joint venture's board of directors will control partners' interests, and how disputes will be resolved. Thus, the formal agreement provides for ways of maintaining the (12) stability of the joint venture. It defines when and how the venture ends, as well. (Control mechanisms are discussed at length in chapter 4, which treats the parent–child side of the model. As chapter 4 will explain, the tradeoffs between coordination and autonomy will affect the integrating mechanisms parents employ, whether the child is horizontally or vertically related to its parents and whether parents share facilities with it. Resource sharing is difficult to manage, but it could yield synergies.)

A Summary of Change Stimuli

A joint venture's *stability* refers to whether changes in terms of the bargaining agreement were necessary before its objectives were attained. The formal agreement is unlikely to capture all of the tensions concerning parents' desires for synergies with the child and the child's needs for autonomy. These tensions will push partners' relationships to change vis-à-vis their child. These dynamics will be destabilizing to joint-venture relationships. Moreover, because joint ventures are formed within dynamic environments, changes in circumstances surrounding either parent (such as (13) changes in parents' strategic missions or in their (14) bargaining power with respect to each other), changes in parents' relationships with their child (such as (19) changes in the joint venture's importance to parents' strategies), or changes surrounding the *child* itself, could precipitate the renegotiation of the (8) bargaining agreement or an end to the (7) joint venture itself.

For example, in figure 3–2 the joint venture's profitability potential will be determined like that of other competitors', in part, by its (16) industry's structure and success requirements therein. The child's strategy determines whether the joint venture has exploited the full potential of its environment. Performance will be determined by the (17) suitability of the child's strategy for serving customers and by its effectiveness in implementing its chosen strategy.

Performance may falter because success requirements change within the child's industry, due to past competitive behaviors or other exogenous forces. The child's abilities to command resources or satisfy its customers may deteriorate or improve depending, in part, on its past performance and its ability to respond to these changes. Changes in competitive conditions in figure 3–2 will influence the (19) child's need for close coordination with the parent that contributed needed resources and skills and its (18) need for autonomous activities.

Since its strategy must accommodate the dynamics of at least three constituencies, the joint venture's relationship with one or both of its parents may change due to changes in the fit between its strategy and that of its parents. The child may evolve in its scope from a sales office into a standalone entity complete with R&D capabilities, plant, and distribution channels, if that development suits its parents.

The timing of changes in the bargaining agreement will depend on the forces motivating a particular parent to cooperate or modify the terms of cooperation. The timing of renegotiation in figure 3–2 will also depend on whether partners can overcome the (6) inertia barriers that may have been created by a variety of impediments to strategic flexibility. Changes in the (19) patterns of coordination between the child and its parents (which may be motivated primarily by the child's competitive strategy requirements) will upset the balance between partners, thereby encouraging changes in the joint venture's status.

The ultimate disposition of the child will depend on (13) changes in its parents' strategic missions, (14) changes in the strategic importance they attached to their child, and (15) changes in their respective abilities to attain their objectives in other ways (a source of bargaining power). If parent firms can no longer agree on the points in their original bargaining agreement, the joint venture will probably be absorbed by the parent that values it most highly. (The child may be spun off, or its configuration as a joint venture may be changed if parents will not sell their interests to each other.)

In summary, both the formation and the stability of a joint-venture agreement in figure 3–2 will depend on the nature of the *bargaining agreement* that can be struck between parents and the impact of *change stimuli* on the perceived attractiveness of their agreement to cooperate. The joint venture's stability will be affected by its *performance*, (which is affected, in turn, by changes in industry success requirements) and by changes in its *coordination patterns* with its parents. Changes in parents' *strategic missions*, changes in the *strategic importance* parents attached to the child, and changes in the *alternatives* parents possess to attain the same benefits that the joint venture may have provided will influence their respective willingness to continue the relationship. Possessing alternatives gives parents a new source of bargaining power to negotiate changes, and that power may be strong enough for them to hurdle the inertia barriers surrounding their cooperation policies and end the venture or change its configuration—including the way in which the child relates to it.

The remainder of chapter 3 presents the determinants of the firm's partnership relationship. First, it examines the single firm's cost–benefit analysis and the weightings that a firm assigns to the forces affecting its decision to form a joint venture. Second, it examines the bargaining agreement whereby firms combine to create a joint venture. Finally it examines the change stimuli that set this analytical cycle in motion again. As conditions change, firms reevaluate their internal analyses. Their conclusions precipitate negotiations among partners to change the bargaining agreement. Consequently, the ownership split, relationships with parents' business units, or other dimensions of the joint venture agreement are readjusted to accommodate partners' evolving needs.

A Single Firm's Perspective: Hypotheses Concerning the Cost–Benefit Analysis

From parent firms' perspectives, analysis of joint-venture strategies encompass *whether* to cooperate, *how* to cooperate (what form of cooperation), and *for how long* to cooperate with a particular partner. Each firm performs its private cost–benefit analysis by weighting assessments of the (1) benefits it expects to receive by cooperating against the (2) costs it sees in joint ventures. Although some costs may be weighted heavily as disincentives to joint ventures when firms assess their private positions on joint-venture formation, changes in their competitive environments may push them into a different, more tolerant position later. Negative weightings of cost may be reduced in consideration of the firm's (5) need to cooperate or increased in light of the (4) attractiveness of alternatives to cooperation that may be available. Firms' initial bargaining positions may be more demanding due to the (3) resources they could use as bargaining chips in forming an agreement to their liking. Potential partners may find it more difficult to find a common ground where firms can agree if firms possess (6) inertia barriers that keep them from cooperating in joint ventures or other strategies.

If firms possess the *resources* needed to compete effectively in the target industry, they will not readily form joint ventures in most cases. Shared decision making is so difficult to manage that firms would rather deal on a contractual basis in short-term relationships with players that cannot be acquired in most cases. (Although there are firms that have chosen a conscious strategy of joint ventures and other cooperative strategies for reasons that are covered in chapter 5, these are exceptions. Firms that welcome joint ventures have enough experience with how to exploit them to overcome the inertia barriers that usually prevent firms from embracing joint ventures as a strategy option.)

Analysis of Shortfalls

The most likely candidates for joint ventures are firms that lack the capabilities, strengths, or resources needed to exploit business opportunities alone. They will attempt to link up with the strongest partners in the target industry, but they will have to settle for the strongest firm that *their bargaining position* qualifies them for. Firms' bargaining positions are determined by the combination of the strengths they offer and their desperation levels. Indifference to whether a joint venture is formed (or not) becomes a negotiating strength if the other firm is eager to form some kind of cooperative agreement.

Benefits and Needs. As chapter 2 has noted, many internal, competitive, or strategic needs could motivate firms to consider some form of joint-venture arrangement. Analysis of competitive conditions may suggest that actions must be taken quickly—for example, to preempt competitors (or simply to catch up). Joint ventures could be a means of preempting suppliers or customers from integrating vertically to become competitors, and they could be used to blunt the abilities of ongoing competitors to retaliate as firms expand their domains.[1] By binding potential rivals to them through joint ventures, firms could make them into allies.

The benefits that a particular firm envisions with respect to its needs will be influenced by competitors' activities. The weightings that firms assign to these benefits will depend on, for example, whether they have promulgated their equipment standards successfully or not. If another firm's designs are becoming the dominant design, the only way remaining for some firms to divert business back to them is to embrace a partner that wants to take on the industry leader. And the benefits of such cooperative strategies appear greater if the dominant firm will not license its standards to other firms or to manufacturers of peripheral equipment until after eighteen months or some other meaningful lag period.

Timing will be an important part of cooperative strategies in situations where environments change rapidly because firms that move first can gain access to *better partners*, set *technological standards*, and exploit *experience curve advantages*. The urgency with which parent firms forge joint ventures (or other forms of cooperative strategy) depends primarily on their assessments of competitive conditions in the market where the child will operate. However, some firms must move earlier than others to secure advantages from cooperation because their bargaining power is less than that of their competitors. Fleeting advantages should be exploited quickly while they are still valuable to provide the means for future innovations, cost reductions, and other improvements.

Joint ventures (or other forms of cooperative strategy) will not occur unless firms need to diversify, acquire new skills and resources, consolidate their positions, or attain other objectives that they cannot reach alone. The likelihood that a joint venture will be formed depends, in part, on the strategic importance that they attach to the proposed activity. Activities that are close to firms' strategic cores—xerography from Xerox, for example—are not likely to be candidates for joint-venture strategies, and the role of strategic importance is discussed further in the two-firm analysis below.

Barriers. Parent firms often reject suggestions to supplement flagging strategic postures through cooperative strategies. Recognition of their weaknesses does not come easily to complacent firms.[2] Their unwillingness to see that the nature of competition is changing creates barriers to firms' effective uses of joint ventures or other cooperative strategies.

The principal barriers to forming joint ventures are *strategic* in nature. Firms are unwilling to share information and access in areas that are of high strategic importance to them. Externally imposed barriers to joint ventures include political restrictions on ownership, patent restrictions, competitor retaliation, or other conditions. These barriers may be easier to overcome than firms' own attitudinal barriers against cooperation. Uncertainties regarding parent firms' abilities to manage operating joint ventures also prevent them from considering this strategy option.

There is an experience curve associated with cooperative strategies. The more that managers have used joint ventures, the better they become at exploiting their benefits. Joint ventures have the potential to leverage firms' abilities, if managers discover how to use them effectively. When firms have overcome their organizational resistance to using joint ventures, and their managers have worked through agreements with dissimilar partners, they become *more adaptive* to competitive challenges because joint ventures permit firms to be *more creative*.

Each firm has a calculus for assessing the attractiveness of opportunities that joint ventures offer. Depending on the weights that firms attribute to their needs to cooperate and the benefits they receive by doing so, firms are inclined (or not inclined) to be courted by potential suitors. When firms' analyses of their needs to form joint ventures are combined with evaluations of their internal strengths, firms' initial *bargaining positions* are created.

Analysis of Strengths

Possessing strengths—resource abundance, opportunities to exploit synergies, strong market position, or many other successes that outsiders may covet—should give firms strong bargaining positions in joint-venture negotiations. Strong firms will be courted by potential partners that want to leverage their strengths for their own benefit, and if such firms were entertaining a takeover bid, their asking prices would be high. Accordingly, the value of their participation in joint ventures—rather than as an acquisition candidate—will be high. There is value in strong firms because their ongoing management systems and organization cultures enable them to solve problems more effectively. Firms' bargaining positions in joint-venture strategies with strong firms must reflect these managerial advantages.

If strong firms entertain negotiations to form joint ventures, they must be clear about what they hope to achieve by cooperating. They must be careful to guard, rather than squander, the competitive advantages that gave them strengths. Joint ventures are the obvious strategy choice for risky undertakings where investments are large and firms cannot afford to bear such risks and costs alone. They are less obvious choices where firms possess internal strengths that enable them to cope with competition adequately on their own.

Resources. Some firms will use joint ventures preemptively to protect turf that is of great value to them. Their secret seems to be their awareness that their sources of competitive advantage are *not* enduring strengths. Consequently, they use their control over crucial resources and their access to technology and markets as bargaining chips to gain timing advantages through cooperation.

The balance of power favors firms that control the resource that is most desired at a particular time. Although bargaining power may come from high-quality products, scarce or proprietary technology, access to markets, resources or capabilities, or high commitment,[3] the most important attribute to control, in most cases, will be market access. Management talent, experience, local contacts, and financial resources will be important, *but secondary,* in determining the balance of power within joint ventures and how to value each firm's contributions. (This premise should not be surprising. Access to geographically remote markets has been the primary motive for many joint ventures within mature economies in the past.)

Market access is usually the most attractive resource because it provides a competitive advantage that is *more durable* than technological resources, especially where product and process technology changes rapidly. Technology-dominant firms seek market access; marketing-dominant firms desire technological skills, especially within industries where patent protection is strong or the knowledge that gives firms technological advantages is *not* highly appropriable. (Technological prowess provides more enduring advantages where proprietary skills *can* be protected, just as marketing and product differentiation skills provide more enduring competitive advantages where products are *not* growing commodity-like and customers are *not* becoming increasingly discerning and powerful as buyers. These points are developed further in chapter 5.)

Firms posssessing high brand-name recognition and a reputation for quality products could effectively expand their product lines (or market access) without creating new competitors; they could use their power to distribute the products of outsiders under their own brand names or parlay their quality image into an equity joint venture to gain new geographic marketing channels. Similarly, firms possessing technological prowess, patents, and an innovative image will have more chips for bargaining advantageously (particularly if their partner cannot evaluate their contributions adequately).[4] Again, if these strengths and resources provide transitory advantages, firms will wish to maximize their benefits *faster.* They will seek licensing agreements, joint ventures, and other ways of leveraging their transitory advantages to gain resources to build generations of products and processes that will provide more enduring competitive advantage.

Alternatives. A firm bargains from a stronger base of strength if it has alternative ways by which it could satisfy the needs motivating it to consider a joint venture. Stronger firms—those with superior resources—will be sought after as a joint-venture partner by more firms. In some cases, such firms may choose to exploit the bargaining advantage of being sought after. As chapter 1 noted, strong firms can exploit their dominant positions to forge "spider's webs" of joint ventures with themselves at the hub, if they wish to do so. They might also be able to force weaker partners to deal with them on an *exclusive* basis—while the strong firm, in turn, plays the field by cooperating with many partners. (Chapter 5 addresses the question of whether firms that possess great bargaining power should exert it. Briefly, it is to the stronger firm's *disadvantage* to require partners to be monogamous in some industries.)

If firms could use their bargaining power to treat suppliers or distributors like extensions of their corporate entity, they need not form joint ventures. If firms can license technologies at reasonable royalties, they need not form joint ventures. If other arrangements are available to give strong firms timing advantages, internal strengths, a steady supply of scarce raw materials, or other internal benefits such as those contained in table 2–1, most firms will *not* make joint ventures their first choice of strategies. (When firms negotiate to obtain needed skills and resources, joint ventures are selected as a *compromise.*)

Fear makes firms more resistant to the forces leading them to form joint ventures. Firms avoid joint ventures because they fear loss of control over strategic resources. If they must cooperate, they prefer positions of high equity ownership. (This bargaining impasse is also modified in subsequent negotiations if a joint venture is to be formed.) If its analysis suggests that a joint venture is needed, the firm will evaluate itself as being a highly attractive partner until it faces its potential partner across the bargaining table and sees the other firm's position.

Initial Bargaining Position: The Cost–Benefit Analysis

The firm establishes its threshold for bargaining based on its internal assessments of the need for cooperation, the amount of risk the firm can cope with alone, and other factors of great importance to it. It assesses what it wants from a joint venture, what resources and strengths it would contribute to receive those benefits, and what constraints on its freedoms to take action will be tolerable. This is the firm's *initial bargaining posture.*

The *strategic importance* that partners assign to their cooperative strategies will suggest how the terms of joint ventures are negotiated. If a business is close to a firm's strategic core, it will be of such importance to a firm that it will *not* want to cooperate at all. The key to maintaining strategic flexibility in using joint ventures is the firms' bargaining power, and care must be devoted to sustaining this power. The firm may come back from its initial position of noncooperation to one of accepting a joint venture if it becomes clear that a firm's need for market access, technology, or certain resources, inputs, or services will not be available in any other way. But it will begin bargaining with a very skittish attitude concerning activities that touch its strategic core.

Firms will be unwilling to accept minority operating positions in ventures that they value highly. Thus they will push to own 51 percent of the equity and to be the "operator"—the partner in charge of day-to-day operating decisions—in such ventures. Indifference (due to holding a business to be of low strategic importance) gives firms bargaining power over partners that care deeply about business activities. Firms that do not hold a business unit to be as important (strategically) as partners do might win other important bargaining concessions from eager partners who want to run the child's operations. These concessions are part of the negotiations that move firms from their initial bargaining posture to a compromise with respect to a particular partner. It is a discovery process. (Firms do not reveal to their potential partners what their true weightings matrix—which comprises the saddle points of cooperation in their bargaining position—looks like.) If firms want to cooperate and think they can agree, they negotiate further.

A Meeting of Minds: Hypotheses Concerning the Bargaining Agreement

Cooperative strategies require giving up some control over strategic activities, especially where the risks and problems of acquiring resources (or of not developing them in-house) leaves few other feasible ways of doing a project. When partners negotiate their bargaining agreement, they provide for the terms of their child's existence. In addition to specifying the target market of the child, partners negotiate (9) who will take the child's outputs—and in what volume; (10) who will provide raw material and supporting services to the child—and on what terms; and (11) how parents will monitor and evaluate their child's performance. (Chapter 4 covers the details of these relationships, as well as parental control mechanisms.) Parents may also provide for the (12) duration of their partnership agreement, or at least provide for "horizon" points (or milestones) for review of their relationship. (As chapter 4 notes, the bargaining agreement contains a divorce settlement, as well.)

Thus firms signal their bargaining positions and work out the details of their partnership in a prenuptial agreement that defines relationships between firms as partners (as well as firms as parents) as explicitly as is necessary in order to make partners comfortable with their affiliation. Each player possesses inherent strengths that give them bargaining power for their negotiations. Firms' strategic missions will determine how they use that bargaining power. Technology transfers, distribution agreements, and other details of parents' relationships with their child will be determined by strategic motivations for the venture and will be subject to ratification by their partners.

Finding a Basis for Agreement

Opposing tensions characterize firms' decisions to embrace a particular form of cooperative strategy. Fears concerning control will motivate firms to seek high proportions of ownership if they believe the child's activity will be of high strategic importance to them. Joint ventures are more likely to be acceptable to firms than arrangements that offer less control over operating decisions. But if a child's activity is far from its parents' core (whether that core is marketing, manufacturing, or innovation intensive)—if it is not of at least *medium strategic importance* to partners—they may form a joint venture, but they will not give their child the attentions it needs to thrive.

Firms will approach the bargaining table desiring high equity ownership and managerial control over any alliance they may form. They will probably start by ascertaining whether their potential partner may be acquired. On learning that their potential partner *wanted to acquire them instead,* round two (which encompasses negotiations that may lead to a joint venture) will probably commence if the resources and skills of the firms are mutually desirable.

Subsequent Bargaining Positions

After partners have assessed each others' valuations of the need to cooperate and the attractiveness of venturing together, some adjustments to firms' initial bargaining postures may be necessary in order to reach an agreement. In reevaluating the attractiveness of cooperation, firms may mitigate their initial demands (1) because they cannot afford their potential partner's price, (2) because they would be unable to manage the joint venture as effectively as it has now become clear that their partners could, or (3) for other reasons. Firms' demands will be mitigated by their relative bargaining weakness in the face of partners that possess the resources and strengths needed to succeed. In the interests of reaching an agreement, each partner may have to concede that its bargaining position is not as strong as it had asserted initially. Otherwise, a bargaining agreement may not occur, since firms have nothing in common and no points of agreement.

Joint ventures are likely to be the equilibrium point that parents will settle on initially as they negotiate if their respective needs for cooperation are high. As figure 3–3 indicates, when firms' bargaining postures have them both valuing a business activity highly, they will reach a stalemate. If firms value potential partners' resources highly enough to negotiate, they would prefer to acquire them (if they were for sale—which they often are not). Joint ventures are their compromise point. If there is enough interest among partners once this is understood, negotiations to flesh out the bargaining agreement will continue.

Partners' relative bargaining power in negotiations translate into market power. If firms have it, they are desirable as partners—so desirable that partners may permit them to be promiscuous. As figure 3–4 indicates, when the resources and strengths of potential partners are compared, the compromise may resemble that shown in figure 3–3, or one (or both) of the partners may

Firm A

	High strategic importance	Low strategic importance
High strategic importance	Stalemate–no cooperation Joint venture	B acquires A B makes minority investment in A
Low strategic importance	A acquires B A makes minority investment in B	Cooperative agreements (no separate entity is created)

Firm B (label at left, between High and Low rows)

Figure 3–3. Strategic-Importance Relationship and Joint-Venture Formation (Assuming Firms Will Cooperate, Ceteris Paribus)

engage in *several* cooperative agreements, joint ventures, minority investments, and so forth, as in figure 3–4. If two weak firms agree to consolidate their resources, they would do best by merging and rationalizing their production facilities to build *one* sleek but more efficient entity. In summary, the firm that possesses the greatest strengths when compared with its partners' needs can exploit positions of bargaining power by forming multiple agreements, even among competing partners. (For example, Rolm could cooperate with IBM, Digital Equipment, Hewlett-Packard, and Data General in setting technological standards for private branch exchanges (PBXs) because its systems were superior to competitors' products.)

When the effects of parents' needs to cooperate are combined with their bargaining power, normative propositions concerning their use of joint ventures may be formed. Partners will cooperate in forming joint ventures primarily where their needs to share risks, costs, and strengths are greater than their concerns about losing their basis for competitive advantage. (Where loss of competitive advantage is not an issue—perhaps because no firm possesses

Firm B \ Firm A	High bargaining power	Low bargaining power
High bargaining[a] power	*A* and *B* can both form constellations of spider's web joint ventures or cooperative agreements at the hubs of their respective webs. One of these ventures will join *A* with *B*	*B* forms spider's web agreements with itself to the hub *A* cooperates exclusively with *B* *B* accepts *A*'s minority investment
Low bargaining power	*A* can form spider's web agreements with itself at the hub *A* accepts *B*'s minority investment *B* cooperates exclusively with *A*	Mergers and capacity-shrinking agreements

[a]Where bargaining power is determined by market position, control of crucial resources, past performances, position in vertical chain of processing, and other attributes.

Figure 3–4. Bargaining-Power Relationships and Joint-Venture Formation Behavior (Assuming Firms Will Cooperate, Ceteris Paribus)

a clear advantage over another within a particular strategic group—firms are free to form as many joint ventures as they wish, as in the example of the oil and other mineral extraction industries.) The balance of power among partners will be apparent in the mechanisms partners use to control their interests in the joint venture, and in the vertical relationships they maintain with their child. The balance of power will be determined primarily by what each partner brings to the party, although some firms will be willing to concede some power in their joint-venture agreement in order to take more home with them.

Successful joint ventures serve their purpose without disrupting their parents' strategic well-being. Like a marriage, partners tolerate their wayward spouses to attain some advantage that satisfies their needs. Until parents find they have irreconcilable differences in their visions for the child, the venture can be a way to implement changes in firms' strategic postures or to defend current postures against forces too strong for one firm to withstand.[5]

The equilibrium point in parents' positions could change if one of the partners backed down and was willing to accept a minority investment from its suitor—or outright acquisition. (A different cooperative strategy could also result over time if parents' perceptions of the activity in question changed.) Assuming in figure 3–3, for example, that firm *A* operated in a geographic market where firm *B* valued a presence highly and that the business activity was of high strategic importance to it, firm *B* would want to control firm *A*'s activities through an equity investment, if possible. If the business activity were not of high strategic importance to firm *A* initially, firm *B* might make a minority investment in firm *A* and exert some influence over *A*'s autonomy. But in doing so, firm *B* could force firm *A* to increase the attentions it devotes to the target activity. If firm *A* devotes more managerial attentions to its relationship with firm *B*, that makes the activity more important for *A*, and the equilibrium point moves to the joint-venture alternative shown in figure 3–3. (In effect, firm *A* spins off its geographic activities in the region of interest to firm *B* to create a jointly owned subsidiary with it.) If the activity's strategic importance does not increase for firm *A*, as it does for *B*, the equilibrium point in these tensions stays in the right cell, and firm *B* will press for the acquisition of *A*'s business unit until they can reach a mutually acceptable price. Whether these shifts occur (or not) depends on the effects of change stimuli on partners' relative bargaining strengths, their changing strategic missions, and their need for the joint venture. These changes will be apparent in the changes that parents make to their bargaining agreements.

Changes in Partners' Viewpoints: Hypotheses Concerning Changes in the Bargaining Agreement

This section addresses how changes over time affect partners' viewpoints concerning their joint venture (as depicted in the single-firm analysis) and the impact of these changes on the bargaining agreement that was hammered out between partners (as depicted in the section above). In figure 3–2, the stability of a joint venture—and timing of changes in its terms—depends on changes in parents' conditions: changes in (13) parents' strategic missions, changes in (14) the importance of the joint venture to parents, and changes in (15) parents' bargaining power with respect to its partners. The joint venture's stability also depends on changes in parents–child relationships: (18) changes in the child's needs for decision-making autonomy and (19) changes in parents' needs for coordination with the child, as well as the child's need for coordination with its parents and other forces discussed in chapter 4. Finally the stability of the bargaining agreement that created a joint venture will depend on changes in the child's successes within its industry: (16) changes in the success requirements of the child's industry, as will be evident by changes in competitors' strategic postures, and (17) the effectiveness of the joint venture's competitive strategy in responding to industry success requirements. The joint venture will not be continued if it has not performed adequately. The child will likely be reconstituted or changed in response to these other change stimuli if it is continued. Figure 3–2 has been recast slightly as figure 3–5 in this section to facilitate its emphasis on (1) changes in partners' positions regarding the attractiveness of their joint venture, (2) changes in parents' relationships with their child, and (3) changes in the child's competitive environment as these forces affect changes in eventual disposition of the joint-venture child.

Successful joint ventures require the correct choice of partners and symmetrical parent outlooks; but because most partners have diverse strategic outlooks and their strategies evolve dissimilarly, the tensions that develop must be managed. It is unreasonable to expect that joint ventures can preserve the relationships that existed when they were first created. Sometimes just a change in managers is sufficient to change how a parent firm values its child. Joint ventures may be terminated at that point, or they may be turned into a new opportunity to cooperate. The key to successful use of these tensions to gain competitive advantage lies in remembering parent firms' sources of bargaining power and their reasons for cooperating.

Joint ventures are a compromise. They will be an inherently fragile and transitory strategy because of the political difficulties inherent in sharing authority for the child's operating decisions with outsiders (described in chapter 4) and because of the changing success requirements of competition (described in chapter 5). Parents will leave joint ventures when they have no need for them, especially when they have learned how to go it alone.

Joint ventures are formed within dynamic environments. Changes in circumstances surrounding either parent, in the relationship of parent and child, or surrounding the joint venture itself could precipitate renegotiation of terms of the bargaining agreement or an end to the joint venture. As partners' strategic missions, expectations, loyalties, and resource mixes change, the balance of power within joint ventures changes. When parents gain (or lose) the power needed to influence their child's activities, the venture will be renegotiated or terminated. Joint ventures may be liquidated, spun off, taken over by one partner, or sold to an outside firm. Alternatively, the venture may go on, but managerial control may pass from one partner to another, or it may open up to include more partners. These are *healthy and inevitable* changes. Because joint ventures are inherently unstable organization forms, they are ideally suited for transitional strategies.

Changes in Parent Strategies and the Child's Strategic Importance

The stability of joint ventures—whether changes in terms of the bargaining agreement were necessary before their objectives were attained—will depend

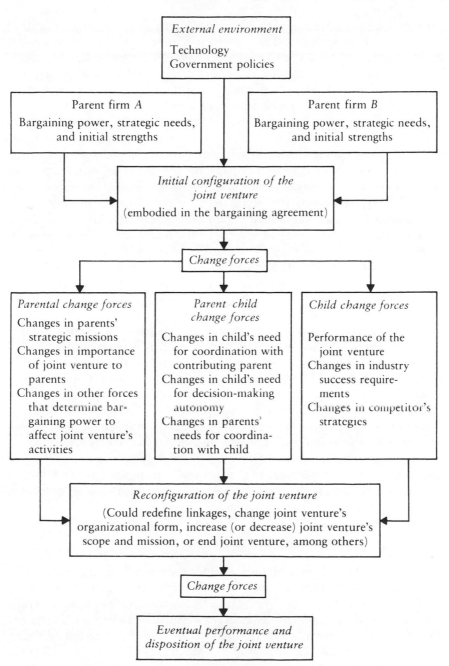

[a]I thank Donald C. Hambrick for suggesting this diagram.

Figure 3–5. A Dynamic Model of Joint-Venture Activity[a]

on how long the need for cooperation embodied in the original bargaining agreement can be sustained. The stability of a joint-venture agreement will be affected by changes in parents' strategic missions, changes in the strategic importance parents attached to the child, and changes in the alternatives parents may possess to attain the same benefits that the joint venture provided.

It will be important to recognize when terms of a joint venture should be changed or the affiliation terminated. Perhaps the child no longer fits well with the parent's diversification plans, or perhaps partners can no longer agree on market allocations, the speed of product introductions, or other points of cooperation. If firms diverge from their original vision for the joint venture, or if their strategies evolve in a manner that lessens the venture's usefulness, it may be necessary to negotiate a "fade out" for one of the partners.

Chapter 1 noted that symmetry occurred where partners possessed evenly matched strategic missions and visions for the role their joint venture would play with respect to their wholly owned business units (as a supplier, customer, or other affiliate). If partners' strategic needs to form a joint venture are symmetrical—if other attributes firms weigh when evaluating the attractivenss of joint ventures are evenly matched among partners—the relationship will be a stable one.

But as chapter 1 cautioned, asymmetries in partners' visions for their child—how quickly they want it to exploit market opportunities, in which direction they want it to move—are destabilizing to joint-venture relationships. The child may be terminated because partners cannot agree on how much autonomy the child should enjoy, for example. They may break the agreement because they now differ concerning how the child will relate to its parents' business units or how the child's strategy should adapt to changes in its competitive environment. The opinions that parents may have held initially on these and other points covered in the original joint-venture agreement change as parents' strategies change, as the strategic importance they attach to their child increases (or decreases), or as they gain (or lose) bargaining power with respect to their joint-venture partner.

Changes in Parents' Relative Bargaining Power

Joint ventures often have a built-in, self-destructing propensity because each parent is continually reassessing the tradeoffs of its investment. Joint ventures can become casualties when firms believe they have made a one-sided bargain that favors their partner unreasonably.[6] When parents become discontent, they may wish to enter markets through wholly owned subsidiaries that they believe they could control more tightly. Much depends on how they value partners' contributions and operating policies.

Inequities could also develop as joint ventures grow and require new infusions of capital because wealthier partners could increase their ownership shares in the child and eventually obtain dominance over it if there was no way of maintaining parity among partners. In oil exploration ventures, for example, when a joint venture seems unprofitable and one partner will no longer put up the cash needed to sustain operations, the other partner can increase its voice in operations and its ownership stake by contributing the full amount that would be needed to continue operations.[7] The latter firm may even acquire the joint venture outright if partners are of unequal financial strength or if one partner becomes ill.

There could be valuation errors. Occasionally, both firms will overestimate the value of a partner's distribution channels or other resources to the joint venture and conclude that they could do as well alone. But more frequently, joint ventures will be terminated as the value of partners' resources evolve asymmetrically because their agreement reflects the balance of power that formerly existed rather than the new balance of power.

Changes in Parent–Child Coordination and Relationships with Wholly Owned Business Units

Because joint ventures are often renegotiated after partners have gained knowledge of markets that they previously did not understand, it is important for domestic firms to find ways of cooperating without losing their competitive advantages to their child, or through it to their partners. For this reason, parents may *think* that they desire passive partners who will not intervene in operating decisions when the child's activities parallel their own. Like a marriage, relationships with assertive partners can be trying to manage, but they often provide greater benefits than those alliances where partners can offer no ideas when problems arise. For this reason, firms should welcome positive changes in their partners' relationships with their child because increased discussions add to the knowledge that the child's managers can utilize in making difficult decisions.

Joint ventures are often created to gain synergies. Because parents' relationships with their child will determine whether they realize desired synergies —and because parent–child relationships exist at the sufferance of partners— it will be important to provide for a means of sustaining good relationships to sustain the chemistry between partners. Without this chemistry, they will not realize the benefits of joint ventures. As chapter 4 points out, synergies will not accrue between parent and child unless they are managed. If differences in strengths, performance, commitment, and other factors lead firms to create management systems (integrating mechanisms with the child) that prevents partners from enjoying desired synergies, their participation in the joint venture will not continue.

This dilemma concerning parent–child relationships is developed at greater length in chapter 4. Briefly, parents could exploit synergies with their child by (1) sharing facilities; they could learn from their child's experiences by erecting (2) parallel facilities. Or parents could grant autonomy by letting their child (3) stand on its own with respect to a particular activity.

Perceived parity in market power will be important to joint-venture stability, but equivalent contributions of knowledge are often more important than many types of asset contributions because innovation permits organizations to renew themselves. In order to maintain parity among partners, employees of the joint venture must learn to work together in creating knowledge, rather than allow their ideas to be blocked by a misplaced loyalty to their respective parents. So long as partners offer each other complementary strengths, which are amplified through their child, each parent firm needs the joint venture. But firms should be wary of developing strengths that are too duplicative of their partners' or child's strengths because jealousies could develop concerning the routing of business opportunities (to the partner or to the joint venture rather than to the firm). For this reason, joint ventures are more stable where partners delineate market territories such that they do not let a child's organization compete against duplicate, wholly owned units of its parents.

Changes in Child's Competitive Environment and Its Need for Autonomy

Industry differences will suggest how quickly joint ventures must evolve from loose cooperation to partnerships to stand-alone entities (if at all). As chapter 5 explains, volatile competitive conditions require shorter-lived and more informal liaisons. High demand uncertainty requires tentative affiliations, modest funding, and pilot plants or test situations. By 1984 few industries' structures were likely to remain unchanged for long, and few ongoing relationships between parent and child matched competitive realities. Change was inevitable, and resilient joint-venture agreements recognized these dynamics.

Summary

Partners must anticipate how their industry could evolve if they hope to provide for all significant contingencies in how their relationships might change in their joint-venture agreements. As chapter 15 notes, even partners that preferred to negotiate decisions as conflicts developed (rather than setting out divorce settlements in great detail in a legal document) found it necessary to agree on the child's purpose initially and to keep updating their expectations vis-à-vis the child and their partners' relationships with their child. Open discussions of these dynamics during the bargaining period often result in partners establishing ground rules for how the child will operate—with how much autonomy the child can proceed as it matures—as strategic milestones are attained. Discussion of these dynamics at the bargaining table during the courtship period often result in management systems—parents' controls and other policies involving the management of the joint venture—that better anticipate these changing relationships and tensions they could create.

Notes

1. Scherer, F.M., 1965, "Firm Size, Market Structure, Opportunity, and the Output of Patented Inventions," *American Economic Review* 55:1097–1125.

2. Harrigan, K.R., 1980, *Strategies for Declining Businesses* (Lexington, Mass.: Lexington Books); Harrigan, K.R., 1983, *Strategies for Vertical Integration* (Lexington, Mass.: Lexington Books).

3. Porter, Michael E., 1976, *Interbrand Choice, Strategy, and Bilateral Market Power* (Cambridge, Mass.: Harvard University Press).

4. Akerloff, G.A., 1973, "The Market for 'Lemons': Qualitative Uncertainty and the Market Mechanism," *Quarterly Journal of Economics* 84:488–500.

5. Edstrom, Anders, "The Stability of Joint Ventures," working paper, University of Gothenburg, Pfeffer, Jeffrey, and Salancik, G.R., 1978, *The External Control of Organizations* (New York: Harper & Row).

6. Franko, Lawrence G., 1971a, "Joint Venture Divorce in the Multinational Company," *Columbia Journal of World Business* 4(3):13–22; Franko, Lawrence G., 1971b, *Joint Venture Survival in Multinational Corporations* (New York: Praeger); Edström, Anders, 1975a, "Acquisition and Joint Venture Behavior of Swedish Manufacturing Firms," working paper, University of Gothenburg; Gullander, Steffan O.O., 1975, "An Exploratory Study of Inter-Firm Cooperation of Swedish Firms," Ph.D. diss., Columbia University; Berg, Sanford V., and Friedman, Philip, 1980, "Corporate Courtship and Successful Joint Ventures," *California Management Review* 22(2): 85–91; Berg, Sanford V., Duncan, Jerome, Jr., and Friedman, Philip, 1982, *Joint Venture Strategies and Corporate Innovation* (Cambridge, Mass.: Oelgeschlager, Gunn & Hain).

7. Bivens, Karen Kraus, and Lovell, Enid Baird, 1976, *Joint Ventures with Foreign Partners* (New York: National Industrial Conference Board); Franko, Lawrence G., 1971a, "Joint Venture Divorce in the Multinational Company," *Columbia Journal of World Business* 4(3):13–22; Franko, Lawrence G., 1972b, *Joint Venture Survival in Multinational Corporations* (New York: Praeger); Edström, Anders, 1975a, "Acquisition and Joint Venture Behavior of Swedish Manufacturing Firms," working paper, University of Gothenburg; Gullander, Steffan O.O., 1975, "An Exploratory Study of Inter-Firm Cooperation of Swedish Firms," Ph.D. diss., Columbia University; Berg, Sanford V., and Friedman, Philip, 1980, "Corporate Courtship and Successful Joint Ventures," *California Management Review* 22(2):85–91; Berg, Sanford V., Duncan, Jerome, Jr., and Friedman, Philip, 1982, *Joint Venture Strategies and Corporate Innovation* (Cambridge, Mass.: Oelgeschlager, Gunn & Hain).

Appendix 3A:
Game Theory and Two-Player Games

From the literature of game theory, a sense of the internal processes that lead firms to enter joint ventures may be gained.[1] Paramount among the forces that determine whether firms will forge joint ventures (and maintain them) is the *strategic importance* that they give to the activities the joint venture would encompass.

Although strategically interdependent firms could compete or cooperate, many of them may be expected to reduce the uncertainty they face through communication (market signaling) and cooperation (information sharing). They do so in order to improve their chances of making nondestructive tactical choices.[2] Firms' exchanges of information (or resources) are guided by their utility tradeoffs for various competitive outcomes and by their analysis of competitors' preferences (or strategic stakes) for these same outcomes. Analysis of the payoffs to both players allow managers to predict, for example, whether specific firms would enter a joint venture rather than go it alone.[3]

Game theory argues that firms will optimize their cost–benefit tradeoffs, subject to uncertain outcomes.[4] In a *zero-sum game*, firms assume that an increase in gain to one firm will be at the expense of all others. In a *cooperative* or *non–zero-sum game*, firms consciously try to maximize their joint gains. Because firms generally operate somewhere between cooperation and competition, they view resources as being neither zero-sum nor infinite. Chapter 3 assumes that firms view joint ventures as non–zero-sum games. Such games could be changed to zero-sum games, however, if firms misunderstand each others' actions.

Misunderstandings occur, in part, because (as the discussion in appendix 2A concerning political theory suggests) nonhomogeneous firms have different payoff matrices (missions) and asymmetric perceptions of risk. Misunderstandings are destructive. Confusion regarding market signals exacerbates harmful competitive behavior, while it saps firms' abilities to regenerate themselves. Firms' perceptions of the costs and benefits of joint ventures (their utility tradeoffs) evolve differently as environmental conditions change to favor one firm or another. For this reason, *industry evolution* is an important force in predicting joint-venture formation (or termination).

Cooption is an attempt to link up with an outsider (or rival) to prevent it from doing harm to the firm or from linking up with the firm's competitors. Cooption is a defensive strategy that often gives a satisficing outcome rather than an optimal one. In chapter 3, competitors who believe they can perform better *alone* will avoid cooption strategies (as well as cooperation strategies). But as growth slows, as markets shrink, as industries become global, and as technological change accelerates to speeds where firms cannot recover their investments alone, firms need a new language of cooperation (not warfare). They think less about capturing market share (a pyrrhic victory) and think more about delivering greater value to their customers. Under these conditions, firms will form alliances to maximize the welfare of all partners jointly.

Notes to Appendix 3A

1. Fellner, W.J., 1949, *Competitive Among the Few* (New York: Knopf); Nash, J.F., 1950, "The Bargaining Problem," *Econometrica* 18:155–162; Schelling, T.C., 1965, "An Essay on Bargaining," *American Economic Review* 65:281–306; Luce, R.D., 1957, *Games and Decisions* (New York: Wiley); Fouraker, Lawrence E., and Siegal, Sidney, 1963, *Bargaining Behavior* (New York: McGraw-Hill); Coleman, J.S., 1966, "In Defense of Games," *American Behavioral Scientist* 10:3–4; Nierenberg, Gerard I., 1968, *The Art of Negotiating* (New York: Hawthorne); Raser, J., 1969, *Simulation and Society: An Exploration for Scientific Gaming* (Boston: Allyn & Bacon); Inbar, M., 1972, *Simulation and Gaming in Social Science* (New York: Free Press); Bell, D.E., Keeney, R.L., and Raiffa, H., 1977, *Conflicting Objectives and Decisions* (New York: Wiley); Osborne, D.K., 1976, "Cartel Problems," *American Economic Review* 66:835–844; Kydland, F.E., 1977, "Equilibrium Solutions in Dynamic Dominant Player Models," *Journal of Economic Theory* 15(2):130–136; Porter, Michael E., and Spence, A. Michael, 1982. "Capacity Expansion and Process Oligopoly: The Case of Corn Wet Milling," in McCall, J.J. (ed.), 1982, *The Economics of Information and Uncertainty* (Chicago: University of Chicago Press). Spence, A. Michael, 1978, "Tacit Collusion and Imperfect Information," *Canadian Journal of Economics* 11:490–505.

2. Schelling, Thomas C., 1960, *The Strategy of Conflict* (Cambridge, Mass.: Harvard University Press); Fouraker, Lawrence E., and Siegal, Sidney, 1963, *Bargaining Behavior* (New York: McGraw-Hill).

3. Von Neumann, J., and Morgenstern, O., 1944, *Theory of Games and Economics Behavior* (Princeton, N.J.: Princeton University Press); Shubik, Martin, 1959, *Strategy and Market Structure* (New York: Wiley).

4. Telser, L.G., 1972, *Competition, Collusion, and Game Theory* (New York: Aldine-Atherton).

4

Interactions between Parent and Child: The Analytical Model Continues

This chapter develops components of the bargaining agreement—the terms, relationships, and management policies that create and define the joint-venture child. It develops hypotheses concerning the horizontal and vertical relationships between parent and child that give rise to the creation of synergies. The integration of parent and child activities represents the second leg in the joint-venture strategy model, as the heavy arrows indicate in figure 4–1, and terms of these relationships are set forth in the bargaining agreement, which is often accompanied by a legal document that defines ownership terms, governance procedures, and divorce settlements. More important than these financial details, however, are the understandings developed between partners concerning (1) what relationships will be maintained between them and their child, (2) what degree of autonomy the child's managers will enjoy to modify those relationships, and (3) what levels of support the child can rely on from its parents.

Chapter 3, which sketched firms' privately weighted cost–benefit analyses, assumed that partners had specific benefits in mind when they agreed to cooperate in joint ventures. Many of these benefits were discussed in chapter 2 as motivations for cooperative strategies. In order for parents to realize these benefits in their dealings with their child, it is necessary for them to agree among themselves on the (1) nature of horizontal or vertical relationships that each will enjoy with their joint venture, the (2) need for close coordination with the child (for synergistic resource sharing) or for (3) operating autonomy (for performance maximization) by the child, (4) which resources will be shared (which will be duplicative of existing resources), (5) how transactions will be channeled among parents' and child's facilities when they run in parallel, and (6) other issues determining how synergies and other benefits of joint ventures will be realized.

I am indebted to William H. Newman for his many suggestions for this chapter.

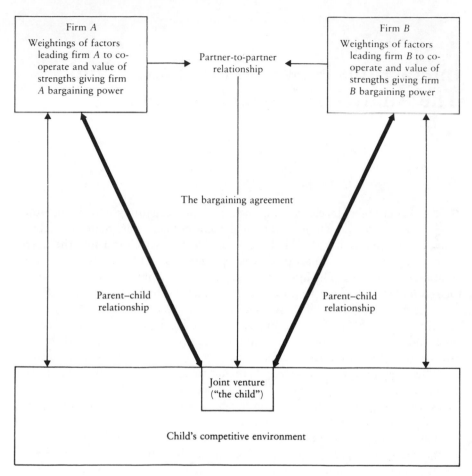

Figure 4–1. Parent–Child Relationships in Managing a Joint Venture

The Bargaining Agreement

The joint-venture framework assumes that the child requires access to certain inputs and a healthy market for its outputs in order to be viable. Access to these inputs and distribution channels is provided for by terms of partners' bargaining agreement, and many arrangements are possible. Parents may specify vertical relationships, as well as horizontal relationships, but some decision must be made concerning where the child obtains inputs and sells its outputs, or the joint venture will not be viable and cannot be expected to survive for long.

Hypotheses Concerning the Bargaining Agreement's Content

The resources and attributes that parent firms will share with the joint venture determines its purpose and what types of synergies (if any) parents expect to enjoy through its operations. These are the benefits that satisfy parents' strategic needs that were discussed in chapter 3. These benefits motivated firms to form joint ventures initially. As the content of the partnership's bargaining agreement evolves, these expected benefits are the touchstones against which parents will compare ongoing operations to ascertain whether the child's operations continue to satisfy their objectives or should be terminated. Details of the joint-venture agreement are shown in figure 4–2, which recasts the dynamic joint-venture framework diagram. Each partner in figure 4–2 possesses resources and skills that could serve as potential inputs to the joint venture. Alternatively, the child's managers may be given autonomy to go to outside markets to obtain needed inputs.

The bargaining agreement, which defines the child's domain of activities, will specify its outputs (and it may specify the child's customers, if one or more parents gives the child a take-or-pay contract for the sale of some of its outputs). Operating relationships with parents are defined by provisions for *sharing facilities.*

The most commonplace sharing arrangement involves the use of parents' sales forces and marketing organizations or the use of their R&D facilities. These are the resources that parents are *least likely* to duplicate in their child because they constitute their respective strategic cores. But if they do not share facilities with their child—if the child will be given plant and equipment, technology, personnel, management team, sales force, or other resources for its exclusive use—partners should agree on whether they will be operating facilities that *duplicate* the child's operations and whether their in-house organizations will have any *choice* in dealing with the child for supplies, marketing services, or other products that the child has been created to provide.

Although this point is frequently spelled out in the bargaining agreement, it is helpful to articulate what *operating autonomy* the child's managers may expect as their experience base increases. Similarly, it is helpful to articulate *how closely* the child's activities will have to be coordinated with those of its parents to exploit the potential for synergies (and this point will be covered in greater detail below).

Finally, the bargaining agreement also specifies the control mechanisms that parent firms will use to ensure that the benefits they desired were indeed received. The control mechanisms provide for how partners develop managerial resources, how the joint venture's board of directors will control partners' interests, and how disputes will be resolved. The formal document specifies

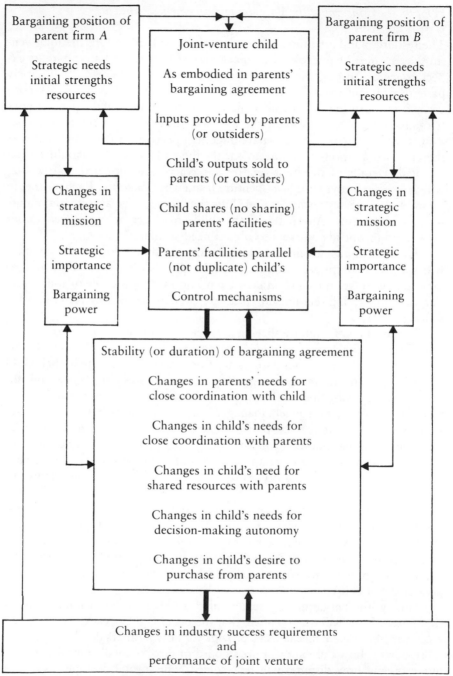

Figure 4–2. A Dynamic Model of Joint-Venture Activity (Child's Perspective)

divorce settlements when the venture ends, and it should also suggest ways of maintaining the joint venture's stability.[1]

In summary, the bargaining agreement document is frequently highly detailed in financial and legal matters. To ensure joint-venture success, more attentions should be given to questions of parent–child relationships and questions of operating autonomy. In particular, managers should devote some attention to questions of how the benefits that are expected of joint ventures will in fact be realized.

Provision of Inputs and Markets for Outputs

Chapter 3 noted that the most likely candidates for joint ventures are firms that lack the capabilities, strengths, or resources needed to exploit business opportunities alone. As table 4–1 indicates, the alliances they create will enable them to (1) share risks and costs with partners; (2) reach the external capital markets using the joint venture as an additional vehicle for raising funds; (3) gain scale economies and operating synergies from shared manufacturing facilities, technologies, and other physical assets; (4) build market share and fill out their product lines by sharing brand names, products, and support services; (5) gain scale economies and operating synergies by sharing distribution channels, sales forces, and marketing facilities; (6) exploit innovation synergies by sharing laboratories and scientific personnel; (7) share components, raw materials, or other supplies that require a plant of a minimum efficient scale far larger than firms' internal component requirements; (8) exploit logistical synergies from shared service organizations, research activities, and other multiplant activities; and (9) gain scale economies through pooled purchasing and provision of services, supplies, and other resources; among (10) other benefits and sources of synergy.

Vertical Relationships. Many other synergies and benefits of joint ventures have been discussed in chapter 2. In table 4–1, these have been depicted in a matrix of synergistic relationships that may be interpreted as inputs $_{(j)}$ and outputs $_{(k)}$ that provide synergy $_{(i)}$ when taken from or provided to parent A (which gives and takes x_{ijk}), to parent B (which gives and takes y_{ijk}) and the outside market (which gives and takes z_{ijk}). The set of synergies was constrained to nine sources in table 4–1 for expositional purposes, and the inputs and outputs were each constrained to four per source of synergy—typically, personnel, technology, physical assets, and capital.

The x_{ijk}s, y_{ijk}s, and z_{ijk}s that partners agree on will determine whether the child is vertically or horizontally related to its parents. In figure 4–3, the vertical stages of processing have been numbered consecutively. If in figure 4–3, for example, synergies accrue when parents A and B share the outputs from (6) their child's plant and market them through their (7) distribution channels or

Table 4–1
Matrix of Synergies by Horizontal and Vertical Relationship of Parent to Joint-Venture Child[a]

Source of Synergy$_{(i)}$	Child$_{(j)}$[b]	Child$_{(k)}$	Parent A$_{(x)}$	Parent B$_{(y)}$	Open Market$_{(z)}$
1. Cost and risk sharing	. . . takes materials from . . . takes personnel from . . . takes technology from . . . takes capital from	. . . sells outputs to . . . gives personnel to . . . sells technology to . . . gives capital to	x_{111} x_{122} x_{133} x_{144}	y_{111} y_{122} y_{133} y_{144}	z_{111} z_{122} z_{133} z_{144}
2. External financial markets	. . . takes materials from . . . takes personnel from . . . takes technology from . . . takes capital from	. . . sells outputs to . . . gives personnel to . . . sells technology to . . . gives capital to	x_{211} x_{222} x_{233} x_{244}	y_{211} y_{222} y_{233} y_{244}	z_{211} z_{222} z_{233} z_{244}
3. Share plant, facilities	. . . takes materials from . . . takes personnel from . . . takes technology from . . . takes capital from	. . . sells outputs to . . . gives personnel to . . . sells technology to . . . gives capital to	x_{311} x_{322} x_{333} x_{344}	y_{311} y_{322} y_{333} y_{344}	z_{311} z_{322} z_{333} z_{344}
4. Share product lines	. . . takes materials from . . . takes personnel from . . . takes technology from . . . takes capital from	. . . sells outputs to . . . gives personnel to . . . sells technology to . . . gives capital to	x_{411} x_{422} x_{433} x_{444}	y_{411} y_{422} y_{433} y_{444}	z_{411} z_{422} z_{433} z_{444}
5. Share distribution channels	. . . takes materials from . . . takes personnel from . . . takes technology from . . . takes capital from	. . . sells outputs to . . . gives personnel to . . . sells technology to . . . gives capital to	x_{511} x_{522} x_{533} x_{544}	y_{511} y_{522} y_{533} y_{544}	z_{511} z_{522} z_{533} z_{544}
6. Share laboratories, personnel	. . . takes materials from . . . takes personnel from . . . takes technology from . . . takes capital from	. . . sells outputs to . . . gives personnel to . . . sells technology to . . . gives capital to	x_{611} x_{622} x_{633} x_{644}	y_{611} y_{622} y_{633} y_{644}	z_{611} z_{622} z_{633} z_{644}
7. Supply materials, components	. . . takes materials from . . . takes personnel from . . . takes technology from . . . takes capital from	. . . sells outputs to . . . gives personnel to . . . sells technology to . . . gives capital to	x_{711} x_{722} x_{733} x_{744}	y_{711} y_{722} y_{733} y_{744}	z_{711} z_{722} z_{733} z_{744}
8. Supply technology, services	. . . takes materials from . . . takes personnel from . . . takes technology from . . . takes capital from	. . . sells outputs to . . . gives personnel to . . . sells technology to . . . gives capital to	x_{811} x_{822} x_{833} x_{844}	y_{811} y_{822} y_{833} y_{844}	z_{811} z_{822} z_{833} z_{844}
9. Purchase products, services	. . . takes materials from . . . takes personnel from . . . takes technology from . . . takes capital from	. . . sells outputs to . . . gives personnel to . . . sells technology to . . . gives capital to	x_{911} x_{922} x_{933} x_{944}	y_{911} y_{922} y_{933} y_{944}	z_{911} z_{922} z_{933} z_{944}

[a]I am indebted to William H. Newman for suggesting this table.

[b]The matrix depicts terms of the joint-venture agreement (child). Its values reflect the interests of its parents.

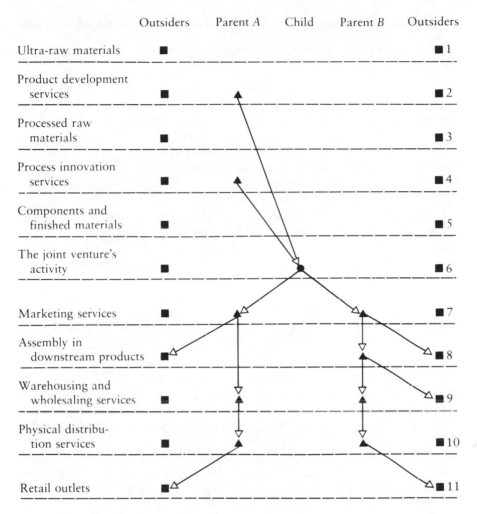

	Outsiders	Parent A	Child	Parent B	Outsiders
Ultra-raw materials	■				■ 1
Product development services	■				■ 2
Processed raw materials	■				■ 3
Process innovation services	■				■ 4
Components and finished materials	■				■ 5
The joint venture's activity	■				■ 6
Marketing services	■				■ 7
Assembly in downstream products	■				■ 8
Warehousing and wholesaling services	■				■ 9
Physical distribu- tion services	■				■ 10
Retail outlets	■				■ 11

Figure 4–3. Example of Vertical Relationships between Parent and Child

sell them to outsiders that use them in subsequent (8) assembly operations, the child operates *upstream* from its parents (at processing stage 6 in figure 4–3) and is *vertically related* to them. Note also in figure 4–3 that the child does *not* sell its outputs to outsiders; the child is a *captive* supplier to its parents in this illustration of vertical relationships. But the larger the value of z_{ijk} in table 4–1—the greater the proportion of outputs the child sells to outsiders, for example—the greater the child's need for *independence* from its parents in its operating decisions. The greater the value of the x_{ijk}s or y_{ijk}s, by contrast—the more dependent the child is on parents for its inputs or as customers of its outputs—the greater need for *close coordination* between parent and child operations in order to maximize vertical integration economies.[2]

The child uses *market prices* as a reference point in most of its vertical dealings with multiple parents to ensure that vertical transfer arrangements are economically justified as well as equitable to them. Forcing the child to take its full requirements from parents (or to sell them all of its outputs) cuts parents off from a useful source of intelligence. Using suppliers' prices to police in-house buyer–seller relationships reduces the heights of vertical integration-related exit barriers when the need for the joint venture's activities ends.[3] (If a vertical relationship exists between partners, care must be taken that discontent and inequities do not develop when each firm realizes what the other's profit margins have been.)

The child will face obsolescence, however, if it is not permitted to advise its parents concerning when the products it merchandizes for them are less in demand. Since a forward-integrated child is closer to the demand of ultimate consumers, it would know more quickly than its parents whether its existence is still economically justified.

Technology Transfer. Chapter 3 noted that technological prowess is a strength in parent's bargaining positions only as long as it is not easily appropriated. Given the perishable nature of this resource, it is scarcely surprising that parents devote substantial attentions to devising technology transfer schemes to *protect* their competitive advantages, especially when effective joint ventures will require ongoing technical relationships between parent and child. Mechanisms must be created to nurture those relationships and allay parents' fears that their competitive advantages will be appropriated if the partnership is to thrive. If patent protection is weak, and parents cannot protect their property rights for the technology that would be used in a joint venture, (1) fewer transfers of knowledge will occur; (2) the difficulties associated with preventing technological bleedthrough will be exacerbated; and (3) the joint-venture relationship will be unstable.

The *proprietary* elements of many parents' resources will probably be sold within joint ventures at arm's-length arrangements that protect their property rights. But for some technologies, even that precaution is inappropriate. Because any information that is transferred to the joint-venture child is no longer under the control of its parents (and no knowledge can be protected adequately once it is shared), the child will often receive the proprietary portions of its parents' technologies (and other resources that give parents bargaining power) just before their half-life has expired. Technology leaders will provide their child with pieces of technology *incrementally* as the knowledge becomes less proprietary or as the firm gains confidence in working with its partners in the joint venture. This will be done because firms have no other satisfactory way to protect the appropriable knowledge that gives them bargaining power.

Market Access. Chapter 3 noted that the most enduring strength that a partner can control is usually *market access,* and partners' negotiations in forming joint ventures often acknowledge that this advantage endures longer than others. Parents are more likely to take the outputs of their joint-venture child to sell through their respective distribution channels (or consume in-house) than they are to pool distribution facilities and permit their child to interface with ultimate customers.

Joint ventures are frequently formed between foreign firms and local competitors to penetrate new markets, but in such arrangements, the foreign firm often contributes products that the U.S. partner sells. Although they may intend for their joint-venture child to evolve into a stand-alone entity that serves its own distinct group of customers, foreign partners will find it exceedingly difficult to realize such development plans if the marketing partner has already established relationships with local customers under its own brand names. Parents' wholly owned business units, in particular, will not appreciate the new competitor that has been created.

Shared Facilities

Shared facilities attain scale economies by pooling firms' individually smaller requirements for manufacturing operations, R&D, or other resources into one facility that enjoys greater economies when operating at a larger, fully utilized scale. Shared facilities are like a bottleneck in the sense that they represent a stage of processing where fewer firms may be operating, but this shortfall of competitors represents an opportunity to exploit technological scale advantages. Briefly, it is *more efficient* for firms to share that stage of processing's outputs than it is to duplicate its facilities to prevent the jealousies created by sharing.

In figure 4–4, the vertical stages of processing are numbered consecutively. In figure 4–4, parent B and the child share a (5) components and finished materials facility. Also, the child has (1) mineral extraction operations to procure ultra-raw materials and (6) operations midway down the vertical chain of processing. In order to enjoy scale economies, the child in figure 4–4 and parent A share a (3) processed raw materials facility and a (8) downstream assembly plant. Their upstream, shared (3) processing plant has a very large minimum efficient scale because the combined inputs of parent and child (1) facilities are insufficient to satisfy its productive capacity; the (3) processing plant also purchases (1) ultra-raw materials from outsiders.

The heavy horizontal line at the level of the (6) joint venture's activity (and the triangles representing its parents, firm A and firm B) suggest that the child in figure 4–4 is *horizontally related* to its parents as well as vertically related to them. Also, the child in figure 4–4 sells some of its outputs ($x_{ijk}s$) to (8) parent A and the remainder of its outputs ($z_{ijk}s$) to outsiders' (8) downstream

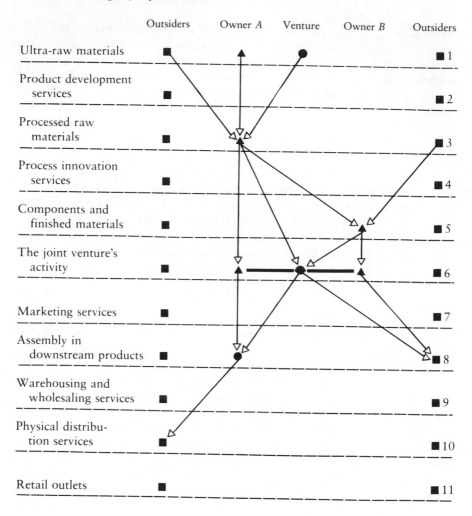

Figure 4–4. Example of Shared Resources between Owners and Venture

assembly operations; the joint venture in figure 4–4 is *not* a captive vendor to its parents because it deals with outsiders.

Parents will share facilities with their joint-venture child to create synergies when they need to protect their technology, their distribution systems, or other resources that give them competitive advantage. Referring to the synergistic matrix of table 4–1, it can be predicted that parents' needs for control over their child's activities will increase as its products $_{(k)}$ are more closely intertwined with their own products $(x_{ijk}s)$.

Horizontal Relationships. *Horizontally related* joint ventures compete in the same industries as their parents. Given the arguments concerning the sources of bargaining power and competitive advantage of chapter 3, it is unlikely that fearsome parents would create duplicate facilities for their child in areas of high strategic importance to them. Their fears of losing competitive advantage to outsiders would lead them to deprive their child of the capabilities in question; parents would instead perform these tasks in-house and share the outputs with joint ventures. Scale economies would accrue from production pooling, and wholly owned business units would enjoy peace of mind because no competitor has been created.

Synergies. Shared resources create synergies if horizontal relationships are managed conscientiously. Wholly owned business units that share resources and facilities can enjoy the synergistic benefits of scheduling advantages, high levels of capacity utilizations, new applications of technological approaches, and other shared knowledge advantages. But synergies between parent and child are difficult to attain without surrendering some knowledge of parents' competitive advantages. To guard against the dangers of bleedthrough of proprietary knowledge into unauthorized hands, parent firms are more likely to provide their child with *parallel facilities* that duplicate their ongoing activities—or to deal only on a buyer–supplier basis at that level of processing—than to allow their child ready access to certain kinds of information.

Whether the relationship between parent and child will be horizontal, vertical, or related (or unrelated) in some other manner, care must be taken to prepare the parents' organization for the notion that resources must be *shared* with the child in order to enjoy synergies. Special care must be given to the reality that firms' competitive advantages in successful joint ventures will be their people and that such resources can be highly mobile. Consequently, the control mechanisms used to coordinate these relationships (discussed below) must be clear in terms of which patterns of loyalties (to the joint venture or to its parent) will be reinforced by the management systems that parents use to control their relationships with their child.

If the child's activities will be coordinated with one or more of its parents, the coordination focal point will have to be on the resources they share. Where parent and child address the same customer needs, for example, synergies will be maximized if sales organizations can share innovations and disseminate knowledge. To attain this benefit, programs and centralized responsibilities for information dissemination (for example, a clearinghouse for materials purchasing, scheduling of available managerial talents, customer information, or other common resources, services, or experiences) are needed to increase opportunities for parent and child to enjoy synergies.

Managers who can devise the most effective means of exploiting relationships between parent and child organizations will have the greatest opportunity to gain a competitive advantage in their child's industry. An effective integration of parent's and child's respective strengths will make the child more than just a new industry entrant. If effective, the synergies they can create will require the child's competitors to seek joint-venture relationships, as well.

In summary, cooperative strategies represent an exciting theory, but they are difficult to implement in practice. The child's viability may be undermined through the relationships parents desire and the control mechanisms they may impose on their joint ventures. If undermined, one of the strongest dimensions of the child as a strategic weapon—the opportunity to realize synergies for its parents—will be negated.

But in order for joint-venture synergies to be realized, parents must reduce the tensions created by parallel facilities, either by placing all of their activities in a particular industry (or market segment) into the child organization (as at level (3) in figure 4–6) or by designing other mechanisms for reducing sibling rivalry. The stability of a joint-venture relationship between parents will be eroded by their respective failures to reduce inter-SBU rivalries, but will be enhanced by their needs for the activities performed by their child, especially if cost advantages are available from such pooling arrangements.

Parallel Facilities

Parents may create facilities for their joint-venture child that parallel their own capabilities in order to ameliorate some of the jealousies the child will encounter from its wholly owned, sister business units. In figure 4–5, the vertical chain of processing is numbered consecutively, and the joint venture is engaged in three vertically related activities: (5) components and finished materials, its (6) core activity, and (8) downstream assembly operations. At each of these stages of vertically related processing, parent A and parent B *also* operate facilities that duplicate the child's facilities. These are *parallel facilities.*

The schema illustrated in figure 4–5 would appear to offer great promise for scale economies, logistical synergies, and other benefits because parent A and the child *share* (2) product development and (4) process innovation services from parent A's centralized R&D facilities. The joint venture is *taper-integrated* to obtain its (3) processed raw materials inputs from both parent A and from outsiders. It sells (5) components and finished materials to parent A, parent B, *and* to in-house (6) processing units of its own. The child's core manufacturing activity is *fully integrated*, selling its (6) outputs on a (7) merchant basis to parents as well as incorporating the child's outputs into parent's respective (8) downstream assembly operations, and into the child's own (8) downstream assembly operations. The child's (8) assembly operations, in turn, are fully integrated downstream, selling outputs only to parent A's and parent B's (9) warehousing and wholesaling facilities at the next stage of processing.

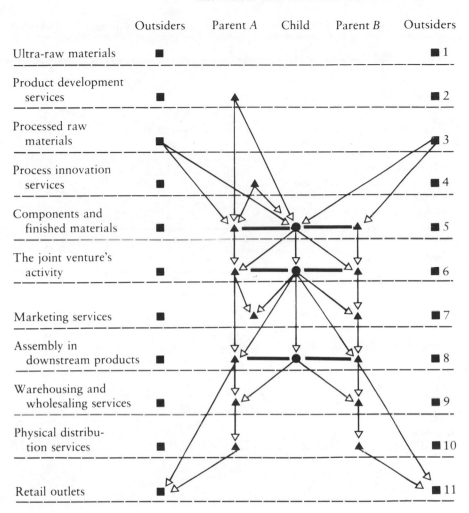

Figure 4–5. Example of Parallel Facilities between Parent and Child

If the joint venture described above had enjoyed greater (but not full) *autonomy* with respect to its buyer–seller relationships, the schema representing the vertical chain of processing would resemble that in figure 4–6, where the vertical chain of processing has also been numbered consecutively. In figure 4–6, the joint venture purchases (1) ultra-raw materials from its parents (firms *A* and *B*) *and* from outsiders and purchases (2) product development services from outsiders. It sells its (3) processed raw materials to its parents, to its own (5) downstream processed components and finished materials operations, *and* to outsiders. Its business unit at level (5) , in turn, purchases

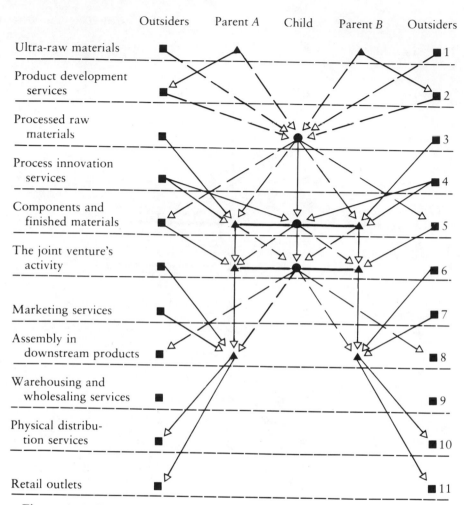

Figure 4–6. Example of Joint-Venture Autonomy vis-à-vis Buyer–Seller Relationships

(4) process innovation services from outsiders and sells its (5) outputs to both parents and to its own (6) core operations. The child's (6) core products unit buys (5) components only from insiders, but it sells (6) outputs to both parents' (8) downstream assembly operations *and* to outsiders. Some of the reasons for creating an autonomous joint venture with facilities that parallel those of its parents are discussed below.

Autonomy and Parallel Facilities. Parents may create facilities for their joint-venture child that parallel their own capabilities when their child matures to an experience level that would enable it to issue securities in its own right. Parallel facilities may also be needed if the child (1) sells similar products to market segments that are *different* from those of its parents, (2) pursues different technological avenues to attain results similar to those of its parents, or (3) must own the property rights for the products and processes it develops. Finally, parallel facilities may be necessary if the child (4) must move quickly in response to competitive needs in technology or marketing areas where parents have been sluggish to react to change in the past. (These points are developed further in another section below.)

Independent facilities are appropriate for the child when its activities are *not parallel* to its parents' activities, where parents have pooled their respective resources and facilities in the child or the child is far from the strategic core of its parents. Stand-alone, autonomous facilities are also appropriate where no vertical relationships exist between parent and child.

If the joint-venture child is to have a life of its own—one in which it may evolve from a loosely structured agreement among partners to work together into a partnership with in-house facilities—it will require assets that either parallel or supplement its parents' capabilities. The child may even evolve into an incorporated entity with facilities to invent, make, and sell products in its own right. By the time the joint venture has developed to that level of maturity, many of the problems regarding synergies and parallel facilities that may hamstring partners' abilities to work together in their early phases of partnership must be resolved. Indeed, vertical (buyer–seller) relationships that once may have existed may be terminated later as they become uneconomic.

Moreover, the child's operations cannot be integrated closely with those of horizontally related parents if parents fear that too much knowledge bleed-through will occur. If it is necessary to design control mechanisms to protect parents' assets or knowledge, this poses a dilemma.

Reducing Tensions. Child facilities that parallel the activities of horizontally related parents will be inherently destabilizing to their joint-venture agreement because of the inter-SBU jealousies such facilities engender, *but a viable joint-venture child will fare poorly without them.*

The child's capabilities (if it is permitted any) will have to be kept apart from the core of its horizontally related parent's competitive advantage, yet creating parallel facilities could mean that a potential competitor has been created. Synergies will *not* accrue in the latter case because, even though firm A is its parent, relationships between personnel within parent and child organizations will be strained over time.

In summary, parents' needs for diverse relationships with their joint-venture children are determined by competitive conditions within the industries where parents hope to use them effectively. Many of these conditions are discussed in chapter 5. In all cases where parents find a need to create facilities within their child that parallel their own, they risk generating animosities between wholly owned and partially owned business units. Sometimes these jealousies can be reduced by dividing marketing territories among competing business units. But if the child develops parallel facilities, it will frequently begin to think (and perhaps act) like a competitor of its parents *unless its domain is restricted.* Thus parents must also devote attentions to issues concerning *when* the competitive challenges the child faces merit high operating autonomy and *when* the synergistic objectives or partners require that the child be reined in by a program of close coordination with its wholly owned, sister business units. The next section considers guidelines for trading between these opposing tensions regarding interbusiness unit coordination.

Integrating Parent and Child

If firms' joint ventures are managed by entrepreneurial executives, parents may find that their child is straining at its tethers. The child's managers may wish to exploit opportunities faster than parents' managers had intended them to move. Alternatively, if joint ventures' managers are not permitted to exercise any initiative, the child will be ill-suited to move quickly and effectively when parents call on it for assistance. In either case, attentions must be devoted to how to ensure that the child enjoys an appropriate mix of autonomy from and coordination with its parents' activities. That mix will depend on the child's strategic mission and how its activities will be integrated with the business activities of wholly owned units.

Hypotheses Concerning Trade-offs between Autonomy and Coordination

As the preceding section has noted, the bargaining agreement between partners must reflect their strategic missions and expectations concerning the benefits they seek from their alliance. Using the synergistic matrix notations of table 4–1 to illustrate these tensions from the child's perspective, the preceding section has argued that relationships with their child provide the benefits $_{(i)}$ that motivated parents to cooperate. Thus, parents will seek to increase their control over activities as their internal consumption of the child's outputs (x_{ijk} and y_{ijk}, for example) increases. As the child's competitive strategy drives it in directions that diverge from those of its parents and it sells more to outsiders (z_{ijk}), the child will agitate for more freedoms. If parents strive to protect technological knowledge (x_{633}, for example) from bleedthrough to unauthorized third parties (z_{633} or z_{833}), they would increase their control over the child. If they seek to protect other shared information that comprised their strategic core $_{(j)}$, they would bind their child closer through their management systems and other control mechanisms (discussed below), as well as through their control over the flows of materials, personnel, technology, and capital $_{(jk)}$ between parent and child.

Tighter controls will be needed when the activities of parent $_{(j)}$ and child $_{(k)}$ are *similar*. When the child develops its own distinctive competences $_{(k)}$ that differ from those of its parents $_{(j)}$, fewer synergies $_{(i)}$ will be enjoyed because fewer resources will be shared. But superior operating performance will be enjoyed by parents as owners of (and investors in) the successful child.

Range of Needs for Parental Control over Venture Child

Parents' needs to intervene closely in the joint venture's decisions increase as the venture's strategic importance to its parent increases, as the value and scope of resources shared with the parent increases, and as the degree of resource transfers between parent and child (vertical integration) increases. The child's need for autonomy increases as the *speed* of competitive response needed increases (and competitive conditions requiring such autonomy are covered in chapter 5) but will decrease as similarities between parent's and child's strategic missions increase or as the value and scope of resources shared among them increase. Figure 4–7, which juxtaposes the intervention needs of parents against the autonomy needs of the child, suggests that in some cases, successful competitive strategies require the child to coordinate its activities closely with one or more of its parents. Figure 4–7 also notes that joint ventures will be highly unstable when these opposing needs for coordination are both high. Yet parents are likely to seek ways of coordinating with their child, even where it would prefer more autonomy.

Need for Tight Controls. The key to determining whether parents must exert strong controls over their child's activities will be in how much interaction with parents' ongoing business units is needed to achieve the child's purpose. The need for parent firms to exert substantial control over their child's activities is greatest when they hope to capture internal benefits involving activities of their ongoing units, such as to share outputs of large minimum efficient-scale plants, to avoid wasteful duplication of facilities, to utilize by-products and processes, or to share brands, distribution channels, wide product lines, and so forth. Relationships are more likely to be either horizontal or vertical when internal strengths are sought; the pattern will be less clear when other benefits are sought.

When competitive benefits are sought through joint ventures (to strengthen their current strategic positions) in response to blurring industry boundaries and globalization, *close* ties to the parent firm will be needed to ease political tensions with host nations (to overcome local trade barriers) and gain access to global networks. Close ties will also be needed in order to create more effective

Child's need for autonomy

	High	Low
High	Very unstable	Parent can intervene heavily High coordination with parents
Low	Child operates like autonomous SBU Financial controls primarily	Joint venture is less likely to offer parent strategic impact

Parent's need to control and coordinate child's activities

Figure 4–7. Parent Coordination and Child Autonomy Needs

competitors by making them hybrids possessing parents' respective strengths, or by making fewer, but more efficient, firms. (*But* looser ties will be appropriate if the joint venture buffers dissimilar partners.)

The *closest* ties between parent and child will be needed to obtain strategic benefits (by augmenting their strategic positions) when it is necessary to create synergies through vertical integration or horizontal linkages. Even where the child will pursue activities that are related to parents' competitive advantages, parents will want linkages to be tight if the activity is of high strategic importance to them.

Need for Intermediate Controls. Parents must ensure some links with their child if they seek intelligence, either to obtain a window on new technologies and customers by gaining superior methods of information exchange or by technological personnel interactions. If parents formed joint ventures to retain entrepreneurial employees, controls over the child's activities (beyond financial controls) would be needed only if it shared resources with an ongoing unit of the corporate parent and needed to interact with personnel of the parent.

The nature of the strategic benefit sought will suggest how tight the cooperation arrangement must be. Some interaction of the child with their ongoing organization will be necessary, where parents hope to influence an industry structure's evolution by pioneering when it is young, reducing competitive volatility when it becomes too bloody, or rationalizing mature industries in the face of excess capacity. If parents seek to preempt competitors' integrations, to link up with the best partners first, a looser arrangement that ties parent to child may be more appropriate. If one of the strategic benefits sought through joint venture was technology transfer, parent and child must have some interactions, but their integrating mechanisms need not be as tight as those used where facilities are shared.

Need for Low Controls. There will be less need to exert control over child's activities where parents seek the internal benefits of cost and risk sharing (uncertainty reduction) or seek to obtain resources where there is no market. If strategic benefits such as diversification were sought from joint ventures, the links between parent and child need not be as tight, particularly if the venture's purpose is to gain a toehold entry into new markets, products, or skills that are unrelated to parents' ongoing activities or if the venture is for rationalization (or divestiture) of parents' investments.

Range of Needs for Child Autonomy and Coordination

The child's needs for autonomy from parental interference are due to competitive requirements within its industry. Its autonomy needs are mitigated by the child's needs for interactions with parents' business units in order to compete effectively. Before the influence of industry structure can be traced in chapter 5, the tensions between needs for coordination and autonomy must be identified, particularly as these opposing pressures will affect parent firms' abilities to match their strategy needs with those of their child.

The child will need to coordinate its activities closely with parents when it shares facilities, personnel, or resources with them, when it is captive in its parents' vertical chains of processing, or when competitive needs for parents' advice, services, and resources are great. As the discussion (below) concerning the sheltered child will suggest, however, tying the child too closely to them will be disadvantageous for parent firms because it harms the child's ability to compete.

The child's needs to coordinate with its parents are greatest, other factors held constant, when technology changes rapidly and prices change erratically, requiring parents' help in modifying products or technologies. Coordination with parents will be important when the child's products are differentiable, markets can be standardized, or excess capacity must be rationalized, due to the scale economies that can be exploited if they work together. If demand grows slowly (or is declining), close coordination will be needed to serve the most promising customers while closing the most appropriate facilities. In this manner, parent and child can be most profitable while keeping capacity in line with demand. If the child is physically interconnected, its activities must be coordinated closely with its parents' activities, since a vertical relationship probably exists. (These points will be developed further in chapter 5.)

Success within some competitive environments requires great strategic flexibility. The child needs substantial autonomy to make its own decisions where these competitive conditions are present. Certain strategies require close coordination between the child and the parents that provide those resources that are crucial for success. The most difficult parent–child interface problems arise where autonomy needs and coordination needs are both high.

The child's needs for autonomy will be greatest, other factors held constant, when competition is volatile, requiring a rapid response to change. Timing advantages will be lost if its decisions must be approved by parents in a cumbersome process of ratification. The child must be autonomous where the resources crucial for competitive success are people-intensive so that parents will not sap the motivation of its personnel and thereby undercut a differentiation strategy based on service. The child needs autonomy where the industry's infrastructure is yet embryonic (hence changeable) in order to adopt alternative product standards, processes, and suppliers (or channels of distribution) that prove to be superior to the approach taken initially. Autonomy to subcontract with outsiders will be needed when demand is growing rapidly. The child can also be autonomous from its parents when the exit barriers associated with its strategic posture are low.

The "Sheltered" Child. Using their child as a guaranteed resource supplier or channel of distribution may seem attractive to parents, but they must beware of "sheltering" it too much from contact with outsiders. Tying the child more closely to parents than is necessary will be disadvantageous to parents because outsiders may be reluctant to deal with entities when they are too closely identified with firms that are their competitors. Parents' business units may become complacent without pressures to innovate or lower costs if their child lacks the autonomy to find outside suppliers or customers.

Without the prod of outside competition, the child's technology may become obsolete or lose any cost advantages. Managers' motivations may be sapped if the child is sheltered because their entrepreneurial efforts to innovate or lower costs are not rewarded. As their enthusiasm wanes, the brightest personnel will abandon positions that are little more than those of caretakers.

The "Boisterous" Child. Unbridled joint-venture managers often wish to expand its scope of activities into areas that parents reserve for their respective, wholly owned business units. The "boisterous" child will be continually waging turf battles with its parents' managers in an effort to gain autonomy where it is not necessary for competitive success. Parents must study the success requirements of various competitive environments to determine whether autonomy should be granted in some areas at a rate faster than they had intended.

Summary of Autonomy Needs. In summary, the child needs autonomy when competition is volatile, but it will also need to coordinate its efforts for rapid competitive response with the parent that contributes crucial inputs to it. For example, when technology changes rapidly in the child's industry, it will need to work closely with its technology parent; if customers are exerting their bargaining power by demanding more features, services, or other product features, the child must work closely with the parent that contributes product styling and marketing services to respond effectively. (High coordination with its marketing parent will be especially important, other factors held constant, when products are marketed to sophisticated consumers.) When managers evaluate the joint venture's needs for autonomy and for coordination with one or more of its parents, they must weigh changes over time in (1) parents' investments; (2) the joint venture's success in its chosen strategy; and (3) the actions of competitors. The dynamics of parent–child and partner interactions should anticipate changes in the respective strategic needs, capabilities, and successes of the other parties to the joint venture.

Control Mechanisms

The child is governed by terms of a bargaining agreement between parents that specifies the nature of information sharing, personnel contacts, representation by parent firms, reporting mechanisms, and other details of the management system created to support parents' strategy objectives. If the purpose of the venture includes innovation and technology transfer, special attentions must be devoted to control mechanisms that protect proprietary knowledge and the child's property rights as well as those of its parents. The bargaining agreement limits the joint venture's autonomy, and it provides for control mechanisms that are used to ensure that parents' objectives are attained. The partnership agreement also provides for renegotiation of terms, including the termination of the joint-venture relationship.

Hypotheses Concerning Joint-Venture Management Systems

In theory, the bargaining contract that forms the joint-venture child will contain the details of the management system that will bind the child to each respective parent. In fact, it is unreasonable to expect parent firms (or their lawyers) to foresee and provide for all of the conditions that could make joint-venture relationships evolve. Many effective firms are in a constant state of fine-tuning with respect to their own management systems. It is unreasonable for these same firms (as parents) to expect their child's system to be cast in concrete. Therefore, adaptive systems are needed to provide for the changes that may occur in the relationships between joint-venture parents, between parent and child, or within the child's domain (discussed below).

Ownership Shares

Earlier studies of joint ventures have devoted a disproportionate emphasis to the balance (or imbalance) of equity ownership. They have asserted, for example, that evenly divided ownership of the child (that is, 50%-50% joint ventures) often encourages deadlocks in decision making, unless one partner is willing to trust the decisions of the other partner on minor issues.[4] For this reason, asymmetric equity controls (such as 51%-49% ownership splits) have been touted as being more effective than joint ventures where ownership (and veto power) was evenly distributed to accommodate managers desires for equal proportions of equity parental ownership.

This issue is a red herring; arguments about the division of ownership have assumed erroneously that ownership is equivalent to management control. The correct balance of managerial controls and autonomy, *not* ownership shares, are the key to effective management of the child. When a decision is reviewed by parents, partners can become deadlocked whether one firm has majority ownership or not. If partners cannot agree, their child simply cannot function. Some firms will take a minority *ownership* position if they can obtain a majority position in *managerial* authority, and they are most likely to compromise in this manner if the child's activities are of high strategic importance to them. Thus, the balance of equity control (and managerial control) will not necessarily be symmetrical because some parents will accept a lesser degree of control to obtain something they seek.

Executive Boards of Directors

Board composition provides parents with a unique opportunity to guide the activities of their child. But instead of placing managers who could help the child to compete more effectively on the executive boards that govern joint ventures, some firms make board directorships an honorary position that is occupied by managers with experiences far from those activities that would be salient to their child. The best candidates for joint-venture boards are often managers operating so far within parent firms' hierarchies that they would never be considered for similar honors within their parent organizations. Yet they may be more compatible with the needs of joint ventures, especially in their early years of start-up, than higher-ranking executives that are more accustomed to dealing with firms' external environments and the complexities of multibusiness enterprise.

A combination of rotation and continuity is needed with respect to parents' representatives on their child's board. Because different operating needs may require attention as the child develops its own capabilities, some of the managers selected to guide the joint venture through the board should rotate in a pattern that reflects these changing needs. For example, as the child graduates into an ongoing entity that issues equity securities in its own right, a different type of board composition will be appropriate than when the child was a struggling start-up venture. As the child acquires more activities that make it tantamount to a stand-alone entity, more general management guidance will be needed, for example, than when parents limited the child merely to manufacturing or research activities.

To maintain some continuity in partners' dealings with each other, some board members must remain in their positions as others rotate off the board. No number of codicils can overcome the benefits of prolonged exposure by the permanent members of partners' delegations to each other. The longer they work together harmoniously, the less need they will feel for recourse to legal documents to establish a homogeneity of vision concerning their child's purpose.

Personnel Rotation

Staffing decisions whereby parents send managers to work within their child will be complicated by an unwillingness to let go. Too many firms permit employees to use the "revolving door" back to headquarters and the security of the parent. Because it will not be possible for the best interest of the child to be served by managers with unclearly focused loyalties and attentions, the child's managers may have to be recruited from outside. Key positions, in particular, must have unswerving loyalties to the child.

The revolving-door policy encourages the bleedthrough of ideas. In some cases, this may be *desirable*. If employees from its parents are frequently rotated through the child, there is a good chance that its parents seek in-house technological capabilities and wish to ensure that knowledge is repatriated to their factories and laboratories. Some aggressive parents will even build parallel facilities and hold in-house seminars to emulate each experiment their child undertakes. If parents want to *encourage* bleedthrough, they will *not* give their child a permanent complement of managers and technical personnel. Parents will treat the assignment of employees to the joint venture as part of their regular career path of experiences and will expect these personnel to disseminate knowledge in both directions.

Trial Marriage

Joint ventures can result in deadlocks if partners have not created equitable mechanisms for resolving day-to-day deadlocks in decision making. For this reason, it is generally more advantageous to draft a *team* of operating managers that can maximize the tradeoffs between synergies (from shared resources) and economies (from centralized facilities). The team should be taken from both parents' personnel.

Joint ventures that hope to maximize synergies by sharing assets, managers, and capabilities with parents increase their abilities to do so by looking at both parents' respective positions within the industries the joint venture will cover before the marriage is consummated. The team should create a proposal for the best use of parents' facilities, without preconceived notions of equitable schedules concerning which plants will be shut down, political solutions for layoffs, and so forth. (Briefly, the ongoing managers in charge of the facilities that each respective partner will contribute should be charged with independently developing the most economic plan for combining them, without knowing *who* will be chosen to run the child's operations after the trial marriage period.) During the trial marriage, teams of managers from all partners work together to implement the best plans for combining operations, adding capabilities and rationalizing the child. Finally, the child's management team is selected on the basis of which managers solved problems together best when the trial marriage evolves into a full-fledged operating joint venture.

Review Points and Child Autonomy

Although the management systems that link parents to child should provide for the ways in which the child's capital requests and budgeting cycle will mesh with that of its parents' planning cycles, parents must be wary of overburdening their joint ventures with excessive reporting obligations. Paradoxically, the management systems used to govern joint ventures are often *more* detailed than the systems of either parent because the child must bridge the cultural differences between parents. The paperwork involved in doing so can stifle creativity within their child. For example, earlier studies indicated that autonomous joint ventures were more innovative than those that were tethered closely to their board's review.[5] Yet, because performance measures, review procedures, reward systems, and other mechanisms used to delegate responsibilities to the joint venture must be designed in a manner that will be consistent with the needs of each parent, a complex management system and organization design (often embodying some version of a matrix organization) has often been embraced.[6] Such a management burden will quickly cancel the expected benefits of cooperation and slow down the child when it must move quickly, as in volatile industry settings (discussed in chapter 5).

Russian Roulette Buy-outs. The fragile nature of cooperative strategies requires mechanisms that ensure that parity among partners is protected. If the relative value of partners' contributions changes, the management systems that govern the child should (in theory) revalue partners' contributions regularly and adjust ownership (and managerial) shares to reflect current market values. Such valuations may be difficult to implement in practice, however, unless a reference point for pricing assets is readily available, as in the example of crude oil. Where there is no market, partners could become deadlocked regarding valuation methods. To overcome such stalemates, partners may have to agree on unorthodox ways of resolving such disputes. Russian roulette buy-outs, for example, are schemes some partners use whereby one firm evaluates the child and proposes a price to its partners who choose, in turn, whether to be buyers or sellers of its joint-venture interests.

Changes in the Bargaining Agreement

As the joint-venture framework above has noted, a bargaining agreement will specify the markets where the child will operate, the outputs it is authorized to produce, and which of its inputs (if any) parents will provide. It should also provide for a means of adjusting the joint-venture relationship to changes in the child's environment.

Joint ventures must revitalize themselves as do other ongoing organizations. Because the industries where joint ventures operate will change over time to accommodate the effects of competition, the manner in which parents integrate the activities of the child with their own must change also. As the sections above have explained, synergies will not accrue between parent and child unless they are consciously managed. Buyer–seller relationships and shared resources must be reinforced by compatible management systems.

If partners expect to enjoy synergies by interacting with their child, they must foster good relationships between their organizations. To do so requires diplomatic skills as well as patience in the managers who represent the child's *parents* as well as in the managers who protect the *child's* interests. Relationships between employees of the parent and child must be managed to ameliorate feelings of envy or excessive competition. Partners' employees may envy the success of the child if it outperforms wholly owned, sister units. Parents' employees may even *sabotage* the child's operations in some manner if they perceive that their future is too dependent on uncontrollable revenues from the joint venture. Scientists in parent-firm laboratories may perceive that excessive rewards are given to innovators within the child organization or that the most interesting projects are farmed out to the joint venture.

Effective management of joint ventures will depend on trust, mutual respect, and a willingness among partners to negotiate any dispute. A policy of open and enhanced communications is necessary in order to air the perceived inequities that could develop within parent–child relationships. These precautions will be particularly important where legal voting control of the joint venture is distributed in a manner that could produce a stalemate, especially if neither partner possesses the bargaining power needed to break the impasse.

Where a joint venture has been formed to marry dissimilar cultures, there is always a risk that the arrangement will fail because partners are too dissimilar and become unwilling to compromise. This impasse is most likely to occur where executives are of dissimilar ages, educational backgrounds, and work experience, if they seek differing personal goals, enjoy differing socioeconomic roots, and aspire to diverse levels of security, or if their concepts of the role of the child differs from that of partners.[7] (If the personalities and styles of two companies are totally different, a successful joint venture between them is doubtful. It may be possible for such parties to cooperate contractually instead.)

Today's partners could become tomorrow's competitors because joint ventures are often reconfigured when partners have gained knowledge of markets and skills that they previously did not understand.[8] Providing for joint-venture disposition is important, or firms may encounter difficulties in recovering the value of their investments in their child. Although a market usually exists for the resources partners have committed, their ability to exit can be ensured better if firms have managed for this contingency.

It is important for partners not to lose sight of their motivations for cooperating. Their management systems and ways of integrating the child with their ongoing operations must continually test and retest the assumptions that motivated them to work together originally. By 1984 few industries' structures were likely to remain unchanged for long. The only certainty that parents could rely on was that competition in the child's industry—as well as in their own industries—would be more trying than it had ever been before. In the midst of such confusion, parents tried to anticipate how industries might evolve when they provided for their joint venture relationships.

When firms form joint ventures, their children can represent important structural changes in an industry's profitability potential because the resources and capabilities of diverse parents can be treated as though they were one. Their child's presence can change the basis for successful competition to the disadvantage of other firms that have no joint ventures. But the severity of the actual threat represented by their child will vary (from the perspective of its competitors), depending on whether the child links parents horizontally, vertically, or in a related (or unrelated) pattern of diversification. Firms create a credible threat *only* if partners can bring their respective powers to bear on competitors through their child's activities.

Effective use of those powers requires partners to tap the strengths that gave them bargaining power in forming their joint ventures. It requires parents to update the role of their child in their respective strategic missions. It requires parents to question the need for them to provide inputs to the child or to absorb its outputs as they have done in the past. It requires parents to be willing to wean their child and send it out on its own when the child's needs to coordinate closely with its parents have diminished. Industry differences will suggest how quickly joint ventures should evolve from loose cooperation to partnerships to stand-alone entities (if at all). Volatile competitive conditions will require shorter-lived and more informal liaisons, for example. Demand uncertainty will necessitate tentative affiliations, modest funding, and pilot plants or test situations. These and other specifics concerning industry differences are covered in chapter 5, which adds the third leg to the joint-venture framework's strategic triangle.

Notes

1. Franko, Lawrence G., 1971a, "Joint Venture Divorce in the Multinational Company," *Columbia Journal of World Business* 4(3):13–22; Franko, Lawrence G., 1971b, *Joint Venture Survival in Multinational Corporations* (New York: Praeger); Edström, Anders, 1975a, "Acquisition and Joint Venture Behavior of Swedish Manufacturing Firms," working paper, University of Gothenburg; Gullander, Steffan O.O., 1975, "An Exploratory Study of Inter-Firm Cooperation of Swedish Firms," Ph.D. diss., Columbia University; Berg, Sanford V., and Friedman, Philip, 1980, "Corporate Courtship and Successful Joint Ventures," *California Management Review* 22(2):85–91; Berg, Sanford V., Duncan, Jerome, Jr., and Friedman, Philip, 1982, *Joint Venture Strategies and Corporate Innovation* (Cambridge, Mass.: Oelgeschlager, Gunn & Hain).

2. Harrigan, K.R., 1983, *Strategies for Vertical Integration* (Lexington, Mass.: Lexington Books).

3. Harrigan, K.R., 1985, *Strategic Flexibility: A Management Guide for Changing Times* (Lexington, Mass.: Lexington Books).

4. Banks, Howard, 1981, "Partners of Necessity," *Europe* 31–33; Bivens, Karen Kraus, and Lovell, Enid Baird, 1966, *Joint Ventures with Foreign Partners* (New York: National Industrial Conference Board); Business International, 1971, *European Business Strategies in the United States: Meeting the Challenge of the World's Largest Market* (Geneva: Business International); Business International, 1972, *Recent Experiences in Establishing Joint Ventures* (New York: Business International); Killing, J. Peter, 1982, "How to Make a Global Joint Venture Work," *Harvard Business Review* 60(3):120–127; Killing, J. Peter, 1983, *Strategies for Joint Venture Success* (New York: Praeger); Reid, William J., 1971, *Interorganizational Coordination: A Review and Critique of Current Theory* (Washington, D.C.: U.S. Department of Health, Education and Welfare); Van de Ven, Andrew H., 1976, "On the Nature, Formation and Maintenance of Relations among Organizations," *Academy of Management Review* 1:24–36; West, Malcolm W., Jr., 1959, "The Jointly-Owned Subsidiary," *Harvard Business Review* 37(4):32–39; Wren, D.A., 1967, "Interface and Interorganizational Coordination," *Academy of Management Journal* 10:69–81.

5. Edström, Anders, 1975b, "The Stability of Joint Ventures," working paper, University of Gothenburg; Gullander, Steffan O.O., 1975, "An Exploratory Study of Inter-Firm Cooperation of Swedish Firms," Ph.D. diss., Columbia University.

6. Davis, Stanley, 1976, "Trends in the Organization of Multinational Corporations," *Columbia Journal of World Business* 11(2):59–71; Pitts, Robert A., and Daniels, John D., 1984, "Aftermath of the Matrix Mania," *Columbia Journal of World Business* 29(2):48–55.

7. Young, G. Richard, and Bradford, Standish, Jr., 1977, *Joint Ventures: Planning and Action* (New York: Arthur D. Little and the Financial Executives Research Foundation).

8. Killing, Peter, 1980, Technology Acquisition: License Agreement or Joint Venture, *Columbia Journal of World Business* 15(3):38–46; Killing, J. Peter., 1982, "How to Make a Global Joint Venture Work," *Harvard Business Review* 63(3):120–127; and Killing, J. Peter, 1983, *Strategies for Joint Venture Success* (New York: Praeger).

5
Viability of the Joint-Venture Child: The Analytical Model Continues

This chapter covers the child's relationship to its competitive environment as these pressures affect parents' joint-venture strategy choices. Industry analysis represents the third leg in the joint-venture strategy model, as is shown by the heavy arrows in figure 5–1. The construction and content of chapter 5 is dramatically different in its specificity and analytical approach from the chapters treating (1) parents' private weightings of the cost–benefit agreement and (2) the child's relationships with its parents with respect to horizontal or vertical relationships, close coordination (for synergistic resource sharing), or operating autonomy (for performance maximization), as it must be, given the role that competitive environments play in the viability of joint venture strategies.

Relating the Child's Competitive Environment to Parents' Joint-Venture Strategies

Most of the arguments contained in chapters 3 and 4 concerning firms' cost–benefit analyses, partners' bargaining agreements, and tradeoffs between coordination and autonomy in relationships between parent and child have been intentionally basic because they can be generally applied to many situations. Only the final discussions of chapter 4—concerning how competitive forces might augment the highly coordinated relationship between parent and child—have foreshadowed the influences of industry traits on the range of joint-venture strategy options that firms might embrace. Chapter 5 demonstrates how specific industry forces will affect applications of the basic concepts presented in chapters 3 and 4. It suggests that parents will face fewer joint-venture options in some competitive environments than within others and that industry traits will make a difference in joint-venture success.

I am indebted to William H. Newman for suggestions concerning this chapter.

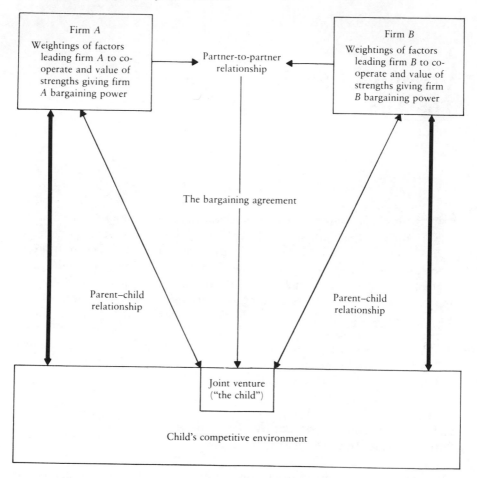

Figure 5–1. Child's Relationship to Its Competitive Environment as It Affects Parent's Joint-Venture Strategy

Chapter 5 is positioned last in the sequence of chapters that describe the joint-venture framework for two reasons. First, a full appreciation of the issues motivating partners to cooperate and to relate their child to their wholly owned business units was needed in order to understand how industry traits affect these fundamental issues. Chapter 5 revives the debate of chapter 3 concerning whether firms should form joint ventures as a means to build new strengths, gain a timing advantage over competitors, enter new markets, gain new products or process, or otherwise diversify from their ongoing scope of activities. It also suggests that close coordination with the activities of parents' business units—when using some of the control mechanisms described in chapter 4—will prove to be stultifying to the child's ability to thrive within some competitive environments. Second, chapter 5 tracks most closely the specifics of situations where joint ventures have been used with varying degrees of success. The joint-venture framework is tested using industry-specific data because the effects of competitive environments are recognized as being important in defining the range of feasible strategies firms might pursue. Industry vignettes that have been stratified by the structural traits described below are presented in chapters 7 to 12 to test the robustness of the joint-venture framework.

The Child Firm's Domain

The tensions between parent and child come to a boiling point in matters of competitive strategy. The child's success requirements will involve issues of autonomy and of resources that evolve as the nature of competition changes. If the child's managers are entrepreneurial and aggressive, they will see opportunities where the child should move *preemptively* to improve its strategic position. As its industry evolves, the strengths and resources needed by the child may be available from a different parent than the one that supplied those resources in the past. Or the best resources may be available from outsiders. Yet managers within parent firms may cling to the notion that the old linkages between the child and its parents must be maintained instead.

The results of these inertia barriers could be disastrous. The preceding chapters have suggested that competition within many industries has become more demanding due to the effects of evolutionary forces that include: the maturation of U.S., European, and Japanese economies, leaps in communications technology, shorter product lives (but larger capital requirements for innovation), globalization of industries (where competition was previously constrained to geographic boundaries), and entry by new players (supported by their respective governments), among others. Chapters 1 and 2 argued that cooperative strategies—and in particular, joint ventures—offer one way of coping with these tensions. The examples that follow suggest how parents' cooperative strategies must adjust to competitive forces if they expect their child to be a viable player within its industry.

This analysis asks how the use of joint ventures differs where demand is uncertain or where competitors have differing expectations concerning product viability. It ponders how joint ventures might best serve both customers and their parents. It considers how attractive joint ventures will be when competition becomes volatile. How will autonomy and coordination needs change when the boundaries separating industries erode?

Domain refers to the industries where the child competes and the type of competition it encounters in its domain. The profitability potential of any venture—jointly owned or not—will be determined by their industry structures and by how firms behave therein. The child's strategy determines whether it has exploited the full potential of its environment, and the child's performance will be determined by its effectiveness in implementing that strategy. Parents will judge performance according to the venture's delivery of value to them. To deliver value, the child must perform well within its domain.

Analysis of the child's domain considers the nature of the markets (and customers) it will serve, the products that competitors might offer to satisfy anticipated demand, differences in the strategic postures firms could embrace to serve attractive market segments, and how firms will protect their competitive advantages from rivals. The key *demand* traits that determine how joint ventures are best used include: customer attributes (including product differentiability, buyer sophistication, and hence bargaining power), supplier expectations, and whether products may be standardized to serve diverse market segments. These relationships hold true whether a venture is jointly owned or not.

The key *competitor* traits that determine how joint ventures will best be used include: how competitors cope with products' technological attributes (particularly with respect to capital intensity and rates of technological change), as well as the kinds of competitive advantages that firms can carve from an industry and protect over time. Effective joint-venture strategies should enable the child to hurdle entry barriers with greater ease while maintaining their abilities to adapt to changing competitive conditions within its industry with greater flexibility (assuming the child's managers can tap into the strengths of its parents effectively).

Demand Traits: Customers and Uncertainty

Two key demand traits that affect joint-venture success are *demand uncertainty* and *customer bargaining power*. Unless cooperative strategies are being forged to permit firms to phase *out* of an industry, demand must be attractive enough to justify firms' investments, whether through a joint venture or by going it alone. Analysis of customer traits will suggest how long a market opportunity may be expected to remain attractive, and the windows of opportunity in some markets may be so short-lived that firms must use joint ventures (or similar alliances) to leapfrog into growing markets to exploit them before their luster fades.

Analysis of *market attractiveness* turns on the study of customers' attributes, particularly on their sophistication in evaluating products and their propensity to exercise their bargaining power in negotiating with vendors. There is a constant tug-of-war between them because suppliers seek to standardize as many of their products' traits as possible, especially where profit margins are low. But customers want as much product customization as they can extract from vendors without paying higher prices. In an effort to spread the overhead costs associated with satisfying demanding clients, some firms form joint ventures by pooling certain types of orders in one factory. The more attractive the perceived reward of serving such customers, the more tempting cooperative strategies will be, particularly where the costs of entry seem too high or the payback period on investment seems too short for one firm to undertake the venture alone. The more attractive the market, the *more autonomy* the child's managers may require.

Demand Uncertainty. As chapter 2 has suggested, when demand uncertainty is high, investments to enter (or shift from one strategic posture to another) will be too risky for one firm to undertake alone. More joint ventures will be formed when the combined resources of partners would make seemingly uneconomic investments acceptable. This risk–return relationship will hold true whether joint ventures are used to enter industries where demand is growing rapidly or to consolidate excess capacity within industries experiencing mature (or stagnant) demand. The differences in how they are managed depends on demand uncertainty and the rate of sales growth (or decline).

Hypotheses Concerning Demand Uncertainty. As figure 5–2 indicates, joint ventures will be used more frequently where demand is uncertain or business risks are high, particularly when demand is growing rapidly or is declining. Joint ventures could enable firms to be more responsive to variations in customer demands, provided parents design their alliances effectively. Joint ventures may be used to ease a firm out of a declining or troubled industry where excess capacity will plague all ongoing firms. One partner to a joint venture may buy out the other, or a firm that previously owned a business outright may create a joint venture as a means of passing ownership to an outsider. Many arrangements *could* be used. But as a partnership agreement, the joint venture offers firms more flexibility in coping with these uncertainties than the corporate form of doing business.

When demand is growing rapidly, other factors held constant, the joint venture's managers need freedom to subcontract production or make other accommodations to satisfy customers. When demand is declining, the joint venture must coordinate its endgame strategy closely with its parents' activities in order to serve the most attractive customer niches without disrupting industrywide price levels.

Rapidly Growing Demand. Vertical joint ventures, whereby parents share their child's outputs (or use their child to absorb their respective outputs) will be particularly useful within settings where demand is growing rapidly as a means of utilizing large plants economically (perhaps by sharing a supplying plant with a competitor, initially) or by reaching target customers to alleviate their fears concerning the new product's or process's viability.[1] Firms will use

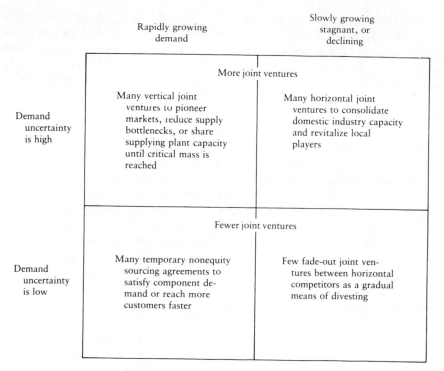

Figure 5–2. Single-Firm Analysis: Hypothesized Effect of Demand Uncertainty and Industry Evolution on Joint-Venture Formation (Assuming Firms Will Cooperate, Ceteris Paribus)

horizontal arrangements later to consolidate excess capacity and focus competitors' attentions (to alleviate wasteful price cutting when demand growth slows). Horizontal joint ventures are embraced when firms would otherwise battle for market share at the expense of each other because demand has become saturated or is primarily for replacement purposes.

Slowly Growing Demand. Demand uncertainty will be lower where demand is growing more slowly, and joint ventures will be particularly appropriate in such settings if significant scale economies are available at large production volumes, particularly if cost reduction is becoming the key to effective competition. (This is often the time when domestic firms will be most vulnerable to offshore competition, and this point will be developed further in the section discussing market standardization, below.) Joint ventures will allow firms who were rivals formerly to retain the most efficient parts of their assets in building a new, world-scale competitive entity. Joint ventures may also be used to permit firms to divest their assets incrementally in situations where they face such high exit barriers that no buyer could afford to purchase them outright.

As demand slows, stagnates, or declines, it will become necessary for some firms to cooperate in order to prevent destructive price wars. Joint ventures will be preferred over nonequity arrangements in such settings if businesses are of high strategic importance because they facilitate divestitures (as well as diversifications) when firms must adapt to changing industry conditions. Then firms will seek to acquire partners' shares (or use *fade-in joint ventures*)[2] to increase their control over joint activities and destroy excess capacity so that the assets will not be resurrected by new firms and continue to plague their troubled industry.

Customer Traits. Whether cooperative strategies are appropriate depends on how well the product can be differentiated, how sensitive service is to the product offering, and whether the market is global. Analyses of these forces may be combined to suggest the relative stability of profits. As long as firms can offer products that retain some dimension of uniqueness for which customers would pay a price premium, their profit margins will be higher. If their product's uniqueness can be eroded easily, their profits will be less stable.

Hypotheses Concerning Customer Traits. Where markets are standardized and coordination needs in serving them are high, joint ventures or other arrangements that impede firms' strategic flexibility will be less attractive than where customers' requirements are varied. As figure 5–3 indicates, firms will prefer to control more of their activities through in-house facilities where many markets could be served by similar product configurations. This preference will be intensified where customers are sophisticated in their abilities to discern differences among vendors' products. Therefore, joint ventures are more likely to be tolerated where customer bargaining power is low but their product requirements, nevertheless, cannot be standardized with those of other markets. If cooperative strategies are forged where product configurations could be standardized across markets, the global partner will seek to control the venture's activities in order to coordinate them with the rest of its network of facilities. Customer sophistication (especially in terms of costs) will be a destabilizing force on the duration of joint-venture relationships, particularly where product configurations change rapidly.

The more demanding the customer, the more autonomy the child will require in responding to customer demands. But close coordination with the child's marketing parent may be needed to satisfy some sophisticated customers. If the products in question are complex and require precision in manufacturing, close coordination with its technology parent will also be needed.

The greater the bargaining power of customers over the firm (by virtue of their large purchase volumes throughout firms' business units), the more

	Product configurations cannot be standardized across markets	Product configurations can be standardized across markets
Customer sophistication and bargaining power is high	Spider's web of cooperative strategies for cost reduction styling Many short-term cross-licensing arrangements for new product features, cost reductions	Few joint ventures, except as required to enter High coordination control by global partner to keep costs lowest
Customer sophistication and bargaining power is low	More longer-term joint ventures (depends on competitors' activities), primarily for new product features	Few joint ventures, except as required to enter (local partner allowed some coordination controls)

Figure 5–3. Single-Firm Analysis: Hypothesized Effect of Customer Bargaining Power and Market Standardization on Joint-Venture Formation and Use (Assuming Firms Will Cooperate, Ceteris Paribus)

important they will be to parent firms. Coordination of customer accounts will be particularly important if parent and child would both be interacting with the same purchasing agents. The greater the percentage of total purchases an important customer makes through a centralized agent, the closer parents will need to work with their child in satisfying customers' demands, other factors held constant. Although they need not be customers themselves, access to viable customers (or autonomy to create its own channels of distribution to reach outsiders) is one of the provisions parents must anticipate in their joint-venture strategy if it is to be effective.

Product Differentiation. Even products that might ordinarily be considered to be commodity-like can be made unique or *differentiated* in the minds of buyers through vendors' attentions to services, uniform quality, or other dimensions. Joint ventures are less risky to undertake where products have the long-term potential to remain differentiated, but conflicts could arise among partners concerning control of the basis for differentiation, access to markets, and product presentation. Briefly, when firms enter joint ventures to make differentiated products, the production tasks that firms entrust to joint ventures will not be the most sophisticated or complex ones, or outsiders could gain control over their sources of competitive advantage. Moreover, firms possessing differentiated products will want complete control over marketing activities, even if a local partner's personnel perform the selling tasks.

Conflicts concerning which partner maintains control will be destabilizing unless domestic firms can use their knowledge of local customers to increase their bargaining power over outside partners to compensate for product attribute changes that undermine their power. Frequent changes in product attributes will also be destabilizing to joint ventures because, although profitability potential will be higher (because firms will emphasize nonprice competition), frequent changes in product dimensions increase the likelihood that partners will become mismatched. To hedge these risks, strong firms will form a spider's web of alliances that are individually easy to dissolve. Joint ventures are too inflexible if the basis for competitive advantage changes frequently unless partners agree that their affiliations must be temporary in nature.

If sellers cannot differentiate their products effectively from those of other firms and price is their major dimension for competition, joint ventures will still occur. But because firms need the lowest-cost technologies to succeed, their joint ventures will emphasize process innovations. Briefly, when joint ventures occur where products are commodity-like, they are the types of arrangements that fill underutilized plants and increase productivity. Such ventures last *longer* because product traits change less frequently and because the large capital investments entailed in cost-reduction joint ventures increase partners' exit barriers. High exit barriers may increase joint-venture stability, but they also decrease profitability potential (because high exit barriers exacerbate competitive volatility).

Figure 5–4, which combines the effects of demand uncertainty and product differentiability, indicates that firms seek sourcing arrangements and other temporary ways of obtaining access to new technology and marketing channels if they cannot adequately satisfy the rapidly growing demand they face by relying on in-house facilities alone. But as demand growth slows, firms need fewer joint ventures because they can move more of their manufacturing responsibilities in-house and develop their own generations of technology. Eventually, joint ventures flourish again, but this time as a means of consolidating excess capacity due to declining demand or import competition. While products are highly differentiable, joint ventures are undertaken primarily to gain access to unique product features as well as new channels of distribution. When products become commodity-like, joint ventures will emphasize process innovations to reduce unit costs rather than marketing attributes.

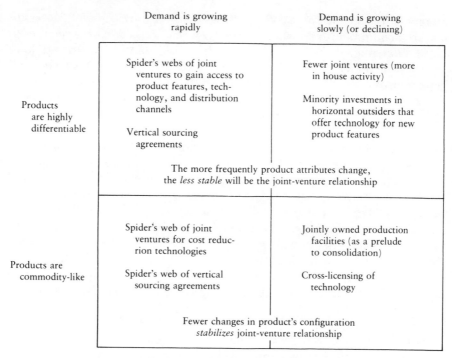

Figure 5–4. Single-Firm Analysis: Hypothesized Effect of Demand Growth and Product Differentiability on Joint-Venture Formation and Use (Assuming Firms Will Cooperate, Ceteris Paribus)

If products can be differentiated in the minds of customers and if both parent and child will offer the products in question, their need to coordinate decisions concerning product features, supporting services, and other attributes increases, other factors held constant. If they do not share products, the child's need for autonomy in differentiating its products increases.

Market Standardization. If customer tastes can be standardized across several geographic markets, investments in the means of satisfying demand appear to be more attractive than where each pocket of demand wants different product configurations and no market segment is of a size large enough to enjoy scale economies in production or distribution. The greatest critical mass exists where customers' tastes are homogeneous throughout the world, and such customers are highly attractive because they enable firms to pursue global strategies.[3]

Global competitors can enjoy significant cost advantages because they possess supply networks that span their many factory locations, assembly plants, warehouses, and distribution systems within several countries. In their quest for *access* to the most desirable locations for the components of their interconnected network of facilities, global firms may offer local partners generous terms in a joint-venture agreement, *provided* the global partner retains managerial control in order to maintain maximum flexibility in the deployment of their international system of operations.

It is unreasonable to expect that firms that have devised an efficient means of serving standardized markets will abandon their traditional networking policies by accommodating cumbersome joint venture arrangements, unless their expected payoff for doing so is great. While local firms control market access, they possess a bargaining chip that they forfeit when foreign competitors have established rival distribution channels in their home markets. Local firms could delay the establishment of outsiders' own marketing systems by offering the use of their marketing networks to global competitors. The advantage of cooperating will yield only short-term gains, however, unless firms use their time together in the partnership to exploit the *other* benefits of joint ventures.

If customers in diverse geographic markets will accept standardized products, firms must move faster to exploit the temporary advantages of joint ventures because it will be more difficult to erect effective entry barriers against other firms where markets are homogeneous. If firms are to be effective, they must devote attentions to detail. Coordinating the logistical aspects of firms' strategies grows more important, and timing in execution becomes crucial, due to the rapid dissemination of ideas within homogeneous markets. Care is needed to ensure that local partners' needs in joint ventures do not become impediments to future strategic flexibility, and there is some evidence suggesting that global firms are divesting those business units that no longer fit their coordination strategies for serving homogeneous markets. Instead of loosely coupled international diversification strategies, for example, global firms instead appear to be consolidating their holdings to focus on rationalization and cost reduction.[4]

Competitor Traits, Industry Structures, and Technological Opportunity

Analysis of the child's domain also considers how competitors elect to satisfy demand. A key determinant of joint-venture stability is the child's effectiveness in coping with the demands of sophisticated customers and tough competitors, and this relationship is dynamic. The key structural changes in firms' industries are precipitated by technological innovations in manufacturing, although innovations in the product's configuration, in channels of distribution, or in other activities could also cause the relationships between buyers and sellers to evolve. These structural changes affect whether an industry's profitability potential will be attractive for joint ventures.

Industry Structures. Joint ventures represent a significant change in industry structures and in competitive behavior. Parent firms embrace joint ventures because they are ways to implement changes in their strategic postures or to defend current strategic postures against forces too strong for one firm to withstand alone. Joint ventures permit firms to create new strengths. They permit firms to share in the use of technologies they could never afford to explore alone. The combinations of talents that effective joint ventures could create have the potential to introduce new competitive vigor into lethargic industries as well as to let embryonic industries develop useful products faster.

Hypotheses Concerning Industry Structure. Joint ventures are transitional strategies. They could be used for entry into, repositioning within, or exit from an industry. Joint ventures could be used to test the waters for entry into mature industries where firms could not enter alone because they could not afford to match the accumulated experience curve advantages of early entrants. Joint ventures may be the only way to match ongoing firms' intelligence advantages when entering *late*. They can be important change agents for launching new products, legitimizing new technologies, and rationalizing capacity as industries evolve. Vertical joint ventures are used to stabilize demand and to introduce new products within young industries, while horizontal joint ventures are used in mature settings to keep abreast of technological improvements and control excess capacity.

Joint ventures to facilitate the learning of new skills are likely, if products are differentiable, particularly if this knowledge fills gaps in ongoing firms' abilities, such as quality-control techniques. If firms cannot focus on standard configurations or other stabilizing points of cooperation, however, joint ventures may be short-lived, since they are too risky for most firms to tolerate within volatile industries. In their efforts to hedge risks within unstable, fragmented, or volatile industries, firms who possess adequate bargaining power forge a pattern of spider's-web alliances, if they decide to cooperate at all.

Thus, volatile competitive environments—those with fragmented structures, commodity-like products, powerful suppliers (or customers), and other attributes that erode firms' profitability potential—diminish the amount of equity parents would be willing to expose through joint ventures. (If the environment is volatile and the activity is not of high strategic importance to them, parents will not waste their efforts on cooperative strategies, as figure 5–5 indicates.) Within environments where competition is not volatile, firms are more willing to use cooperative strategies, but they still favor greater control over those activities that are of high strategic importance to them. Thus joint ventures could become the agent that *stabilizes* industry conditions by introducing standard product configurations, creating lowest-cost production processes, or facilitating improved competitive intelligence, if used effectively.

	High strategic importance	Low strategic importance
Volatile competitive environment and fragmented structure	Spider's web of cooperative agreements between firm and horizontal and vertical players	No interfirm cooperation
Stable competitive environment and concentrated structure	Acquisitions Joint ventures	Cooperative agreements Will accept minority investments from outsiders

Figure 5–5. Single-Firm Analysis: Hypothesized Relationship between Competitive Conditions and Strategic Importance in Joint-Venture Formation (Assuming Firms Will Cooperate, Ceteris Paribus)

Embryonic Industries. When an industry is embryonic, demand is uncertain and product standards are not yet established. Frequently infrastructures must be built within embryonic industries. Firms use vertical arrangements in such settings to build infrastructures, legitimize new products, and educate customers. Often these vertical arrangements are jointly owned by horizontally related parents, especially if the costs of creating distribution channels, transportation systems, or other supporting activities are substantial.[5] Vertical joint ventures will provide market access and are most appropriate as a means of joining industries when basic relationships between buyers and sellers are evolving. A presence within at least two stages of a vertical chain of processing gives partners a "listening post" to assess and communicate competitive intelligence back to the child's parents if the joint venture is structured effectively. (This sort of intelligence is necessary in order for firms to respond quickly to changes in demand, to develop new technologies, and to incorporate others' innovations into their products.)

Embryonic industries pose a potential source of conflict between parent and child concerning risk taking. If an industry is embryonic, great uncertainty remains concerning which competitive approaches will be most successful. Product and marketing standards are not established; neither are relationships between suppliers and customers. Until successful strategies become evident, some firms hedge their bets by trying several approaches. Managers within a "boisterous" child often want the freedom to move in directions that seem more promising as uncertainty is reduced. But their venture's parents may hedge their bets concerning which approach will prove most successful instead, by creating a spider's web of joint ventures. If parents diversify, they will expect the managers of each respective joint venture to act as champions of their respective strategies until another is proven to be superior rather than to diversify (in technologies or product configurations) for their parent.

Established Industries. Joint ventures are useful within slowly growing, established industries. As projects grow large and more risky, as technologies become too expensive to afford alone, and as the challenges of global competition increase, managers will find it difficult for numerous firms to survive independently. Joint ventures are one means of accommodating new competitors within markets where capacity has been overbuilt and demand is growing slowly at best. Under these circumstances, firms must either shrink capacity themselves or through marriages in order to avoid debilitating price warfare. The recent burst of U.S. joint ventures in some industries suggests, in part, that managers would prefer to enter into joint ventures *voluntarily* (rather than follow federally directed policies of industry rationalization) because such strategies permit them to decide which portions of a business unit to divest.

Tensions concerning infrastructure uncertainty are reduced when an industry matures, other factors held constant. If the joint venture shares no resources with its parents, its managers can act autonomously in matters of competitive strategy, subject to the financial controls imposed by the venture's parents. Where the venture shares resources or parallels those of its parents, other industry factors may make close coordination necessary.

Timing of Joint Ventures. In summary, because small but timely investments made early in an industry's development could give firms important leadership positions later, joint ventures are frequently used when industries are embryonic to gain first-mover advantages. Pioneering investments in research are also appropriate reasons to form joint ventures in embryonic industries, particularly where expectations of commercial success are low and firms are reluctant to invest heavily until uncertainties regarding product standards, commercial viability, or other factors have been reduced.[6] Joint ventures are a way to spread the costs of innovation when the risks of obsolescence are high due to rapid rates of technological change. Pioneering strategies are often risky, however, because late entrants that are more powerful could make the product configurations, standards, and other attributes of early entrants obsolete. Accordingly, firms engage in a mutual spider's web of alliances to test many technologies while an industry is still young.

Strong and highly determined competitors can piggy-back on the infrastructures built by early entrants if pioneers have not created standard product configurations for the industry or sustained other first-mover advantages. But if effective pioneers can defend their early investments from the incursions of late entrants, joint ventures within embryonic industries would be well justified. Moreover, if firms could effectively move their industries in directions that late entrants would find difficult to match, joint ventures may be their best means of acquiring the skills and resources needed to precipitate these changes.

As industry structures evolve and the nature of competition changes, the capabilities that firms will need to compete effectively will change.[7] When the structure of an industry is well established, less uncertainty will exist concerning product standards, buyer–seller relationships, and other means of competing. Structural relationships between buyers and suppliers will be better established. Although new competitors could still enter mature industries, their behaviors will be more predictable in such settings.[8] Fewer joint ventures will be necessary, but those that endure will assume greater importance in firms' corporate strategies.

When competition is volatile and prices fluctuate erratically, the child needs autonomy and yet it also needs to coordinate closely with the parent that provides its marketing support, if either parent does so. When competition is not volatile, when nonprice competition prevails, the child's autonomy and coordination needs are lower, other factors held constant.

Success within changeable environments demands rapid responses and high strategic flexibility. The child's flexibility can be greater when exit barriers are lower if parents grant it the autonomy needed to respond to pricing, product feature, or technological changes quickly. If pioneering does not provide strong competitive advantages, the child's response need not be as rapid, nor must its autonomy from parental activities be as high.

Technologies. Joint ventures enable firms to capture more profits than they would enjoy if they merely licensed their technologies. Moreover, joint ventures provide more control over how firms' resources will be used. But technology leaders will not readily share those kernels of knowledge that are central to their competitive advantage, and parents would be unwise to transfer all of their technological expertise to their child (since knowledge is highly appropriable and joint ventures do pose problems of bleedthrough). But firms can use joint ventures to exploit much of their highly perishable knowledge rapidly and can fine-tune their pace of technology sharing more easily through joint ventures than nonequity arrangements.

Where industries are people-intensive, rather than capital intensive, the forces driving firms to exploit their perishable technological advantages are subdued by the reality that firms' competitive advantages reside in highly mobile assets. Short of chaining these resources to their desks, firms protect their rights to intangible assets gained by developing new processes, taking risks as pioneers, or setting product standards by forming joint ventures *with their entrepreneurial employees.* More cooperative strategies are pursued, and they are of shorter durations to restrict outsiders' personnel to one generation of knowledge per agreement, if technologies are people-intensive. Where parents might have contributed critical technological knowledge earlier to their child in capital-intensive industries, they will withhold such knowledge longer than in people-intensive settings and instead will use more arm's-length licensing agreements to exploit perishable competitive advantages.

When outside suppliers are powerful, by virtue of the importance of their products to the joint-venture child or the lack of alternative vendors, the child's need for close coordination with its parents purchasing activities increases, other factors held constant, in order to mitigate the power of outsiders. Although they need not be suppliers themselves, access to an economic source of raw materials or components (or autonomy to negotiate for them from outsiders) is one of the provisions parents must anticipate in their joint-venture strategy if it is to be effective.

Hypotheses Concerning Technologies. If firms wish to seize a competitive advantage, they must be prepared to take risks. Technological innovation is a major way to change an industry's structure to a firm's advantage, but many processes that firms invest in are very expensive failures. Joint ventures permit firms to share those risks by hedging their bets concerning which products, processes, or configurations will become industry standards. Moreover, they permit firms to keep abreast of technological innovations by providing a means of sharing development costs. But firms must exert care in their use of joint ventures for technology acquisition. Although technology is one of the major bargaining chips that firms possess in forging cooperative strategies, it is a more perishable advantage than market access and is a particularly fragile asset where technologies are people-intensive. Accordingly, firms share less knowledge of this bargaining advantage with outsiders (through their child) if they cannot replenish this strength, as chapter 4 suggested.

Rates of Technological Change. Technological joint ventures enable pioneers to capture more of the value added by their research efforts where knowledge grows obsolete quickly. Joint ventures help technological followers also because they spread risk and bring an infusion of new ideas from innovative partners. Rapid technological change often increases firms' needs to cooperate, but it may also create an arrangement that is too inflexible to adapt to the volatile competitive environment if structured incorrectly.

HYPOTHESES CONCERNING RATES OF TECHNOLOGICAL CHANGE. Joint ventures are formed among technology leaders within environments of rapid technological change. Because volatile competitive settings may squeeze down profit margins and prevent such firms from reinvesting in the R&D needed to sustain a competitive rate of innovation, they need a means of producing the cash needed to fund their next generation of discoveries. Technologies are obsolesced so quickly within some industries that paybacks cannot be earned on a single generation of products. This means that even where firms might prefer the greater control of wholly owned ventures, they team up with a strange collection of bedfellows (including foreign competitors) if other desirable objectives could be attained.[9]

In eras of scarce resources and rapid technological change, technological leaders should have great interest in using cooperative strategies to gain competitive advantages or sustain leadership. The magnitude of harm created by choosing the wrong cooperative strategy depends on how rapidly firms' advantages might be eroded by competitors' innovations if they did not engage in some program of cooperative strategies. If substantial, the form of cooperation matters less.

Technological changes involving the child's physical assets (to gain cost advantages in production processes) cannot be implemented as quickly as changes involving the use of subcontracting (to modify product features, for example). If an industry is embryonic and the best technologies (product features, styling, or means of distributing a product) are yet unknown, the child will want autonomy to move in the directions that seem most promising. But since technologies are most frequently obtained from one or more parents (at least initially, until the child can develop its own technologies), close coordination with technology parents will be necessary in order to modify the child's products to suit the evolving demands of attractive market segments.

TECHNOLOGY LEADERS. In settings where technological strengths could rapidly become obsolete, innovating firms must exploit their discoveries as quickly as possible. Where technologies change rapidly, technology leaders who fear that their investments will be obsolesced before the costs of developing them can be recovered will license many firms and share technology with their child faster, in order to exploit their resources rapidly. (If technologies change slowly, by contrast, firms will not share their cutting-edge, proprietary knowledge with their child until they have developed a new generation of technology to hold in reserve as a competitive advantage.) Furthermore, technology leaders will seek market access in exchange for their technology in settings where rapid exploitation of their resources is not imperative. Even where technology changes rapidly, leaders may be choosy concerning which firms they will allow to use their newest processes and designs.

Technology Followers. Technological followers seek a spider's web of partnerships, where available, to supplement their obsolescing technology. (Since they have little strength to bargain from, however, technological followers are rarely at the hub of any webs of cooperation.) Since their bargaining positions as technology followers are not strong, but their needs for new generations of technology are substantial, followers hedge their bets to reduce uncertainties regarding which technologies eventually become industry standards, especially within volatile settings where technologies are changing rapidly. If followers cannot offer coveted assets (such as market access) in exchange for the technology they require, they will not keep apace of competitors, especially within environments of rapid technological change.

Capital Intensity and Scale Economies. Some industries' technological scales are so large that smaller firms could exploit those economies only by sharing a plant's outputs. Schemes to share large-scale plants have a stabilizing effect on competition because they bring industry capacity more closely in line with demand. In this manner, joint ventures could be used to increase concentration by rationalizing capacity, neutralizing disruptive players, or introducing other structural changes. The opportunities to exploit these information- and asset-sharing economies will be exploited with less frequency, however, if an industry is people-intensive, as figure 5–6 indicates.

Entry Barriers, Mobility, and Cooperation. Joint ventures can be a potent evolutionary force on industry structures because they provide a means for firms to enter industries (or adopt strategic postures) where ongoing competitors were previously protected by high entry (or mobility) barriers. Because potential entrants do not have to enter de novo and surmount the barriers that might deter stand-alone firms, the old concept of entry barriers must be updated when discussing joint ventures to take into account the changing structural traits and competitive dynamics such alliances create. Internally, the management systems used to guide joint ventures must adapt quickly to the dynamics of the child's industry, or they may act as exit barriers by impeding its ability to reposition its strategy with respect to customers or vertical linkages with its parents.[10]

Hypotheses Concerning Entry, Mobility, and Cooperation. Consideration of the effects of joint ventures on ease of entry (and exit) suggests that a new type of entry barrier will be created. When it is operative, an astute and timely joint venture could preempt competitors from linking up with those entrants that are most likely to succeed. For entering firms, competitive advantage is also gained by allying with the best local partners first (provided the early joint venture is mutually an exclusive one). The need to cooperate is especially acute—on both sides—if entry is inevitable, as in the example of industries where technological or economic forces are eroding old boundaries.

If entry barriers protect the child's strategic posture from easy emulation by outsiders, its need for close coordination with its parents increases, other factors held constant. But if entry barriers are high, the joint venture may need to coordinate its entry-deterring responses closely with parents (particularly if they share facilities), or it may injure their respective strategic postures.

New Concept of Entry Barriers. For outsiders seeking cooperative strategies with ongoing domestic firms, the price of admission is embodied in the terms of their joint-venture bargaining agreement, not in the strong brand name, high capital costs, access to channels of distribution, control of scarce resources, or other attributes that comprise entry barriers when firms enter

	People-intensive technology	Capital-intensive technology
Embryonic industry structure	Spider's webs of cooperative strategies Objective: hedge bets, exploit many avenues quickly	
	Venture capital arrangements Many cooperative (nonequity) agreements Many short-lived arrangements to recognize asset mobility	Many short-term "project-basis" ventures to spread risks Many partners in capacity sharing to scale economies
Well-established industry structure	Fewer, but larger cooperative strategies	
	More in-house venturing with entrepreneurs taking equity More development of technology in-house Less sharing of critical kernels of knowledge with venture Slow technology transfer to venture	More acquisitions as critical mass sales volume is attained Longer-duration joint ventures Equity transfer ventures to consolidate industry capacity and keep abreast of technolog- ical innovations

Figure 5–6. Single-Firm Analysis: Relationship between Industry Evolution and Capital Structure in Joint-Venture Formation (Assuming Firms Will Cooperate, Ceteris Paribus)

alone. Instead, many of the relevant entry barriers surrounding joint ventures are mental. They will exist in managers' outlooks—their ways of conceptualizing market demand, ways of competing, and ways of working with suppliers and distributors.

Parents' needs represent the salient entry barriers for analysis of industry attractiveness. If all potential entrants seek the same capabilities from potential partners, those capabilities are the barriers that best protect ongoing firms from entry by new players, or best prevent easy emulation of their strategic postures by competitors.[11]

Maintaining Flexibility. Firms must guard against inflexibility created by joint ventures, particularly if their strategic postures require rapid modification. Being flexible means being willing to create flexible systems where people (an important differentiating factor in joint venture success) are given autonomy to make economic decisions for the child's well-being. These issues are exacerbated by changing attributes in their customer base, by changes in buyer knowledge, and hence by changing heights of customer-switching cost barriers, as in the case of embryonic industries where demand uncertainty is high. In settings where structural traits are yet unestablished, firms' postures must remain flexible. As chapter 4 noted, that means that the management systems accompanying joint ventures must not become an exit barrier.[12] Changing technology can increase interdependencies between activities that were previously conceptualized as being separate. (For example, changing technologies and factor costs coupled with the information technology revolution have resulted in more industries becoming global.) If a game moves so quickly that there is less tolerance for error, then perhaps the "true" barriers to mobility or exit in joint ventures are in systems, management, and people. If a wrong control system emphasizes wrong targets, then partners will have the wrong means of mobilizing resources. If the terms of the bargaining agreement do not provide adequately for decisions regarding whether and when to shut down excess productive capacity, these mobility barriers will impede parents from diversifying out of stagnant industries or from modifying an ineffective cooperative strategy.

Evolutionary Changes in Competitive Advantage

As chapter 3 indicated when it introduced the joint-venture framework, a joint venture's *stability* refers to whether changes in terms of the bargaining agreement were necessary before its objectives were attained, and the stability of joint ventures will be determined, in part, by the attractiveness of the market opportunities they were created to exploit. Some joint ventures will be of short duration because partners can attain their objectives with only a brief period of cooperation. Others will be short-lived because market conditions were (or become) so unattractive that renegotiation (including termination) of terms of the joint-venture agreement was necessary.

Changes in firms' missions change their needs for joint ventures, just as industry evolution alters the need for firms to cooperate in a particular way. Joint ventures can better fulfill some missions *later* in an industry's development than when demand uncertainties or other risks are high. Technological change will be particularly germane to the role that joint ventures may play in firms' competitive strategies at varying times during an industry's evolution because technological changes accelerate the pace by which product standards change, customers become more sophisticated, and assets become obsolete. Because it is particularly difficult for numerous firms to survive independently as industry structures evolve rapidly, joint ventures are often used to shrink capacity and avoid price wars. But even in this example, the tensions mentioned in chapter 3, which make partners' interests and abilities diverge, will exert a destabilizing force on shared ownership arrangements. If the joint venture no longer provides its parents with competitive advantages, it has outlived its usefulness. Even within the most stable competitive environment, shared ownership and management inputs are difficult to sustain.

Joint Ventures and Industry Evolution. Even when their effects on industry structure are most dramatic, the time when particular types of joint-venture strategies are appropriate is brief. The many, short-lived joint ventures created when demand fluctuated erratically are replaced by a few, larger joint ventures of greater permanence as demand slows and stabilizes. The vertically related capacity that partners once shared becomes insufficient even to satisfy the throughput requirements of one parent.

As customers become more discerning in their abilities to distinguish among vendors' products, the number of joint ventures firms maintain decrease, and those remaining emphasize cost reductions and processes for adding value to products without increasing their cost. As customers become *more similar* across the globe, the need for joint ventures *falls* if firms are pursuing global strategies (unless one partner is willing to play a passive role in coordinating the child's activities with its own). But if customers' preferences cannot be standardized and they become ever more demanding in their expectations of vendors, more *short-term arrangements* such as licensing agreements or sourcing arrangements will supplant firms' preferences for jointly owned ventures.

Briefly, the more volatile the competitive environment, the less attractive joint ventures become over time. The more flexible the assets that provide firms with competitive advantage, the more transitory are parents' uses of cooperative strategies with a particular partner. (Firms continue to forge joint ventures and other arrangements for pooling skills, intelligence, and resources but they become more fickle in their alliances. The more experienced a firm becomes in the use of cooperative strategies, the greater the advantage it can carve for itself when negotiating joint ventures because it understands better when shared ownership ventures no longer meet the requirements of an industry better than going it alone.)

Hypotheses Concerning Evolutionary Changes in Competitive Advantage. Therefore, if joint ventures provide firms with competitive advantages, they will be continued. If the use of joint ventures can stabilize an industry's structure, standardize the products that customers accept, or create scale economies (or other means of cost reduction), they will become a part of the strategies that effective firms embrace within an industry. If the needs for risk-sharing activities do not abate, joint ventures will be a durable strategy for all phases of an industry's development (but the identities of partners may change over time).

Summary

The arguments above suggest that demand traits are important when assessing whether joint ventures are needed. Customer attributes affect firms' abilities to differentiate their product offerings from those of competitors while standardizing their respective product configurations across markets. The actions suppliers undertake by relying on their expectations concerning future demand traits determine an industry's competitive environment. Taken together, these forces determine the attractiveness of a child's domain for the formation of joint ventures.

Firms will use joint ventures when products are first introduced to share in the risk that customer acceptance for them may never materialize. Later, they will use joint ventures as a means of divesting their facilities to others that may be better suited to compete in environments of mature, stagnant, or declining demand. Market access, a major source of bargaining power when forging terms of joint-venture agreements, will be less critical to obtain through joint ventures where customer attributes enable firms to standardize their products across market boundaries.

The arguments above suggest that fragmented industries will be less attractive settings for joint ventures than concentrated ones because firms within fragmented settings focus on short paybacks for quick profits. They also suggest that concentrated settings will be more attractive settings for joint ventures because firms operating within oligopolies can focus on mutually desirable goals with greater ease. The ability to identify such focal points will permit parents to accept longer paybacks in testing new products, undertaking research, or making other expenditures because competition takes forms that firms can predict with greater ease. If joint ventures can consolidate a fragmented industry, price competition could be replaced with rivalry in new product features, services, and other nonprice dimensions, making the industry more attractive for joint ventures. But price wars (or activities that change firms' competitive standings rapidly) will increase uncertainty and exacerbate the political pressures that already divide partners with dissimilar backgrounds, motivations, and values. This will be especially so when the venture links parents who are *not* competitors because they will have different outlooks concerning how to compete. Such ventures are difficult to monitor by parents and difficult for them to evaluate.[13]

Therefore, joint ventures with *horizontally related* partners will reduce some forms of price-cutting pressures because partners who have served the same markets with similar products will find it easier to focus on other ways of alleviating volatile competition. This ability to agree is important because changes in the structural relationships within the child's industry and in the nature of competition will affect the joint venture's stability, as well as its profitability potential. If the child's initial strategic posture no longer addresses customer needs adequately, change will be necessary. Joint ventures that face high mobility barriers due to their parents' inability to agree will be unable to augment their strategies to fit new competitive realities. They are more likely to use price as their primary dimension for competition, and such actions will make their industry less attractive for all players—whether jointly or wholly owned.

Conclusions Regarding Importance of Child's Domain on Parents' Joint-Venture Strategies

In summary, joint ventures are assuming greater importance because product lives are shorter, cost advantages are becoming more pronounced, and greater numbers of firms who operated formerly only in domestic markets are becoming global competitors. These changes could have ominous ramifications because managers are likely to be offered partnership in joint ventures by others who covet their firms' strengths (transitory though they may be). A timely analysis of how joint ventures fit the interests of their firms could help managers to forge configurations that leave their firms better off.

In the past, joint ventures have often been read as a signal of lesser corporate commitment to the project in question (unless firms purposely signaled high commitment to the markets in question in other ways). Firms have been particularly loathe to use joint ventures where local governments did not require them as a condition of entry for domain-expanding multinational players. In environments of scarce resources, rapid rates of technological change, and massive capital requirements, however, joint ventures may be the best way for some firms to attain better positions in businesses they deem to be of great strategic importance. As long as managers recognize the dangers and limitations of cooperation and manage these shortcomings, there will be a chance that firms can use joint-venture strategies effectively.

Notes

1. Hymer, Stephan, and Pashigian, Peter, 1962, "Firm Size and Rate of Growth," *Journal of Political Economy* 70:556–569; Ijiri, Y., and Simon, H.A., 1964, "Business Growth and Firm Size," *American Economic Review* 54:77–89; Weiss, Leonard W., 1963, "Factors in Changing Concentration," *Review of Economics and Statistics* 45: 70–77; Ornstein, S.I., Weston, J.F., Intriligator, M.D., and Shrieves, R.E., "Determinants of Market Structure," *Southern Economic Journal* 39:612–625; Wilson, John W., 1975, "Market Structure and Interfirm Integration in the Petroleum Industry," *Journal of Economic Issues* 9(2):319–336; Kydland, F.E., 1977, "Equilibrium Solutions in Dynamic Dominant Player Models," *Journal of Economic Theory* 15(2): 130–136; Caves, Richard E., Porter, Michael E., 1978, "Market Structure, Oligopoly and Stability of Market Shares," *Journal of Industrial Economics* 26:289–313; Porter, Michael E., and Spence, A. Michael, 1982, "The Capacity Expansion Process in a Growing Oligopoly: The Case of Corn Wet Milling," in McCall, J.J. (ed.), *The Economics of Information and Uncertainty* (Chicago: University of Chicago Press); Scherer, F.M., 1979, "The Causes and Consequences of Rising Industrial Concentration: A Comment," *Journal of Law and Economics* 22:191–208; Justman, Moshe, 1982, "Dynamic Demand Functions: Some Implications for the Theory of Firm and Industry Organization," Ph.D. diss., Harvard University.

2. Meeker, Guy B., 1971, "Fade Out Joint Venture: Can It Work for Latin America?," *Inter-American Economic Affairs* 24:25–42.

3. Hout, Thomas, Porter, Michael E., and Rudden, Eileen, 1982, "How Global Companies Win Out," *Harvard Business Review* 60(5):98–108.

4. Davidson, W.H., and McFetridge, D.G., 1984, "Recent Directions in International Strategies: Product Rationalization or Portfolio Adjustment," *Columbia Journal of World Business* 19(2):95–101.

5. Nelson, R., and Winter, S., 1975, "Factor Price Changes and Factor Substitution in an Evolutionary Model," *Bell Journal of Economics* 6(2):466–486; Porter, Michael E., 1979, "The Structure within Industries and Companies' Performance," *Review of Economics and Statistics* 61:214–227; Eaton, B.C., and Lipsey, R.G., 1979, "Theory of Marketing Preemption: Barriers to Entry in a Growing Spatial Market," *Economica* 46:149–158; Spence, A. Michael, 1979, "Investment Strategy and Growth in a New Market," *Bell Journal of Economics* 10(1):1–19; Caves, Richard E., Porter, Michael E., Spence, A. Michael, 1980, *Competition in the Open Economy* (Cambridge, Mass.: Harvard University Press); Hergert, Michael L., 1983, "The Incidence and Implications of Strategy Grouping in U.S. Manufacturing Industries," Ph.D. diss., Harvard University.

6. Tennant, R.B., 1950, *The American Cigarette Industry* (New Haven, Conn.: Yale University Press); McKie, J.W., 1955, "The Decline of Monopoly in the Metal Container Industry," *American Economic Review* 45:499–508; Phillips, C.F., 1963, *Competition in the Synthetic Rubber Industry* (Winston-Salem: University of North Carolina); Hunt, Michael S., 1972, "Competition in the Home Appliance Industry, 1960–1970," Ph.D. diss., Harvard University; Newman, H.H., 1973, "Strategic Groups and Structure-Performance Relationship: Study with Respect to the Chemical Processing Industry," Ph.D. diss., Harvard University; Porter, Michael E.,

1980, *Competitive Strategy: Techniques for Analyzing Industries and Competitors* (New York: Free Press); Davidson, William Harley, 1980, "Corporation Experience Factors in International Investment and Licensing Activities: Study of International Business," Ph.D. diss., Harvard University; Hunker, Jeffrey Allen, 1982, "Structural Change in the U.S. Automobile Industry, 1980–1995," Ph.D. diss., Harvard Business School; Stuckey, John Alan, 1982, "Vertical Integration and Joint Ventures in the International Aluminum Industry," Ph.D. diss., Harvard Business School; Harrigan, Kathryn Rudie, 1985, "Vertical Integration and Corporate Strategy," *Academy of Management Journal* 28: forthcoming; Tushman, Michael, and Romanelli, Elaine, 1985, "Organizational Evolution: A Metamorphosis Model of Convergence and Reorientation," *Research in Organizational Research* (7). Greenwich, Conn.: JAI Press.

7. Carter, Charles, and Williams, Bruce, 1957; *Industry and Technical Progress* (London: Oxford University Press); Mansfield, E., 1962, "Entry, Gibrat's Law, Innovation and the Growth of Firms," *American Economic Review* 52:1023–1051; Menge, J.A., 1962, "Style Change Costs as a Market Weapon," *Quarterly Journal of Economics* 76:632–647; Scherer, F.M., 1967, "Research and Development Resource under Rivalry," *Quarterly Journal of Economics* 81:359–394; Winter, S.G., 1971, "Satisficing Selection and the Innovating Remnant," *Quarterly Journal of Economics* 85:237–261; Mansfield, E., 1968, *Industrial Research and Technological Innovation* (New York: Norton); Greer, D.F., 1971, "Product Differentiation and Concentration in the Brewing Industry," *Journal of Industrial Economics* 19:201–219; Myers, Summer, and Marquis, Donald G., 1969, *Successful Industrial Innovation* (Washington, D.C.: National Science Foundation); Wasson, Chester R., 1974; *Dynamic Competitive Strategy and Product Life Cycles* (Chicago: St. Charles); Lambin, Jean Jacques, 1976, *Advertising, Competition and Market Conduct in Oligopoly Over Time* (Amsterdam: North Holland); Abell, Derek F., 1978, "Strategic Marketing," *Journal of Marketing* 42(3):21–26; Comaner, W.S., and Wilson, T.A., 1979, "Advertising and Competition: A Survey," *Journal of Economic Literature* 17:453–476; Spence, A. Michael, 1981, "The Learning Curve and Competition," *Bell Journal of Economics* 12(1):49–70; Ghemawat, Pankaj, 1982, "The Experience Curve and Corporate Strategy," Ph.D. diss., Harvard Business School; Liberman, Marvin B., 1983, "Capacity Expansion, Firm Strategy and Market Structure," Ph.D. diss., Harvard Business School.

8. Daniels, John D., 1971, *Recent Foreign Direct Investment into the U.S.: An Interview Study of the Decision Process* (New York: Praeger).

9. Gabriel, Peter P., 1967, *The International Transfer of Corporate Skills* (Boston: Harvard Business School, Division of Research); Baldridge, Malcolm, 1983, "Testimony on Government Policies to Promote High Growth Industries Based on New Technologies and to Increase U.S. Competitiveness" (Washington, D.C.: Committee on Finance, U.S. Senate, January 19).

10. Porter, Michael E., 1976, "Please Note Location of Nearest Exit: Exit Barriers and Strategic and Organizaitonal Planning," *California Management Review* 19(2):21–33; Harrigan, Kathryn Rudie, 1980, "The Effect of Exit Barriers upon Strategic Flexibility," *Strategic Management Journal* 1(2):165–176; Harrigan, Kathryn Rudie, 1982, "Exit Decisions in Mature Industries," *Academy of Management Journal* 25(4):707–732; Harrigan, Kathryn Rudie, 1981, "Deterrents to Divestiture," *Academy of Management Journal* 24(2):306–323; Harrigan, Kathryn Rudie, 1983 and 1985, "Exit Barriers and Vertical Integration," in Chung, Kae, ed., 1983,

Proceedings, Dallas: National Academy of Mangement Conference, and 1985, *Academy of Management Journal* (29): forthcoming.

11. Bain, Joe S., 1956, *Barriers to New Competition* (Cambridge, Mass.: Harvard University Press).

12. Porter, Michael E., 1976, "Please Note Location of Nearest Exit: Exit Barriers and Strategic and Organizational Planning," *California Management Review* 19(2):21–23; Harrigan, Kathryn Rudie, 1980, "The Effect of Exit Barriers on Strategic Flexibility," *Strategic Management Journal* 1(2):165–176; Harrigan, Kathryn Rudie, 1982, "Exit Decisions in Mature Industries," Academy of Management Journal 25(4): 707–732; Harrigan, Kathryn Rudie, 1981, "Deterrents to Divestiture," *Academy of Management Journal* 24(2):306–323; Harrigan, Kathryn Rudie, 1983 and 1985, "Exit Barriers and Vertical Integration," in Chung, Kae, ed., 1983, *Proceedings*, Dallas: National Academy of Management Conference, and 1985, *Academy of Management Journal* (29): forthcoming.

13. Galbraith, J.R., 1971, "Matrix Organization Designs—How to Combine Functional and Project Form," *Business Horizons* 14(1):29–40; Davis, Stanley M., 1976, "Trends in the Organization of Multinational Organizations," *Columbia Journal of World Business* 11(2):59–71; Davis, S., and Lawrence, P.R., 1978, "Problems of Matrix Organizations," *Harvard Business Review* 56(3):131–142; Cascino, E., 1979, "How One Company 'Adapted' Matrix Management in a Crisis," *Management Review* 68(11):57–61; Egelhoff, W.G., 1980, "Matrix Strategies and Structures in Multinational Corporations," paper presented before the Academy of International Business and Management, New Orleans; Berg, S., Duncan, J., and Friedman, P., 1982, *Joint Venture Strategies and Corporate Innovation* (Cambridge, Mass.: Oelgeschlager, Gunn & Hain).

6
Research Methodology of the Joint-Venture Study

This brief chapter has two purposes: (1) to explain the research methodology employed to test the strategy framework introduced in chapter 3 and developed in chapters 3, 4 and 5 and (2) to present an overview of the industry chapters that follow. Chapters 7 through 12 focus on industries where joint ventures were formed. Their inclusion in the sample design was dictated by the three major dimensions of the joint-venture framework presented in the preceding chapters, as is explained below.

The Predictive Power of the Framework

Scholarly tests of the joint-venture framework rely primarily on examination of *observable* traits, and particularly on traits within the child's industry. Each industry vignette sketches (1) partners' needs for joint activities, (2) which joint activities were announced and consummated, and (3) how closely the children's activities were coordinated with those of their parents. Some of this factual information is readily verifiable through several corroborating data sources. As the section describing data collection (below) explains, field interviews also generated substantial anecdotal information, which addressed salient points developed in chapters 3, 4, and 5 that were less readily testable within the scope of this study. Insights gathered on these topics have been distilled and presented in summary chapters 13 through 16, but they were not subject to the same stringent rules of scientific inquiry that guided the industry studies.

Partner-to-Partner Relationships

Tests of the partner-to-partner hypotheses ask whether cooperative arrangements are likely to be formed, and predictions concerning the likelihood of

I am indebted to William H. Newman for his many suggestions concerning this chapter.

joint-venture formation were driven by a consideration of the target industry's traits. Without knowing the structure of the target industry, it is difficult to predict whether particular types of cooperative arrangements are more (or less) likely to occur. Partners determine whether they can or are willing to go it alone on the basis of information about the target industry.

Depending on that industry's traits, (1) a technology partner may team with a marketing partner to exploit a fleeting technological advantage, while a firm with local market access may fill out its product line; (2) competitors may pool their requirements for a stable supply of a particular component or raw material to create an upstream child; (3) potential competitors may pool their complementary resources to pioneer a new type of distribution channel, technology, or product; (4) competitors may pool cash and risks to undertake a very costly venture that none would care to face alone; (5) competitors may rationalize ongoing facilities to reduce excess capacity, gain scale economies, or upgrade obsolete facilities to new technologies representing larger minimum efficient volumes of utilization; (6) vertically related firms may form a joint venture for a processing step intermediate to their respective activities; or (7) other combinations of firms may become partners in joint activities. Tests for patterns of opportunistic behavior by firms in choosing their partners draw on information concerning the traits of competitors, suppliers, distributors, other potential partners, and other *observable traits* that are particular to the child's industry.

Parent–Child Relationships

Questions regarding the nature of parent–child relationships also probe partners' strategic purposes in forming joint ventures. In testing the robustness of this dimension of the joint-venture framework, patterns relating the child to its parents and to outside suppliers, customers, and competitors are sought. These patterns include: (1) whether the joint venture purchases from (or sells to) its parents; (2) whether its activities duplicate those of its parents; (3) whether the child shares facilities with its parents; (4) whether the child is a captive supplier or customer of its parents; (5) how much autonomy the joint venture is permitted in selecting its own suppliers, customers, or other dancing partners; (6) how far the child progresses in its evolution from a loose agreement among firms to work together to an entity that issues securities in its own right; and (7) other patterns of parent–child relationships.

Because knowledge of the child's industry is necessary in order to test normative hypotheses concerning whether the child should be closely coordinated with one (or more) of its parents or should enjoy operating autonomy, the focus in gathering data must be on *observable industry traits* within industries where joint ventures were formed. These patterns may be detected by an input–output analysis of the x_{ijk}, y_{ijk}, and z_{ijk} relationships between parents, their child, and outsiders, as described in table 4–1.

Child's Relationship to Its Industry

The joint-venture framework's central argument is that different cooperative strategies are appropriate for diverse industry contexts. Heterogeneous patterns of cooperative behavior are expected where industries differ in their (1) demand uncertainty and growth rates, (2) product differentiability and customer sophistication, (3) market standardization, as compared with other geographic markets, (4) age and stability of industry's structural relationships, (5) rates of technological change, (6) competitor behaviors and (7) other industry characteristics. Tests of these hypotheses rely on findings of patterns of *observable industry traits*.

Construction of Industry Chapters

A standard format was adopted for each industry examined in tests of the joint-venture framework. This procedure facilitated the presentation of factual information in a structure that separated data presentation from comments regarding the predictive power of the framework's hypotheses. The efficacy of the framework with respect to each dimension of the research design is summarized at the end of each chapter.

Partner-to-Partner Relationships: Need for Joint Activities

Each industry is identified briefly with respect to its products, technologies, and other structural traits. Reasons that were common across the industry for firms to take partners in forming joint ventures are sketched. Specific patterns of partners' traits are presented in the subsequent section of each industry vignette.

The need for cooperative activities within a particular type of industry suggested the need for particular types of firms to join forces, as well. These expectations are compared with observed patterns of joint ventures in the section explaining which partners were chosen in response to particular industry challenges.

Child's Relationships to Its Industry: Choosing Partners

Specific partnerships, their durations, and dispositions are listed in the second part of each industry vignette. The child's mission is explained and child activities are sketched. Space constraints limit the detail with which specific parent–child relationships are described.

Joint-venture histories are grouped by *parent* firms and are presented chronologically. This structure illustrates patterns of (1) partners' spider's webs of joint ventures, (2) with varying (or the same) partners, (3) over time—especially as industry structures evolved—with (4) varying successes and with (5) diverse patterns of competitor imitation. This format illustrates (1) how the challenges of competition made certain types of cooperative strategies more (or less) necessary over time, it (2) suggests which types of firms (leaders or followers, for example) formed joint ventures (with what success), and it (3) suggests whether the structural dimensions held constant in each industry were good discriminators in predicting joint-venture behaviors.

Parent–Child Relationships: Child Activities

Patterns of close coordination between parents and child and of operating autonomy are sketched for each industry. If a particular partner—the one possessing marketing strengths, for example—was more likely to be chosen as the "operator" of the joint venture within certain industries, that pattern is also noted.

Field Research Procedure

This section sketches the data that was collected, the method of collection, and the processing of these data to create industry chapters. The details of the sample design and site selection are explained. Finally the advantages and disadvantages of this particular research methodology are reviewed.

Description of the Data

Information concerning the relationships between parent firms and their joint-venture children was obtained in three stages: (1) construction of background papers on each industry using archival data; (2) validation using field interviews and survey questionnaires (completed in advance of the interview); and (3) a three-round delphi-method questionnaire. The framework sketched in chapters 3, 4, and 5 concerning the three perspectives of joint-venture strategies was tested by studying 884 cooperative strategy decisions within 25 industries (as categorized in table 6–1) during the years 1960 through 1984. Those joint ventures operating within the target industries described in table 6–1 were the units of analysis, although measures for upstream, downstream, or horizontally related, wholly owned business units of parent firms were also gathered, depending on the type of strategic relationship the joint-venture child enjoyed with each of its respective parents.

Table 6–1
Joint-Venture Sample Composition[a]

Industries	Total Cooperative Arrangements	Joint Ventures
Mining	19	19
Metals processing	10	10
Metals fabrication	8	8
Heavy machinery	21	18
Light machinery	3	1
Programming packaging	29	27
Programming (entertainment)	8	8
Videodisc players and videotapes (videodiscs)	21	21
Precision controls, robotics	28	13
Software, databases	22	17
Communications services—satellites, voice	23	23
Communications services—CATV	17	16
Communications services—teletext, videotex	12	7
Financial services	85	62
Electronic components	68	18
Computers and computer peripherals	59	31
Office equipment	28	12
Communications equipment	52	26
Petrochemicals	137	113
Steel	33	19
Farm and industrial equipment	11	6
Medical products	35	23
Pharmaceuticals	97	27
Engines	37	3
Automobiles	21	1

[a]Note that cooperative arrangements were *less* likely to include joint ventures within industries like electronic components, engines, pharmaceuticals and automobiles. These are global industries.

Selection of Sample

It would have been unwieldy to encompass in a single research design the many traits that chapters 3, 4, and 5 have suggested are important to the formulation of effective joint-venture strategies. Instead, seven *observable* industry traits were used to stratify the research sample. In doing so, it is possible to hold constant some elements of joint-venture strategies while varying others. Joint ventures were selected to obtain observations that varied in the dimensions depicted in table 6–2. Briefly, because child industries varied according to their capital intensity, product differentiability, asset durability, rate of technological complexity and obsolescence, structural evolution, demand uncertainty, and market standardization, a mix of industries could be selected to showcase these traits and facilitate comparisons while testing the framework.

Table 6–2
Industry Traits of Interest in Studying Joint-Venture Strategies

Capital intensive	*Labor intensive*
Examples: metals processing, metals fabrication, light machinery, electrical equipment, communications equipment, and pipelines	Examples: precision controls, ethical pharmaceuticals, medical products, electronic consumer products, and videotape recorders
Commodity-like products	*Differentiable products*
Examples: coal extraction, oil extraction, chemicals, steel, and cable communications services	Examples: light machinery, aerospace, electronic equipment, communications systems, and software
Durable, physical assets	*People-intensive assets*
Examples: chemicals, metals processing, heavy machinery, aerospace, and communications equipment	Examples: motion pictures, financial services, advertising services, databases, and wholesaling, retailing, and distribution
Low technological complexity and rates of change in technological configuration or processes	*High technological complexity and rates of change in technological configuration or processes*
Examples: pulp and paper, metals processing, wholesaling, retailing, and distribution	Examples: medical products, electronic components, computers and peripherals, photocopy, and office equipment
Young industries, with embryonic structures	*Mature industries, with well-established structures*
Examples: genetic engineering, robotics, communications services, and alternative energy	Examples: metals fabrication, heavy machinery, engines, and petrochemicals
Rapid sales growth	*Slow sales growth*
Examples: computer software, communications services, financial services, and electronic components	Examples: steel, oil extraction and refining, automotive, and coal extraction
Global industries	*Localized industries*
Examples: chemicals, pharmaceuticals, medical products, automotive, videotape, and videodisc players	Examples: printing, publishing, cable communications, and pipelines

Sample Design. Table 6–1 identifies the industries of the target joint ventures and the sample's distribution among the twenty-five industries. Table 6–2 represents the taxonomy that was developed from *observable* traits, including both consumer and producer goods industries, as well as those of varying ages. This taxonomy was used to ensure that various features that make industries relatively attractive or unattractive environments for cooperative strategies of various forms would be represented in the sample of joint ventures. The sample was also stratified to allow comparisons of industries having high capital intensities with those that were labor intensive, comparisons of industries experiencing rapid rates of technological change with those where product and process technology changed slowly, and comparisons of industries that were becoming global with those where competition was primarily local, regional, or national in its scope. Finally, the sample was stratified also to compare those industries where the product was a service with those where the product was not a service.

Data Collection. Target firms were selected from announcements of joint ventures contained in *Mergers & Acquisitions* and from a special compilation of joint ventures contained in the *Funk & Scott's Index* of business periodicals. Verification inquiries yielded 746 announcements of joint ventures that were hand-sorted into 52 industry categories. Low response rates in some industries (like public utilities and waste disposal, for example) eliminated them as candidates for further study. The first-stage questionnaires were sent to all parent firms mentioned in connection with a particular joint-venture announcement. Questionnaires were also sent to parent firms identified in connection with another 2,094 cooperative arrangements that did *not* involve shared-equity arrangements. (The reason for contacting firms with no joint ventures within the same industries where joint ventures had been announced was to ascertain *why* managers preferred one form of cooperative strategy over another.) Helpful managers verified announcements of joint ventures and volunteered information concerning additional joint ventures that had not been announced in either source periodical. This process yielded a total of 884 cooperative arrangements, of which 492 (or 55 percent) were joint ventures.

Data Collection

Field studies used to gather data progressed in several stages and employed a variety of corroborating sources. Preliminary hypotheses had been generated from a literature search concerning the use of joint ventures by U.S. firms—in mature economies, both overseas and in the United States. The hypotheses were pretested and refined in 1983 by interviewing strategists in a variety of firms; some of these firms were included in the subsequent delphi sample (explained below). Background papers on target industries were then constructed from archival sources that included annual reports, other financial disclosure documents, trade journals and trade association publications, and government documents. Details concerning joint-venture activities contained in these background papers were later refined through field interviews, telephone conversations, follow-up letters, and revisions suggested by managers who participated in the study. It was not necessary to interview managers within all of the entities—parents and children—in order to gather estimates concerning joint-venture activities, as is explained below.

Data Processing

Information concerning joint ventures (or other cooperative strategies) was obtained and refined from interviews and questionnaires using an iterative, delphi-like procedure. Initial estimates for descriptive factors—percentage shared facilities, relative strategic importance of the child's activities to parent A (or B), and other factors used to build the joint-venture frameworks of chapters 3, 4, and 5—were developed as a starting point for the interview from materials in the public domain and were scaled *relative to competitors*. Initial interviews concerning 444 joint ventures and cooperative arrangements were primarily face-to-face, and managers invariably volunteered materials from their files that were not available in the business press concerning themselves and their competitors. Interviews, telephone conversations, follow-up letters of clarification, transcripts, and comments on preliminary drafts of each industry vignette provided revised estimates of these factors, until estimates for the 492 joint-venture child's contexts (including attributes of their parents) were developed. Informants also provided information concerning the strengths and flexibility of suppliers, customers, technologies, and other competitive features of their industries. Newspaper accounts of price wars, divestitures, changes in joint-venture ownership, including acquisitions documented changes in joint ventures that had occurred over time; interviews with industry participants—and observers—corroborated my interpretations of the meanings of these events and estimates of these factors.

The delphi-like procedure provided estimates for variables that were not in the public domain and that firms might not collect routinely. By incorporating the opinions of expert judges, it is also possible to refine estimates based on imperfect information. In this study, the judges included the players—the managers of children and parent business units, executives familiar with the target industries (and with the players), outside suppliers, outside customers, trade association executives, industry analysts, and industry observers. Since a delphi procedure was employed, it was not necessary to talk with all of the participants within an industry in order to develop estimates of variables concerning their respective joint ventures. By piecing together information provided from these many sources—who all dealt with nonresponding firms—it was possible to verify and fill in profiles of competitors that had been constructed from archival data. In this manner, interviews with 40 percent (197 of the 492) joint ventures comprising the total sample—plus the other cooperative arrangements—facilitated estimates of variables for firms that were not interviewed. (Note that because the data had been sanitized, disguised, and scaled relative to competitors, confidentiality problems were reduced. None of the informants had access to source files other than their own. They were given average estimates per joint venture and were not advised of judges' identities or of their individual scalings.)

Preliminary estimates of each variable for each SBU were revised by the appropriate judges three times. Each time, they were informed of the average value obtained from judges on the previous round. As the judges reassessed each variable, they discussed their reasoning (thereby providing additional insights concerning joint-venture relationships). Since the scales and measures developed were revised in the delphi rounds three times, respondents often converged in their estimates of the relative rankings of firms along various attributes. The resulting estimates for each child are scaled relative to competitors. Since the scalings were constrained to values between .01 and .99 for most variables, problems with heteroscadasticity have been reduced, and observations can be pooled across industries in statistical analyses, undertaken subsequent to this study.

Limitations of the Data

In a study such as this one where there were many differences across industries in structural and strategy variables, one must be conservative in the degree of confidence asserted. These data were constructed from field interviews. The study's findings should be interpreted with great caution despite the care that was taken in implementing the delphi study. (It is an inherently subjective research methodology.)

The frameworks of chapters 3, 4, and 5 pose numerous challenges to the way in which joint ventures have been conceptualized in the past. Nevertheless, despite the robustness of the framework's propositions and the many data sources used to test them, some key factors affecting joint-venture success could have been omitted. Joint ventures are a strategy for times of turbulence and change that merit *more* managerial reflection than they have received in recent years. Joint ventures are readily recognized as the price of admission into foreign markets where sovereign governments can demand local participation. They have long made sense as a risk and cost-sharing strategy. This study suggests that joint ventures can be used effectively in firms' domestic mature economies, as well. It focuses upon the decision to use a joint venture, given that some form of cooperation will be necessary.

Advantages of the Research Methodology

Scholars of strategic management follow rules of science in their research. The care that they exert in their research methodologies ensures objectivity in their results. This section discusses the research approach embodied in the chapters that follow.

Strategy research needs sophisticated research methodologies because it treats a complex topic. *Business strategy* is a difficult-to-measure construct that can differ from competitor to competitor within the same industry. One approach to understanding business strategy is to investigate why firms within the same industry pursue different strategies to attain similar objectives. Understanding a particular firm's business strategy requires knowledge of its history and corporate strategy, its management team, and its competitive environment. The essence of these relationships can be captured in the results of large sample studies, but statistical analyses lose (in their error terms) the unexplained variances that could offer richer insights concerning business strategies. For this type of research a *hybrid methodology* is needed.

In much existing research, insights gained using "fine-grained" methodologies (such as case studies) lack generalizability and statistical rigor, but "coarse-grained" methodologies, such as the Profit Impact of Market Share (PIMS) studies, lose the nuances and insights concerning individual firms' strategies that a contingency approach seeks to capture. The finest detail concerning strategies is attained with cases treating individual firms, an expensive methodology (usually based on field studies) that may be difficult to replicate. Cases have great potential as illuminating vehicles for studying questions of corporate strategy, if coupled with *other* data gathering methodologies and integrative analysis, because cases include meticulous attention to detail, relevance to business practice, and access to multiple viewpoints. Case studies can capture the complexities of corporate strategy, competition, and uncontrollable environmental factors surrounding strategy formulation if they are done well. But their value alone as a research methodology is limited (due to shortcomings in hypothesis generation, replicability, and statistical summaries, all features that are the hallmark of careful and objective research).

Contingency approaches to strategy formulation require hybrid designs, incorporating attributes of both fine- and coarse-grained research methodologies. One could straddle the gulf between these extremes in strategy research by devising a medium-grained methodology wherein the detail of case studies is combined with the rigor of large-sample methodologies. Such research methodologies need a carefully structured sample design—one permitting the investigator to hold key dimensions of industry settings constant while varying others in order to scrutinize how various firms in each of several types of industries handle the problems under study.

Research designs that sample multiple sites are expensive in time and travel costs. They require robust data collection designs that could include published materials, field interviews, and archival materials, delphi panels, databases, and researchers' inferences, among other sources (including survey data). Using several data sources and measures of phenomena provides cross-checks on data accuracy and enrichment of the conclusions researchers might present. Juxtaposing multiple data sources increases the likelihood that convergence will be reached between the subject's perception of its environment and competitive position and its actual (or measured) position. Also, using better measures or descriptions of the phenomena studied enhances the replicability of researchers' findings concerning them.

In summary, strategy research needs many sources of information to reconstruct firms' business strategies and comprehend their strategy choices. Hypothesis generation and testing benefit from tightly defined research designs and numerous perspectives regarding the variables under study.

For students of corporate strategy, the benefits of using cross-sectional, time-series designs and multiple research sites to study competitive histories suggest that new vistas of intellectual inquiry can be opened by using hybrid methodologies to verify academic hypotheses concerning the appropriateness of various strategic responses to industrywide challenges. This avenue of research should be of interest to corporate strategists. The monitoring of competitive histories using such methodologies is an additional tool, which belongs beside scenario analysis in the corporate arsenal of planning tools.

Industry Chapter Overview

The hypotheses of chapters 3, 4, and 5 were tested by examining the histories of joint-venture formation (and dissolution) within many industries by using such hybrid methodologies. Insights were sought concerning why, for example, in table 1–3, so many joint ventures were used over time in both the petrochemicals and financial services industries. Comparisons among competitors were sought to understand why so many joint ventures were announced in the communications services industry in 1983. The research methodology explained above was chosen as the most appropriate way to gather relevant information about the use of cooperative strategies. By contrasting the resulting patterns of joint-venture use and performance, it should be possible to evaluate the robustness of the framework that has been advanced to suggest the effective use of joint ventures.

Chapters 7 through 12 use the research schema shown in table 6–3. Thus, joint-venture practice is examined in (1) capital-intensive industries (oil exploration, mining, metals processing, metals fabrication, heavy and light machinery); (2) industries where products are differentiable (cable and home video programming and programming packaging, videotape and videodisc hardware and software, precision controls, factory automation, and robotics); (3) service industries (software, databases, communications services, and financial services); (4) industries of varying rates of technological change (electronic components, computers and computer peripherals, office equipment, and communications equipment); (5) those where industry structure has evolved (chemicals—including genetic engineering—and steel and farm and industrial equipment; and (6) industries where customer needs were very similar across geographic markets (medical products, ethical pharmaceuticals, engines, aerospace, and automobiles).

Table 6–3
Industries Comprising Sample

Chapter 7: Capital-intensive industries	Oil exploration metals extraction metals processing metals fabrication heavy and light machinery
Chapter 8: Industries where products are differentiable	Cable and home video programming and programming packaging Videotape and videodisc hardware and software Precision controls Factory automation Robotics
Chapter 9: Service Industries	Software and databases Communications services Financial services
Chapter 10: Rate of technological change	Electronic components Computers and computer peripherals Office equipment Communications equipment
Chapter 11: Industry structural evolution	Chemicals (including genetic engineering) Steel Farm equipment Industrial equipment
Chapter 12: Market standardization	Medical products Ethical pharmaceuticals Engines Aerospace Automobiles

Capital Intensity

Many early domestic joint ventures were found in capital-intensive industries, for these were most likely to require the pooling of capital costs and risks. These industries represent the traditional notion of joint-venture strategies and are presented in chapter 7 as a *touchstone*, to suggest how some of the most experienced managers have coped with the problems of shared ownership and decision-making authority. These industries include costly technologies, durable and specific physical assets that create high barriers to strategic flexibility, and other conditions that necessitate cost sharing. (Special attentions are given to the differences in joint-venture strategies for service businesses in chapter 9—as contrasted with the capital-intensive industries of chapter 7.)

Labor-intensive industries encourage joint ventures that pool knowledge and technologies to gain market access. Because labor-intensive industries depend on skillful management of highly mobile resources for success, they pose a vexing problem for effective joint-venture management.

Product Differentiability

Differentiable products can be sold to discriminating customers for higher prices. But when customers see no differences among competing vendors' products, their increased bargaining power forces suppliers' prices to become more similar. Discriminating customers see products as being more commodity-like (unless the products *are* truly different in quality, configuration, or other attributes that matter to the customers in question).

Where customers can force vendors to compete on the basis of price, the need for joint ventures to reduce operating costs will be substantial. But when products are differentiated, other cooperative strategies have been favored over joint ventures, as chapter 8 explains.

Technological Complexity and Obsolescence Rates

Industries characterized by low technological complexity and slow rates of change in technological configurations or processes differ in their needs for joint activity from those where economies can be driven to very large-scale industries with less risk of obsolescence. The high obsolescence and coordination problems of rapidly changing technologies that favor a job-shop orientation and frequently changing product configurations (or manufacturing processes) make joint ventures short-lived, as chapter 10 explains.

Industry Structural Evolution

Demand, product standards, buyer–seller relationships, and the basis for competition are highly uncertain within embryonic industries. Structural relationships are also unclear, such as the value-added chain of processing, the identities of competitors (due to frequent entries and exits of players), and the nature of competitive advantages that would ordinarily function as entry barriers. More vertical joint ventures are used within such settings to develop the infrastructure and resolve these uncertainties.

Most industries within mature economies have well-established structures. Little uncertainty remains concerning product standards, buyer–seller relationships, and the basis for competition, although underdog competitors may try to change the value-added chain of processing, the cast of competitors, or the nature of barriers that protect their market positions. Joint ventures within established industries recognize the advantages of ongoing firms as key bargaining chips, as outsiders try to gain market access and underdogs try to upset the competitive equilibrium.

When demand grows rapidly, joint ventures are forged by firms that fear being left behind. Rapid-growth industries are characterized by capacity shortfalls and uncertainties concerning what customers want, rather than by the capacity surplus problems of established industries or endgame industries. Joint ventures to obtain sources of components (or finished products) are commonplace strategies for mature settings. But capacity surpluses also motivate joint ventures for different reasons. Within slow growth industries where basic product configurations change slowly and demand is primarily for replacement purposes, horizontal joint ventures are used to shrink capacity with increasing frequency, as chapter 11 explains.

Market Standardization and Global Strategies

If product configurations, marketing practices, and other business activities can be standardized across markets, joint ventures give way to the needs of global strategies. If products and activities cannot be standardized across markets, joint ventures can follow traditional notions of shared ownership and decision-making authority. Chapter 12, which illustrates how cooperative strategy practices differed in these different international environments, notes that *fewer joint ventures* were used in globally coordinated systems.

7
Joint Ventures in Capital-Intensive Industries

The industries in this chapter represent the typical cost- and risk-sharing uses of sixty domestic joint ventures. These are representative of the oldest uses made of joint ventures in the United States. Accordingly, analyses of how these firms coped with the problems of joint ownership and shared decision-making control should be of interest when younger industries or other uses of joint-venture strategies are examined in subsequent chapters.

Motives

Many U.S. joint ventures described in this chapter were made when industries' outlooks were significantly more attractive than they were in 1984. The motives for joint-venture formation in capital-intensive industries has not changed, but the arenas where they now occur have become those of newly industrializing economies.

Overcome Entry Barriers

Joint ventures provide a means for firms to enter industries (or adopt strategic postures) where entry barriers are high. The barriers of capital costs and access to scarce resources are examined herein.

Share High Capital Costs. The oldest domestic U.S. joint ventures were used in capital intensive industries, such as railroads and offshore oil exploration, where the costs of entry (and uncertainties surrounding success) were so great that firms pooled their interests to share these costs and risks. More recently, joint ventures were established in the 1970s to mine the mineral riches of the

---

I am indebted to John Richardson Thomas (M.B.A. 1983) for industry background materials prepared for this chapter.

ocean floor. Partners hoped to recover nickel, cobalt, and manganese, using costly and untried technologies.

Risk Sharing. Many processes firms invest in are very expensive failures. Joint ventures permit firms to share those risks by hedging their bets concerning which products, processes, or configurations will become industry standards. Moreover, they permit firms to keep abreast of technological innovations by providing a means of sharing development costs.

Scale Economies

As a further economic inducement, partners sought economies. Some industries' technological scales were so large that smaller firms could exploit those economies only by sharing a plant's outputs. Thus, the combined pressures of plant scales too large for single firms to absorb plus expensive technologies made joint ventures within capital-intensive industries in the United States seem appropriate.

Industries

Oil and Gas Exploration

Joint ventures have been a key structural feature of the oil and gas industry (particularly in exploration) for so long that many firms interviewed did not think of them as joint ventures. For these managers, joint ventures were merely standard operations. Cost- and risk-sharing had long been major motivations for partnerships in activities like offshore exploration, where one well, for example, may cost between $10 and $20 million to complete and offer a 10 percent chance of economically recoverable findings at current oil prices. By taking a partial interest in several properties, firms believed they would reduce their exposure to big losses while increasing their chances of acces to crude oil.

Need for Joint Activities. In addition to the cost- and risk-sharing aspects of the oil industry, technological factors also necessitated some form of cooperative strategy. Contiguous acreage owned by diverse parties was *unitized* (treated as a unit) to enhance the amount of recoverable oil in a particular geological formation. Sharing a common gathering facility offered firms the benefits of scale economies. Transportation of crude oil and refined product was also carried out through joint ventures because the capital costs of pipelines were very high and the scale economies of building a slightly larger-diameter pipeline increased geometrically. Given this technological fact, investing in duplicate pipeline facilities for identical geographical routes would be wasteful.

Joint ventures were preferred where risks were high or the firm possessing mineral rights lacked the technology to develop acreage in inhospitable regions (for example, in the Arctic or in regions prone to earthquake). Terms of joint-venture agreements were strongly influenced by (1) decades of experience in using joint ventures and (2) homogeneity of interests among partners. Because firms had often been both operators and nonoperators in the past, they saw each others' perspectives more easily. Provisions of their agreements strived for equitable treatment of partners' interests, and since their industry was closely knit, their conduct became widely known.

Farm in (or *farm out*) agreements enabled firms possessing yet-unexplored mineral rights to take on partners that typically offered cash and exploration technology. The entering partners could pay for exploration costs to obtain a 50 percent interest in the oil field. Alternatively, the partner possessing mineral rights may have drilled to a certain depth with discouraging results and lacked the means to drill further. Partners could be farmed in at this point if they made contributions up to some portion of sunk costs (sometimes plus a premium) to obtain a position of parity in the acreage under exploration.

Choosing Partners. There were over 13,000 U.S. oil exploration firms in operation during the 1970s. They formed many joint ventures. Rather than report on each partnership individually, this section distills findings from many field interviews conducted within the oil industry from 1980 to 1984.

Oil firms preferred partners that offered a technological complementarity and geological experience in oil production. When they decided to take partners, oil firms sought others that had an interest in developing the same geographical area that they were interested in developing. An ideal partner offset other firms' strengths and had experience in working with oil firms in other exploration joint ventures.

Negotiations between parents determined the child's activities as far as possible in advance, and once exploratory and development wells were completed successfully, the venture became a passive one until enhancement decisions were made years later. Partners reached agreements concerning (1) bases for valuing each partner's contributions, (2) how to interpret geological maps, (3) which technologies to use, and (4) how to divide interests in the reservoir being developed. Because partners expected to venture together again, their negotiations were smoother than in other industries described below.

Oil exploration joint ventures have been and will continue to be an important means of developing promising oil fields. Overseas, joint ventures were commonplace in the oil industry at all stages of the vertical chain of processing because (1) governments demanded local participation, (2) ownership by partners of various national origins defused anger against a particular nationality that may have resulted in expropriation of those multinationals' properties, and (3) partners' individual product needs in one country could not absorb the output of an efficient-size refinery or other facility, in addition to other reasons sketched above.

Child Activities. Parents exerted substantial control over their child's activities in oil exploration through terms of their partnership agreement. Because the daily operating expenses in oil exploration were very high, delays due to decision-making stalemates among partners were costly. Instead, *side-payments* were made to disgruntled partners (as covered in partnership contracts) if they disagreed in an action taken by their child so that exploration could proceed.

Exploratory drilling could be undertaken by a firm under a *sole risk* provision if partners wished to stop a venture from going forward. The entire costs of drilling were borne by subscribing partners in this case. But if the venture struck oil and some partners had not paid their share of drilling costs, subscribing partners were indemnified for their costs (plus a penalty that was often 200 to 300 percent of their costs) before partners shared equally in the venture's findings. The stiff penalties of not participating reduced deadlocks once joint ventures were formed.

The partner in oil exploration joint ventures that was designated as the operator took charge of the physical work and made presentations to a *planning committee* (composed of other partners' personnel) concerning where and how to drill. This was the single most important decision in oil exploration, and parents devoted significant time and energies to it. The operator had budget authority to cover most day-to-day expenses, and parents differed substantially concerning how involved they were in monitoring those activities. There appeared to be an inverse relationship between parents' experiences in joint ventures and their demands to be consulted on minor expenditures.

Firms that were frequently partners used *offsets* to maintain equality between them by forming a series of joint ventures. Each served as operator in one venture and as nonoperator in the others. Thus, partners had equal ownership shares but different management responsibilities per venture.

The Alaska Pipeline joint venture provides an example of how partners adjusted to unforeseen events in their agreements. The agreement (which was written in 1977) provided maximum flexibility in terms of how much crude oil each partner would ship through the pipeline, how to handle additional Prudhoe Bay oil discoveries, and other events that could occur when resources were commingled. The capacity of the pipeline was determined by *estimated* reservoir capacity, and each partner's ownership share paralleled the proportion of capacity it would use in shipping crude oil. If partners' relative shipping volumes changed, the contract provided for them to adjust their ownership shares, as well. (This was done to ensure that no partner was predominantly a shipper or predominantly a customer. Conflicts were avoided by making all partners' tradeoffs as both shipper and customer relatively equal.) If another large oil basin were discovered in acreage adjacent to that originally covered by the Alaska Pipeline agreement, the contract provided that original partners had a right-of-first-refusal to invest should the pipeline be expanded to accommodate the new crude oil capacity.

Joint ventures in the oil industry were done on a project-by-project basis. Because they were structured as stand-alone units, there were relatively few opportunities for shared resource synergies between the child and organizational units of its parents within the oil exploration industry. Seismic information (which was close to the strategic core of parent firms) was shared between parent and child, but other resources were less likely to be shared due to the coordination difficulties that were created.

Mineral Extraction

By 1984 metals mining had become a distressed industry within the United States. High labor costs and expensive-to-recover U.S. reserves had forced much mining activity overseas to developing economies, and newly formed U.S. joint ventures were primarily divestitures in 1984. Mining joint ventures formed in an earlier era were languishing, while new ones were being forged overseas with foreign partners.

Need for Joint Activities. Mining operations were costly and complicated activities that could cost $1 to $2 billion to launch. Technologies did not change rapidly, and lead times of seven to ten years were required to assemble resources, design and develop a mine, and begin production. Many oil companies invested in mining (especially coal) during the 1970s when crude oil was scarce.

Choosing Partners
Coal Mining. Hanna Mining formed a coal mining joint venture with W.R. Grace in 1975. Subsequently, the partners joined in additional mines. A large U.S. coal partnership was created when Scallop Coal (with Shell Coal International) purchased an interest in the A.T. Massey Coal Company, a subsidiary of St. Joe Minerals Corp. (now part of Fluor Corp.) in 1979. The venture represented seventy-five coal mines with a capacity of 5 million tons of steam coal annually. Demand was not as large as expected, and Fluor was in financial difficulty in 1984.

Conoco formed a 76%-24% joint venture with Rheinische Braunkohlenwerke to work five coal mines in Pennsylvania producing a total of 12.5 million tons annually. When DuPont digested Conoco, interests in many of

Conoco's coal properties were sold. (Conoco also formed a uranium mining joint venture with Pioneer Nuclear in 1971. Each partner sold finished product until the venture was ended in 1982, when prices became uneconomic.) Ashland Coal formed a 75%-25% joint venture with Saarbergwerke. The German partner in this alliance sought a stable source of fuel. In 1981, Petrofina offered American Natural Resources (ANR) access to the scale economies of a project larger than it could undertake alone as well as access to Petrofina's worldwide marketing network. (Petrofina established a marketing organization for the coal with the West German firm, Krupp Handel.) In 1977 Panhandle Eastern Pipeline Co. formed a joint venture with Peabody Coal, a firm that controlled substantial coal reserves. Coal prices fell within four years after the venture was formed, as customer demand softened. By contrast, Union Pacific (through its Rocky Mountain Energy subsidiary) formed a coal mining partnership with Dravo Corp. that was very successful. (Union Pacific also mined soda ash in a partnership with Stauffer Chemical.)

Phosphate and Uranium Mining. In 1971 Kerr-McGee Corp. formed a joint venture with American Cyanamid in phosphate mining, Brewster Phosphates. Each parent marketed outputs through their respective distribution channels. Investments were made to modernize facilities and the venture thrived, despite increasing pressures from competitors that were state-owned enterprises. One of its major domestic competitors in 1980 was a joint venture of W.R. Grace and International Minerals & Chemicals. Nuclear Dynamics formed a uranium exploration joint venture with a privately held partner in 1975 to explore its nuclear land holdings in Colorado. The unnamed firm paid for all of the activities up to and including initial drilling; after that costs were shared on a 50%-50% basis. Nuclear Dynamics also had a 25%-75% uranium exploration joint venture with Bethlehem Steel Corp. at that time.

Copper Mining. In 1974 AMAX and Anaconda formed Anamax Mining Company to operate the Twin Buttes open pit copper mine in Arizona, which had formerly been owned by Banner Mining Company (but leased to Anaconda). AMAX acquired Banner Mining and Tintic Standard Mining Company in 1973 and sold the bulk of its shares in the Twin Buttes mine to Nippon Mining Co. Their mine was closed in 1983.

Under a 1979 Federal Trade Commission (FTC) order, Atlantic Richfield was required to divest certain Anaconda properties it had acquired in 1976, and as a part of that decision, Anaconda was ordered to sell its interest in Anamax Mining. A copper joint venture between Anaconda and Asarco in Montana was also announced in 1976, but under its 1979 decree, Anaconda could form copper mining joint ventures with leading U.S. copper producers only with FTC approval. By 1984 the U.S. copper mining was in its death throes, and there were few buyers for these firms' joint-venture (or wholly owned) interests. Poor performance was experienced across the entire mining industry (except perhaps in gold) and was not limited solely to mining joint ventures.

Undersea Ocean Mining. In the late 1970s, when there was great interest in undersea mining ventures whereby nodules could be gathered off the ocean floor by surface vessels, Kennecott Copper formed a joint venture for underwater mining with Rio Tinto-Zinc Corp., Consolidated Gold Fields, Ltd., British Petroleum, Mitsubishi, and Noranda Mines, Ltd. Similarly, U.S. Steel, Sun Company, and Union Minière (of Belgium) created a joint venture in 1977 called Ocean Mining Associates to purchase majority ownership of Tenneco Inc.'s Deepsea Ventures Inc. Another undersea mining consortium included Inco Ltd. (seeking sources of nickel), a group of German companies, six Japanese companies, and Sedco (possessing offshore exploration expertise). The lure of undersea riches also encouraged Lockheed Missiles & Space, Billiton International Metals (of Royal Dutch/Shell), Amoco Minerals Co., and Bos Kalis Westminster Group of the Netherlands to form a joint venture. These partnerships had intended to begin mining in the early 1980s but became uneconomic due to the cyclical nature of their industry, as well as to technological problems. (Many of the consortia were still in existence in 1984 but were not active and had not attained commercial success.)

Synfuels. Several firms pooled costs and risks in coal-gasification, oil shale, and other energy projects involving risky technologies that would prove but marginally economic (given crude oil prices in the early 1980s) if they worked at all. Their commercial viability was heavily dependent on crude oil prices and federal funding. The Great Plains coal gasification project was one of the few projects that moved beyond the proposal and demonstration plant stages. When the energy crisis abated, criticism of this joint venture intensified due to its dependence on federal funding.

Child Activities. Because the technologies used in mining activities were similar to those used in oil exploration, the nature of key operating decisions and the need to consult parent firms was also similar. Relationships between parent and child in many joint mining activities were managed in a manner that was similar to the operating committees of oil exploration parents.

Like oil exploration joint ventures, mining partners could buy into ongoing operations by compensating firms that bore the original risks of development. Their child was often vertically related to their processing operations, and parents marketed their child's outputs through wholly owned distribution channels. Partners were usually homogeneous in their outlooks regarding the venture and were willing to grant their child operating autonomy for all but major expenditures.

Partners typically met quarterly in mining joint ventures to give direction to their child. (Technology changed so slowly that little more was needed.) In one of these meetings, annual budgets were established. Since the child had its own facilities and dealt in an arm's-length manner with the parents that purchased its outputs, few synergies were realized between parent and child.

Metals Processing

Several U.S. joint ventures involving nonferrous metals processing were announced during the 1960s and 1970s. (Joint ventures in the steel industry are covered in chapter 11.) Many of these partnerships involved substantial capital investments in plants with very large output volumes. Compared with ongoing technologies, the processes they used were often highly risky or their outputs were sold to customers, such as nuclear plants, that faced uncertain futures. Like the joint ventures in the mining industry, described above, precipitous price declines made the new processes uneconomic.

Need for Joint Activities. Aluminum smelters required investments of $700 to $800 million for an efficient scale plant, requiring at least two potlines (at a cost of $350 million each) that produced approximately 180 million pounds of metal. Since this volume would be difficult for one firm to absorb alone, vertical joint ventures were formed by aluminum firms to share a large facility's outputs.

Uranium and titanium facilities were less costly than aluminum smelters, but they often utilized untried, capital-intensive technologies. Risk-sharing and cost-reduction motivated these alliances.

Choosing Partners.
Aluminum Smelting. AMAX and Howmet (the U.S. subsidiary of Pechiney-Ugine-Kuhlman) formed an aluminum smelting joint venture, Intalco, in 1967 when AMAX purchased 31 percent of Howmet's interest. (AMAX's interest had increased to 50 percent by 1975.) AMAX wanted Pechiney's excellent smelter technology at a partnership price, and Pechiney wanted access to metal in the United States to further its strategy of global expansion. The financial risk of the project and large plant scale also influenced their decision to cooperate. Together they operated a 254,400-ton reduction plant in Washington and formed Eastalco to construct and operate an 176,000 ton potline in Maryland at a cost of $103 million (to double the capacity of Howmet's plant there).

In July 1975 AMAX approved equal participation with Mitsui & Co. Ltd. in the ownership, construction, and operation of a two-potline, 187,300 ton per year primary aluminum reduction plant in Oregon at a cost of $175 million each. Mitsui & Co. Ltd. was AMAX's partner in an aluminum fabrication venture, ALUMAX (described below). Mitsui took the output from one potline of the jointly owned aluminum smelter to sell in Japan or elsewhere. ALUMAX and Alsas Inc. (a wholly owned subsidiary of Mitsui) owned a South Carolina aluminum smelter that produced approximately 199,000 tons in 1982. ALUMAX's share of this production was 75 percent; Alsas owned 25 percent. The smelter was operated by a subsidiary of ALUMAX.

In 1968 National Steel and Southwire Corp. formed an aluminum reduction joint venture in which each partner took half the output from the large facility. For Southwire, the venture was a backward integration because it could use the ingot to produce aluminum rod, wire, and cable. Southwire's continuous casting process—which it had originated for aluminum—was applied to copper in a 1963 joint venture with Western Electric Co. For National Steel, then fourth-largest U.S. producer of steel, the venture was a diversification. National had no semifabricated aluminum operations but acquired fabrication operations shortly thereafter.

Uranium Reprocessing and Zirconium Production. In 1974 Pechiney-Ugine-Kuhlman (PUK) and Burns & Roe formed a joint venture to design and build a uranium ore reprocessing plant. In 1976 Howmet Turbine Components (a subsidiary of Pechiney-Ugine-Kuhlman that produced precision cast parts and superalloys for the aircraft and other industries) and Western Zirconium announced a joint venture to produce zirconium for the nuclear energy market and other industrial applications. Project costs were estimated at $30 to $40 million. As market conditions deteriorated in the year that followed, Howmet backed out of the venture, citing other investments its parent wanted to pursue. Nuclear plants comprised 90 percent of demand for zirconium at that time, and PUK (the parent) was one of two producers of it. Western Zirconim, which sought to continue the venture with other partners, was acquired by Westinghouse Electric, which later tried to divest the zirconium facility unsuccessfully.

In 1979 Beker Industries and Western Cooperative Fertilizers announced a 50%-50% joint venture, Conda Partnership, which would own the company's phosphate ore reserves and associated beneficiation facilities in Idaho. Beker also formed a joint venture in 1980 to enter the uranium industry with Mono Power Company, a Southern California Edison subsidiary. The venture would have extracted uranium oxide from Beker's phosphoric acid production (the Conda Partnership), but subsequent uranium market conditions made the venture uneconomic.

Titanium Sponge. In 1979 Howmet Turbine Components and Dow Chemical formed a $10 million joint venture, D-H Titanium Company, to scale up and commercialize an electrolytic cell process for the production of titanium sponge, a porous, solid product of the electrolytic dissociation of titanium tetrachloride that could be melted to make ingots or alloys. Their venture would have been a backward integration for Howmet.

The D-H Titanium partners had studied the electrolytic process together since 1973, but prices fell to one-third of the 1973 level by the time commitment to a $40 million scale-up stage was reached. At that price level, their process would not be economic so the venture ended. Dow Chemical retained the facility and technology.

Child Activities. Aluminum smelting technology changed slowly; some processes were almost 100 years old in 1984. Parents would not have to intervene often in the operations of their child in such industries. Parents were often vertically related to their children in metals processing ventures and purchased their outputs for internal consumption. Needs for coordination among them for this purpose were not high due to the predictable nature of their technology.

Metals Fabrication

Metal fabrication activities are not as capital intensive as those discussed above, and the entry barriers associated with capital requirements for this industry are not high. The primary needs for joint ventures are to obtain access to marketing channels or to scale up new technologies beyond pilot plant levels to test their commercial value. Partners in these ventures during the 1970s were often foreign firms. Many of them were vertically related to their child's activity.

Choosing Partners.
Ball Bearings. In 1972 Hoover Ball & Bearing Co. and Nippon Seiko K.K., a leading Japanese ball bearing maker, formed a joint venture, Hoover NSK Bearings Inc., to operate former Hoover plants in Michigan and New Jersey. Hoover and Nippon Seiko had cooperated in a marketing agreement since 1958 whereby Hoover distributed Nippon Seiko products in the United States. As the market grew more important to Nippon Seiko's total sales and as Japanese bearings captured over 50 percent of the U.S. market for some applications, it wanted to produce bearings in the United States as part of its strategy of global expansion.

Anodes. In 1970 Union Carbide and Engelhard Minerals & Chemicals Corp. joined to form Metal Anodes Associates, a venture to sell anodes to the chlorine industry. Engelhard provided production facilities (to plate corrosion-resistant titanium with platinum), and Carbide provided marketing and technical service to make a gridlike titanium anode with an electrically conductive coating (a dimensionally stable anode that resisted erosion in use).

Aluminum Fabrication. Because successful joint ventures with Pechiney in the Intalco and Eastalco aluminum smelters assured it a supply of metal, AMAX expanded downstream and entered the foil business in 1962, opened a general extrusion line, and built a sheet mill through a wholly owned subsidiary, ALUMAX. The aluminum business grew rapidly, requiring massive capital investments (but was not highly profitable). So in 1974 AMAX sold to Mitsui & Co. a 50 percent interest in its aluminum fabrication business (ALUMAX) for approximately $135 million. Mitsui & Co. (Japan's second-largest trading company) purchased AMAX's interest to gain a U.S. source of aluminum at a time when capacity expansion was constrained in Japan. Mitsui & Co. sold a 5 percent interest in ALUMAX to Nippon Steel Corp.

With Mitsui's funding ALUMAX was able to expand capacity when others were holding back, and its parent, AMAX, was able to pursue an aggressive strategy instead of that of an underdog. Its plants were newer than most competitors, and it was quite profitable initially. Because ALUMAX was vertically integrated, it did not have to sell tonnage aluminum. It sold proprietary end products, instead, using ingots that ALUMAX obtained from Intalco and Eastalco, both joint ventures of AMAX and Pechiney-Ugine-Kuhlman (through Howmet Aluminum).

The aluminum fabricating business gave AMAX an investment tax credit when it was fully owned, but it could not be tax-consolidated with its parent as 50 percent of a joint venture. In 1984 the venture was restructured to provide AMAX with 80 percent ownership (to permit AMAX to consolidate ALUMAX's taxable profits with AMAX's accumulated tax losses). The Japanese partners received slightly more than 50 percent of ALUMAX's profits as compensation.

In 1978 Hayes-Albion Co. and Honsel-Werke A.G. of West Germany formed a joint venture, Honsel-Hayes, to make aluminum castings in the United States. The venture was successful initially because the technology was new, but Hayes-Albion personnel quickly learned and improved on their partner's contributions. As competitors like Ford Motors opened their own plants and competition began to tax goodwill within the partnership, Hayes-Albion purchased Honsel-Werke A.G.'s interest in the venture in 1980.

In 1983 ALCOA and Continental formed a joint development venture to test the economic, technical, and manufacturing feasibility of two-piece, aluminum food cans. Their alliance ended one year later as Continental reassessed the strategic importance of multisize aluminum food cans to its product line. ALCOA continued development work with another partner.

In 1983 Amacast Industrial Corp. and Dynamark formed a joint venture to manufacture aluminum wheels for the original equipment manufacturer

(OEM) market. As the partner that controlled marketing, Amacast was the operator in an activity that was so well received that plant expansions were needed within a year of the venture's formation. Prospering from the depressed state of supplier industries, the venture invested in the latest, computer-controllable casting technology and ploughed back its profits to improve the technology it shared with both parents.

Copper Foil. Oak Industries, Anaconda Co., and Mitsui Mining formed an electrolytic copper foil manufacturing joint venture, Oak-Mitsui, in 1976. (Oak owned 68.6 percent of the new firm, Mitsui 19.1 percent, and Anaconda 12.3 percent. Mitsui had the option to increase its investment ratio to 39 percent, with Oak and Anaconda revising their holdings to 41 and 20 percent respectively. Instead, Anaconda backed out of the venture as the funding requirements of the rapidly growing business unit became too substantial. By 1980 Oak-Mitsui was 78.2 percent owned by Oak Industries and 21.8 percent owned by Mitsui Mining.)

Oak-Mitsui was formed to develop and manufacture high-specification copper sheet and foil in support of parent Oak Industries' Materials group, including copper-laminated boards for PC-board applications. Technology was provided by Mitsui (originally licensed by Anaconda in 1967). The Oak-Mitsui venture grew rapidly in 1979. Before its original plant and equipment was completed, work began to double its capacity to keep pace with the growth of Oak Industries' laminating business. In response to a trend toward the use of thinner foils in the printed circuit industry, Oak-Mitsui developed two parallel technologies for producing ultra-thin copper. Its productive capacity was more than sufficient to satisfy Oak Industries' internal requirements in 1980 when Oak-Mitsui became the third supplier of copper foil for laminate producers in the United States. By 1984 it provided foil to outsiders as well as its parents.

Titanium Fabrication. In 1981 Nippon Mining Co. and C. Itoh & Co. set up a joint company called Nikko Wolverine Inc., with UOP Inc., an oil refining and engineering firm, to operate UOP's Michigan plant from its titanium division (Wolverine), which produced seamless titanium pipes for chemical plants and titanium-coated copper bars for soda electrolysis electrodes. Nippon Mining purchased 51 percent interest, C. Itoh took 24 percent, C. Itoh & Co. (America) purchased 5 percent, leaving UOP with 20 percent. Because of shortages of titanium sponge and billets, the Wolverine division had been operating at only 50 percent of capacity. Under the joint venture, however, titanium billets were obtained from parent, Nippon Mining in Japan through its subsidiary, Toho Titanium, and the child's capacity was fully utilized.

Child Activities. Many joint ventures in metals fabrication were vertically related to one or more of their parents. Initially, they served as captive suppliers or distributors for their parents. If they thrived, they served outside markets also. Survival and satisfaction seemed to be higher among joint ventures in this industry, perhaps because capital requirements and technological risks seemed lower than in other capital intensive industries. Greater use of cooperative agreements and licensing arrangements was made in metals fabrication activities than in mining and metals processing, and this pattern is repeated below in the case of light machinery. Alternatively, these joint ventures may seem longer-lived because some of them were, in fact, incremental divestitures of assets and goodwill by one of their parents to outsiders seeking entry. (The divestiture phenomena is examined further in chapter 11.)

Heavy Machinery

Heavy machinery includes turbine generators, nuclear reactors, drilling platforms, and other complex, fabricated metal products with numerous moving parts and a power source. It may also include farm and industrial equipment, machine tools, and other capital-intensive machinery, but these products are discussed in chapters 8 and 12.

Need for Joint Activities. The heavy machinery industry was highly risky because of the customers it served, as well as the long lead times of seven to ten years required to judge whether new products were successful or not. When technologies that had been transferred from overseas were not well-accepted in the United States, an industry leader was needed to demonstrate the new processes or products' viability. Doing so was costly. If foreign partners were unknown entities in the United States, the riskiness of such joint ventures was compounded. When customer viability was in doubt, only large firms acting in joint ventures could afford to bear such risks. (Risk and cost sharing were necessary in the nuclear energy business, for example, where investments often exceeded $500 million. Entry barriers were also quite high in the dredging industry.)

Choosing Partners.
Nuclear Power Plants. In 1955 Scallop Nuclear Inc. (a subsidiary of Royal Dutch/Shell) and Gulf Oil Corp. formed General Atomic Company (GAC), a 50%-50% joint venture, to pursue opportunities in the field of nuclear energy. In 1975 General Atomic and Allied Chemical Nuclear Products (a subsidiary of Allied Chemical) formed a joint venture, Allied-General Nuclear Services (AGNS), to reprocess light-water reactor (LWR) fuel. General Atomic developed gas-cooled reactor technology as a safer and more efficient alternative to LWR.

In 1973 Gulf General Atomic (a subsidiary of Gulf Oil) and Foster Wheeler Nuclear Equipment (a subsidiary of Foster Wheeler) formed a joint venture, Nuclear Power Products, to manufacture steam generator equipment for high-temperature gas-cooled reactor (HTGR) nuclear power plant systems. Gulf Oil took majority interest in the joint venture, and an operating services contract for the child's Florida facility was awarded to Foster Wheeler. Investment for the start-up phase was approximately $10 million.

The parents of GAC bore substantial operating losses through their child due to several contract cancellations by customers concerned with the uncertainties generally surrounding the development of nuclear power. In 1975 and early 1976 General Atomic agreed to the termination of its remaining commercial reactor commitments.

In 1976 Arizona Public Service and its six partners received Nuclear Regulatory Commission (NRC) approval to proceed with a mammoth, $2.8 billion nuclear power generating plant, the Palo Verde Complex. Other partners included Arizona Electric Power Cooperative, El Paso Electric, the Salt River Project, Southern California Edison, and Public Service Co. of New Mexico. When completed, Palo Verde included three 1,270 megawatt nuclear units that were managed and operated by Arizona Public Service Co. (All of the partners had the necessary expertise to do so.) A hot functional test of the first unit occurred in spring 1983.

Electrical Equipment. In 1968 the High Voltage Power Corp. formed a joint venture with Reynolds Metals Co. to develop and sell gas-insulated transmission systems to the electrical power industry. For Reynolds, a large producer of aluminum cable, the venture was a vertical integration. For High Voltage Power, it was an opportunity to expand its product line to satisfy customers for pressure-insulated underground power transmission systems.

In 1971 RTE Corporation (a manufacturer of power distribution systems) formed a 50%-50% joint venture, RTE-ASEA, with Allemana Svenska Elektriska Akteibolatet (ASEA) to make and sell medium-size power transformers. RTE's products included three-phase power transformers, and it sought ASEA's help in substation power transformers because that market was dominated by General Electric and Westinghouse Electric, among others. ASEA's technology proved to be the best and RTE-ASEA was a highly successful joint venture.

RTE sold its 50 percent interest back to ASEA in early 1984 because ASEA had several other electrical equipment products it wanted to sell in the United States (such as high-voltage circuit breakers, power transformer bushings, and other components that ASEA had formerly sold to its child). ASEA continued to use RTE Corp.'s sales force to distribute its products after the joint venture ended. Consequently, RTE offered a wider product line to its customers (and to firms that were once its competitors) through this arrangement. ASEA did not create its own U.S. sales force.

In 1977 Allis-Chalmers and Siemens A.G. formed a 50%-50% joint venture, Siemens-Allis, to revitalize Allis-Chalmers' U.S. market position for electric utility equipment, such as switchgear. Siemens wanted a foothold in the U.S. market but was reluctant to go alone against the two major competitors—General Electric and Westinghouse Electric. Siemens-Allis intended to sell a substantial portion of Siemens's innovative motors line. Their child, Siemens-Allis, continued to offer electrical equipment and power engineering technology in 1984, but Allis-Chalmers's ownership share had dwindled to approximately 15 percent because it had become too strapped for cash to keep abreast of its funding obligations to the child. Allis-Chalmers had also formed a 15%-85% joint venture, Utility Power Corp. (UPC), with Siemens's Kraftwerke Union previously, but its results had been mediocre. (UPC constructed turbine-generator plants.)

In 1980 Research-Cottrell Inc. and Transamerica Delaval Inc. (a subsidiary of Transamericas Corp.) formed a joint venture to market systems for power generation and energy utilities. The child operated from Research-Cottrell's Biphase Energy Systems unit in California.

In 1980 Combustion Engineering and Mitsubishi Heavy Industries formed a joint venture, C-E-MHI Fan Co., to sell, install, and service axial flow fans for utilities and large industrial applications, such as supplying air to fuel burning equipment. (Technology for the venture was supplied under a license agreement with Mitsubishi Heavy Industries.)

RTE Corporation and Zellweger Uster A.G. formed a 50%-50% joint venture in 1980 to introduce peak-load power management equipment to U.S. electrical utilities. The child was uneconomic because U.S. customers were unwilling to accept the new technology. It was a small part of RTE's business, and the venture eventually folded.

In 1981 Combustion Engineering Inc. (a supplier of equipment and services for the utility and oil and gas industries) and Neyrpic (itself a 65%-35% joint venture between Creusot-Loure S.A., a major French manufacturer and Alsthom-Atlantic, a French engineering company) formed a 50%-50% joint venture to make and sell hydropower turbines in the United States. Neyrpic licensed turbine technology to the joint venture, and Combustion Engineering provided manufacturing services.

IN 1982 Garrett Corporation and Wheelabrator-Frye Inc. formed a joint venture, GWF Power Systems, to build small-to-medium-size power plants. As a leader in developing cogeneration systems, Garrett had lengthy experience in heat transfer and gas turbine technology. (Cogeneration is a process of producing electricity and another form of energy at the same time.)

In 1983 Westinghouse Electric and Steel Improvement & Forge Company (SIFCO Industries Inc.) formed a joint venture, SIFCO Turbine Component

Services, for the rebuilding of worn jet engine and land-based combustion turbine components used by airlines and electric utilities. For Westinghouse, this was a vertical integration because its Combustion Turbine Systems Division had more than 7,600 large combustion turbines in operation around the world.

The technology SIFCO Turbine Component Services employed was somewhat risky because land-based combustion turbine vanes were often ten times as large as the jet engine vanes its parent, SIFCO, had been remanufacturing before its joint venture with Westinghouse. The joint venture was a means of pursuing a global expansion strategy for SIFCO.

Paper Machinery. In 1975 Ingersoll-Rand received a marketing license from Escher Wyss GmbH to manufacture, market, and service a selected number of paper machinery products in the United States. (The agreement between Morden Machine Co. and Escher Wyss had not been renewed, yet customers were quite familiar with Escher Wyss products through that former affiliation.) The license was a faster way for Ingersoll-Rand to enter the secondary fiber- and stock-preparation equipment market segment. (Ingersoll-Rand was well established in the chemical pulp area of the pulp and paper industry.) Voith had entered the U.S. market through a similar agreement with Allis-Chalmers in an era when the increasing cost of fuel oil prompted paper users to demand a higher proportion of cheaper secondary fiber content. Escher Wyss later acquired Manchester Machine as a means of entering the U.S. market when Ingersoll-Rand did not meet the sales quota it had set.

Materials Handling and Processing Equipment. In 1976 Chromalloy American Corp. and Victor Laurich-Trost formed a joint venture, Industrial Applications International Inc., to engineer, develop, manufacture, and market production systems and material handling equipment for the chemical, petrochemical, and foundry industries. (Victor Laurich-Trost was a designer and innovator for the process industries.)

In 1976 Mesta Machine Co., producer of heavy rolling machinery, and Production Machinery Corp., maker of processing lines and machinery, formed an agreement whereby the two companies designed, manufactured, and sold processing lines to the metal producing industries. They shared engineering technology in electrolytic tinning, pickling, galvanizing, continuous cleaning, and annealing lines. As a part of the arrangement, Mesta Machine Co. was granted an option to purchase a minority interest of about 25 percent in Production Machinery common stock. Mesta Machine also forged a long-term licensing agreement with Pahnke Engineering Co. of Dusseldorf, West Germany, in 1980 to cooperate in the design and sale of hydraulic forging presses, forging press manipulators, and forming and extrusion presses.

Tankers and Drilling Vessels. In 1976 Overseas Shipholding Corp. (OSG) and the Continental Grain Company formed a 50%-50% joint venture for the ownership of two 60,000 dwt dry bulk carriers. Both vessels were placed on long-term charter to Continental Grain, a substantial user of bulk vessels. The joint venture represented a new customer for OSG that built, owned, and operated a fleet of various types and sizes of bulk vessels.

In 1977 Zapata Corporation and Bos Kalis Westminster Construction, the Dutch-based dredging and construction company, formed a joint venture, Zapata Westminster Dredging, to design, build, and operate trailing hopper suction dredges. (This was a third-generation pipe-laying barge designed to lay 36-inch gas pipeline in the inhospitable environment of the North Sea above 60 degrees north latitude.) The venture was terminated when the vessel was constructed. (It was sold to a third party.) The project was accomplished ahead of schedule with outstanding results. Partners applied their experiences from this venture to subsequent undertakings.

In 1976 subsidiaries of Panhandle Eastern Pipeline, Moore McCormack Resources, and General Dynamics formed a partnership, called Lachmar, to construct, own, and operate two cryogenic tankers for use in the transportation of liquified natural gas (LNG) from Algeria to the United States. Pelmar Co. (Panhandle Eastern) and Pantheon, Inc. (General Dynamics) each took a 40 percent interest in Lachmar, and Morgas, Inc. (Moore-McCormack) took a 20 percent interest. Lachmar was suspended when demand for LNG dropped by over 50 percent by 1984, resulting in conditions of excess supply. Moss Rosenberg Verft A.S. (a member of the Kvaerner Group of Oslo) also formed such a venture with Columbia LNG Corp. and the National Iranian Gas Company, but it was terminated in 1978.

Child Activities. This section has illustrated parent firm responsibilities for ventures undertaken in arenas with uncertain futures, like nuclear power, where partnerships are necessary to bear their associated risks. Performance in these products was often dependent on uncontrollable events (like the energy crisis). Even in highly successful joint ventures like RTE-ASEA, partnerships did not last long in their original forms. Because partners judged each other on the basis of their joint venture experiences (however short they may be), this result suggests that parents seeking longer affiliations with their partners should permit their child the autonomy needed to perform well.

Light Machinery

Light machinery was fabricated from metal, but it was an activity that did not require as large an investment to enter as other activities discussed above. Its exit barriers were also lower, making the activity less risky for one firm to bear alone. Technology changed infrequently, and competition was often stable but vulnerable to offshore competition.

Need for Joint Activities. Fabrication of light machinery was an activity where more licenses, cross-licensing arrangements, and marketing agreements were used than joint ventures. This pattern existed because there was less need for joint ventures that created a separate entity. Moreover the technologies associated with these activities often did not require a separate, dedicated facility. Accordingly, joint ownership of a parent's ongoing research facilities, factories, and sales force was unlikely to occur in an activity like light machinery unless the arrangement was an incremental form of divestiture.

Choosing Partners.

Coating Equipment. There were many more cooperative ventures in the light machinery industry where capital costs were not as high, technologies were less risky, and economies were available at smaller production scales. In 1976 Geotel Inc. and Eutectic Corp. formed a cooperative venture in the research and marketing of plasma spraying equipment used for solar-cell coating, insulating surfaces, and other applications. Their agreement provided for joint research and development between Plasmadyne, a division of Geotel, and Eutectic in areas of plasma technology, including transferred and nontransferred arc plasma, special powder technology in plasma spray, and flame spray technology. A second cooperative agreement by the partners made Eutectic the worldwide (non-U.S.) distributor of the Plasmadyne equipment line.

Slot Machines. In 1980 Elsinore Corp. and Interscience Systems, Inc. formed a joint venture to make electronic slot machines. Each firm contributed $1 million to the venture. Elsinore controlled access to gaming casinos that it owned, and it sought a microprocessor-based conversion package adaptable to most existing electromechanical slot machines so as not to be obsolesced by a new generation of slot machines utilizing microprocessor technology. Interscience Systems, Inc. was a computer equipment manufacturer, and through its subsidiary, Summit Systems, Inc., was a developer of microprocessor applications for gaming devices.

In 1978 Vendo Co. and Coordinated Systems Corp. agreed to exchange technology for a variety of applications. Vendo was the leading manufacturer of vending machines. Coordinated Systems developed data acquisition systems using micromputer technology.

Child Activities. Cooperative agreements were more appropriate than joint ventures where the child did not have to control or develop new technology in order for these ventures to succeed. Moreover, if the activities covered by such agreements could be performed in partners' facilities, joint ventures were not necessary. In the two examples involving the application of microprocessor technology to formerly electromechanical products, the key difference in circumstances pertained to market access. The slot machine venture represented a new undertaking for each partner. In the latter venture, the vending machine firms possessed their own respective facilities.

Summary

The capital-intensive, metal-bending industries used as examples in this chapter suggested that as the magnitude of capital investments required to enter an industry *decreased*, joint ventures were *less* likely to be embraced. Where the minimum efficient scale of upstream technologies was vast, joint ownership of them was necessary for all except the largest firms in order to alleviate their riskiness by guaranteeing a market for their outputs.

The relative ease with which partners in the extractive industries operated joint ventures offers suggestions for partner selection and venture structuring that may be applied in other situations involving large capital expenditures and high uncertainties concerning success. Firms in these industries chose to join forces often, even in their home economies. Partner homogeneity and a willingness to grant their child operating autonomy in routine decisions contributed strongly to the abilities of their ventures to succeed.

Because entry barriers for the child's industry were high in most of the capital-intensive industries examined, its need for close coordination with its parents was lower—except when the child shared facilities, personnel, or resources with parents, when it was captive in its parents' vertical chains of processing (especially when the child was physically interconnected), or when competitive needs for parents' advice, services, and resources were great. Coordination with parents was also important in these industries when excess capacity had to be rationalized (and this point is covered further in chapter 11).

The poor outlook for many of the capital-intensive industries examined confounded analyses concerning whether using the child as a guaranteed supplier or distribution channel harmed its parents. Demand was so depressed in many of these industries that it was difficult to determine whether outsiders were reluctant to deal with partners' children because they were too closely identified with competitors. Similarly, it was difficult to ascertain whether making the child a captive supplier or customer made parents' business units become complacent because they faced no outside pressures to innovate or lower costs.

Dissatisfaction with joint ventures occurred most frequently where partners had never ventured together with any other firm, had misunderstandings concerning the roles each would play in making the venture succeed, or were unable to make significant contributions (beyond cash) to their child's operations. Operating committees in the most successful ventures delineated clearly when their child had to gain approval before actions were taken. In the less successful ventures, partners used their child's managers as a medium for expressing dissatisfaction with their partners. In brief, in activities where close coordination *between partners* may well have been more critical to success than close parent coordination with their child, partners in unsuccessful joint ventures failed to manage this side of the triangle effectively. Worse, they communicated these hostilities to their child, thereby increasing the tensions borne by their child's managers.

8
Joint Ventures Involving Differentiable Products

The ninety-one joint ventures and other cooperative strategies in the industries of this chapter involved products that were differentiable—in the perceptions of relatively unsophisticated consumers (such as households that purchased products through retail outlets) or to relatively sophisticated industrial customers that devoted substantial attentions to the purchasing function. Product differentiation skills were often close to firms' strategic cores. Accordingly, analyses of how firms coped with customer bargaining power in activities affecting their products' images (and other attributes of great importance to them) should be of interest in addressing questions of joint-venture duration and parent–child coordination.

Motives

Product Traits

Whether joint ventures were appropriate depended on how well the product could be differentiated and how sensitive service was to the product offering. Joint ventures seemed less risky when products could be differentiated effectively, but frequent changes in product attributes were destabilizing to joint ventures because frequent changes in product dimensions increased the likelihood that partners would become mismatched. While products were highly differentiable, joint ventures were undertaken to gain access to unique product features as well as to new channels of distribution. (Cost reduction concerns became more important motivations as customer bargaining power increased.)

Parent and child had to *coordinate* decisions concerning product features, supporting services, and other attributes closely when both firms intended to offer the same products, so that the child's activities would not in

---

I am indebted to Nida T. Backaitis (Ph.D. candidate, Columbia University), for industry background materials prepared for this chapter.

some manner harm the goodwill and image its parent has created. If they were not sharing products, the child's need for operating *autonomy* in decisions pertaining to how it differentiated its products increased.

Customer Traits

When highly differentiated products were sold to highly sophisticated customers, a *mix* was needed of high coordination with relevant parent-firm operations and high child-firm autonomy (to make other marketing decisions). The more demanding the customer, the more operating autonomy the child required in responding to customer demands. But close coordination with the child's marketing parent was also needed to satisfy some customers. If the products in question were complex and required precision in manufacturing, the child needed close coordination with its technology parent, also.

The greater the bargaining power of customers over their vendors, the more important these customers were likely to be parent firms. If parent and child were both interacting with the same purchasing agents within such customer firms, coordination of customer accounts was so important that parents would not permit their child to have its own salesforce.

Control of Differentiation Advantage

Conflicts arose among partners concerning control of the basis for differentiation, access to markets, and product presentation if both firms already possessed such expertise in-house. Moreover, they were not likely to entrust the most sophisticated or complex tasks to their child because then outsiders could gain control over their source of competitive advantage. Although they behaved passively in marketing decisions initially, partners possessing differentiated products often wanted control over marketing activities, even if the parent in question was a foreign firm and the local partner's personnel were performing the selling task effectively. (Control of distribution channels was an enduring competitive advantage that partners sometimes sacrificed needlessly.)

Industries

Programming for Entertainment and Communications Services

Programming could be distributed through several channels, including commercial television, pay-television, and home videotape recorders or videodisc players. A major source of programming was the motion picture industry. (Television networks also created programming through their in-house studios.) Like the oil industry, the movie business was cyclical. Each project was unique and perishable. There were periods of substantial excess capacity as well as periods of great scarcity. The distribution system had a huge capacity, and one project alone was insufficient to fill the distribution system's throughput volume. There was always demand for good feature films, but if good features were not available, the distribution system worked with lesser quality programming. (But it was often more costly to do so due to the lower yields from inferior raw material quality. Lower-quality programming commanded lower licensing fees and could not be used as effectively as "blockbuster" programming.)

Need for Joint Activities. Motion pictures (*programming*) were distributed to satellite communications firms and cable system operators by *programming packagers*, like Home Box Office (HBO). (Motion picture studios themselves were not vertically integrated to programming packaging in the early 1970s.) The capital costs of entering the programming packaging business were not so high that a large firm could not afford to go in alone, but the capital costs of programming (movie-making) were large. Nevertheless, there were many joint ventures in the programming packaging part of the industry in the late 1970s because of the many changes that the industry was going through. The industry was new and still developing, and parents believed that partners were needed to share losses and other risks while they experimented with a new kind of distribution channel that might experience growing demand. Like firms in the oil industry, even large players preferred to invest in several projects to hedge their bets concerning which one would be successful and to lower their exposure to "dry holes." There were many crossover relationships in which the composition of partnerships changed in programming. This pattern carried over to programming packaging. Many firms were engaged in spider's webs of joint ventures in both industries.

Some joint ventures were inspired by a desire for vertical integration to create countervailing bargaining power against the programming packagers. HBO, for example, had entered early and built a strong distribution franchise that gave it substantial bargaining power over the motion picture studios. (By 1983 HBO had 12.5 million subscribers compared with a combined total of 6 million subscribers for Showtime and The Movie Channel; its bargaining power was immense.) Much like the nonintegrated oil exploration firms during periods of excess crude oil supply, the movie studios found that they had to accept the terms that programming packagers dictated to them until they could find a way of changing the balance of power.

Some joint ventures were motivated by a need to create more and better programming. During the 1960s and 1970s theatrical films had been a staple of network television. Firms like Universal controlled over 11,000 motion picture titles, but newer films (and blockbusters) commanded the largest audiences. By 1982 these movies were becoming overexposed, and theatrical films began doing so poorly on the commercial networks that their ratings no longer justified their costs. Channels were cannibalizing each other as satellites, pay-per-view, dish antennas, and videocassettes all competed for viewers by offering exclusive programming. As the costs of good programming skyrocketed, the need for film-makers to capture greater value-added margins became acute. Moreover, resentment of their treatment at the hands of the new distribution technologies caused some movie studios to jump into joint ventures in cable TV, home video, and other distribution systems that they scarcely understood. They engaged in many ventures because the movie studios were hedging their bets. (If any of them had possessed clear insights concerning how the industry would evolve, it would have invested alone.) As the motion picture studios were pressed for more good programming, more limited partnership financing ventures were created, even among firms like Universal Studios, which had financed their own movies historically.

Cable television was in only 30 percent of all U.S. households in 1982. By 1987, 12 million households were expected to enjoy cable TV. By the end of the decade, cable television services were expected to be in over 50 million households. Programmers of software for teletext and videotex watched these developments with great interest because demand for their products would follow acceptance of cable TV and personal computers (which used telephone lines to link and interact with their programs). Teletext and videotex services are discussed in chapter 9.

Choosing Partners.
Home Box Office. Home Box Office (HBO) of Time Inc. had become so successful by 1980 that it financed much of the programming it packaged and arranged for rights to *exclusive* showings of a growing number of pictures in exchange for some up-front financing of their films. Many joint ventures (described below) were motivated by HBO's early dominance of programming packaging services for cable television operators. Motion picture studios were seeking the high value-added margins enjoyed by programming packagers.

HBO was providing increasing amounts of funding for exclusive rights to made-for-cable feature-length programming in the 1980s. In 1983 Metromedia and HBO joined forces to develop and broadcast programming made for cable TV that could be licensed for broadcast on commercial television networks. This was a desirable alliance for Metromedia because most cable television companies that created their own programming had no way of selling them to the lucrative after-markets of commercial television. The Metromedia deal allowed cable television firms to spend more money on their original productions at lower risk by pre-selling their distribution, much the way producers of theatrical films and network television had done.

Subscription Services. In 1979 four motion picture studios and an oil company (Columbia Pictures, Universal (MCA), Paramount (G + W), Twentieth-Century-Fox, and Getty Oil) formed a joint venture, Premiere, to offer new films nine months before they would have been made available to other pay-TV networks. About half of the new movies would have been provided by the joint-venture partners (Columbia Pictures, Universal (MCA), Paramount (G + W), and Twentieth-Century-Fox). The remainder would have been obtained from other motion picture studios on a *non*exclusive basis.

The other programming packagers, including HBO and Showtime (a joint venture of Viacom International and Teleprompter, a unit of Group W of Westinghouse Electric), protested bitterly to the U.S. Department of Justice against the creation of the Premiere network. Following its defeat in the Premiere venture, Columbia Pictures licensed HBO to air several of its feature-length films on an exclusive basis. The Movie Channel and Showtime entered similar agreements with other motion picture studios.

Warner-Amex (a joint venture of American Express and Warner Communications) was a cable operator. By 1981 Warner-Amex had 863,000 subscribers in 27 states for 146 cable systems and had been somewhat successful in its interactive (videotex) QUBE demonstration project. Its subsidiary—the Warner-Amex Satellite Entertainment Corp. (WASEC)—aggressively marketed The Movie Channel (which it owned), Nickelodeon (children's programming), and advertiser-supported MTV (Music Television—the fastest growing service in cable television history) through Warner-Amex and other cable operators. As a result of the substantial costs associated with the simultaneous building and development of a number of new Warner-Amex cable systems and the marketing of new WASEC cable programming packaging services, the joint venture realized a net loss of $46.6 million during 1981, which its parents believed would be temporary. In one of its packaging ventures, WASEC had collaborated with ABC Video Enterprises to present cultural programming for cable TV. Their joint venture, Alpha Repertory Television Service (ARTS network), was devoted to the performing and visual arts.

Despite the built-in advantage of having Warner-Amex as a parent, The Movie Channel had not done well in the fiercely competitive pay-cable market up to 1982. In 1982 Warner Brothers, Universal Studios, and Paramount tried to form a joint venture (with Warner-Amex) to purchase 75 percent of its interest in The Movie Channel. Their motivation was the same as that of the Premiere partnership; the motion picture firms wanted to capture the higher value-added margins of pay-cable programming packagers.

The Department of Justice refused to permit The Movie Channel merger until the joint venture was restructured to include only Warner-Amex and Viacom International (half owner of Showtime) as partners. Viacom International had significant expertise as a developer, builder, owner, and programmer of cable systems through its Viacom Cable subsidiary. It was also a partner in Lifetime, an advertiser-supported network owned with Hearst/ABC Video. (Lifetime, a casualty of the cable programming packager shakeout, was a merger of Viacom's Cable Health Network and Hearst/ABC Video's Daytime Channel.)

In 1981 Walt Disney Productions and Group W Satellite Communications announced the formation of a joint venture, the Disney Channel. Although the joint venture was discontinued in 1982 (due to creative differences), Disney Productions proceeded with its plans to launch the Disney Channel alone.

In 1982 RCA broadened its role in the home entertainment market by forming a 50%-50% joint venture, RCTV, with Rockefeller Center, Inc. to furnish programming (The Entertainment Channel) to cable systems via satellite. After RCA bought its partner's interest and the venture continued to operate at a loss, RCA merged it with ARTS (a joint venture between ABC and Hearst Corp.). The new service was called the ARTS and Entertainment Network, or A&E, and it was owned equally by the Hearst Corp., ABC Video, and RCA Cable.

In 1981 Time Inc. purchased a 50 percent interest in USA Cable Network (an advertising-supported cable television programming packager that was making substantial demands for capital on its parents) from UA-Columbia Cablevision Inc. for $15 million. It became a joint venture of Paramount, Universal, and Time Inc. in 1983. (UA-Columbia Cablevision and Madison Square Gardens had been the original joint-venture parents.)

In 1981 Wometco Enterprises, Inc. terminated its joint venture with Universal Subscription Television, Inc. to operate Wometco Home Theatre of New York. Wometco chose to own the Smithtown, New York, station (WWHT) completely and to operate the Home Theatre with a remaining, minority partner, Blonder-Tongue Laboratories. Wometco Enterprises had interests in broadcasting, cable TV, bottling, automatic vending, and entertainment at that time.

In 1983 Times-Mirror Cable Telecom dissolved Spotlight, a jointly owned, pay-TV programming packager. Times-Mirror Cable Telecom was a subsidiary of Times-Mirror of Los Angeles (the publishing, paper products, commercial television broadcasting, and cable-TV firm). (The other Spotlight partners were Storen Communications Inc., Cox Communications, and Tele-Communications Inc.)

In 1983 Group W Satellite Communications (GWSC) and several regional sports networks and professional sports teams—including the Sonics Superchannel, the Wisconsin All Sports Network, Pro Am Sports, and the Baltimore Orioles baseball team, among others—joined forces to form The Sports Network, a multiple region pay-TV sports service that linked (via satellite), regional sports channels located across the nation. Group W coordinated programming from the regional sports channels, provided the wrap-around national programming and handled sales, marketing, affiliate relations, program distribution, and administration, as well as management in each region.

In 1983 Mattel Toys and Group W Productions (Westinghouse) formed a partnership to develop a first-run, syndicated television program, "He-Man and the Masters of the Universe" (based on a similarly named set of Mattel action figures). Group W's animation house, Filmation, produced the program for syndication to commercial television networks. Mattel also planned a joint venture, called Playcable, to broadcast video games to subscribers. (Mattel held the second-largest market share in video games in 1983.) Its partner in the Playcable venture was General Instrument Corp., a firm that made equipment for cable television. Users purchased a Mattel Intellivision game player and a General Instruments decoder, for a total cost of $225, to receive and use Playcable. Many other firms contemplated joint ventures to distribute video games over cable systems, including the Game Network (International Cablecasting Co.), Atari (with Activision and Philips N.V.), and Coleco (with A.T.&T.), among others. But their enthusiasm waned when it became apparent that Playcable was unsuccessful. At best, it had signed on 10,000 subscribers by 1984.

Service Broadcasting. In 1981 Group W Satellite Communications (a subsidiary of Westinghouse Electric) and ABC Video Enterprises formed a joint venture, Satellite News Channels, to provide news broadcasting services that were delivered by its parent's satellite. Its principal competitor was Cable News Network (CNN), the pioneering all-news network owned by the Turner Broadcasting System Inc. Less than a year after launching the service, Satellite News Channels was acquired by arch-rival, the Turner Broadcasting System.

In 1981 the Taft Broadcast System formed two joint-venture partnerships with Tele-Communications, Inc. (TCI), the largest U.S. operator of cable systems. The first child, TCI-Taft Cablevision Associates, acquired and operated cable systems, and the other child, Taft-TCI Programs, developed original programming and packaged existing programming from others for cable television. Taft-TCI took an equity interest in Black Entertainment Television (BET), the only cable satellite network providing black-oriented programming at that time. Four pilot programs were in production.

Pay-Per-View Programming. In 1983 Reserved Seat Video Productions (RSVP) offered its first sporting event broadcast. RSVP was a pay-per-view cable programming joint venture between ABC Video Enterprises and ESPN (at that time, a 85%-15% joint venture between Getty Oil and ABC). The venture lost $2 million, and ABC purchased Getty Oil's interest in ESPN for $202 million in 1984. (ESPN was the largest cable service at that time, reaching 30 million homes. It was also considered to be one of the more viable services.) In 1984 ABC and ESPN took a minority stake in Screen Sport, the U.K. cable television sports channel. Through it, ABC and ESPN gained coverage of British sporting events, while Screen Sport gained access to ABC's sports coverage from around the world.

In 1983 four partners—American Television & Communications Corp., Tele-Communications Inc (TCI), Group W Cable, Inc., and Caesar's World Productions, Inc.—formed an equally owned (25 percent each), pay-per-view (PPV) sporting events joint venture called EventTeleVision. Earlier, in 1981, Cox Communications (through its subsidiary, Cox Cable) and ABC Video Enterprises had formed a joint venture, FIRSTICKET, to test pay-per-view sporting events cable television services. The viability of PPV services remained uncertain through 1984.

Movie Studios and Home Video. CBS/Fox was a highly successful joint venture with operations in cable TV. It created, packaged, marketed, and distributed original products for video cassette recorders, and it operated the former CBS Studio Center film production facility—which was fully equipped to make motion pictures and television series. (CBS Studio Center was leased to outsiders, although CBS/Fox could produce original programming for television, pay-TV, and videocassettes there if it wished to do so.) CBS/Fox had also operated CBS Cable, a cultural programming service that flopped in 1982.

Twentieth-Century-Fox Film had been looking for a partner to help it to produce original, quality movies for pay-TV at prices that would be higher than the pay-TV programming packagers would pay in 1982. Fox's alliance with CBS gave it a means of reselling their films' rights for network or syndicated local-TV use and for possible release overseas. (Twentieth-Century-Fox was also engaged in a cable TV joint venture with the former head of American Television and Communications (the leading cable TV multiple systems operator), and it held a 50 percent interest in PRISM, the regional pay sports and movie service for cable systems in Philadelphia.)

Many movie studio joint ventures had been launched, cancelled, then renegotiated as the film companies realized belatedly that the tidal wave of new technologies for distributing movies was diminishing their bargaining power. In 1972 Columbia Pictures and Warner Brothers had formed a joint venture, Burbank Studios, to operate the former Warner studio and production facilities. The venture was a means of keeping production facilities from being retired so that capacity shortfalls would not develop. They also formed an international motion picture venture, Warner-Columbia.

In 1982 CBS, Columbia Pictures, and HBO formed a film company and motion picture studio, TriStar Pictures, with an initial investment of $300 million. Through TriStar, HBO was guaranteed an additional source of feature films. CBS obtained a toehold in cable TV services (and gained a source of feature films for commercial broadcasting). Columbia Pictures obtained a new source of films and an extra studio when space was scarce. (Columbia

Pictures and Gaumont S.A. had also formed a motion picture joint venture, Triumph Films, to develop additional programming for these new outlets.)

TriStar leased its motion picture studio, which it had acquired from Warner Brothers Studios, to outsiders when it was not filming its own feature length films. Although TriStar operated completely separate from its parents, it did not have its own distribution system. Its parents distributed TriStar's films through their respective distribution systems. TriStar Pictures was notable because the child was preparing to issue securities in its own right as a stand-alone entity in 1984. (After the public offering, TriStar's parents would each own a 25 percent interest in the studio.)

The most important function of the motion picture companies historically had been the distribution of films. If they lost control of distribution, they lost control of their raison d'etre.

Overseas Ventures. In 1984 Paramount, Universal Studios, and MGM/UA offered cable television programming packaging overseas through The Entertainment Network (TEN), a joint venture that included Rediffusion and Visionshire (two of the United Kingdom's largest cable system operators), Plessy (an electronics manufacturer), and Rank (a major distributor of theatrical films). Because the movie companies had sold pay-TV rights to their films in the United States to programming packagers like HBO, they did not have direct access to subscriber revenues there. (They were paid a flat licensing fee instead.) But U.S. movie companies had held back foreign rights to their films when they negotiated prices for U.S. pay-TV rights. HBO and the other big pay-TV programming packagers could not repackage their U.S. products for overseas markets without taking the movie studios as partners.

HBO, Columbia Pictures, Twentieth-Century-Fox, and CBS formed a joint venture (for a 49 percent interest) with London-based Goldcrest Films and Television, Ltd. (51 percent), but after six months, CBS withdrew from that joint venture because foreign pay-TV ventures did fit well with its other business plans. Thorn-EMI reorganized the partnership—in 1984—with Goldcrest Films and Television, HBO, Showtime, Columbia Pictures, Warner Brothers, and Twentieth-Century-Fox as partners. Thorn-EMI held a 51 percent interest in the newly formed venture. (The others held 9.6 percent each.)

Child Activities. Joint ventures in the programming and programming packaging businesses were closely coordinated with their horizontally and vertically related parents, respectively. Because the child's activities were important to parents, parents kept a relatively tight rein over the child's decisions, sometimes not permitting the child to buy the rights to a movie, for example. Not infrequently, parents' personnel managed the child's activities as well as that of its parents. In the example of ABC Video, anchor personnel were taken from commercial broadcasting assignments to revitalize the cable services.

The many programming formats that the narrowcasting medium of pay TV or cable TV permitted encouraged parents to form many joint ventures. Spider's webs of alliances pitted parents' children against each other as the networks and motion picture studios tested new media to assess which of them would be the most important distribution channels in the future.

Home Video Products

The home video industry was developed through teamwork. Japanese firms cooperated to establish standards for videotape recorders; they formed joint ventures to introduce the riskier videodisc player. Programming for the tape and disk players was provided by joint ventures and other alliances, as well.

This pattern of cooperation was scarcely surprising. Joint ventures of all types had abounded in the entertainment industry, including (1) co-production of motion pictures (Burbank Studios and Warner-Columbia, a jointly owned international programming distributor), (2) joint production of phonograph records (such as Polygram, a joint venture of N.V. Philips of the Netherlands and Siemens A.G. of West Germany, and CBS/Sony Inc., the Japan-based joint venture that produced digital audiodisks for sale in the United States), and (3) joint ownership of manufacturers of broadcast video equipment (such as Fernseh Inc., a joint venture of Bell & Howell and Robert Bosch Corp.)

Need for Joint Activities. During the 1970s, home video entertainment was still a developing industry. Technical standards had not yet been established, and there was little software (programming) for videotape recorders and videodisc players. Establishing standards was imperative in order to get programming because software producers were unwilling to incur the cost of producing disks for three or more different formats. Moreover, the distributors of the large-ticket videocassette recorders and videodisc payers were not sanguine about handling the small-ticket discs. New distribution channels were needed (like record stores to distribute software for stereo phonographs).

Choosing Partners.
Videotape Recording Systems. Compared with the history of videodisc players, that of videotape recorders is fairly straightforward. The pioneering firm (Sony) formed joint ventures to convince customers of the viability of its products. Early U.S. programming joint ventures hedged their bets concerning which videotape format would ultimately prove to be the industry standard by producing programming in both formats.

In 1973 Imperial Chemical, Ciba-Geigy, and Nippon EVR Ltd. (whose members included Teijin, Ltd., Hitachi, Ltd., Mitsubishi Electric, and

Mainichi Broadcasting System Inc.) formed EVR Systems Inc. to market electronic video recording systems in the United States and Canada. In the same year, Mitsubishi Chemical Industries Ltd. and Kalvar Corp. formed a 50%-40% joint venture, Kasei Kalvar Ltd., to engage in research, manufacturing, and distribution of vesicular film. (Cannon Inc., the exclusive distributor for Kalvar films in Japan and Southeast Asia, owned the remaining 10 percent.)

The early front runner in the videotape recorder contest was Sony with its Betamax system, and Sony used joint ventures to coax retail users into adopting its products. In 1972 Sony and Teletronix established their joint venture, ST Duplicating, to provide commercial Betamax customers with a way to duplicate tapes. In 1977 ST Duplicating offered a similar service to retail customers, permitting them to convert home movies and 35-mm slides to half-inch Betamax cassettes for playback. In 1976 Sony joined with Paramount Pictures to develop pre-recorded material (including movies and educational programming) for sale to owners of Betamax.

Sony was unseated from its position of dominance in videotape recorders when the Victor Company of Japan (JVC) introduced its Video Home System (VHS) in a configuration that was not compatible with that of Betamax. (Sony was considered to be a maverick in the Japanese electronics industry. JVC, by contrast, had technical cooperation agreements with Sharp, Hitachi, Mitsubishi, and the powerful Matsushita.)

In 1980 CBS and MGM formed a joint venture for the worldwide marketing of video cassettes and videodiscs. Both parents had film libraries that represented a vast potential for home video programming. But MGM terminated the agreement and began programming home video products on its own when CBS agreed to form a similar, 50%-50% home video joint venture with Twentieth-Century-Fox Video Corp. (CBS/Fox Co.) in 1982. (Twentieth-Century-Fox Video was one of the largest manufacturers of prerecorded videocassettes and distributors of cassettes and videodiscs at that time.) CBS and Fox each continued individually to be an independent supplier of programming for the home video operations of the joint venture, and CBS/Fox packaged the films of other motion picture studios for the home video entertainment market, as well. Pressing of videodiscs (discussed below) was done as part of the new venture in Georgia.

Paramount and MCA formed a very successful joint venture, CIC, to control distribution of motion pictures through theatrical outlets and home video distribution channels. CIC Video (its subsidiary) made and distributed Paramount and MCA products in cable, videotape, and videodisc formats outside the United States and Canada. CIC and UA/MGM formed a joint venture called UIP for theatrical distribution overseas.

In 1981 RCA and Columbia Pictures launched two successful joint ventures in the area of home video entertainment. One joint venture, RCA/

Columbia Pictures Home Video, distributed prerecorded video cassettes in the United States and Canada; the other joint venture, RCA/Columbia Pictures International Video, distributed them overseas. Bell & Howell/Columbia Picture Video Services was formed in 1981 to combine the videocassette duplication business of Bell & Howell with Columbia Pictures' EUE/Screen Gems Division videocassette duplication and editing facilities. The RCA joint ventures in videocassette programming and packaging were quite successful, as was the Bell & Howell videotape postproduction joint venture with Columbia Pictures.

Videodisc Players. The history of the videodisc player is a more tortured one than that of the videotape recorder. Many firms used joint ventures to try to develop markets for the videodisc home entertainment system. Three configurations that were *not* compatible with each other fought to become the industry standard. These included an inexpensive grooved capacitance technology (CED, which was championed by RCA), a grooveless capacitance technology (VHD, championed by Matsushita, General Electric, Thorn-EMI, and JVC), and a more expensive laser optical technology (championed by Philips N.V.).

In 1974 Germany's Telefunken and British Decca formed a joint venture, TED, based on the capacitance videodisc technology. Their prototype system played ten-minute disks priced at approximately twenty cents each. Also in 1974, MCA Inc. (parent of Universal Studios) and Philips N.V. formed joint ventures to market the laser optical videodisc player and develop compatible plastic disks. (Both firms had been developing similar technologies independently. Videodisc players seemed to be so risky that they thought it best to pool their knowledge and to work together to establish standards.) MCA was developing disk technology and Philip's Polygram planned to press them in Europe. Philips (with its subsidiary, Magnavox) concentrated on developing hardware. In 1977 MCA also formed a joint venture with Pioneer Electronics Corp. (a special acoustics equipment manufacturer) called Universal Pioneer Corp. to manufacture videodisc players in Japan.

By 1975 MCA had licensing agreements to use programming developed by Paramount, Warner Brothers, and Twentieth-Century-Fox with its videodisc technology. The arrangements were speculative, since it was not clear that videodisc technology would be successful. But firms licensed their titles, nevertheless, in case videodiscs ever did achieve economic volumes. (Ever pragmatic, MCA licensed RCA to use its film programming with CED videodisc technology while it raced to develop rival technology.) In 1978 MCA Discovision opened a plant to press disks for the Magnavox (Philips) laser optical videodisc player (which had not yet been introduced).

IBM had also been researching the laser optical videodisc system since 1975 because, in the long run, videodisc systems were expected to be used in home computers and home information systems, particularly as electronic component manufacturers developed laser-optic memory devices. (A smaller potential market for videodisc players was envisioned for industrial applications, where they could be used to train employees, teach students, demonstrate, and sell products, as well as to store and retrieve information.)

In 1979 IBM purchased half of MCA's videodisc technology interests, thereby forming a 50%-50% joint venture, DiscoVision Associates (DVA), to develop, manufacture, and market videodisc players and their discs. IBM pooled its patents, technology, and cash with those of MCA. (Universal-Pioneer made industrial videodisc players for DiscoVision in Japan. Distribution of entertainment disks was handled by a separate MCA business unit.) In 1980 MCA transferred its 50 percent ownership in Universal-Pioneer Corp. to DiscoVision, giving IBM a 25 percent interest in Universal-Pioneer, and DiscoVision signed a cross-licensing agreement with Philips N.V. for an exchange of licenses on patents relating to videodisc players. DVA devoted research to the use of videodisc players as *both* storage peripherals for computers (to give operators direct access to any of the 54,000 video frames stored on either disk side using two-way digital communications) and as entertainment medium.

In 1982 DiscoVision Associates decided to suspend further R&D and marketing activities within the joint venture.The child's assets were sold to Pioneer, and all obligations of the survivor were lifted. Pioneer closed the U.S. videodisc manufacturing plant and transferred disk production to a plant in Japan. DVA also sold its 50 percent interest in Universal Pioneer to its partner, Pioneer Electric. DVA licensed patents and transferred technology thereafter. MCA maintained its rights to the thousands of film titles in Universal's library. Pioneer Electric was allowed to license them like any other packager of home video entertainment after the child was disbanded. MCA was thought to have spent more than $100 million in trying to get DiscoVision off the ground. Sony and Thomson-CSF had each announced that industrial laser optical videodisc players would be available from them by 1982, but both of them eventually abandoned their projects.

In 1980 Matsushita Electric, Victor Company of Japan (JVC), Thorn-EMI, and General Electric (GE) formed three joint ventures to penetrate the U.S. market for videodisc systems. The ventures included a program distribution and artistic production firm (VHD Programs Inc.), a disk manufacturing company (VHD Disk Manufacturing Co.), and a videodisc player manufacturing company (VHD Electronics Co.), and they combined GE's retail distribution strengths, Thorn-EMI's programming, and Matsushita's and JVC's experience in developing and manufacturing videodisc players. The spider's web of joint ventures utilized the VHD (video high-density) formula developed by JVC. Introduction of the VHD system was hampered, however, by the group's slowness in negotiating rights to programming. To overcome this shortfall, the Matsushita/GE/Thorn-EMI consortium offered to press disks for movie studios under their own respective labels. (Control of labels was important to the programming firms who would not license their most popular titles to RCA or DiscoVision in case the market for videodisc players took off.) The U.S. venture collapsed two years later when General Electric withdrew from it.

In Europe JVC formed a VHD-format videodisc manufacturing joint venture with Thorn-EMI, Thomson-Brandt, and AEG-Telefunken in 1981. Unfortunately, uncertainties concerning the policies of the French government discouraged (or precluded) joint ventures with French firms. For example, Thomson-CSF (which is 41 percent owned by the Thomson-Brandt Group) had a joint-production agreement with TEAC Corporation of Japan to make disks and one with Minnesota Mining & Manufacturing (3M) to make videodisc players, but these ended when French workers seized shipments to partners, arguing that jobs were being exported.

In 1981, when the Matsushita/Thorn-EMI/General Electric joint venture was first formed, MCA and Thorn-EMI also formed a joint venture, MCA/Thorn-EMI Programs International, to produce programming for the home video market. Programming included both the VHD format (of Matsushita and JVC) and the optical laser format (of Philips N.V. and DVA). That same year, MCA's Universal Studios took over the U.S. theatrical distribution activities of AFD, a Thorn-EMI unit.

After Thorn's joint venture with Matsushita soured, MCA and Thorn-EMI formed another joint venture (TEM Productions), which blossomed into an entity that made programming for network television, satellite television, and theatrical distribution. Their child was given substantial autonomy to develop and distribute its programming in the most appropriate manner, even if programming was obtained through outsiders. Like an independent film studio, the child was cut loose to find the best deals available for its products. In 1984 Thorn-EMI Video Inc. (which distributed videocassettes in the United States) was absorbed in a joint venture with Home Box Office, Thorn-EMI/HBO Home Video.

By 1980 RCA Corp. had obtained more nonexclusive licenses for software titles in the CED-videodisc configuration ("SelectaVision") than any other competitor. These included films from United Artists, Paramount, Avco Embassy, and Disney. RCA had also gathered an impressive consortium of consumer electronics firms to back its SelectaVision system, including Zenith, CBS, Sanyo, Hitachi, Toshiba, Sears, and JCPenney. RCA had spared no expense in its efforts to make SelectaVision a success, but in 1984 (after absorbing $575 million in losses) RCA announced that it would stop making videodisc players. (It planned to press CED-format disks at least until 1987.)

Child Activities. For many parent firms, the manufacture of videodisc players represented a different and risky activity that was significantly different from their core of activities. Only *marketing* activities for their videodisc joint ventures were coordinated closely with parents' ongoing activities because control of distribution was close to their strategic cores.

Since the technological configuration that dominated the videotape recorder market had been developed overseas, there was little need for U.S. joint ventures except in the area of programming, and this activity was of great strategic importance to the firms that formed these ventures. Not surprisingly, these ventures were coordinated closely with their parents' activities, leaving joint-venture managers little autonomy in decision making. Videodisc players were especially conducive to joint ventures. No one partner controlled all aspects of the technology, manufacturing, and marketing skills needed to make the venture succeed. The technology was risky and costly to start up alone. A global partnership was desirable in order to penetrate several key markets simultaneously (and attain breakeven economies).

Precision Controls and Robotics. Numerical controls were used to moderate processing operations within industries such as chemical, petrochemical, pulp and paper, power metal processing, oil and gas production, and refining, among others. Numerical controls operated machine tools and other equipment electronically, according to predetermined programs. (Programmable controllers were the heart of automated factory systems. But increasingly, these were controlled with software rather than hardwired microcomputers in 1984.) Robotics use was rising in the United States, particularly within the machine tool industry, which was attempting to increase productivity and overcome shortages of skilled machinists and operators.

Robots combined mechanical, computer software, and electronics technologies. Some robots were equipped with artificial intelligence (sophisticated sensors and computer software) to respond to outside changes, make judgments, communicate with human operators, and process information. Robots could be programmable or nonprogrammable. Programmable robots were capable of moving robot hands to any position in the workspace. (Nonprogrammable robots were capable only of a small, finite number of movement positions without mechanical readjustment.)

Need for Joint Activities. Joint ventures (and other forms of cooperative strategy) were used to respond to customers' demands for more sophisticated products and a broader range of services. Some alliances were created to serve large, multinational customers wishing to standardize their instrumentation in several plant locations. Others were undertaken to acquire capabilities to make products that used new technologies that parents did not control in-house. Licensing was commonplace because technology grew obsolete so rapidly.

Development of effective numerically controlled machine tools and robots required the assistance of electronics firms and software houses. Computer companies were logical allies for this affiliation. Many of the firms that possessed the necessary knowledge were European or Japanese. Consequently, a variety of licensing and joint-venture agreements with diverse partners occurred in the early 1980s.

Choosing Partners.

Precision Controls. In 1980 Monsanto and GEC Marconi Process Control Ltd. and International Control Valves Ltd. (both divisions of General Electric Ltd. of England) formed a 67%-33% joint venture, Fisher Controls International, to make control valves and regulators. The venture included an expanded offering of electronic and pneumatic field instrumentation, control room instrumentation, and digital control systems, as well as process control instrumentation for sale to the energy and processing industries. (Monsanto's Fisher Controls subsidiary made control valves and process controls. It was interested in moving into the electronics fields where Marconi already had a worldwide reputation. General Electric Co. Ltd.'s strength was in process controls and instrumentation, particularly in electronics.)

General Electric Co. Ltd. (GEC) had little stake in the U.S. process control market prior to the joint venture, and Fisher was weak in Europe. Together, they combined marketing strengths, particularly when dealing with multinationals headquartered in the United States with subsidiaries in Europe. The instrumentation and process control side of the joint venture was run by GEC (because it had the electronics expertise), and the control valve side was managed by Monsanto's Fisher subsidiary. In 1981 Fisher Controls ranked number two in sales of process control equipment, surpassed only by Honeywell.

Factory Automation, Numerical Controls and Robotics. Metal parts can be fabricated using machine tools. *Computer numerical control* units (CNC) contained a minicomputer and memory capacity for hardwired programs. *Direct numerical controls* (DNC) made flexible machining systems and flexible transfer lines possible. (DNC was a fundamental part of the growing area of computer-aided design and computer-aided manufacturing (CAD/CAM) activity covered in chapter 9. With direct numerical control units, a central computer ruled over a hierarchy of computers, machining centers, single-purpose machine tools, materials handling equipment, and robots to run much of a manufacturing system.)

In 1981 the major U.S. CNC manufacturers were General Electric (which dominated the medium-price numerical control market with a market share of 13 percent of the U.S. machine tool market), Allen Bradley Corp. (which catered to larger machines requiring more sophisticated and expensive numerical controls with a market share of 16 percent), Autonumerics, Inc., the Bendix Industrial Controls Group (including Warner & Swasey with a 6 percent share of the U.S. machine tool market), Cincinnati-Milacron Inc. (with a 12 percent market share), Giddings & Lewis Electronics, Matuura, Yamazaki, and Makino. General Numeric, a joint venture of Fujitsu Fanuc and Siemens A.G., had a market share of 8 percent of the U.S. machine tool market.

Robots combined the fabrication capabilities of machine tools with the capabilities of numerical controls. Differences in robots were attributable both to mechanical flexibility and to software content. For example, relatively simple, two-axis *factory automation units* were programmable for continuous process, assembly-line operations, and their programming changed once a year (or less). Electromechanical content comprised most of their value. At the other polar extreme were robot products comprised of twice as much value in software as in mechanical and electronic content. Such robots were programmable for a different task with each use.

Although there were over sixty firms making industrial robot products in 1984, five firms represented 78 percent of the U.S. market in 1983. As the U.S. robotics industry became increasingly competitive, pioneering firms' market shares dwindled. For example, Unimation's 1983 market share of 27 percent had been 42 percent in 1980. (Cincinnati-Milacron's share decreased from 33 percent in 1980 to 20 percent in 1983; ASEA's share increased from 5 percent to 7 percent. Devilbiss's market share remained at 6 percent from 1980 to 1983, but Prab's share fell from 7 percent to 5 percent.)

In 1965 Fujitsu Fanuc gave Siemens A.G. exclusive rights to manufacture and sell its numerical control devices in Europe. In 1975 Fujitsu Fanuc engineers went to West Germany to help Siemens to develop software for CNC devices, and six Siemens engineers went to Japan to help Fanuc to develop hardware. Each parent developed its own precision controls manufacturing facility, but they shared technology and patents. In 1976 Fujitsu Fanuc and Siemens A.G. formed a joint venture, General Numeric, to sell and service numerical control devices in the United States.

In 1976 General Electric, Warner & Swasey (Bendix) and Allen-Bradley dominated the U.S. numerical controls market. Given this competitive reality, General Numeric seemed to be the best way for Siemens and Fanuc to penetrate that market. By 1977 General Numeric produced over 30 percent of all of the numerical controls installed worldwide, and by 1979 Fujitsu Fanuc was the world's largest numerical control systems builder. Both firms built U.S. facilities and coordinated General Numeric's activities between them. By 1980 General Numeric's U.S. market share rose to 8 percent.

Unimation made industrial robots for welding, foundry work, forging, metal handling, assembly, and inspection applications. Unimation was a subsidiary of Condec Corp. until it was acquired by Westinghouse Electric in 1983. Unimation robots possessed vision capability for identifying parts (for sorting or transporting) through the use of a Machine Intelligence Corp. binary vision system developed in conjunction with General Motors in the PUMA robot project.

By 1983 Unimation lead the industry with an installed base of over 4,000 robots, despite its poor profit record. Westinghouse had entered the robot business in 1982 through an exclusive five-year license with Olivetti to manufacture, sell, and service its Sigma assembly robots before it acquired Unimation. By 1984 Westinghouse was seeking equity partners to bolster Unimation's position in factory automation systems. It no longer wanted to be Unimation's only parent.

Devilbiss (owned by Champion Spark Plug) first became involved with industrial painting robots in 1974 through an agreement (with Unimation) to market the industrial robots of a European affiliate, Trallfa, in the United States. The Trallfa robots were capable of painting, welding, picking and placing parts, stapling, and hot melt- or bead flow-glueing operations and were considered extremely reliable by customers. Devilbiss took exclusive North American distribution rights for the Trallfa robots in 1976 and U.S. manufacturing rights in 1980.

In 1974 Ex-Cell-O Corp. and CKN Windsor Ltd. of England formed an exclusive manufacturing and marketing agreement whereby CKN's injection molding machines were sold under the Ex-Cell-O trade name and manufactured at the firm's XLO micromatic plant in Michigan. In 1978 the 600 Group and the Clausing Corp. formed a joint venture to distribute and market machine tools imported from the 600 Group together with Clausing's drill presses and comparators. Alba-Waldensian Inc. and Selective Electronic Co. A.B. (of Sweden) formed a joint venture, Sensitive Electronic, to distribute optoelectronic measuring devices in the United States.

In 1978 Acme-Cleveland and Leuze Electronics formed a joint venture, Namco-Leuze, to market photoelectric controls that performed control functions not possible any other way (such as detecting a missing bottle cap on a production line) in North America. Namco-Leuze was expected to manufacture these controls in the U.S. later.

In 1979 Harnischleger Corp. and Allemana Svenska Elektriska Akteibolatet (ASEA) formed a 49%-51% joint venture, ASEA Industrial Systems, to engineer, manufacture, and market industrial electrical control systems and parts. Harnischleger, which made industrial, mining, and earthmoving equipment, contributed electric control technology. It viewed the joint venture with ASEA as an important step in terms of its ability to design, manufacture, and integrate its own mechanical, structural, and electrical components. Harnischleger had been a licensee of ASEA's technology (which was recognized as being among the best in the world) since the mid-1960s.

With its technology, Harnischleger had been able to develop electrical controls into its structural and mechanical designs that contributed greatly to the acceptance of its products. Kobe Steel owned a 10 percent interest in Harnischleger in 1984.

Through its U.S. subsidiary, ASEA imported robots and specialized in the sale of complete turnkey robot installations. ASEA had obtained some of its materials handling technology when it acquired Electrolux (a large Swedish manufacturer of household appliances), which had developed robots for internal use. In Japan, ASEA manufactured welding robots.

Several U.S. and European robot manufacturers (including Unimation and Prab) had signed agreements to market their robots in Japan by 1980. Others licensed their technology for use in Japanese markets as well. For example, Prab had licensed Murata Machinery to make and sell its robots throughout the Far East. (Prab began as a supplier of scrap-handling conveyor and processing systems. Its robots were used in machine loading/ unloading, die casting, forging, and material handling. Prab used a series of licensing agreements with companies in Canada, Japan, and Europe to exploit its robot technology in those countries quickly.)

Warner & Swasey (a subsidiary of Allied Corporation's Bendix Corp.) had a very successful joint venture with Murata Machinery Company Ltd. in Japan to manufacture and sell Bendix lathes and punch press machines in Japan. (Warner & Swasey was acquired by Cross & Trecker in 1984.) In 1980, Bendix had transferred production of standard grinding and turning machines to its 50 percent owned Japanese affiliate, which delivered a typical turning machine to Bendix in Cleveland for $65,000 (about $20,000 less than it cost for Bendix to make one). Bendix's 1982 agreement with Yasakawa Electric Manufacturing Co. Ltd., which allowed it to sell three computer numerical controls and materials-handling robots, also went very well. Its joint venture with Leica Camera gave Bendix visual inspection products. Its agreement with Toyoda Machine Works Ltd. allowed Bendix to make and sell Toyoda machining centers in the United States and Canada. A 30%-70% joint venture with Comau S.p.A. (a subsidiary of Fiat) would have allowed Warner & Swasey to manufacture and sell flexible manufacturing systems in the United States and Europe, but the venture was disbanded. Comau sought a new partner as a means of entering the U.S. market, and Allied Corporation retained the 30 percent interest it had acquired in Comau even after it sold Warner & Swasey. Although Toyoda proved to be an excellent partner for Warner & Swasey, the venture was disbanded because Cross & Trecker had a rival line of products.

In 1980 Ransburg Inc. and Renault Industries Aquitementes et Techniques formed a 51%-49% joint venture, Cybotech, to develop, make, sell, and service industrial robots. Cybotech offered a line several heavy-duty servo robots for arc welding, cutting, heavy part and transport loading, among other uses—all highly programmable. In the United States, Cybotech specialized in serving the aerospace industry; its parent, Renault, had a share of over 50 percent in the French spot-welding robot market and had pursued painting and resistance welding applications through Cybotech to automate its U.S. affiliate, American Motors Corp. (AMC). In 1984 Renault's substantial losses in AMC diverted funds from its factory automation campaign. By contrast, Ransburg had accumulated the resources needed to continue R&D funding in its aerospace applications.

Cybotech had captured 5 percent of the general U.S. market for industrial robots by 1984 and was thriving in its specialized markets. By the end of the year, partners' investments in Cybotech had shifted majority ownership to Ransburg (90 percent). Earlier, Ransburg had formed a joint venture in painting robots with Tokiko to take Ransburg's technology to Tokyo. Their partnership thrived and the technology they developed surpassed that developed by Cybotech for Renault. By 1984 Ransburg used the painting robot technology developed with Tokiko in its U.S. products, rather than that developed for Cybotech's painting robot.

In 1981 General Motors and Fujitsu Fanuc formed GMFanuc Robotics to develop, manufacture, and sell flexible automation systems, a field of great interest to General Motors. General Motors had made significant contributions to robotics development earlier. For example, the PUMA robot was developed by General Motors (with Unimation) for use in automotive assembly operations. General Motors also developed its own spray painting robot (in a cooperative effort with Bendix) for use in many General Motors automotive plants. GMFanuc Robotics Corp. had enjoyed a fourfold sales increase in 1984 and was one of the few U.S. manufacturers that prospered while the rest of the robotics industry suffered.

In 1984 General Motors purchased a minority interest in three machine-vision firms: Diffracto Ltd., View Engineering Inc., and Automatix Inc. Developing machine-vision technology was considered crucial to General Motors in order to reduce its manufacturing costs. Machine vision would permit robots to see by adding sensors that allowed robots to adapt to changing conditions. These investments reinforcd the thrust of General Motors' acquisition of Electronic Data Systems (EDS), a firm that possessed technology that might be used to connect GMFanuc's factory automation devices.

Makino Milling Machine Ltd. bought a 51 percent share in LeBlond Co. (a metalworking lathe maker) in 1981, renaming the firm LeBlond Makino Machine Tool Co. By 1984 LeBlond Makino also assembled Makino-designed machining centers and sold highly automated lathes built by a West German supplier.

Acme-Cleveland developed machine tools jointly with Mitsubishi Heavy Industries of Japan in 1982. It was still struggling to incorporate CNC designs into its designs in 1984 and was moving into computer-aided design and manufacturing and robot applications through seven small affiliated companies in which Acme-Cleveland made minority investments. Acme-Cleveland also had a joint venture with Karl Hertel GmbH to make carbide cutting tools and work holding devices to be sold in the United States.

In 1983 General Electric Co. (GE) and C. Itoh & Co. announced a 60%-40% joint venture, General Electric Industrial Automation Ltd., to market GE factory automation products in Japan. General Electric had captured 1 percent of the U.S. industrial robots market by 1983. Their child marketed computer-aided design systems from Calma as well as other factory automation products (including precision controls). General Electric had licensed robot technology from Volkswagen and Allegro Robots (of Italy). An earlier manufacturing and marketing tie up with Hitachi Ltd. in 1981 had provided GE with robots. Before the General Electric alliance, Hitachi had sold robots on a private label basis to Automatix Inc.

In 1983 Allen-Bradley Co. and Olivetti SpA formed a 32%-68% joint venture, Olivetti Sistemi Automasione Industriale A.B., to market numerical controls and automation systems. Allen-Bradley contributed its European numerical controls sales and service network to its child. In 1984 Allen-Bradley put itself on the auction block and was purchased for $1.65 billion by Rockwell International, a firm involved in a variety of commercial businesses using advanced electronics technologies.

In 1984 Houdaille Industries sought access to Okuma Machinery Works Ltd.'s computer numerically controlled lathes and other new technology through a joint-production agreement. An alliance with Okuma would provide Houdaille with a quick way to offer flexible manufacturing systems.

In 1984 General Electric announced a 40%-60% joint venture with Ungermann-Bass, a network vendor based in Santa Clara, California, to develop factory-floor computer networks. Ungermann-Bass provided technology for developing the factory-based local area network (LAN) that tied together computers, robots, machine-tool devices and other products within a manufacturing complex. In 1982 General Electric introduced GEnet, a means of tying together many GE-made factory devices such as electrical motors and programmable controllers. The General Electric and Ungermann-Bass joint venture went much further than GEnet, however, because it was compatible with computers, robots, machine tools and other devices from a variety of vendors. In 1983 GE had committed $1.5 billion for its automation campaign and had earned a 1 percent market share in the robotics market.

In 1984 Caterpillar Tractor purchased a 20 percent interest in Advanced Robotics Corp. with the aim of diversifying and of applying factory automation to its own depressed industry. (Arc welding was a major and costly part of Caterpillar's manufacturing process.) Other links between heavy machinery makers and factory automation firms were expected.

Child Activities. Cooperation was necessary in all parts of the precision controls, factory automation, and robotics industry because of the long payback periods required to prove experimental technologies. The drain on parent firms' resources was immense, and industry leaders had not shown a profit after twenty years of activity. Consequently, marketing agreements, licenses, and cross-licensing agreements abounded in precision controls and robotics, yet there were relatively few joint ventures.

Balanced ownership shares in high technology joint ventures were considered desirable by parents in order to ensure that partners remained interested in and involved with the child's technological development activities. Innovation was enhanced by sending engineers from each parent to the laboratories of partners, through frequent visits to partners' plants and through on-line communications links. (Once prototype hardware was commercialized, subsequent innovations often involved software development, and this activity is discussed in chapter 9.) Parents that were closer to the market tended to control their child's operations while technology parents were involved with customer responses primarily when product modifications were required. Selling tasks were usually performed by the marketing parent's own sales force. The child's managers were granted substantial day-to-day autonomy in manufacturing activities but coordinated design and other technical details with parents closely.

Parents differed in how they controlled technology developed within their child. Ownership was a nettlesome problem because all of the child's technology originally came from its parents. Many patterns of coordination existed. Some firms let their child be the royalty-collecting intermediary when partners wanted permission to license technology that may have been contributed by another parent. But other firms prohibited any ownership of technology by their child. Some parents insisted only on a licensing right-of-first-access for technology developed by their child and allowed their child to license technology to others, as well. Other parents did not allow their child to license its knowledge to outsiders.

Having a high technology child be both supplier and customer to its parents was an especially complex situation because simply holding transactions to arm's-length relationships did not suffice in situations where quick responses were needed. Several rounds of negotiation between partners were often necessary to resolve which actions their child should undertake in the face of competition.

Summary

This chapter has examined cooperative strategies involving highly differentiated products sold to retail consumers and to sophisticated industrial customers, respectively. Although there were many cooperative arrangements in these industries, patterns regarding the use of joint ventures differed significantly between the consumer and industrial businesses. There were many joint ventures in the programming, programming packaging, and home video entertainment businesses. There were relatively few joint ventures in the high technology businesses.

The framework predicted that fewer joint ventures would be formed in precision controls, factory automation, and robotics than in cable and home video entertainment because the industrial products did not possess the potential to remain differentiated as long as those in the consumer industries. In fact, there *were* more equity joint ventures in the consumer products industries. Firms cross-licensed technology, marketed outsiders products through their respective distribution channels, and cooperated in a flurry of nonequity ventures in the industrial products industries, but they created few joint ventures. To hedge the risks that one configuration would win out over another, the framework predicted that firms would form a spider's web of alliances, as they did in cable TV programming, videotape programming, and programming packaging. This pattern was indeed observed.

Close coordination between parent and child was necessary within the industries involving differentiable products that were examined here because (1) no firm could ensure that competitors would not enter their market niche and erode their competitive advantage; (2) the child shared facilities with parents, as in the programming and programming packaging joint ventures; (3) technology was changing rapidly; and (4) prices were lower than many firms' costs. Although the cable TV programming packaging, home video, and robotics industries were embryonic (and the framework predicted that such children would need high operating autonomy), the effects of high product differentiability and rapid technological change made the need to coordinate relatively greater.

9
Joint Ventures in Service Industries

T he 160 joint ventures in the industries of this chapter involved products that were services. They were highly labor-intensive and could be differentiated in the perceptions of customers through the efforts of firms' personnel, particularly as they interacted with customers. Scale economies were attainable in these industries because certain tasks could be routinized or fixed costs could be spread for the tangible assets used in providing services.

Products were often customized for a class of customers depending on their sophistication and bargaining power over vendors of services. Software customers were more sophisticated, for example, in evaluating products than were retail financial customers. Thus the patterns found in chapter 7 concerning capital intensity and in chapter 8 concerning differentiable products are contrasted herein with those of service joint ventures where employees were more (or less) effective in satisfying customers.

Motives

Perishable Competitive Advantages

Joint ventures were a way for parents to enter these markets faster. This motivation was illustrated most graphically in the example of joint ventures to provide communication services. Referring back to the tables of chapter 1, which depicted joint-venture announcement frequency by industry, the effects of deregulation of communications services on joint venture formation become most clear. Prior to 1983, joint ventures for communications were used infrequently. As the window for offering communication systems and services opened, firms rushed in to exploit this opportunity before it evaporated. For many firms, the only way they could achieve rapid entry was through joint ventures.

I am indebted to Nida T. Backaitis and John G. Michel (both Ph.D. candidates, Columbia University) for industry background materials prepared for this chapter.

But if an industry was people-intensive, fewer opportunities existed to exploit asset-sharing economies. Instead more opportunities existed to exploit *information-sharing* advantages. It was necessary to move faster when competing in service industries because the forces driving firms to exploit their competitive advantages were highly perishable and mobile. Thus, joint ventures were needed to pioneer new service offerings and to pool knowledge faster in response to others' innovations.

Arm's-Length Coordination

The highly mobile nature of assets in service businesses affected relationships between parent and child significantly. Coordination between parent and child was higher when firms' competitive advantages resided in highly mobile assets, but less *proprietary* information was shared among them. Instead, parents either pooled their capabilities in their child (to team up against stronger competitors) and gave their child full autonomy for the activity in question; or partners used cooperative strategies that did not create a separate entity. Critical technological knowledge did not pass to the child as quickly in service industries, and the child became reluctant to pass knowledge back to its corporate parent. Legal solutions were an imperfect way to safeguard parents' intellectual property rights in service businesses, especially where employees frequently walked out on their former employers.

It was sometimes necessary (for competitive success) to inculcate a culture within the child that was substantially different from that of its parents. When parent and child developed different cultures, interactions among them inevitably grated on each organization's nerves. Shared resources, for example, provoked these cultural clashes between parent and child. If the cultural differences between potential partners were dramatic, contractual links supplanted equity ties. If partners' cultures were similar, they were more willing to enter joint ventures rather than some other form of cooperative strategy.

Joint ventures to provide services were formed to prevent firms' brightest former employees from going elsewhere, but if these employees were culturally dissimilar to their former employer, the resulting child reflected these differences. The relationship between partners—firm and former employees—was uneasy. The relationship of parent firm to entrepreneurial child functioned more like that in minority investments where parents could not influence their child's activities *directly*.

Industries

Software, Databases, and Computer-Based Management Services

Scale economy advantages were enjoyed in services that depended on computer hardware. But as the costs of software outpaced those of hardware, and as the technology of data communications improved, the distributed data-processing concept (which underlay many of the earlier software, database, and computer-based management joint ventures sketched below) grew *less* economic for large customers as a way to provide these services in-house when compared with vertical integration arrangements. Moreover, as hardware became a relatively less expensive part of the total package, programmers started their own firms with increasing frequency.

Need for Joint Activities. Many database joint ventures were established at a time when technologies were risky and demand was uncertain. Partners were needed to share these costs and risks at that time. By 1984 communications links and costs were the most expensive portion of many computer-based services, and links with partners possessing communications facilities became more desirable.

A new motivation for joint ventures had developed. In the past, computer companies had sold hardware, and their customers (or third parties) wrote the applications software. By 1984 customers wanted computer vendors to supply them with software as well as hardware. The ability of computer manufacturers to respond to this demand depended on firms' R&D capabilities, the personnel they could hire, and their abilities to fund scale up campaigns during compressed time periods. Cooperative strategies provided them with rapid access to these needed skills.

Choosing Partners.
Software. Software tells computers what to do. Its value is in the program, not the media on which it is stored. In the 1960s computer firms gave away software to sell hardware. In the 1980s the cost of programming rose so dramatically—because it was labor-intensive—that smaller computers were becoming like the razors that once sold razor blades. Software was customized (created for a specific customer) or packaged. Programs for factory automation tended to be customized. Programs for personal computers were primarily packaged.

In 1975 NCR and Control Data Corp. (CDC) formed a joint venture with NCR, Advanced Systems Laboratory, to develop software that would be compatible with its parents' mainframe computers. CDC concentrated on large mainframe products, while NCR emphasized small- and medium-size mainframes. Partners recognized the value of designing standards that would make their products compatible with each other.

By 1981 a number of computer makers had turned to joint ventures as a way to obtain packaged software for their products because ready-to-run software had become an important selling point. Large mainframe and minicomputer vendors (like Texas Instruments, Data General, Burroughs, Hewlett-Packard, and IBM) found they were unable to produce all of the software needed in-house. Joint marketing arrangements were formed with independent software companies to supplement their in-house software writing activities.

By 1984 IBM's impending dominance of the personal computer software market motivated firms like Comshare, Artificial Intelligence, and Interactive Systems to form distribution alliances with IBM. The Japanese Ministry of International Trade and Industry (MITI) backed a project to encourage Japanese computer makers to standardize their software on Unix, AT&T's operating system that worked with many kinds of software. (This effort was necessary after IBM began to withhold its source code and sued copyright infringers like Hitachi and Fujitsu.)

Computer-aided design (CAD) systems were used to draw and analyze physical structures. In 1977 Cetec Corp. (a manufacturer of computer peripherals, broadcasting equipment and industrial products) and Ferranti Ltd. (United Kingdom) formed a 25%-75% joint venture, Ferranti Cetic Graphics, to produce computer microfilm systems. As computer-aided design and computer-aided manufacturing (CAD/CAM) capabilities became more commonplace by 1981, customers began to suggest that their suppliers be equipped with CAD/CAM technology and that they swap CAD/CAM software to maintain component compatibility and standards across vendors. Firms like McDonnell-Douglas Corp.'s McAuto and Ronningen Research & Development Co. were among those leading the CAD/CAM exchange campaign.

General Electric purchased Calma (a leading CAD/CAM firm) in 1981. (That same year, Schlumberger acquired Applicon, while IBM continued to sell Lockheed CAD/CAM software on an OEM vendor basis.) General Electric formed a joint venture with C. Itoh to gain overseas market access of Calma's CAD/CAM software in 1982. After Calma failed to launch an effective computer-aided engineering (CAE) product on its own, General Electric teamed up with SDRC (through a minority interest and joint venture) to gain access to CAE software.

Computer-aided engineering workstations simulated electronic prototypes by relying on stored information about electrical characteristics of the components represented on computer screens by symbols. The CAE business was nonexistent in 1981; by 1984 it had become a $200 million industry. It had the potential to replace some hardware businesses—such as the logic analyzer used to test the internal operations of electronic components, for example—and to reduce design time for prototypes by as much as 90 percent. Interest in developing CAE software was intense. Twelve of the eighteen members of the Microelectronics and Computer Technology (MCC) joint venture (described in chapter 10) sponsored joint research to develop faster ways of building very large scale integrated circuits (VLSI).

In 1981 Honeywell and SESA (of France) formed a joint venture to offer a packet-switching network in the United States. SESA was a systems engineering firm that specialized in "packet-switched" data communications networks.

In 1984 Cox Enterprises Inc. purchased a minority interest in Creative Software. Cox owned twenty newspapers and anticipated circulating them to subscribers through computers.

In 1984 General Motors purchased Electronic Data Systems (EDS), a computer service firm that specialized in streamlining chaotic computer systems. General Motors was a major user of CAD and CAM systems, but its systems were incompatible and not integrated. Each of its robotic centers or computer systems stood alone. One product that emerged from General Motor's integration efforts was the development of a manufacturing automation protocol (MAP), a set of standard communications rules that were devised in consultation with other computer-assisted manufacturing users. In 1984 General Motors announced that its computer equipment vendors would have to observe the MAP standard or lose the General Motors account. With that sort of an incentive, the development of software standards for manufacturing operations was expected to be accelerated.

Similar integration efforts were afoot in the banking industry. In 1982, thirty banks contributed technical staff (and funding) to Anacomp Inc. to create an integrated system for banking to satisfy a plethora of needs for remote-access services, more efficient back-office operations, updating services to meet changing regulations, and other integrating services. By 1984 Anacomp had lost $90 million and had not yet delivered its integrated product.

By 1984 artificial intelligence (AI) was viewed by many firms as being the next frontier in software development. Merrill Lynch and its partners backed Inference Corp., one of many fledgling AI software firms. Schlumberger developed its proprietary artificial intelligence system in-house. More joint ventures in artificial intelligence were expected later among firms that had to catch up with the pioneers.

Databases. On-line database services offered information held in computer files to subscribers for a fee. Users of on-line databases needed a terminal (that is, a CRT or a hard-copy terminal) in order to be able to communicate with the computer containing the information and a modem to interface with the computer itself. Demand for database services was highly dependent on the terminal population (regular terminals, personal computers, and videotext terminals) and on a well-developed telecommunications system (discussed below).

In 1974 Dow Jones & Co. and Bunker-Ramo Corp. formed a joint venture to introduce the Dow Jones News/Retrieval service. At that time, a joint venture made sense because a host computer system constructed locally would cost over $2.5 million (including the land purchase or lease, construction and start up costs, hardware/software, personnel, and so forth necessary to make the new child facility operational). When personal computers became commonplace and could be linked to these information sources, the economics of ventures changed. Dow Jones took control of its on-line service to offer it over cable communications systems in 1983 in a joint venture with Group W.

In 1980 Automatic Data Processing Inc. (ADP) and Townsend-Greenspan & Co. formed a joint venture, Econalyst, to provide clients with a wide range of Townsend-Greenspan economic forecasts and reports on the U.S. economy. Customers accessed the service through computer terminals (supplied by ADP's data-processing subsidiary) that were installed in their offices. Historical databases were used in analysis and forecasting. Econalyst enabled users to receive economic information and forecasts and to assess the effects of economic charges on their businesses.

In 1983 AT&T and Wang announced a joint venture into electronic publishing. Wang had been buying the electronic publishing rights to various reference standards such as dictionaries and Roget's Thesauraus. AT&T owned the Yellow Pages directories, which it could offer to its service venture.

Computer-Based Management Services. Computer-based management systems included services developed for specialized customers (or vertical markets) such as dentists, hardware stores, warehouses, or other businesses requiring customized software and access to specialized databases. Firms like Triad Corporation formed joint ventures to gain market access by providing turnkey inventory control systems for vertical markets, such as dental offices. Control systems like Triad's incorporated the requirements of different insurance reimbursement programs, for example, to aid physicians' offices in filling out forms.

In 1970 Xerox Data Systems and Data Architects formed a joint venture to offer Dai-Secure, a computer programming system for automating the entire back office of a stock brokerage firm. The distributed data processing version of the service was offered to small- and medium-size brokerage firms that could not justify the acquisition of large computer-based stand-alone systems on the basis of their sales volumes. The dedicated version was offered to larger brokerage firms and financial institutions.

In 1976 Standard-Alliance Industries and Schiller Industries formed a joint venture, ScanVeyor Systems, to design and sell automated data collection and handling systems for use in the magazine and paperback distribution industry, as well as in automated warehousing systems and in automated manufacturing processes.

In 1980 Reynolds & Reynolds and Baxter Travenol Laboratories Inc. tried to form a joint marketing venture to sell computerized management systems to U.S. hospitals. (Baxter Travenol sold intravenous solutions and hoped to provide automatic reordering of their products within the inventory control programs. Reynolds & Reynolds made and sold computer systems and services.) The venture fell through and Reynolds & Reynolds went on alone.

In 1980 Quotron Systems Inc. (proprietor of Quotron information services), American Information Development (a software concern), and Continental Corp. (an insurance holding company) formed a highly successful joint venture, Insurnet Inc., to provide data processing services—including word processing and communications—to independent insurance agents. Their child acquired the business assets of American Information Development (making it a fade-out venture for that parent) and used Quotron's telecommunications network and computers to establish an electronic interface between agents and insurance companies.

In 1981 Informatics Inc. (a marketer of software, professional services, and information processing services) and Management Analysis Co. (a management services company) formed a 51%-49% joint venture, Infodynamics Inc., to provide computer-based information management systems and support services to the power industry. Its parent, Informatics, provided various computer-related products and services to industry and government, while the child, Infodynamics, offered software systems development, on-site implementation services, network service center processing support, and turnkey hardware.

In 1981 Computer Sciences Corp. (a provider of data processing management and technical services) and BSL Technology (manufacturer of medical computer systems) formed a joint venture to create and sell a clinical laboratory system, Clindata 7100, to be used as a component of Computer Science's hospital information system.

By 1984 access to markets had become more important to success in selling computer-based management systems than proprietary operating systems. Computer-based management systems were becoming increasingly similar because programmers were each able to improve on the previous generation of programs sold by their competitors.

In 1984 IBM and Merrill Lynch formed a joint venture, International MarketNet, to build and operate a computerized market information service for brokerage firms. Using windowing software, the service allowed personal computer users to (1) follow up-to-the-minute stock quotes while calling up (2) research reports from mainframe computers and (3) producing investment reports for clients, simultaneously. Merrill Lynch was the largest user of Quotron services in 1984; its MarketNet services would compete with Quotron's computerized stock market information service. IBM was also developing brokerage services with Automatic Data Processing in 1984; its child also competed against Quotron and MarketNet. IBM, Merrill Lynch, and the Public Broadcasting System were developing a teletext system to deliver financial data.

In 1985 Lotus Development Corp., a leading personal computer software house, engaged in a series of start-up ventures in software. Lotus sought to ally itself with companies that could develop promising new computer programs rather than rely completely on in-house development. It made minority investments in some of these ventures. Lotus and UST Capital Corp. invested $1 million in Arity Corp., one such start up software house that was founded by four former Lotus employees. Lotus Development formed a joint development venture with Iris Associates to create a new line of integrated business software. Lotus received licenses and the right to market and support Iris's products.

Child Activities. Parallel facilities had been a major impediment to continued software writing relationships, while firms refused to market outsiders' software that competed with their own products. This jealousy was compounded when market access became most important to software products' success. Few firms wished to share this access with rival products or with duplicate products developed by their children.

Joint ventures were given authority to package hardware and software provided by parents. Arm's-length buyer–seller relationships ascertained the economic viability of joint ventures, and many of them were short-lived, given these jealousies. The highly competitive, marketing-intensive business environment of 1984 changed all of this. Even IBM was forming a spider's web of joint ventures in software and other services.

Communications Services

Communications services included: telephone service, telex, fascsimile, teleconference, data transmission, cellular radio telephone, paging, telecast, private networks, electronic mail, and packet switching, as well as cable communications, teletext, and videotex services. By 1984 product life cycles were shorter, and competition was becoming keener—in part due to deregulation and in part due to successes in marrying telecommunications with data processing. Joint ventures were necessary in telecommunications because of (1) the convergence of computers and telecommunications; (2) shorter product lives driven by rapid technological improvements; (3) huge R&D expenditures made by ongoing and new competitors; (4) intensification of global competition; (5) deregulation of telecommunications; (6) expectations concerning a boom in the office automation equipment industry; and a (7) potential breakdown of trade barriers as a result of technological changes and political activities.

Need for Joint Activities. Satellite communications changed the minimum efficient scale for competitors because with them, distances no longer mattered. (The cost of delivery services was the same within a radius of 9,000 miles.) Sharing of satellite capacity was mandatory for almost every player, except AT&T, because of the large volume of traffic that one satellite could handle.

Choosing Partners.

Satellite Communications. Satellites were costly and risky, costing $25 million each plus $30 million to launch in the 1970s. In addition to their substantial capital costs to build and launch, if they were launched unsuccessfully, owners lost the "bird" itself. Because the life of a satellite was unknown in the 1970s, owners could not evaluate the riskiness of offering satellite communications services. When the Federal Communications Commission (FCC) asked for applications to launch communications satellites, it was flooded with proposals for joint ventures.

Satellite Business Systems originated in 1971 as a 50%-50% joint venture called MCI Lockheed Satellite Corp. MCI Communications Corp. (representing sixteen affiliated carriers) and Lockheed joined forces to build and operate a $168 million domestic satellite communications network. Communications Satellite Corp. (COMSAT) joined the venture in 1972 (by acquiring an equal interest from the venture's ongoing parents). Joint venture participation appeared to be the only way that COMSAT could be involved in domestic satellite activities in 1972, due to an FCC policy that prohibited AT&T and COMSAT from entering alone.

In 1974 COMSAT General and IBM proposed to take over CML Satellite because MCI Communications and Lockheed Aircraft were encountering financial difficulties. The FCC refused their request until they found a third partner, Aetna Life & Casualty Insurance. Complaints from (1) RCA's domestic satellite subsidiary, American Communications Inc., (2) Western Union Telegraph Co., and jointly by (3) American Satellite Corp. and Fairchild Industries, Inc. delayed the joint venture's operations until 1981. The COMSAT-Aetna-IBM joint venture conducted intracompany communications experiments with Rockwell International, Texaco, Montgomery Ward, and others while it was awaiting permission to begin commercial operations. Losses accumulated as the years passed, and by 1982 the SBS partners had contributed $591 million.

In 1984 COMSAT agreed to sell its interest in Satellite Business Systems (SBS) to its joint-venture partners, IBM and Aetna Life & Casualty. SBS had suffered heavy losses that COMSAT could not afford. It continued to use SBS's satellites under previous contracts.

In 1973 Western Union reduced its interest in American Satellite, a 50%-50% joint venture with Fairchild Industries, to 20 percent when it declined to invest any more capital in the venture. By 1978 American Satellite had established the first wideband digital data transmission service via domestic satellite for the Defense Meteorological Satellite Program. Its future satellite transmission capacity was assured through a 20 percent ownership interest in Western Union's WESTAR satellite system. American Satellite also had the right to use up to 50 percent of the commercial capacity of the tracking and data relay satellite system (TDRSS) being built by SPACECOM (described below).

In 1979 Fairchild Industries had sold half of its interest in American Satellite to Continental Telecom because Fairchild could not handle the funding requirements associated with the rapid growth it anticipated in satellite communications services by itself, given Fairchild's other expansion plans. By 1984 American Satellite operated the largest U.S. transceiver satellite communications network with more than 100 earth stations in operation, under construction, or under contract. Unlike Satellite Business Systems, American Satellite earned a modest profit for its parents.

SPACECOM, a joint venture of Western Union (50 percent), Fairchild Industries (25 percent), and Continental Telecom (25 percent), depended primarily on government contracts for satellite communications services. SPACECOM designed, constructed, and operated the tracking and data relay satellite system (TDRSS) for NASA. Capacity on the TDRSS satellite was also leased to commercial users. In 1983 Fairchild and Continental Telecom acquired Western Union's interest in SPACECOM, and the system was reserved exclusively for NASA's use.

Oak Industries had several communications services joint ventures. As chapters 7 and 10 explain, Oak Industries' increasing joint-venture activities reflected its commitment to the greater growth and profit promised by new markets. Oak tended to choose privately held or foreign firms as its partners. As a manufacturer of communications equipment, its move into communications services seemed like a logical diversification step. Oak's new emphasis on services included an over-the-air subscription television service, commercial television broadcasting, satellite network communications, a multipoint distribution pay television service, and a financing service for firms in the communications industry. Thus Oak Industries was involved in both the hardware and software for communications services through its spider's web of joint ventures.

In 1977 Oak, Microband National Systems, and Satellite Network Systems formed an equally owned joint venture, Satellite Network, Inc. (SNI), to operate a ground distribution system for satellite communications. Oak supplied converters for cable television, equipment for MDS systems, JV tuners, switches, crystals, potentiometers, controls, and materials for the electronics industry. Its 50 percent owned subsidiary, Oak Broadcasting Systems, Inc., and Chartwell Communications formed a 51%-49% joint venture, National Subscription Television (NST) in 1977. Oak had developed much of the technology utilized by NST, including the decoder, the equipment for broadcasting scramble signals and the related computer system. (The success of the NST joint venture resulted in the partners' separating to pursue these services at their own respective paces.) In 1977 Oak Industries used a joint venture, Multipoint-Texas Co., to determine the potential of the emerging multipoint distribution communications technology by providing pay-TV service to large apartment buildings in Houston. Oak was a minority partner in the venture and maintained that position while determining when and how future involvement in multipoint distribution systems might be profitable. Oak supplied the decoder equipment as well as the scrambler equipment for this market.

In 1979 Oak Industries formed a 50%-50% joint venture with Capital Cities Communications, Inc. to purchase from Video 44 a 49 percent interest in Chicago television station, WSNS. When that deal fell through, Oak entered the joint venture with Video 44 on its own and converted the station to a partial pay-TV format (like NST). Oak Industries also took a 65 percent interest in a subscription TV (STV) venture in the Dallas/Fort Worth area. In 1980 Oak and Walter E. Heller International Corp. formed a very successful joint venture, Heller-Oak, to provide financing services for the communications industry.

In 1981 Satellite Business Systems (SBS) and Tymnet (a national and international value-added carrier owned by Tymshare, a subsidiary of McDonnell-Douglas, that offered intercity packet-switched communications services) requested permission from the FCC to establish digital termination systems (DTS) networks in fifty cities by 1987. DTS rates were expected to be much lower than those charged for digital wideband offerings such as AT&T's Dataphone Digital Service (DDS). (This service paralleled one that SBS planned to offer on its own. Moreover, Tymnet and SBS proposed to use virtually the same technology in their respective wide-band, local distribution networks.)

In 1981 subsidiaries of MA/Com and Aetna Life & Casualty Insurance formed a partnership, LDD, for the purpose of providing transmission equipment for the local distribution of business communications. The first phase, conducted in conjunction with the SBS and Tymnet test, included the development and demonstration of the technical, practical, and commercial viability of a local data distribution system.

COMSAT General and AT&T had long held equal shares in the U.S. earth stations used by the International Telecommunications Satellite Organization (INTELSAT), a consortium of 109 member nations whose satellites carried most international telephone and television transmissions. In 1983 SBS and the international division of British Telecom offered joint transatlantic services, using the satellite facilities of INTELSAT. The venture was created in response to requests from several customers (including IBM) for transatlantic wide-band channels for data communications, high-speed electronic mail, and video teleconferencing. SBS also filed for permission to form a similar international venture with ITALCABLE (Italy).

In 1983 Satellite Business Systems (SBS) and Geosource formed a joint venture, Geosource/SBS Communications, to provide communications services from the Arctic to Houston for the oil industry. Geosource provided its expertise in erecting structures in regions with harsh weather. SBS provided its communications expertise. In 1984 Aetna Life & Casualty sold its Geosource interest to Gerhard Industries in exchange for Gerhard stock.

In 1982 American Satellite Co. (the child of Continental Telecom and Fairchild) and Tandem Computers formed a joint venture to develop, market, and implement INFOSAT, the first fail-safe satellite data transmission system for continuous on-line data processing. Also in 1982 American Satellite formed a partnership with Mitel to establish a specialized new carrier, providing switched, long-distance voice, data, and video conferencing services via satellite. American Satellite formed an agreement with Trans-Canada Telephone System to provide transborder satellite communications services into Canada.

National Public Radio (NPR) was entering a variety of joint ventures in 1982 in order to find new sources of funding for its nonprofit broadcast operations. It formed a joint venture with National Information & Utilities to build a nationwide data communications network called INC Telecommunications. NPR and Mobile Communications Corp. of America (a large paging concern that covered thirty-seven cities in fourteen states) formed a 40%-60% joint venture, National Satellite Paging, Inc., to provide nationwide paging services. The child offered satellite paging through local radio common carriers (RCCs) that subscribed to the service. (Between 10 and 30 percent of the 1.3 million paging service subscribers were expected to want nationwide paging services in 1982.) In 1982 Field Enterprises and Paging Network, Inc. formed a joint venture to provide telecommunications services. The owners of Field Enterprises liquidated the firm, and Paging Network acquired its partner's interests.

In 1983 Merrill Lynch and Western Union formed a 60%-40% joint venture, Teleport Communications, to build and operate a satellite communications service on Staten Island. Financing, land, right of way, and buildings were provided by the Port Authorities of New York and New Jersey to create the office park, which provided high capacity, multiple-access data-, voice- and video-communications services. Teleport Communications was expected to become the information processing back office of the New York City financial community. Its satellite port was connected with offices in New Jersey and New York through a fiber optic network that connected with telephone and television coaxial cables.

United Satellite Communications was a joint venture formed in 1983 between United Satellite Television, Prudential Insurance (40 percent, rising later to 51.9 percent), General Instrument (which supplied $600 million equipment), and Francesco Galesi, chairman of Galesi-Corp., a closely held real estate investment concern. United Satellite Communications Inc. (USCI) was responsible for marketing, installing, servicing, and programming a new satellite system in 1983. General Instrument hoped to install earth stations on roofs of houses to receive USCI programming.

Satellite Television Corp. (STC) was owned by COMSAT General. In 1984 COMSAT and CBS discussed opportunities in direct-broadcast satellite (DBS) program packaging. The primary purpose of their talks was to find other potential partners and ascertain the start-up costs of such ventures. COMSAT announced a five-channel, low-power direct-broadcast satellite service for late 1984, and Satellite Television Corp. (STC) announced a DBS service for the eastern United States with national expansion by 1986.

In 1984 several firms that had intended to launch direct-broadcast satellite services backed down, including the STC-CBS direct-broadcast satellite joint venture. CBS had also intended to launch a high-powered direct-broadcast satellite, but it backed away from that project in 1984 (as did Western Union and RCA Corp.). COMSAT's Satellite Television Corp., one of the few firms that still intended to launch DBS service, discussed a merger with the other DBS service provider, United Satellite Communications (USCI) in 1984, but that also fell through.

In 1983 many firms planned to use satellites to offer a variety of services, and a mad scramble erupted among competitors to get the best orbital slots, best programming, and other advantages. If all of the announced services were actually offered, there would be thirty-nine channels of DBS TV available in 1984. It was scarcely surprising that some of the announced joint ventures got cold feet by the end of 1984.

In 1983 COMSAT and Intercontinental Hotels formed a joint venture, Intelmet, to provide international satellite communications services. Communications Satellite (COMSAT) and Holiday Inns formed a joint venture, Hi-Net Communications, to offer pay-TV services and teleconferencing by satellite. Neither venture went forward. In early COMSAT's Satellite Television Corp. (STC) also cancelled all plans to launch DBS services.

In 1984 COMSAT decided to sell its interest in Satellite Business Systems (SBS) to its partners. SBS posted a loss of $123 million on 1983 revenues of $142 million and invested capital that exceeded $1 billion. IBM and Aetna wanted to invest up to $1 billion more in SBS to expand its long-distance service to a total of 200 cities by 1990. The joint venture was reconfigured to give IBM 60 percent of the child's equity.

Early in 1985 General Motors (GM) indicated that it would consider selling communications services to outsiders. The combination of GM's and EDS's telecommunications networks gave the firm substantial excess capacity.

Cable Communications. In the late 1970s, joint ventures in cable television systems proliferated in markets of all sizes. The growth in demand for cable services stemmed from the fact that it could provide a multitude of channels and therefore many viewing options to television homes. The growth in joint ventures was also due to the scale economies of cable television systems.

Firms carved out empires in the fragmented cable television industry piece by piece, regional franchise by regional franchise, until they had attained a critical mass of franchises. But as they did so, customers demanded increasingly favorable terms, making the creation of cable systems increasingly expensive. A shakeout among cable operators seemed to be inevitable by 1983 because local authorities exerted such bargaining power over cable companies that they could demand high percentages (89 percent) of revenues for themselves and low subscription fees for their residents. By 1984 cable companies had to "buy" their way into major markets.

Cablecom and Century Colorado Corp. were both joint ventures, owned in part by Time Inc.'s American Television and Communications. Its partners were Cablecom-General Inc. and Century Communications, respectively. In 1974 Cablecom's wholly owned subsidiary, Vumore-Video Corp. of Colorado, was sold to Century-Colorado Corp. in a typical transaction between cable companies that were trying to stitch together a patchwork quilt of regional franchises to attain scale economies. By 1983 American Television and Communications had over 2 million subscribers as a result of its successful "clustering" strategy. (A clustering strategy enabled firms to reduce costs by hooking up a string of isolated small systems to a computer and other centralized equipment. Following their acquisitive clustering phases, cable companies often pursued a consolidation phase.)

Tele-Communications Investments Inc. was created in 1977 by Tele-Communications, Inc. (TCI) and Kaufman & Broad, Inc., a life insurance and housing company, to consolidate TCI's cable TV investments. The financing arrangement permitted TCI to acquire more cable TV systems to expand its existing systems of cable TV and common carrier microwaves. TCI concentrated almost exclusively on buying and running cable systems. (As chapter 8 explains, TCI's joint ventures provided programming).

By 1981 Tele-Communications, Inc., had become the largest operator of cable systems in the United States. Its spider's web of reciprocal joint ventures with Taft Broadcasting gave both firms a competitive edge in the scrappy cable television market. TCI-Taft Cablevision Associates acquired, developed, and operated cable television systems, while Taft-TCI Programs developed programming to transmit over its parents' systems and for sale to other cable operators. The joint ventures combined Taft's experience in commercial broadcasting and program production with TCI's vast experience in operating cable systems that served 1.9 million subscribers in forty-three states. TCI-Taft Cablevision Associates acquired its first cable system in January 1982, using a clustering scheme whereby it purchased several adjacent cable systems in Michigan and Arkansas and subsequently in other regions.

In 1982 TCI formed a 50%-50% joint venture with Knight-Ridder, TKR Cable Co., to acquire, develop, and operate cable television systems. By the end of 1982, the TKR systems had a total of 91,000 subscribers and 1,888 miles of plant in place. In 1983 Knight-Ridder developed its cable systems fifteen-year franchise to serve Long Beach, California, and was building a $32 million, 112 channel system.

In 1983 Tele-Communications (TCI) and E.W. Scripps formed a joint venture, TeleScripps Cable, to acquire and develop cable TV systems. TCI managed the child, initially, with the intention of making it a stand-alone cable operation by mid-1984.

In 1981 Rogers Cablesystems (a Toronto cable TV firm) and United Artists Communications (a movie exhibition concern) formed a 51%-49% joint venture called Rogers UA Cable Systems (formerly UA-Columbia Cablevision) by outbidding Knight-Ridder and Dow Jones. (Dow Jones owned 25 percent interest in Continental Cablevision, a privately held Boston firm founded in 1964.) In 1983 Rogers Cablesystems and United Artists Communications split their interests in Rogers UA Cable Systems. Their child had 600,000 subscribers in 16 states and revenues exceeding $100 million per year at that time. Its name reverted to United Artists Cablesystems Corp., and no reason was given publicly for the dissolution of what appeared to be a profitable joint venture.

In 1984 General Electric Cablevision (a subsidiary of General Electric Co.) was folded into United Artists Cablesystems Corp. (a subsidiary of United Artists Communications Inc.) to create a 37%-63% joint venture, the United Artists Cablesystems Corp. The sale of General Electric's cable television system was viewed by observers as a means of divesting the business unit incrementally to a buyer that could not afford GE's full price. (It was also a way of focusing GE's efforts on businesses that were closer to its strategic core.)

In 1982 United Cable Television and Tribune Cable Communications Co., a subsidiary of Tribune Co. (of Chicago), created a 50%-50% joint venture, United-Tribune Cable, to serve the cable TV franchise for California's greater Sacramento area. The child, United-Tribune Cable, also pursued cable TV franchises in suburban communities in the Washington, D.C., Los Angeles, Sacramento, Minneapolis, Detroit, and Baltimore areas.

In 1983 Viacom Cable Television participated in an experiment with Satellite Business Systems (SBS) to transmit and receive financial data via satellite between San Francisco and New York. A sister business unit, Viacom World Wide, Ltd., formed an agreement with Visionshire Cable, Ltd. in 1983 to provide it with a broad range of cable television services.

In 1977 Warner Communications first tested QUBE (its two-way cable television service). Unlike passive cable television services that offered only news, movies, and educational programming, QUBE permitted viewers to participate in programming by punching buttons on a console. (QUBE was not yet a true videotex service, however, because it did not offer home shopping, banking, information retrieval, and electronic mail services in 1977).

The apparent success of QUBE outstripped its parent's abilities to fund its growth adequately, and so in 1979 Warner Communications sold a 50 percent interest to American Express, thereby forming Warner-Amex. The child constructed and operated cable systems that provided video programming and other services to residential and commercial subscribers, including satellite broadcasts of its programming. But these expenditures for capital-intensive assets and major franchise-building campaigns in metropolitan areas created short-term losses for Warner-Amex in 1980.

By 1982 Warner-Amex reached 1.2 million households with 147 systems in 27 states and 8 major cities. It introduced a new QUBE III home console for its two-way cable services that was capable of handling more channels of programming plus interactive transactions. By 1983 Warner-Amex had 1,362,000 subscribers, but it had taken on more than $700 million in debt and lost well over $100 million through its strategy of pursuing costly big-city franchises because Warner-Amex was the only big cable system operator that continued to woo them. Warner-Amex had rushed in to meet the demands of powerful cities when rival cable operators backed away and promised customers too many services at prices that were too low. By 1984 Warner-Amex was in trouble, and it cut back on ninety minutes of interactive programming planned for QUBE. Contracts were renegotiated in Milwaukee, while Warner-Amex tried to sell its St. Louis, Dallas, and Chicago franchises. For example, Tele-Communications, Inc. took Warner-Amex's Pittsburgh franchise.

In early 1985 Warner Communications and American Express Co. were seeking the means to break up or dispose of Warner-Amex, following months of streamlining their child to make it profitable. Warner-Amex owned a 67 percent interest in MTV Networks, Inc., which was valued near $225 million as well as cable subscriptions valued near $800 million. Termination of the joint venture was provided for under a "Russian roulette" buy-out clause, but its execution was deterred by a curious exit barrier. Neither parent seemed to want the child.

Voice Communications. Deregulation injected adrenaline into the voice communications business, as firms as diverse as General Motors and Eastman Kodak announced their intentions to provide communications services. In 1982 Western Union held a 50 percent interest in Airfone, Inc., a joint venture to provide an air-to-ground telephone service on commercial airlines. Continental Telephone filed applications to offer cellular mobile radio service and joined Advanced Mobile Phone Service, Inc. (a wholly owned subsidiary of AT&T) in a venture to provide cellular mobile telephone service in Los Angeles. Partners included AT&T (6 percent), GTE Mobilnet (20 percent), Continental Contel Mobilcom (10 percent), and Telephone & Data Systems' U.S. Cellular Inc. (5 percent). Continental Telephone also launched its videotex experiment, Conte/Vision in 1982, but did not take partners.

In 1983 CSX Corp. and Southern New England Telephone formed Light-Net, and other railroad-communications ventures were announced, including

Cable & Wireless with the Missouri-Kansas-Texas Railroad and Norfolk Southern Corp. with Santa Fe Southern Pacific. AT&T responded in 1984 with a $2 billion expansion of its long-distance network. Enormous over-capacity in fiber-optic cables was expected to result in a massive industry shakeout. Satellite network services would be affected most severely because fiber-optic technology was technologically superior and price competitive to satellite transmissions.

Data Communications. Electronic mail is a term that was applied to any communications service that permitted the transmission and storage of messages by electronic means. In 1984 it was a $1.5 billion a year business. The most prevalent electronic mail devices had been the telex machine (which had been used commercially since World War I) and the facsimile machine, which transmitted not only the text of a message but also its photographic image. But electronic mail services were expected to be dominated in the future by the computer-mailbox services (offered by firms such as General Electric, ITT, and GTE) that used a computer to transmit messages over telephone lines, through a central computer, to the recipient's computer. With their sizable memory banks and instantaneous transmission, computers enjoyed an enormous advantage over the telex and facsimile machines.

Local area networking (LAN) was a dedicated cable service for transport-ing information to and from different computers within the same office area. Local area networks could link users within an area of approximately three kilometers. The GEnet tied together computers, robots, machine-tool devices, and other products within a manufacturing complex. The Ethernet (as well as products by Datapoint, Systek, Ungermann-Bass, IBM, Network Systems, and many others) tied together office machines. Data communica-tions services were a fruitful area for joint-venture formation.

Teletext and Videotex Communications. Videotex was a form of interactive computer system that used a home computer to send and receive information over the telephone lines or two-way cable systems. Linked to a computer data-base, the videotex system displayed information on the screen in both text and graphics. Included in its services were electronic banking, teleshopping, adver-tising, computer-based education, interpersonal message transmission (electronic-mail and -bulletin boards), entertainment features (videogames), and specialized information retrieval. Teletext was *not* interactive.

Demand for teletext and videotex services were expected to follow the ac-ceptance of cable TV and personal computers into homes, making it possible to reach 25 to 30 million households by the mid-1990s. In 1984, however, confusion surrounding the commercial viability of videotex services had left a long string of corpses belonging to firms that could not afford to hang on any longer. The videotex industry was no longer expected to be profitable quickly, and customer resistance was becoming apparent in matters such as the price of videotex terminals. (Users needed a $600 dedicated terminal to receive the full graphics version of videotex from services like Knight-Ridder's. Although it was possible to rent terminals and would eventually be possible for users to modify their personal computers to display full graphic videotex, such technology was not available in 1984.)

Because teletext services (text only) could be fed to users' personal computers, they attracted more subscribers than videotex by 1984. These services included H&R Block Inc.'s CompuServe (140,000 customers), Dow Jones & Co.'s Dow Jones News/Retrieval (155,000 subscribers), and Readers Digest Inc.'s the Source (58,000 customers).

Knight-Ridder was a pioneer in offering videotex services, and it used joint research programs and joint ventures to do so. Knight-Ridder and AT&T had experimented together with the viability of offering videotex services in the early 1980s. AT&T provided the Sceptre terminal and phone line necessary to receive Knight-Ridder's Viewtron service. Knight-Ridder controlled the database and computer system needed to provide the full graphics version of the service. By 1984 Knight-Ridder had spent an estimated $17 million to prepare for commercial offerings of videotex services in southern Florida in 1984. Its Viewtron service became a gateway for other databases provided by Knight-Ridder and outsiders.

In 1981 CBS forged an agreement with AT&T, the Canadian government, and Telediffusion de France to create a technical standard for teletext transmission. In a videotex venture with AT&T, CBS provided program content by utilizing information resources that were both local and national in scope and by involving advertisers, retailers, banks, and others. AT&T provided the head-end computer software. (The standards AT&T announced for its videotex system were mostly compatible with the Telidon standards that were being tested by Times-Mirror Videotex Services and Informart in 1982. Telidon was an advanced videotex system that connected a television set to a computer databank by using telephone lines.)

In the second phase of their joint market test of computerized home information systems in 1983, CBS and AT&T offered edited news, personalized computer services, and home shopping, as well as home banking services (provided by Automatic Data Processing and the Treasurer). CBS remained responsible for the assembly of the information used in the service, while AT&T furnished the computer equipment, including home terminals.

In 1982 Times-Mirror Videotex Services Inc. and Informart formed a joint venture, Videotex America, to market and operate Telidon videotex systems in the United States. (Informart was an electronic publishing joint venture of Torstar Corp. and Southan Inc., both Toronto-based communications companies.) Videotex America obtained its programming from a Times-Mirror database of more than 70,000 pages called Gateway, and it planned to form partnerships to operate consumer videotex systems in local markets, like cable television franchises. Its test involved 350 households in which Telidon users could bank, purchase theater tickets, make hotel and airline reservations, and order merchandise from certain retailers, but Videotex America had not been commercialized by the end of 1984.

Times-Mirror offered its Gateway videotex service commercially in Orange County, California, in 1984. It hoped to have 20,000 to 30,000 videotex subscribers by 1987. (In 1983 Times-Mirror and the Washington Post Co. formed a joint venture to develop and introduce videotex service in the Washington, D.C., area.)

In 1982 Matsushita Electric Industrial Co. Ltd. and Time Inc. formed a joint research venture to develop hardware for consumer information services that Matsushita would manufacture and market (under the Panasonic name). Their first product was a terminal for Time Inc.'s cable teletext service that was being test-marketed by its American Television and Communications Corp. (ATC) in late 1982.

In 1983 a videotex joint venture, Keycom Electronic Publishing, was formed by Centel (54 percent), Honeywell (30 percent), and Field Enterprises (16 percent). It had originally been a venture between Honeywell and Field Enterprises (then the owner of the *Chicago Sun-Times*), which later opened to admit Centel. Keycom planned to offer a text version of its full-graphics service for most personal computers but missed its intended startup date of 1983 after investing $15 million. When News America Publishing Inc. (which acquired the *Sun-Times* and Field Enterprises' interest in Keycom) decided to pull out of the joint venture, the Keycom partners had to restructure the venture yet again.

In 1983 Coleco Industries and a unit of AT&T announced a joint venture to distribute video games and entertainment software by telephone. The AT&T Consumer Products unit designed a modem to enable the AT&T-Coleco subscriber to receive video games on home computers or videogame players. It was not commercialized. When teletext was authorized for broadcasting by the FCC in 1983, Zenith Radio Corp. and Taft Broadcasting announced a joint venture to produce teletext receiving equipment. Taft would develop programming while Zenith made teletext decoders for Zenith color television. By the end of 1984, this venture had also not been commercialized.

In 1983 Group W began offering the Dow-Jones News/Retrieval service on some of its cable systems. (Most of Dow-Jones's 80,000 subscribers used telephone lines in 1983.) The interactive service allowed subscribers to interface the cable system, contact the Dow-Jones database to pick information (from broad topics to statistics), and retrieve the information. Dow-Jones offered a subject search of *Wall Street Journal* articles, stock quotations, an encyclopedia, world, sports, and weather news, movie reviews, a home shopping system, business and financial information.

In 1984 Chase Manhattan Bank and Cox Cable Communications agreed to develop electronic home financial services that would be made available to other financial institutions. The services would be delivered to customers' home via two-way cable TV systems that were installed by Cox. (The system used a home terminal developed by Cox and the Jerrold Division of General Instruments.)

Both Cox Communications and Chase Manhattan Bank were also testing other home banking services during this time. Chase Manhattan Bank was offering its own home banking services using telephone lines and personal computers, but it wanted the joint venture with Cox Communications to become familiar with other distribution systems such as cable, as well. Cox Communications had a home banking pilot program in California with HomServ (then a subsidiary of American Can). Funding was withdrawn by Cox's partner because the penetration rate for two-way cable services was deemed too low to justify further testing in 1984.

In 1984 IBM, CBS, and Sears, Roebuck joined forces to introduce Trintex, a home videotex service that they hoped to introduce nationally in the future. The service was a flexible system, open to the widest possible variety of personal computers and providers of information, merchandise, and transactions. Other videotex firms were glad to see the creation of Trintex because it added credibility to the videotex business (as IBM's entry into personal computers had done). CBS's decision to sever its alliance with AT&T, in favor of one that used personal computers as videotex terminals, was attributed to its belief that dedicated videotex terminals would not be accepted by customers.

By early 1985, only 5,000 dedicated videotex terminals capable of receiving full-text, color services had been sold. Instead, the most successful services were the text only (no graphics) products that could be received by personal computers over telephone lines. (Such services allowed subscribers to bank and shop at home. In earlier years, they would have been considered to be on-line database services because they did not feature graphics.)

Child Activities. Most of the communications services joint ventures were closely coordinated with their parents' operations. Coordination among the joint ventures in cable communications was necessary from a capital and risk-sharing perspective, but as the case of Warner-Amex illustrates too vividly, they incurred larger losses when the child became too boisterous. In the Warner-Amex example, neither parent possessed the wherewithal to assess whether the child was running wild (and it was).

There were many more joint ventures in the area of videotex (where demand was dubious or would take a long time to realize) than in teletext, where the commercial viability of the offering was more uncertain, and the videotex ventures did not seem to be as closely coordinated with their parents' activities as other communications services joint ventures. A key difference that may explain this pattern was the *differences* between parents' activities and those of their child in the videotex ventures.

Financial Services

Financial services included brokerage, underwriting securities, lending, banking, portfolio management, advisory, real estate, insurance, reinsurance, leasing, and electronic funds transfer (EFT) services, among others. Some regional banks had organized consortia long ago to strengthen their defenses against competition from money centers as the financial services industry grew increasingly competitive. This pattern of cooperative strategies was prevalent before deregulation turned the financial services industry topsy-turvy. Boundaries between players in the financial services industry were blurring in 1984, as banks invaded brokerage and commercial paper underwriting, while money management firms invaded banking.

Need for Joint Activities. The financial services industry had become a global one by 1984. As chapter 1 noted, financial services firms had used joint ventures earlier and more frequently than many other industries prior to 1984. Because the only significant barriers to emulating other firms' competitive advantages were human and financial resources, small firms used consortia and other cooperative strategies to match the scale advantages and capital advantages of their larger competitors as they expanded their domains.

In order to succeed in the financial services industry, firms needed an image of leadership that could be established only through decades of customer contact. A large distribution network was required for success to take advantage of scale economies in serving desired customers. Because there were few economies in serving many small and diversified accounts, successful firms marketed their products aggressively but selectively to attain scale economies in processing. Telecommunications assets could be used to reach some customers, but control of customer access was nevertheless the key resource to control. (Software capabilities were important, but these could be purchased. R&D skills were needed to develop a wide range of new products, but these could also be obtained through cooperation.) Thus, firms used their successes in serving local markets to expand globally and supplement their product lines by swapping market access to offer the products of others.

Choosing Partners.
Securities. In 1974 Amminet Inc. and Remote Computing Corp. (RCC) formed a joint venture to create a nationwide, computer-accessed communications network that linked buyers and sellers of mortgages. Amminet was a nonprofit corporation formed to increase the liquidity of mortgage

investments by making it easier to buy, sell, stabilize, and increase the flow of money into the housing industry by attractive investors.

In 1976 Merrill Lynch & Co. and bullion brokers Samuel Montagu and Co. (London) formed a joint venture, Merrill Montagu Inc., to trade precious metals in the United States. The joint venture was formed by purchasing from Handy & Harmon its interest in a predecessor company called Merrill, Montagu, Handy & Harmon.

In 1979 Bache Halsey Stuart Shield Inc. cooperated with Citibank, Republic Bank of New York, and First National Bank of Chicago to market gold certificates to their customers. Citibank obtained competitive quotes from leading bullion dealers and provided discounts on commissions for large volume purchases.

In 1982 Fidelity Management & Research and Security Pacific National Bank formed a joint venture to provide discount brokerage services for Security Pacific's 660 branches. Many mutual funds, like Fidelity, formed packages of services to offer through banks that offered access to their depositors.

Many overseas investors took minority interests in U.S. securities firms. Since 1978, for example, First Boston Inc. had been one-third owned by Financière Crédit Suisse-First Boston, a European holding company. In 1982 Smith Barney, Harris Upham & Co. sold 24.9 percent of its stock to Lama Holding Inc., a Middle Eastern group of thirty-four individual and corporate investors. Belgium's Cie Bruxelles Lambert owned an interest in a securities firm that was re-christened Drexel Burnham Lambert Inc. Competrol Ltd. (Saudi Arabia) purchased a 24 percent interest in Donaldson, Lufkin & Jenrette. Security Pacific Corp. (Los Angeles) purchased a 29.9 percent share in Hoare Govett Ltd., a London stockbroker in 1982. In 1983 RIT and Northern PLC (London) increased its interest in L.F. Rothschild, Unterberg, Towbin to 50 percent from its earlier investment in 25 percent of Rothschild, an investment banking firm that specialized in underwriting the stock issues of new firms, particularly those in high technology fields.

In 1983 S.G. Warburg & Co. (a merchant bank) purchased a 50 percent interest in Akroyd & Smithers' ongoing U.S. stockbroker subsidiary. For Akroyd (a dealer in British government bonds on the London Stock Exchange), a joint venture with Warburg (a major Eurobond dealer) enhanced its position in the international bond market.

In 1983 Compagnie Financière de Paris et des Pays Bas (Paribas) purchased the 25 percent interest in Warburg Paribus Becker-A.G. Becker held by its partner, S.G. Warburg & Co. Paribus and Warburg had purchased 40 percent interest in A.G. Becker initially, as a toehold entry, then increased their holdings to 50 percent in 1982 as financial conditions deteriorated. In 1984 Paribas was seeking to purchase the remaining 43 percent of Becker Paribas that it did not own. Operating management shifted from partner to partner, and outsiders were brought in to rectify A.G. Becker's problems without success. The partners were unable to agree on the mission their child should have pursued. Merrill Lynch purchased Becker Paribas, instead.

Management by committee at A.G. Becker had become burdensome because key decision makers could not act with authority. Top management needed instantaneous information concerning the value of the firm's inventories to decide whether to liquidate a position or make other crucial and time-sensitive decisions. The shared management perspectives at A.G. Becker were often in conflict, and this prevented them from making fast decisions.

In 1983 Citicorp entered the discount brokerage business through a cooperative strategy with Q&R Clearing Corp. (a unit of Quick & Reilly Inc., a New York brokerage concern). Similarly, the banks of Society Corp. (Cleveland) began offering discount brokerage services through a joint venture with Third National Bank of Dayton in cooperation with Donaldson, Lufkin & Jenrette Inc. Meanwhile, Citicorp (London) tested a variety of financial services that Citibank NA was prohibited from offering in 1984. It purchased a 29.9 percent interest in Vickers da Costa (Holdings) P.L.C., a London-based stockbroker with offices in Tokyo and Hong Kong, and it participated in securities underwritings to develop a strong in-house corporate finance group.

In 1984 Pallas Group, an international investment banking firm, acquired a 50 percent interest in Dillon, Read Overseas Corp., the British subsidiary of investment banker Dillon, Read. The jointly owned business unit (which was re-christened Dillon, Read Ltd.) was better enabled to expand its European corporate finance and trading activities as a result of this cash infusion.

In 1984 the independently run Lazard financial houses of London, New York, and Paris agreed to form a closer relationship that would give financier Michel David-Weill effective control of (and ability to coordinate the activities of) the group. The three houses agreed to form a Delaware-based partnership in which the entities controlled by Mr. David-Weill owned a 50 percent interest.

Money Management. In 1970 Dreyfus and Marine-Midland Banks, Inc. (Buffalo) formed a 50%-50% joint venture, Dreyfus-Marine Midland Management Corp., to engage in business as an investment advisor to the bank's large institutional accounts and manage investment portfolios for them. In 1973 First Chicago Corp. (parent of First National Bank of Chicago) and Starwood Corp. formed a 40%-40% joint venture, Starwood Associates, to offer specialized investment services to pension and similar funds and wealthy families. (The remaining 20 percent interest was given to Starwood Associates managers as an incentive.)

In 1973 Fidelity Corp. (Pennsylvania) and Connecticut Commercial Travelers Mutual Insurance Co. formed a joint venture, CCT Financial Services, to market financial services to institutional clients of CCT Mutual Insurance. By 1982 federal regulations had changed such that the real estate financing, commercial financing, money market transactions, and management consulting services provided by the child could also be provided by its parents on their own.

In 1976 Goldman Sachs & Co. and Kleinwort Benson Ltd. (a large London-based merchant bank) formed a 40%-40% joint venture, Kleinwort Benson McCowan, to form an independent investment management company. (The remaining 20 percent interest was owned by Goldman Sachs senior investment management personnel who resigned to join Kleinwort Benson McCowan.) The joint venture was created to anticipate federal legislation (ERISA) that severely restricted the ability of securities houses, like Goldman Sachs, to manage institutional investment advisory accounts and collect brokerage commissions from them, as well.

In 1980 Gartmore Investment (a British international funds management organization) and Investors Diversified Services formed a 40%-60% joint venture, IDS Advisory-Gartmore International Inc., to manage pension, profit sharing, and endowment funds investing outside the United States. The joint venture was created to provide the capability for international investment services for U.S. corporate pension clients and Gartmore received a research contract fee in exchange for the money management expertise it provided to its child. In 1981 IDS purchased the 40 percent interest of its partner, but it retained their research affiliation.

In 1981 Mellon National Corp. and Pictet & Cie formed a joint venture, Mellon-Pictet International Management, Ltd., to manage money on an international scale. Pictet & Cie was a Swiss banking firm. Through it, the child offered global investment of equities and fixed-income in the major capital market of the world. International investments were an area of strong interest on the part of the U.S. pension plan sponsors in the 1980s. In 1982 Midlantic Banks and Florida Coast Banks formed such a joint trust venture in Florida, called Florida Coast Midlantic Trust Co. In 1983 Aetna Life & Casualty and Samuel Montagu (the London merchant bank) formed a 50%-50% joint venture, Aetna Montagu Asset Management, to provide international investment portfolio management services to U.S.-based pension funds and other institutional investors.

In 1984 Merrill Lynch, Nomura Securities, and Lombard Odier & Cie formed two joint ventures to offer investment services and trust funds covering industries in Japan, Europe, and the United States. The partners jointly owned Merrill Lynch International Holdings Inc. (which was offered in the United States) and World Fund S.A. (which was offered outside the United States). Actual management of the funds was provided by subsidiaries of the ventures' parents in their respective domestic markets. In 1983 the partners had formed Sci-Tech Holding Co., an investment trust in high technology stocks.

Inventory Financing. In 1974 Texas American Bancshares and Shawmut Corp. (both bank holding companies) formed a joint venture, The American Cattle and Crop Services Corp., to create a cattle-feedlot financing firm in the Southwest. For both partners, the joint venture represented a geographical diversification that enabled them to circumvent regulatory restrictions on their scope of operations. The joint venture, which was renamed American AgCredit Corp., enjoyed very profitable operations, and Texas American Bancshares became more active in the cattle-feedlot business following its success.

Leasing. In 1974 Commercial Credit Co. (CCC) of Baltimore (the third-largest independent finance company and affiliate of Control Data Corp.) and Nippon Shinpan Co. Ltd. (a consumer credit company) formed a 40%-40% joint venture, International Leasing Corp., to provide computer leasing services. (The remaining 20 percent interest was owned by fourteen leading Japanese industrial and financial firms.) The joint venture offered a full range of leasing services in Japan, in Hong Kong, and throughout Southeast Asia.

In 1975 Citicorp Leasing International (a subsidiary of Citicorp) and the Hamilton Group (Canada) formed a 60%-40% joint venture, Citicorp Leasing Canada, to acquire Hamilton's leasing operations. (Citicorp Leasing International previously held a 35 percent interest in the Hamilton Group.) The partnership enabled its joint venture to finance more costly capital equipment throughout Canada. (Hamilton had traditionally dealt with small-ticket equipment, while Citicorp had traditionally dealt with aggregate purchases over $25,000.)

In 1984 IBM Credit Corp. formed partnerships with Merrill Lynch, General Mills, and Metropolitan Life, among others, to offer computer leasing services. The credit unit gave IBM greater flexibility in selling computers and provided tax shelters for its partners. In a similar move, Sears, Roebuck and First National Bank of Chicago formed a joint venture for product and market research and merchandise acquisition in which First National provided financing support.

In 1984 Cigna Corp. and United Motor Works formed a 50%-50% joint venture, Cigna UMW Finance, to provide short- and medium-term financing services for non-U.S. corporations and governments, including export financing and merchant banking. Cigna owned AFIA (a foreign insurer based in the United States), INA Corp. and Connecticut General Corp. United Motor Works (Singapore) was a manufacturing, assembling, trading, and distribution service firm with operations in the United States and Asia.

Insurance. Risk-sharing was very commonplace in the insurance industry, but when partners encountered adverse business conditions, they were less likely to cooperate. Coalitions of insurers dissolved when risks became too high.

Attempts by life insurance companies to penetrate the property and casualty insurance business were motivated by a desire to find new products for agents to sell to maintain their historic compensation based on constant commission rates. Compensation based on life insurance sales was declining because fewer women were staying home (where life insurance agents could reach them), more marriages were breaking up, and birthrates were declining. Regulations prevented life insurance firms from simply raising prices to cover higher commissions.

In 1970 Prudential Insurance Co. and Kemperco, Inc. formed a joint venture, Kemperco-Prudential, to permit Prudential (a life insurance firm) to enter the property and liability insurance business. Kemperco provided underwriting, administrative, and claim services for a fee. For Prudential, the arrangement was like renting administrative services until it could develop its own systems in-house. A major cultural clash developed as it became clear that management of independent or part-time agents (Kemper's sales force) was dramatically different from using salaried employees (Prudential's agents) to attain strategic objectives. After a brief trial marriage, Prudential terminated its joint venture with Kemperco in 1972. Kemperco had sold Prudential its American Protection Insurance Co., a specialty auto insurer, to permit Prudential to enter the property and casualty business. Although it had been stripped of all existing business when it was transferred to Prudential, American Protection was licensed to operate in many states. Kemperco wanted it back when the venture ended. Consequently, Prudential had to charter its own organization and procure local licenses—exactly what it had hoped to avoid when Prudential formed the joint venture with Kemperco initially.

In 1971 John Hancock Mutual Life Insurance Co. and Sentry Insurance Group also formed a joint venture, Hanseco, under which John Hancock agents marketed property and casualty insurance underwritten by Sentry. The venture permitted John Hancock's licensed life insurance agents to be licensed rapidly and to add property and liability products to their portfolios faster than if they had had to develop them on their own.

The products that Hanseco sold reflected its parents' respective marketing strategies, and these were sometimes in conflict with each other. When the respective law and marketing departments of Hanseco's parents were not responsive enough to their partners' needs (as represented through Hanseco), they decided to disaffiliate, effective in 1985. John Hancock purchased Sentry's interest in Hanseco and created two new companies—John Hancock Property & Casualty and John Hancock Indemnity Co.—to continue serving Hanseco customers as their policies came up for renewal.

In 1977 the brokerage firm Bache Halsey Stuart cooperated with Bankers Security Life Society to offer its clients low-cost, guaranteed-issue life insurance coverage by direct mail. Insurance coverage was underwritten by Bankers Security, and Bache received a percentage of the premiums from Bankers Security.

In 1978 American International Group (AIG) and seven other insurance companies formed Transatlantic Reinsurance (Transreco) to provide reinsurance services to primary insurance companies. Transreco was a wholly owned business unit that served as a conduit for passing reinsurance business through the reinsurance companies of AIG, a major reinsurance firm that offered global programs to Fortune 500 firms. Transreco was recapitalized when Metropolitan Life, Swiss Reinsurance, Walden Insurance Ltd. (Bermuda), U.S. Fidelity and Guarantee Co., Compagnie Financière (Belgium), Daido Mutual Life, and Nichido Fire & Marine Insurance Co. Ltd. were invited to participate in its level of reinsurance activity. AIG sold a partial interest in Transreco to its partners to give them an opportunity to participate in the international market, and in doing so AIG increased its risk participation capacity. The Transreco partners also took reinsurance business from other sources because although relationships were incestuous, very few business relationships were exclusive in the insurance business.

In 1979 Alexander & Alexander Inc., Donald Kramer, and Shearson Hayden Stone Inc. formed a joint venture, KCC Syndicate Managers Inc., to provide management services to members and prospective members of the New York Insurance Exchange. KCC managed a number of syndicates of various corporate and partnership firms.

In 1979 the Continental Corp. (an insurance holding company) in conjunction with the Phoenix Assurance Co. of New York (a subsidiary of Phoenix Assurance of London), La Préservatrice, S.A., of France, and Toro Assicurazioni, SpA (Italy), formed a joint venture, the Maiden Lane Syndicate, to underwrite insurance as a member of the New York Insurance Exchange. Continental owned a 24 percent interest in Phoenix and managed Phoenix's underwriting accounts in the United States. Syndicate membership increased as additional companies decided to participate.

In 1979 Continental Corp. purchased a 20 percent stake in Stenhouse Holdings, a British insurance broker. Stenhouse owned 54 percent of Reed Stenhouse Co., a publicly listed Canadian insurance brokerage concern and formed a joint venture with Continental Corp. called Continental Reed Stenhouse Management Co. Their child provided underwriting management services to New York Insurance Exchange syndicates, including the Maiden Lane Syndicate organized by Continental earlier in 1979. Stenhouse subsidiaries were members of Lloyd's of London, the British insurance trading floor, which prohibited non-Lloyd's insurance companies, including U.S. concerns, from owning controlling interests in its member companies.

In 1980 Quotron Systems Inc., American Information Development Inc., and the Continental Corp. formed a joint venture to provide data processing services to independent insurance agents by acquiring American Information Development's existing business assets. Quotron provided management and field support services as well as telecommunications experience to set up an electronic interface between agents and insurance companies.

In 1981 Continental Corp. and Reed Stenhouse Cos. (a Canadian insurance brokerage firm) formed two 50%-50% joint ventures, Continental Life Insurance Co. and Continental Pensions Ltd., to offer unit-linked pension products, as well as other classes of life, pension, and permanent health insurance. In 1983 Continental Corp. and Phoenix Assurance Co. (London) formed a joint venture, Phoenix-Continental Services Ltd., by merging their Canadian property and casualty insurance operations. Their child operated with an increased capacity to exploit scale economies and improve services.

In 1982 Continental Corp. acquired a 60 percent interest in the Lombard Insurance Group unit of Hong Kong-based Jardine, Matheson & Co. Ltd. Jardine sought to strengthen its insurance underwriting operations, while Continental sought to consolidate its Asian operations. Lombard became the sole property and casualty underwriting arm for both Continental and Jardine in Asia.

In 1980 American International Group Inc. (AIG) and People's Insurance Co. of China formed a joint venture, China-American Co., to write insurance and reinsurance worldwide. The child wrote insurance in connection with China's international trade activities and was the first joint venture between People's Insurance and any foreign insurer.

In 1980 Swiss Union-General Insurance Co. Ltd. of Geneva and Constellation Reinsco (a subsidiary of Constellation Reinsurance Co. of New York) formed a joint venture, Galaxy Reinsurance Co., to write all lines of domestic reinsurance business in the United States. Constellation Reinsco, the minority partner, provided management and underwriting services for the child.

In 1980 American General Corp. sold its subsidiary, Fidelity and Deposit Co. of Maryland, to Swiss Reinsurance Co. and Zurich Insurance Co., both of Zurich. Its new parents allowed the child to continue operations under existing management as an independent unit within their worldwide organizations.

In 1982 Transinsco Inc. (a domestic underwriting subsidiary of Gulf Oil) and Hartford Specialty (a subsidiary of ITT's Hartford Insurance Group) formed a joint venture to write specialized property and casualty policies. The child complemented Gulf's Bermuda-based international reinsurance company, Insco, Ltd.

In 1983 Johnson & Higgins and Willis Faber (two of the world's largest insurance brokers) formed a 51%-49% joint venture to develop the reinsurance business in North America through Johnson & Higgins' subsidiary, Wilcox Incorporated Reinsurance Intermediaries. The joint venture's London subsidiary, Willis Faber & Willcox Ltd., was a Lloyd's broker and handled North American business developed by Willcox. The partners also operated jointly in Canada, New Zealand, and Australia, and offered surplus lines brokerage services in the United States through Neal, Lloyd & Co. The partners also jointly owned Johnson & Higgins Willis Faber (U.S.A.), which managed underwriting syndicates on the New York Insurance Exchange.

In 1984 Johnson & Higgins and Kirke-Van Orsdel Inc. (KVI) formed a joint venture, Johnson & Higgins Kirke-Van Orsdel Inc., to offer life insurance and merchandising coverage for employer-sponsored groups and associations. KVI was a major player in the associations market. Johnson & Higgins also formed a cooperative strategy with Arthur J. Gallagher & Co. (a major international insurance broker) to broaden its product lines by marketing products developed by Gallagher.

In 1984 Charterhouse J. Rothschild PLC (United Kingdom) and Reliance Holdings agreed to sell Target Group, their 60%-40% life insurance joint venture. Morgan Grenfell & Co. (United Kingdom) purchased a 20 percent interest, and Charterhouse's investment units purchased a 12 percent stake in the newly created Target Group PLC. Charterhouse had acquired Target in 1980 as part of another acquisition. It sold a 40 percent interest in Target to Reliance, a U.S. insurance holding company, as part of its restructuring to become a broadly based financial services group. Charterhouse took a 25 percent interest in Hambros Life Assurance PLC, one of Target's larger competitors, in 1984.

In 1984 American International Group (AIG), Phibro-Salomon Brothers, and several other partners formed a joint venture to offer insurance for municipal securities. (This line of business had increased in attractiveness after major defaults of obligations by issuers of municipal securities had occurred.) AIG also participated in international joint venture insurance activities with Citicorp. A joint venture was necessary because Citicorp was not allowed to participate in the insurance business in 1984. Bank of America was seeking a similar affiliation, and more financial institutions were expected to seek joint ventures with insurance companies as their holding companies expanded the scope of their activities beyond banking.

Electronic Funds Transfer (EFT). Joint ventures in electronic funds transfer shared cable interconnections and clearinghouse facilities and automated teller machines (ATMs). Such joint ventures were necessary because (1) certain elements of electronic funds transfer were too expensive for many individual firms to purchase and (2) it was inefficient under some circumstances for more than one firm to provide certain services. There were other benefits to sharing electronic funds transfer facilities. These included: (1) the ability to overcome capital requirements needed for participation in attractive markets; (2) increased competition (due to more participating firms); (3) a system directed by market forces rather than by one or more government regulators; and (4) the prospect of more rapid advances in technology as systems competed for customers.

In 1972 Mellon National Bank and Bradford Computer & Systems Inc. (a shareholder servicing firm that operated computers and machine-based clerical systems and provided computer services to banks, mutual funds, and other financial institutions) formed a joint venture to run the bank's transfer agency business. Earlier in 1972, Bradford Computer & Systems Inc. and Bankers Trust Co. had formed a joint venture, BT Bradford Stock Services, Inc., to apply Bradford's data processing capabilities to the securities transfer agency, registry, and related shareholder services of the bank. Bradford already had joint subsidiaries operating the stock transfer departments for Marine-Midland Bank and Franklin National Bank when it formed the Mellon alliance. Through them, Bradford had the potential to develop a national stock transfer service for shareholders and bank customers.

In 1974 Bradford Computer & Systems Inc. and Crocker National Corp. formed a 49.9%-50.1% joint venture, Western Bradford & Trust Co., to provide stock transfer and automated business services to Crocker National Bank's customers throughout the United States. By 1975 Bradford also provided transfer services for Chase Manhattan Bank N.A. In 1977 Pacific Stock Exchange Inc. and Bradford signed an agreement whereby Bradford assumed of the exchange's data processing facilities in Los Angeles and San Francisco. After Bankers Trust discontinued its stock transfer business in 1978, Bradford Trust Co. was named agent and registrar in place of Bankers Trust for several companies.

In 1973 Security Pacific Corp. and U.S. Datacorp (a subsidiary of U.S. Bancorp of Portland, Oregon) formed a joint venture, Security Pacific Datacorp., to provide computer output microfilm (COM) services to commercial customers in California. Computer output microfilm technology involved placing computer generated transactions directly onto microfilm or microfiche, thereby bypassing conventional paper systems. The service offered cost and time savings in the storage and retrieval of information.

In 1973 Hartford National Bank & Trust Co. and Martin-Marietta Corp. formed a joint venture, Financial Industry System, to offer data processing resource management and related services to banks, insurance companies, and other financial institutions in the New England states, New York, and Maryland. It operated for seven years but was marginally profitable during that time. In 1980 the systems business was sold to a third party.

In 1975 Omaha National Bank and First Federal Savings and Loan Association (Nebraska) formed a joint venture to share computer terminals for electric funds transactions at nineteen retail locations in Omaha (supermarkets and department stores) by using plastic bank cards. The joint venture was the first instance of terminal sharing by a commercial bank and thrift institution at the retail point of sale.

In 1976 American Express (Amex) cooperated with Docutel Corp. to form an electronic funds transfer (EFT) system that allowed its cardholders to obtain travelers checks twenty-four hours a day. Chase Manhattan Bank acted as a clearinghouse to collect payment from the cardholder's bank.

In 1977 Banc One (a Columbus bank) helped Merrill Lynch start its Cash Management Account (CMA), which combined the use of a credit card, checking account, securities account, and money market fund. Banc One benefited from the cooperation because the bank cleared account checks and processed credit card transactions. In 1984 Merrill Lynch advised Banc One that it would perform the credit card processing activities and process its own checks, as well, by 1985. Banc One processed CMA-type accounts for over 200 other firms—including Prudential-Bache Securities and Dean Witter Reynolds Inc.—at that time. Banc One had also formed an alliance with Comp-U-Card International Inc. to issue special VISA cards for customer transactions by telephone or computer.

In 1980 Data-Sys-Tance Inc. (a data processing subsidiary of Kansas City Southern Industries) and the Midwest Stock Exchange formed a joint venture, Buckingham Financial Services, Inc., to provide processing support for stock transfer and record-keeping activities for its parent. DST used joint ventures with partners having complementary capabilities and resources to distribute its services. DST Inc. and State Street Bank & Trust Company formed a joint venture, Boston Financial Data Services, Inc. (BFDS), to provide money market fund services. DST Inc. and Kemper Financial Services, Inc., formed a 50%-50% joint venture, Investors Fiduciary Trust Company (IFTC), to recapitalize their child (which was formerly a wholly owned subsidiary of DST Inc.).

In 1984 IBM joined with Merrill Lynch to form International Market-Net, to build and operate a computerized market information service for brokerage firms. IBM preferred to venture with partners when it entered businesses that were unfamiliar or had long payoffs. For example, it joined COMSAT and Aetna Life & Casualty in launching Satellite Business Systems in 1975 and joined with CBS and Sears in launching Trintex, a network for home computer owners to provide information, entertainment, and electronic shopping. Citicorp was involved in information joint ventures with Reuters Ltd. and Dun & Bradstreet, respectively in 1984.

International Banking. In 1976 a group of twenty Arab, U.S., and European banking concerns jointly formed the UBAF Arab American Bank, a U.S. commercial bank that was based in New York. The U.S. parents included Bankers Trust, First Chicago, Security Pacific, and Texas Commerce Bancshares. (Each held a 5 percent interest because the Bank Holding Act prohibited them from owning more than 5 percent of another bank.) Eleven Arab banks (including some Arab central banks) controlled 64 percent. The remaining 16 percent was controlled by Union de Banques Arabes et Françaises, which was itself a consortium of twenty-six Arab and French financial institutions. The bank acted as a funnel for Arab investment in the United States, with the bank's staff providing management services for investments ranging from short-term money market and Treasury bills to long-term direct investment. The bank also acted as a window for U.S. corporations looking into the Middle East.

In 1978 Hong Kong & Shanghai Bank acquired an equity interest in Marine-Midland Banks, Inc. Midland-Marine and Wardley Investment Services Ltd. formed a joint venture, Wardley Marine International Investment Management. The child united the international investment expertise of Wardley with Marine Midland's service capabilities in the United States.

In 1980 the Interbank Card Association (ICA) of the United States cooperated with three Japanese bank-related credit companies (Diamond Credit Co., Million Card Service Co., and Union Credit Co.) to issue one credit card for use both in the United States and abroad. The consortium designed their card to resemble the basic pattern of Mastercard, which was issued by ICA. The partnership was created to compete with the VISA card, which was issued jointly by Sumitomo Credit Service Co. and VISA International, the world's largest credit card organization.

In 1981 Massachusetts Financial Services Inc. (MFS) and Lombard Odier International Portfolio Management Ltd. (a London-based subsidiary of Lombard, Odier, & Cie, a bank in Geneva) formed a joint venture to create the first U.S.-based international bond mutual fund, Massachusetts Financial International Trust-Bond Portfolio, capable of speedily switching its holdings from country to country. MFS held majority interest and managed investments in the United States. Lombard Odier managed investment decisions overseas. In the United States the fund invested in money market instruments and medium-term and long-term fixed-income securities issued by the government and corporations. Overseas, the fund purchased government bonds.

Real Estate. Joint ventures were often used in real estate as a means of sharing risk and capital requirements. Like oil exploration partnerships, these joint ventures were done on a project-by-project basis. Many real estate ventures were passive joint ventures because one partner contributed only cash (financial partners). Passive partners were less attractive to experienced real estate firms because capital was the least difficult resource for them to obtain. Partners with previous experiences in real estate development ventures (development partners) were valued most highly by them.

The many types of joint-venture arrangements used in real estate development projects varied in their use of general and limited partners. They differed also in partners' relative involvement in decision-making activities. Passive financial partners expected an equity share of at least 50 percent. They contributed money, did not make policy decisions, and received royalties from the joint venture when the project was completed. Landowners could contribute properties and receive an interest like that of the financial partner. (Passive financial partners were guaranteed a completion price and rate of return by the developer. If there were cost overruns, the developer received no proceeds until the financial partner had received its guaranteed return.) Experienced financial partners wanted a decision-making share of at least 50 percent, as well as a majority in equity interest. Such financial partners took positions on the executive committee that ran the child and dictated terms to the management firm. (The management firm was usually a subsidiary of the development partner.)

In co-development joint ventures in real estate, financial partners with experience in developing real estate properties received a part of the development fee in exchange for their development expertise and contributions. The developer's guarantee of cost—a guarantee that completed costs would be some amount or less—was a risk shared with the financial partner in co-development joint ventures. The financial partner controlled the executive committee and owned in excess of 50 percent of the equity (since it was often contributing most of the cash resources). The assets contributed by partners had to be valued explicitly before the venture began in order to prevent the development partner from appropriating the financial partner's investment when the venture dissolved later.

Child Activities. Access to a desirable customer base was the key competitive advantage needed for success in the financial services industry. The assets used to supply financial services in joint ventures were often the same assets used by parents to supply financial services. Consequently, joint-venture children were more often organizations on paper than in fact. Personnel from parent and child might be the same, but their product lines were wider, and they were trained to offer new services to the same customer base as a result of the joint venture.

The effective provision of financial services required significant investments in computer systems and paper processing facilities. Systems shortfalls could be rectified through acquisitions, but problems remained concerning how to teach both new and existing personnel how to sell each others' products. Consequently, synergy increases between parent and child were realized slowly (if at all), since another sales force was often added to the original one, and both organizations were expected to sell the products of their combined parents. Computer systems also had to be wed if personnel were expected to increase their product line breadth—whether the new products were acquired through mergers or joint mergers. Thus close coordination between parent and child was needed in the financial services business. The joint-venture child enjoyed little (if any) autonomy in developing or marketing products, since it had to coordinate so closely with parents' ongoing activities in most cases.

Summary

Using the patterns of joint ventures described above in the software, database, computer-assisted management services, communications services and financial services industries, as well as the patterns of joint ventures in programming and programming packaging sketched in chapter 8, some conclusions may be drawn concerning the use of joint ventures for service businesses. Key among these is the finding that the uses of joint ventures in service businesses were very similar to those in other industries, *except where the industry's technology was labor-intensive*. When the key strategic assets were people, different patterns of joint-venture strategy were found.

Fewer equity joint ventures were found where the key assets needed for success were human resources. Where joint activities were used, they were more likely to occur as personal service contracts of limited durations than as equity joint ventures. Several reasons for these patterns existed. First, contractual relationships reduced the cultural frictions between potential partners. Creative talent—whether in motion pictures, computer programming, or other entrepreneurial activities—did not mix well with the management systems needed to run the activities of most complex corporate entities.

Second, the high mobility of labor resources made it more difficult to transfer the key technological assets necessary for success without danger of appropriation in service businesses. Licenses and other protections of intellectual property (discussed in chapter 10) were inadequate where human resources made the difference between success and failure in the provision of services.

Third, scale economies could be exploited in the provision of communications services (especially in satellite communications) and other automated activities where capital requirements were high. Joint ventures were motivated by risk- and cost-sharing in those examples, as they were in the capital-intensive industries described in chapter 7. But scale economies were more elusive where the fixed costs of salaries had to be spread over production volume while *also* maintaining high service quality.

Thus, there were fewer joint ventures in activities where services were provided by technologies that were truly labor-intensive, particularly where the knowledge in question could not be protected adequately and the rate of technological change was rapid. A spider's web of joint ventures developed in the programming and programming packaging industries because critical resources (film libraries) were owned by parents and securely protected under licensing provisions. Close coordination was necessary between parent and child in the programming, programming packaging, databases, communications services, and financial services industries because facilities were shared among them. Coordination with parents was also important when the child tried to differentiate its products from those of competitors in service businesses. But efforts to differentiate services often created frictions between parent and child because people-intensive businesses preferred to be autonomous. The heavy hands of parents that tried to draw their children more closely to their own activities could sap the motivations of key person-nel—thereby undercutting differentiation strategies that were based on ser-vice. Parental intervention could be so potentially harmful to the child's strategic success where critical resources were people-intensive, that arm's-length dealings were used if children were created at all.

10
Joint Ventures in High Technology Industries

Technological prowess is the key to attaining competitive advantage when technologies (1) change frequently; (2) are highly risky; and (3) require extremely high creativity in design and precision in manufacturing. Products changed rapidly in the 197 examples of this chapter, making them useful for examining questions of technology transfer within joint ventures. (Many of the cooperative strategies discussed in this chapter were *not* joint ventures, for reasons explained below.)

Innovation can change an industry's structure to a firm's advantage (because it affects entry barriers and buyer–seller relations, as well as the number of surviving players), but many processes that firms invest in can be very expensive failures. Joint ventures permitted firms to share those risks by hedging their bets concerning which products, processes, or configurations would become industry standards. Moreover, they permitted firms to keep abreast of technological innovations by providing a means of sharing development costs.

Motives

Technology as Competitive Advantage

High technology products would seem to be a logical arena for joint ventures because they usually carry worthwhile profit margins if partners can get in and out of them quickly enough. Rapid technological obsolescence would seem to be another reason to form joint ventures. Partners can better share the development costs of multiple generations of products, particularly when they are supplanted by competitive technologies before such costs can be recovered.

I am indebted to Nida T. Backaitis and John G. Michel (both Ph.D. candidates, Columbia University) for industry background materials prepared for this chapter, and especially to John Michel, who provided his analyses of joint-venture patterns in the electronic components industry.

Cooperation was indeed a fundamental structural trait of high technology industries. Yet, as the industry examples below indicate, *licenses and informal agreements* were more commonplace than joint ventures in the United States, except where technologies were poorly understood. Difficulties in managing parent–child relationships provided one explanation for this pattern of cooperative strategies. For example, because technology leaders wanted to guard the kernels of knowledge that were central to their competitive advantages, they devised ways to share proprietary knowledge with their child and their partners while maintaining peace of mind. The very nature of competition in high technology industries made this sharing activity difficult to manage.

Technology Transfer

Patents were poor protection for knowledge within high technology businesses, and firms expected to have only two or three years before competitors copied their products (with or without authorization). Some firms filed patents on technology to protect themselves (so that they could not be accused of violating another firm's technology), not because they believed patents were a safe way to transfer knowledge between parent and child.

The implications of this environment for joint ventures were straightforward. If no knowledge could be protected adequately through cooperative strategies that created a child, and if any information transferred to a joint venture was no longer under the control of the child's parent, firms pooled their knowledge, but they licensed their intellectual property only where there was mutual trust among players. In high technology industries, mutual respect among players was difficult to maintain because reverse-engineering and improvements on pioneers' designs (such as unauthorized borrowing of intellectual property rights) was commonplace. Firms had to develop cooperative strategies to cope with these practices while they established technical standards to persuade customers to adopt their products' configurations. Pragmatic solutions concerning how to transfer technology to joint ventures encompassed what information to provide (and when) as well as how partners' personnel interacted with those of the child—assuming a joint venture was created.

Timing and Coordination

Some firms had to move earlier in forming joint ventures than others because their bargaining power was less than that of their competitors. Some firms formed alliances early to set industry standards. But joint ventures rarely lasted long within industries that were as volatile as the examples in this chapter. That meant firms had to devise arrangements to get in and out of ventures before their knowledge became obsolete. Given their need to move quickly and to reposition if they were wrong, firms eschewed arrangements that seemed to be too inflexible.

If an industry was embryonic and the best technologies (product features, styling, means of distributing a product) were yet unknown, joint ventures needed autonomy to move in the directions that seemed to be most promising. But since their technologies were most frequently obtained from one or more parents, close coordination with them was necessary to modify that technology to suit the evolving demands of the child's markets. Frictions between parent and child were exacerbated if it was necessary to reject parents' technologies and go to outsiders. Few parent firms were willing to allow their joint ventures that much autonomy in industries characterized by rapid technological change.

Industries

Electronic Components

Electronic components included *active* devices that convert electrical current by emitting electrons (transistors, integrated circuits, and microprocessors) and *passive* devices that did not emit current (resistors, capacitors, transformers, connectors, and inductors). Active component technology changed more frequently than that of passive components, and more joint activities involved microprocessors (the "brains" or logic chips of computers) than memory devices, due to differences in their scale economies.

Need for Joint Activities. Capital requirements to introduce a new generation of electronic components were large, and risks of failure (or premature obsolescence) were great. Patent protection was insignificant, and firms enjoyed a brief window of advantage (eighteen months or so at best) before their designs were incorporated into others' products. Technology changed rapidly in the electronic components industry, and successes were quickly outmoded. Technology was subject to a steep experience curve in memory devices (random-access memory, RAMs, and read-only memory, ROMs); but production of logic chips seldom approached volumes where such economies could be exploited as they could be for RAMs and ROMs.

Profit margins on electronic components were thin because prices dropped rapidly as unit volumes accumulated and as firms pressed their cost advantages. Yet firms felt obliged to participate in each technological generation to apply their experience to the next iteration of product designs. They typically obtained this knowledge through *cross-licensing agreements,* if not through internal development. Second-source vendor licenses were used frequently to assure customers that each product was available from at least two vendors. Thus, electronic components quickly lost their differentiated status and became standardized (hence commodity-like) products that could best be made by large, global competitors.

Choosing Partners. In 1973 Sprague Electronics and Goodman Electronics formed a joint venture, Sprague-Goodman Electronics, to make trimmer capacitors. The joint venture was sued for patent infringement and theft of process secrets and did not last long.

In 1974 Fairchild Camera & Instrument and Applied Materials formed a 45%-55% joint venture, Great Western Silicon Corp., to produce and sell semiconductor-grade polycrystalline silicon. (Texas Instruments and Motorola both made their own polycrystalline silicon, but Fairchild did not. It wanted an assured supply in the event of future shortages.) When the joint venture's plant was completed in 1977, two-thirds of its annual capacity was consumed in-house by its parents, but Applied Materials phased out of the silicon wafer business in 1978 because it could not afford the child's cash demands. Great Western Silicon was sold to General Electric in 1980 after Fairchild was acquired by Schlumberger.

In 1973 General Electric and Solid State Scientific formed a 60%-40% joint venture, Integrated Display Systems (IDS), to manufacture liquid crystal displays (LCD) and complementary logic modules for digital watches (which were selling for $150 to $250 in 1973). In 1975 Integrated Display Systems and Bulova Watch Co. formed a 50%-50% joint venture, Bulova-Computron, to produce and market a full line of digital watches, but the deal fell through because Stelux Manufacturing, IDS's competitor, bought a 26.8 interest in Bulova.

In 1976 General Electric took a 13.4 interest in Solid State Scientific in exchange for its interest in Integrated Display Systems. Solid State Scientific, in turn, sold 25 percent interest of its stock to VDO Adolf Schindling (a privately held German manufacturer of instrument panels, which had planned to develop semiconductor and display technology jointly with Solid State Scientific). In 1979 Integrated Display Systems and Gillette formed a joint venture to make digital watches, but the deal fell through, and seven months later, Solid State Scientific divested IDS.

The IDS experience illustrates the riskiness of undertaking joint ventures to reduce technological uncertainty. Neither parent knew which technological standards would develop and when critical mass in demand would be attained. By the time a product was developed, manufactured, and marketed, digital watch prices had fallen from their lofty 1973 levels. Competition had been whittled down to Texas Instruments, Fairchild Camera & Instrument, and Timex by 1977, and Texas Instruments had precipitated much of the subsequent shakeout with its aggressive price-cutting tactics.

In 1974 Unitrode (a semiconductor firm that served military customers) and Solid State Scientific had planned to merge, creating Solid State Scientific-Unitrode. But instead, in 1976 Unitrode Corp. acquired a 20 percent interest in Synertek, a producer of memory and microprocessor devices to develop VMOS technology. (Other Synertek shareholders included American Telecommunications, Bulova, and General Automation, each of which held 15 percent.) Synertek had been explicitly created in 1974 by its four backers to be a manufacturer of custom chips. It had been so successful, initially, that it could not keep up with demand. In 1978 Honeywell acquired all Synertek stock. In 1981 National Semiconductor licensed Synertek, Inc. as a second-source vendor of its products and provided it with photomasks for making microprocessor devices. Unfortunately, under Honeywell's ownership the cultural tensions of big firm versus little firm were exacerbated, and in late 1984 Honeywell finally put Synertek on the auction block. All but one of the original founders and officers of Synertek had departed from the newly acquired Honeywell unit by 1980, and its replacement personnel were involved in fewer collaborations with designers from Rockwell International, Mostek, and its other usual "dancing partners" due to conflicts of interest with Honeywell's other projects.

In 1977 Siemens purchased a 17 percent interest in Advanced Micro Devices (AMD), a U.S. semiconductor maker, to gain access to U.S. technology and the large U.S. semiconductor market. It had already tried both technology-exchange and marketing agreements but found them unsatisfactory. In addition to this minority investment, Siemens formed a joint venture with Advanced Micro Devices in microprocessors.

Advanced Micro Devices gained a necessary cash infusion to support its ambitious growth plans in microprocessors through Siemens's 1977 investment. Joint ventures were one of the few ways that a moderate-size company like AMD could hope to survive in the volatile microprocessor systems business because it required massive capital resources, systems experience, and the type of worldwide marketing operations that Siemens offered. The two partners transferred their microprocessor operations to a 60%-40% joint-venture company that concentrated on designing, manufacturing, and selling microprocessors to original equipment manufacturers of telecommunications gear.

One year later, Siemens and Advanced Micro Devices mutually agreed to terminate their joint venture in microprocessors due to a conflict of interest. Siemens had become licensed as second-source vendor for Intel's 8086 microprocessor, and AMD was licensed as second-source vendor for Zilog's Z-80, a direct competitor to the 16-bit Intel 8086. Advanced Micro Devices purchased Siemens's U.S. interests in the joint venture, and Siemens purchased AMD's European interests. Siemens teamed up with Philips N.V. to produce 256K random-access memory chips in 1984.

In 1977 Robert Bosch GmbH (a West German auto parts firm) acquired a 25 percent interest in American Microsystems Inc. Later that year, Bosch shared its AMI ownership with Borg Warner in a 50%-50% joint venture. In 1981 Gould acquired American Microsystems.

In 1974 American Microsystems had bought out its Japanese partner in a joint venture to market its integrated circuits in Japan that had not gone well. In the 1977 low-power logic chips war, it had aligned with Intel. In 1978 American Microsystems had formed a semiconductor joint venture with Gold Star of Korea, Goldstar-Microsystems Inc., to design and make MOS large-scale integrated circuits, primarily for the Korean market. AMI licensed Wang Laboratories to make electronic logic devices using its manufacturing process and computer-aided design software packages in 1981.

In 1978 Fairchild Camera & Instrument and General Electric (United Kingdom) formed a joint venture in England to make large-scale integrated circuits, microprocessors, and complex computer memory devices. Fairchild was far behind its U.S. competitors, and was in need of help. Although it had signed a twenty-two-year technological pact that licensed Mostek as a second-source vendor of its F-8 microprocessor family in 1975, such alliances were valuable only as long as customers purchased the F-8 products. (Mostek hedged its bets by also serving as a second-source vendor for Zilog's Z-80 microprocessor, thereby covering both the low-cost/high-volume end of the market, with the F-8, as well as the low-volume/high-price end, with the Z-80.) Fairchild was second-source vendor for Motorola's MC 6800 microprocessor family, which meant it used photomasks and other technical aids provided by Motorola. (Unauthorized second sources were on their own to copy designs.) Fairchild was also licensed to make a 4-bit Motorola microprocessor (the MC 10800). (Motorola served as a second-source vendor for Fairchild's family of lower-power microprocessors, but Motorola would manufacture another firm's devices if better technologies were made available to it.) Signetics (Philips N.V.) had agreed to serve as second source for Fairchild's FAST line of bipolar circuits, but stronger firms, like National Semiconductor and Motorola, had already agreed to serve as second sources for Texas Instrument's line, which was competitive with Fairchild's FAST line.

Fairchild and Micro Inc. signed an agreement in 1977 for joint development of large-scale integrated circuitry for electronic games, but that adventure was a short-term solution to Fairchild's problems because such games were fads. Fairchild supplied Robert Bosch GmbH with process technology and assembly know-how for solid state automotive ignitions similar to those supplied by Fairchild to General Motors. But Fairchild knew that was also a temporary solution. The automotive firms had a history of backward integrating to make high-volume, high-value components in-house.

In 1977 Intel and American Microsystems introduced MOS technology to make memory devices that were as fast as bipolar memory technology (which

Fairchild dominated), used less power, and were cheaper to manufacture. Meanwhile, suppliers for single-chip 8-bit microprocessors were split sharply into two camps in 1977, signaling the start of a major battle for the high-volume markets over the next few years. Motorola aligned with the Mostek 3870 (which was interchangeable with Fairchild's F-8), while Advanced Micro Devices and National Semiconductor aligned with the Intel 8048.

In 1979 Schlumberger purchased Fairchild Camera & Instrument for $360 million. Schlumberger (a French instrument and test equipment firm) was a major user of semiconductors. As a leading well-logging supplier to the oil exploration industry, Schlumberger was in a position to fund Fairchild's semiconductor business adequately.

In 1979 Intel and Texas Instruments were leading U.S. competitors in bubble memory. Rockwell and Burroughs agreed to exchange technical information and manufacturing assistance and to produce each other's bubble memory products. Rockwell had also licensed Siemens as a second-source vendor for its double memories. In exchange, Siemens had cross-licensed Rockwell to make Siemens devices and funded its research. After failing to line up other electronics firms that would use its devices as standards, Rockwell dropped out of the bubble memory market in 1981, after investing over $15 million in its unsuccessful development. Texas Instruments also departed from the bubble memory market in 1981.

Rockwell's arrangement with Burroughs was part of its scramble in 1979 for promising products. Earlier, in 1974, Rockwell had decided to take on Texas Instruments in the hand-held calculator competition because it made the semiconductors used in calculators for others under private-label agreements. In 1978 Rockwell was allied with MOS Technology (owned by Commodore International) and Synertek as a second-source vendor for the 6500 microprocessor family. (The 6500 was used for consumer products, like personal computers.) Rockwell and Synertek personnel had been meeting periodically, on an informal basis, to discuss extensions of the 6500 family and other technologies prior to 1978. But that alliance was upset when Honeywell acquired Synertek, since Rockwell and Honeywell were tough competitors on several product lines.

Rockwell was badly in need of second-source vendors for its 8-bit 6500/1, since the intended second source, Electronic Memories and Magnetics, had fallen through. In 1981 Motorola took as second-source vendors for its 16-bit microprocessor, the 68000, Mostek, NCR, Hitachi, Rockwell, Signetics/Philips N.V., and Thomson-CSF in its imminent showdown against Intel, Hitachi, and other competitors. Each firm was responsible for tasks concerning the designing of clusters of support chips for Motorola's 68000. The agreements marked the first time in the ritual of second sourcing that *six* companies had received masks and tooling on a proprietary microprocessor, and it suggested that Motorola was fighting very hard to unseat the dominance of Intel's 8086.

In 1977 Philips N.V. purchased Signetics, then the sixth-largest U.S. semiconductor firm. Intel cross-licensed its patents for microprocessor products to Philips N.V., North American Philips, and Signetics (and provided photomasks) in exchange for very-large-scale integrated circuit (VLSI) technology. In 1981 Signetics and Philips N.V. were licensed as a second-source vendor of the Motorola 68000 16-bit microprocessor family. Under terms of the Motorola agreement, Signetics and Philips could develop and manufacture whatever parts they desired as long as they adhered to a common architecture. Also in 1981 Signetics exchanged technology with Advanced Micro Devices for bipolar microprocessor products. They agreed to act as second sources for each other in microprogrammable microprocessors and in error detection (and correction) units and dynamic memory controllers, respectively.

In 1979 United Technologies acquired Mostek, another semiconductor firm that had been bloodied by the hand-held calculator and digital watch war. In 1976 Mostek had allied with Zilog and Synertek to make microprocessors that were software-compatible with Intel's logic chips. An intense price battle erupted in the single-chip microcomputer market in 1977, which caused firms to ally behind the standards of either Motorola or Intel, and Mostek had gone with Motorola. (Intel took Fujitsu as a second-source vendor for the 8086 microprocessor when Mostek joined the Motorola 68000 alliance.)

In 1981 Advanced Micro Devices and Mostek agreed to develop and produce jointly two key circuits for use in Xerox's Ethernet local networking system. (Xerox had pioneered the Ethernet concept (described elsewhere below), but it joined with Digital Equipment and Intel partners to promulgate the use of its local area network (LAN) systems and to develop specifications for the Ethernet.) IBM worked with Texas Instruments in 1981 to develop VLSI circuits for its local area network system because with Intel committed to the Xerox (Ethernet) product, Texas Instruments became the logical partner to work with for IBM in developing standards and supplying chips. Fujitsu formed a similar joint venture briefy with Ungermann-Bass in 1982 to develop VLSI circuits for local area networks. (General Electric and Ungermann-Bass formed a LAN joint venture in 1984.)

In 1983 IBM purchased a 12 percent minority interest in Intel, which quickly became a 13.7 percent interest. By 1984 IBM held a 20 percent interest in Intel with an option to acquire a total of 30 percent. (Sales to IBM represented more than 10 percent of Intel's 1981 revenues and 9 percent of its 1983 revenues.) Intel had become IBM's primary supplier of microprocessors for products like the Personal Computer. IBM wanted to ensure that Intel would be capable of sustaining high levels of R&D expenditures. The infusion of cash gave Intel the wherewithal to compete against Texas Instruments, Motorola, and Japanese electronic components firms in the area of microprocessors.

IBM was the world's largest semiconductor manufacturer in 1983, but it did not sell chips on the open market. (Western Electric was testing the option of selling its 256K RAM to outsiders in 1983.) Among the reasons cited for IBM's decision to take a minority interest in Intel was that independent semiconductor companies were unable to finance innovations adequately because their products were obsolesced before earning paybacks on their initial investments. Aggressive pricing strategies by Japanese competitors spoiled profit margins for all players in 1983. (Synergy reasons were also cited, but it was not clear how IBM would use its new status. If IBM personnel were to coordinate research efforts with Intel's scientists and engineers, their alliance could possibly provide IBM with previews of forthcoming Intel approaches and products.)

In 1983 fifteen major companies formed a joint research venture, Microelectronics & Computer Technology Corp. (MCC), to quicken gains in technology. Its goal was to share the expense of developing advanced semiconductor, computer, and software technology that the partners could use in their products. Its membership included twenty firms in 1984, and partners included Advanced Micro Devices Inc., Allied Corporation, BMC Industries Inc., Boeing Co., Control Data Corp., Digital Equipment Corp., Eastman Kodak, Gould Inc., Harris Corp., Honeywell Inc., Lockheed Missiles & Space Co., Martin-Marietta Corp., 3M Co., Mostek Corp., Motorola, NCR, National Semiconductor, RCA Corp., Rockwell International Corp., and Sperry Corp., among others. (A research consortium owned by the Bell operating companies had also applied for membership.) The venture was fashioned after the Japanese practice of pooling corporate R&D money and disseminating results. A second major joint research consortium, Semiconductor Research Corp. (SRC), had been created in 1982 to coordinate semiconductor research.

The MCC experiment illustrated problems that were commonplace to partners' relationships with each other and with their child in high technology joint ventures. Initially, partners balked at surrendering their very best personnel and proprietary ideas to a consortium that would help domestic competitors. But the child's manager had negotiated the right to reject personnel that were contributed by parents if these engineers did not meet the venture's high standards. After rejecting 90 percent of the applicants parents submitted in the first round of staffing, MCC was finally staffed with outsiders when parents would not send top-notch in-house talent. (Six of the seven key project directors were outsiders, for example.) When parents protested that they would have no way to repatriate knowledge back to their laboratories from MCC if its employees were outsiders that loyal to the child, they were advised to submit better in-house candidates or forever lose that chance. The caliber of parent-sponsored applicants improved abruptly. Several parent firms developed organizational mechanisms to move MCC technology into their laboratories.

In 1979 Energy Conversion Devices (ECD) formed a joint-venture and licensing agreement with ARCO Solar (Atlantic-Richfield) to develop and commercialize ECD's proprietary ovonic photovoltaic cells. ECD also licensed this technology to Sharp Corp. (Japan) and Burroughs. In 1980 Energy Conversion Devices and A.B. Dick formed a joint venture, A.B. Dick-MicroOvonics, to develop a micrographics system. Their microfilm venture was mutually cancelled in 1981.

In 1981 Control Data Corp. (CDC) formed a joint venture with Ampex to produce ferrite core memory products for CDC. Core memories had been a relatively small business for Control Data, and it was reducing its investment in them as semiconductors replaced ferrite cores for most applications. Ampex produced core memories for Control Data and for its OEM customers, and it agreed to repair and refurbish the existing base of CDC core memory installations. As a part of the venture, Ampex purchased Control Data's core memory production equipment and inventories. Thus, the alliance looked like a fade-out joint venture.

In 1984 National Semiconductor and Texas Instruments formed a joint research venture to commercialize a 32-bit microprocessor developed by National Semiconductor. Texas Instruments contributed its manufacturing capacity and experience plus design capabilities to develop peripheral chips for the new microprocessor system. Partners produced the microprocessor together but sold them through their separate, respective distribution channels. Their agreement was similar to an alliance between Intel and Advanced Micro Devices to expand production of Intel's microprocessors and was expected to become an increasingly commonplace business practice in the electronic components industry.

By 1984 five U.S. semiconductor firms had 50%-50% joint ventures with Tokyo Electron Ltd. (TEL), a semiconductor machinery maker. TEL sold chip-making equipment for twelve others and manufactured two product lines under licenses from another U.S. semiconductor firm. The U.S. firms provided technology, and TEL made highly reliable equipment for their needs.

In 1984 Wang Laboratories closed its internal chip-making operations and purchased a 15 percent interest in VLSI Technology Inc. Wang had tried to make its own custom semiconductor chips and telephone switching equipment (PBXs). It formed a technology-sharing agreement with VLSI Technology, instead.

In 1985 RCA Corp. and Sharp (Japan) formed a $200 million joint venture to make semiconductors in the United States. The cost of building new semiconductor plants had risen so high that all but the very largest firms sought ways to share the costs and risks.

Child Activities. The electronics industry faced short product lives, global competition, and scanty patent protection. There were few joint ventures but many other types of cooperative agreements within it. Partners coordinated their activities closely, as would be expected in settings where competition was highly volatile in terms of both price and product innovation. Close affiliations often meant that firms "borrowed" each others' ideas, and that practice contributed to the industry's volatility. No firm could hope to exploit a position of advantage for long.

The need for firms to cooperate increased in areas where the industry was relatively young and characterized by rapid technological obsolescence. Such settings squeezed profit margins such that firms could not afford to reinvest in R&D or new plants to sustain innovation. Their need for close coordination was also high. Accordingly, many firms preferred to acquire the technology they needed or to cross-license it, rather than work through the extra levels of managing shared decision making that joint ventures embodied. With over 200 firms competing for a slice of the global semiconductor market, cross-licensing arrangements and joint ventures were expected to be increasingly important in the future.

Computers and Computer Peripherals

Product offerings for computer systems included: mainframes, peripherals, software, and support. By 1984 many heretofore noncompeting supplier groups vied for customers in the arenas of small and medium-size computers, as well as in large mainframe computers. They were also forced to compete in the area of computer peripherals, software, and communications when they served the office automation customer. The worlds of the large mainframe computer manufacturers, the general-purpose minicomputers makers, and the microcomputer firms were converging to become one and the same as software and data transmission skills became increasingly important to competitive success.

Need for Joint Activities. Prior to 1984 manufacturers of mainframes, minicomputers, microcomputers, and communications equipment competed in separate markets. By 1984 the boundaries separating these markets had blurred as sophisticated customers pressed for compatibility between all parts of their information systems. Moreover, by 1984 computer companies no longer merely sold hardware; customers expected them to write applications software, as well. Computer companies found themselves undertaking new tasks or relying on outsider vendors to provide products for resale under their own labels. They scrambled to form alliances and partnerships with firms that were once their bitter competitors in order to broaden their product lines (while keeping prices low) and to interconnect the pieces of their systems.

Many U.S. computer and computer peripheral joint ventures were motivated by Japanese computer manufacturers, either as a means of letting them enter the United States or as a way of keeping them out. The first commercial Japanese computer was made in 1958, and domestic producers there were aligned into three joint research groups in 1973—Fujitsu-Hitachi, Nippon Electric (NEC)-Tokyo Shibaura Electric, and Mitsubishi Electric-Oki Electric Industry. They cooperated in their efforts against IBM Japan (a wholly owned subsidiary of International Business Machines) and Nippon Univac (a joint venture of Sperry-Rand, Mitsui & Co., and other Japanese investors). In 1984 Fujitsu was moving to become the world's second-largest computer mainframe manufacturer, through its strategy with respect to Amdahl and other computer makers that were using it as an OEM vendor. A combination of minority investments, joint ventures, OEM vendor agreements, technology cross-licensing, marketing and manufacturing agreements, and other cooperative arrangements permeated the computers and computer peripherals industry by 1984.

Choosing Partners.

Computers. In 1964 Martin-Marietta and Thomson-Ramo-Woolridge (TRW) formed a joint venture, Bunker-Ramo, to produce computer control systems for the military and industry. Their child absorbed the computer divisions of TRW and the Electronic Systems and Products Division of Martin-Marietta. TRW went back into computers in 1976 by acquiring Singer's data processing business.

In the early 1970s, Telex and Hitachi terminated discussions of a joint venture to market a mainframe computer made by Hitachi. Telex made peripheral machines for use with IBM computers but did not market a central processing unit (CPU) or mainframe machine itself. Their arrangement called for Hitachi to provide Telex with technical information and know-how associated with its new computer.

In 1970 the Heizer Corp. (a venture capital firm) and Fujitsu formed Amdahl, a manufacturer of large computers. Fujitsu owned a 26.7 percent interest in Amdahl in 1979. Amdahl operated autonomously, but three Fujitsu representatives sat on its board. International marketing rights to Amdahl's large-scale computers (outside the United States, Canada, Japan, and Spain) were held by Amdahl International Ltd., a 50%-50% joint venture of Fujitsu and Amdahl.

Fujitsu's response to Amdahl's attempt to acquire Storage Technology (STC) in 1980 illustrates how conflicts could develop between parent and child. (Earlier in 1979 Amdahl's attempt to acquire Memorex was also thwarted by the actions of its Japanese partner.) Fujitsu did not have a large market presence in the United States in 1980, but it wanted to penetrate the U.S. market for computers peripherals, with Amdahl's help. Fujitsu shared semiconductor technology with Amdahl and liaisoned closely and regularly with its personnel. Amdahl engineers traveled on a regular basis to Tokyo.

Observers believed that Fujitsu opposed Amdahl's diversification efforts because Storage Technology and Memorex both made computer peripherals that would have competed with Fujitsu's own devices. In 1984 Fujitsu increased its ownership in Amdahl to 49.5 percent.

In 1980 TRW and Fujitsu formed a 49%-51% joint venture, TRW-Fujitsu Co. (TFC), to sell Fujitsu's computers in the United States. TRW had not been successful in data processing, even after trying twice, and yet it considered the computers, computer peripherals, and computer maintenance businesses to be very important. Under their venture agreement, TRW products were phased out, and new ones from Fujitsu were introduced. Their first joint-venture product was a business computer—priced at $25,000 (and capable of supporting fifteen terminals). One-third of the joint venture's employees were devoted to writing applications software appropriate for the U.S. market. (TRW had a modest reputation in applications software.) TFC built a national sales network to supplement TRW's existing sales and service organization, but the distribution that TRW provided was inadequate for Fujitsu's needs, and TFC did not get the penetration it had hoped for. In 1983 Fujitsu purchased TRW's 49 percent interest in TFC, renamed it Fujitsu Systems of America, and the child's personnel became Fujitsu employees.

Fujitsu also had a joint development venture with International Computers, Ltd. (ICL)—which had been created from two failing computer companies—to supply a wide range of computers, particularly for distributed computing networks. ICL's alliance with Fujitsu allowed it to span the entire mainframe product line while reducing its in-house R&D expenditures.

In 1983 Nippon Electric had a 45 percent share of the personal computers market in Japan. A substantial proportion of NEC's mainframe computers were exported in the form of OEM sales to an increasing number of overseas companies for software, maintenance support, and resale. These firms included Amdahl Corp (United States), Siemens A.G. (Germany), Nasco (United States), Olivetti (Italy), BASF (Germany), and ICL (United Kingdom). NEC established joint ventures with Honeywell USA (for marketing computers), with 3M (for the development and marketing of information storage systems) in the United States, and with Honeywell Bull in France.

In 1976 Digital Equipment (DEC) joined with the Norden Division of United Technologies to build military minicomputers for the hostile environments encountered in tactical applications. DEC did not want to develop the highly specialized machine alone, and United Technologies had a good track record in selling complex equipment to the military.

In 1979 Matsushita Electrical Industrial Co. Ltd. and Friends-Amis, Inc., formed a joint venture to develop and make a hand-held microcomputer with a compressed memory that held more than twice the data of conventional systems. Friends-Amis was a computer research and development firm.

Hitachi and Itel had formed a joint marketing venture to sell plug-compatible computers similar to IBM's products. When Itel withdrew from the computer business in 1979 and National Semiconductor assumed its computer leasing and sales operations, Hitachi agreed to supply its medium and large computers and memory products to its subsidiary, National Advanced Systems Corp. (Nasco). But Hitachi made it clear that it intended to open *its own*, fully owned U.S. marketing division that would compete against Nasco. In 1983 National Advanced Systems quit trying to build its own version of a 4300-class processor and devoted itself to marketing and servicing computers supplied by its Japanese joint-venture partner, Hitachi.

IBM's use of cooperative strategies was a part of its dramatic change in policies regarding the use of outsiders' components in the early 1980s. Minolta provided IBM with copiers for resale in 1981, and Sanyo Seiki and Hitachi provided robots and printers for resale, respectively, in 1982. Matsushita and Oki provided components for the IBM work station in 1983. IBM's success with its Personal Computer illustrated graphically how to use cooperative strategies effectively. Its designers were given great autonomy to penetrate the personal computers market quickly by using an Intel microprocessor, Microsoft operating system, and readily available parts from outsiders rather than developing proprietary components in-house.

In Europe, IBM recognized the value of consortia to achieve timely entry by bringing together suppliers from different backgrounds. IBM used joint ventures in Japan with Mitsubishi Trading Company and with Cosmo Corp., a software concern, to develop software for the telecommunications field. IBM formed a joint venture with Kanematsu Gosho, a medium-size trading company, to form a nationwide network of computer sales and service dealerships for middle-of-the-line products. In 1984 IBM arranged for Triumph-Adler A.G., the office-equipment subsidiary of Volkswagenwerk A.G., to supply electronic typewriters that could be modified for use with IBM computers. IBM used other European manufacturers to provide personal-computer printers and other peripheral equipment. Doing so afforded IBM greater flexibility in embracing the newest and best technologies for use in its products.

IBM persuaded value-added resellers to buy its units and components to write software or build peripheral equipment, thereby harnessing the software-writing efforts of thousands of independent businesses that traditionally purchase hardware, add specialized software, and then resell their products to specific market niches (*vertical markets*). To overcome its late start in the microcomputer market, IBM embraced an "open architecture" strategy, whereby it publicized the standards for its PC interfaces to competitors to encourage them to build compatible software and peripheral products for it. But simultaneously, IBM sued competitors, such as Hitachi, for theft of trade secrets in mainframe computer products, where it adhered to a policy of closed architecture.

By 1984 other major computer firms were also embracing cooperative strategies. AT&T linked up with Philips N.V. and Olivetti, respectively, in 1984 (Philips was not a major player in telecommunications equipment or in computers and data processing. AT&T's interests with Philips were primarily in marketing in Europe). AT&T purchased Olivetti computers (and other office equipment) and Convergent Technologies microcomputers for resale. Its 1984 personal computer (an Olivetti product) offered a standard telephone modem, and capabilities were rumored to exceed even those of the newly announced Rolm-IBM offering (described in another section below). Olivetti purchased a 49 percent interest in Acorn Computer Group PLC in early 1985 to help rescue the troubled microcomputer maker. The acquisition was part of Olivetti's efforts to become a global computer firm. Olivetti expressed some dismay early in 1985 at AT&T's lack of aggressiveness in marketing its microcomputer product line. The joint venture's duration was threatened as Olivetti discussed the creation of a parallel marketing effort.

In 1984 computer makers like Sperry and Honeywell were relying on outside vendors to provide many products in their mainframe product lines. By doing so, firms hoped to attain scale economies that would permit them to compete with IBM. Honeywell used NEC's large mainframes, and Sperry marketed Mitsubishi Electric Corp.'s small- and medium-size mainframe computers. Sperry also took a 15 percent interest in Trilogy Systems, a large mainframe maker that boasted the founder of Amdahl Computer as its chief executive.

Computer Peripherals. In 1970 Pitney-Bowes, Inc. and Alpex Computer Corp. formed a 50%-50% joint venture, Pitney-Bowes-Alpex, to make and sell computerized point of sale (POS) register systems developed by Alpex. Virtually all of Alpex's assets were put into the child, making it look like a fade-out joint venture. Pitney-Bowes's Monarch Marking Systems subsidiary provided devices to make ticket-imprinters to prepare machine-readable tickets for use with the POS equipment of the child.

Since its founding, Control Data had expected to grow and prosper through cooperative strategies. By 1984 CDC had been engaged in over 200 cooperative ventures (of varying forms) throughout the globe and within several industries. In 1974 Control Data Corp. (CDC), International Computers, Ltd. (United Kingdom), and NCR formed a joint venture, Computer Peripherals Inc. (CPI) to make computer peripheral products, including tape drives, card equipment, and printers. CPI was the first computer hardware combine, and its mission was reformulated in 1983 when ICL sold its interest back to CDC. CPI's remaining parents sold the printer portion of its business, leaving only the magnetic tape drives business, and Syntronics (an outsider) was merged with the spun-off printers venture to create an entity capable of attaining critical mass in sales volumes. The merger gave the parents of CPI a 40 percent interest in a newly formed printers company.

In 1976 Control Data Corp. (CDC) and International Computers Ltd. (United Kingdom) formed a 24%-76% joint venture, Control Dataset Ltd., to transfer knowledge concerning computers and computer peripherals. The child made magnetic disks, ribbons, and other computer wares, and it was prosperous. But when the minority partner (which managed the venture) encountered adversity rather than its partner's cooperation, the venture was terminated.

In 1975 Control Data Corp. (CDC) and Honeywell formed a 70%-30% joint venture, Magnetic Peripherals Inc. (MPI), to design, develop, and make rotating mass memory products for the computer industry, such as disk and drum products. Honeywell and CDC contributed their respective computer peripheral assets to create a child that could compete with IBM. Magnetic Peripherals had lower costs than either parent had alone because it eliminated duplicate activities and exploited economies of scale. CII-Honeywell Bull later purchased a 3 percent interest in MPI from Honeywell. Sperry became a partner in 1983 with 17 percent, making the ownership split CDC (67%) and Honeywell (17%). Magnetic Peripherals was a captive supplier for its parents. (It sold on an OEM basis only to them.) MPI's parents did not purchase their magnetic memory devices from other in-house business units. Nor did they maintain parallel facilities that competed against MPI as long as its products were updated and competitive with those of outsiders.

Magnetic Peripherals Inc. was used as a vehicle to enter other joint ventures on behalf of its parents. Magnetic Peripherals and Memorex formed a set of 60%-40% joint ventures to develop a magnetic plating for MPI's memory devices in 1981. The joint venture invested in generations of technology to develop thin-film heads and applications for them in semiconductor technologies. These joint ventures were also captives that sold only to their parents, which used their respective market access to sell the ventures' outputs. As the ventures became increasingly successful, partners relied on them to be major suppliers, especially where other firms failed to commercialize similar products.

In 1982 MPI and Philips N.V. formed a set of joint ventures to develop laser optimal memory devices. Philips was a majority owner (52 percent) in their partnership to develop the substrate for the memory device. MPI was majority owner (52 percent) in their partnership to develop the drive, its rotation mechanism, and its read/write head. Although CDC was strong in magnetic memory devices, it wanted to have access to knowledge concerning alternative technologies that could supplant its ongoing products. The joint ventures were structured to provide complementary bargaining power while putting one partner in charge of each child's activity. When their development phase was completed, the two ventures were melded into one 51%-49% joint venture, Optical Storage International (OSI), with Philips N.V. as majority owner and CDC as its partner. (Control Data obtained the rights to the OSI technology from Magnetic Peripherals, the original venture partner.) Optical Storage International was permitted to have both manufacturing and marketing facilities of its own, but it was expected to contract for marketing and distribution services from Control Data initially.

In 1979 Reynolds & Reynolds (a maker of business forms and provider of computer systems for business establishments) and Zonic Technical Laboratories formed a 70%-30% joint venture, ReyZon Computers, to manufacture intelligent computer terminals to be marketed primarily to Reynolds' computer services customers. Zonic Labs offered Reynolds & Reynolds access to a piece of equipment it needed to replace, one that its previous vendor had discontinued. The venture started as a contract, but Zonic Labs lacked capital, so a joint venture was formed as a way of financing it. When one of the Zonics principals left the firm, Reynolds & Reynolds acquired its 30 percent share of ReyZon in 1980.

In 1979 Tandy/Radio Shack and Datapoint formed a joint venture to make disk drives for personal computers. When the venture did not work out, Tandy replaced Datapoint with Tandon and formed a joint venture, Texas Peripherals, to produce disk drives for sale under the Tandy brand name.

In 1980 Floating Point Systems arranged a cooperative marketing program with Digital Equipment to combine the capabilities of Floating Point's extended precision array processors and the large memories of DEC's PDP-11 and VAX computers. As part of this affiliation, Floating Point launched a software development program to reach markets neither partner serviced adequately alone. In 1983 the Autologic subsidiary of Volt Information Systems and 3M formed a similar venture to develop a paginating system, utilizing an array processor, with applications for the printing industry.

By 1983 Storage Technology (STC) had spent $12 million to bring a generation of disk computer memories into production. But by the time it prepared its next generation of optical data storage units for sale, costs had shot up to $80 million. To raise the $40 million it needed, STC formed a limited partnership for research and development with private investors, and it formed a research joint venture with DuPont to perfect the optical storage media. (DuPont was emphasizing electronic products as its film-based storage media grew obsolete.) But in 1984 Storage Technology filed for bankruptcy protection.

In 1984 Polaroid Corp. formed a joint venture with Permabyte Magnetics Inc. and PerfectData Corp. to produce the flexible disks on which software is written. The technology was compatible with Polaroid's expertise in photography. (It developed the coating for the disks and distributed them through drug stores where it sold photographic film cartridges.) PermaByte Magnetics made the disks, and PerfectData distributed them to traditional outlets, such as computer stores.

Also in 1984, Westinghouse Electric and Toshiba formed a joint venture to produce color cathode ray tubes (CRTs) in the United States. Earlier in

1984 Westinghouse had announced a ten-year partnership with Sanyo Electric and Nissho Iwai to make and sell electronic communication products for cable television systems.

In early 1985 AT&T and Electronic Data Systems (EDS) agreed to market jointly specially designed computer and communications systems. The marketing agreement provided for 150 EDS employees to work with 100 AT&T employees to generate sales leads and design integrated computer and communications systems. Teams of sales representatives from both parents solicited specifications from customers for private branch exchanges, integrated systems (for automatic order placement), and local area networks that linked computers, and teams of communications and computer specialists from both parents formulated bids to satisfy their requirements. A third team of EDS and AT&T engineers put together the hardware and software for systems purchased by customers. The venture's announcement followed on the heels of one stating that Apple Computer and General Electric would cooperate in marketing computerized systems using the GE communications network (GEnet).

Child Activities. Although there were few joint ventures to make computers, minority investments, OEM vendor arrangements, and other types of cooperative agreements abounded in this industry. The activity in question (making computers) was so important to major players that they would not cooperate with outsiders or tolerate the extra layers of negotiation needed to manage a joint venture child.

There were many joint ventures, as well as many other types of cooperative arrangements, in the computer peripherals business. The high-scale economy advantages available from manufacturing computer peripherals in large volumes made close coordination between parent and child necessary unless partners pooled their assets in the child and permitted it to be totally responsible for their in-house peripheral development. As the example of Magnetic Peripherals indicates, parents could choose alternative sources for their peripherals if their child did not perform adequately, and the child's failure signaled its demise since it had no marketing assets of its own.

Minority investments were popular among U.S. computers and computer peripherals firms because they carried the illusion that owners could control their child's activities and gain advance knowledge of its product decisions. Only Fujitsu (in its relationship with Amdahl) provided tangible evidence that it was acting as a marionette master in the examples examined herein.

As increasing numbers of information processing and electronics companies joined forces to cooperate, two patterns emerged: (1) Horizontal cooperation did *not* create a child. Instead, partners learned how to cooperate in developing common standards because no firm had enough research money to risk and enough good results in-house to offer every product needed to compete effectively. The "not-invented here" (NIH) syndrome that had plagued efforts to transfer knowledge from division to division within a single firm (not to mention between autonomous firms) had to be surmounted. When it became clear that coalitions *would* be important in hurdling the chasm between computer technology and that of telecommunications, (2) firms scurried to form alliances. But as the next section explains, no competitors possessed the necessary resources and knowledge to bridge this product gap in a timely fashion alone. Separate joint-venture entities were formed more frequently to bridge this gap because partners were not head-to-head competitors and because a single repository was needed to pool the knowledge that was germane to the task.

Office Equipment

Office equipment included machinery for typing, word-processing, tabulating, record-keeping, record-storage, filing, photocopying, dataprocessing, and transmitting information. Computers (covered above) comprised a costly portion of office equipment budgets. The private branch exchanges (PBXs), covered in another section below, represented an increasingly important part of this business.

Need for Joint Activities. The nature of office automation was changing in the 1970s as electronics permeated the office. Products were changing faster and were offering more features. Joint ventures were formed to permit firms to introduce new products faster.

Choosing Partners. One of the earliest and most successful joint ventures in office products was the formation in 1960 of Rank-Xerox to make and sell xerographic equipment in England. Ownership in the venture was shared on a 51%-49% basis (Xerox had the majority) and was so well integrated with ongoing operations that it was considered to be a part of the Xerox organization by customers. The Rank Organization joined with Xerox to make and sell copier and duplicator products for sale throughout the eastern hemisphere. Because Xerox provided technology to the child, it received a larger proportion of Rank-Xerox's profits. Rank-Xerox formed a 50%-50% joint venture in Japan with Fuji Photo Film in the early 1960s.

Xerox and the Rank Organization formed another 51%-49% joint venture in 1979 to make and sell office equipment, including high-speed printers, word-processing equipment, small business systems, and document finishing products. In 1980 Xerox formed marketing agreements with CompuScan Inc. for optical character recognition equipment and with Mathematical Applications Group, Inc. for computer-based 35 mm slide product equipment.

There were many joint marketing agreements covering office products. Apeco Corp. formed a joint marketing agreement with Clark Copy International Corp. to gain worldwide distribution of photocopy machines in 1978. Nolex formed a joint marketing agreement with Tokyo Aircraft Instrument Co. Ltd. in 1976 to sell its plain-paper copier in the United States. SCM Corp. formed a joint marketing agreement in 1978 with Kip Corp. of Japan to sell its photocopy machine. SCM formed a similar joint marketing agreement in 1977 with Olympia Werke A.G. of Germany to distribute its dry-copiers in the United States. Nashua formed a joint manufacturing and marketing agreement in 1976 with Matsushita Electric Industrial Co. Ltd. covering electrothermosensitive recording paper for photocopying. Nashua formed a joint marketing agreement in 1975 with Savin for electrostatic copy products. Bell & Howell Co. and Mamiya Camera Co. formed a joint marketing agreement in 1975 to sell Mamiya's photographic products in the United States. (Bell & Howell and General Electric formed a joint venture, Microx Corp., in 1976 to develop and make an instant microfilm imaging system.) Minnesota Mining & Manufacturing Co. (3M) formed a marketing agreement with Energy Conversion Devices in 1976 to sell imaging products, including a microfiche card system. In 1977 Honeywell formed an agreement that permitted it to develop Advanced Computer Techniques's word processing system. TRW Inc. formed a joint marketing agreement in 1977 to sell Lexitron's word processing equipment. Dennison formed a joint marketing agreement to sell Wordplex Corp.'s word processing equipment.

In 1975 A.B. Dick and Scott Graphics Inc. (a subsidiary of Scott Paper) formed a joint venture, A.B. Dick/Scott, to market a new record processor. It was part of a data storage and retrieval system that enabled users to add a single image to a microfiche in a practical and cost-effective way through the use of a special film. The original record processor equipment was developed by Scott Graphics and was manufactured by A.B. Dick for the child. Scott Graphics produced microfiche film and suppliers for it.

A.B. Dick formed a joint research venture in 1979 with Data Products to develop nonimpact inkjet printers, a technology that printed characters by projecting minute ink droplets through the air at very high speeds. A.B. Dick formed a joint marketing agreement with Hendrix Electronics in 1979 to sell Hendrix's word processing line. (Hendrix had held an exclusive license since 1977 to market Digital Equipment's mainframe computer system for new typesetting functions.) Macrodyne Industries Inc. formed a joint manufacturing agreement with Uppster Corp. covering high-speed nonimpact printers. In 1984 Ricoh Corp. introduced five photocopier models. Concurrently, Savin announced a line of photocopiers made for it by Ricoh. Both product lines were designed to challenge Xerox's market position in xerography, as were a number of the joint ventures, joint marketing agreements, and other cooperative strategies sketched above.

In 1978 Savin and Conrac formed a joint venture, Savin/Conrac, to sell and service photocopier equipment. Savin and Conrac provided manufacturing, engineering, and development of copiers for their child. Savin/Conrac acquired the assets of Conrac's Cramer Division, making the venture a fade-out for it. The child produced accessories for Savin's copier line and manufactured line of liquid-toner plain-paper copiers now under development by Savin.

In 1981 Bunnington Corp. and Sumitomo formed a 67%-33% joint venture, Magnetic Systems, Inc., to manufacture precision magnetic assemblies for the photocopying and electronic printing markets. Sumitomo Special Metals Co. Ltd. had supplied Bunnington's Fannon Industries with ferrite materials for use in magnetic heads, which are contained in copiers, word processors, and high-speed printers. Under terms of their joint venture, Magnetic Systems manufactured the heads for shipment to customers for later assembly. It also performed final black box assembly for customers.

In 1981 Memorex Corp. and Dainippon Ink and Chemicals Inc. formed a 57%-43% joint venture, Memorex DIC Corp., to supply products for word processing equipment. Memorex, which made computer peripheral equipment, computer media products, and blank magnetic tape, marketed the child's products. Dainippon Ink and Chemicals provided the child with technology.

In 1983 less dominant manufacturers were entering into joint ventures to strengthen their product lines to survive in the competitive environment of office automation and computerization. Nippon Electric Corp. (NEC) and Honeywell Bull formed a joint venture in office automation. Software development was crucial for the office automation strategy NEC had chosen. Without it, NEC's strengths in communications and computers could not be fully exploited. Honeywell Bull provided that missing skill. Similarly, NEC formed a joint venture with 3M (for the development and marketing of information storage systems) in the United States.

Child Activities. There were more cooperative agreements than joint ventures in the office equipment business because these products were changing rapidly during the 1970s and firms were reluctant to enter arrangements that they believed would stymie their flexibility. Of the joint ventures listed above, over half were formed to permit a foreign competitor to access distribution channels in new geographic markets. There were fewer technological risk-sharing motives in this group of joint ventures than in the other industries of this chapter. OEM arrangements allowed firms with established market positions in office equipment to supplement their product lines faster than they could do in-house.

Communications Equipment

Communications equipment consisted of network equipment and customer premises equipment. Network equipment included: switching systems, submarine cables, satellites, fiber optic cables, microwave, mobile radio systems, satellite earth stations, and coaxial cable. Customer premises equipment included: telephones, facsimile machines, word-processing equipment, teletype-writers, PBXs, work stations, pagers, and teleconferencing systems.

Major groups of customers included: (1) domestic end-users, original equipment manufacturers (OEMs), specialized common carriers, international record carriers, newswire services and governmental agencies (such as Quotron, Xerox, and Intel) that required high standards of on-line performance; (2) domestic telephone and telegraph common carriers and railroads; (3) international buyers; and (4) corporations seeking to link data processing and communications equipment in offices and automated factories.

Need for Joint Activities. The communications industry was characterized by substantial capital requirements, pressures to reduce costs (by exploiting scale economies), and increasing sophistication of products in the data transmission industry. Excess capacity was a continual threat as the telecommunications industry was deregulated and vendors each strived to offer complete, compatible network systems.

New technologies were constantly being developed, and as each generation of equipment appeared on the market, older versions were rendered obsolete. In order to succeed, firms needed: (1) technological expertise; (2) large amounts of capital; (3) the ability to adapt technology to customers' needs and partners' configurations; (4) distribution networks (or ways to access to others' networks); (5) cost structures that permitted firms to offer attractive pricing and acceptable quality; and (6) willingness to hook up with other vendors.

The U.S. telecommunications industry changed rapidly and was volatile because of (1) the convergence of computers and telecommunications; (2) shorter product lives driven by rapid technological improvements; (3) huge R&D expenditures by ongoing and new competitors; (4) intensification of global competition; (5) deregulation of telecommunications; (6) an expected boom in the office automation equipment industry; and (7) a potential breakdown of trade barriers as a result of technological changes and political activities. These conditions triggered an early shakeout among some players.

Choosing Partners. By 1984 many electronics, information processing, and telecommunications firms were teaming up to develop new technologies and products. Some firms were forming joint ventures because a self-centered, vertically integrated approach to the business did not seem to be appropriate any longer. Moreover, because no firm could develop in-house every product needed to compete effectively in 1984, firms were moving swiftly to find appropriate partners. Collaboration had become so important to the interface between communications and data processing that some companies were investing in partners to cement their relationships and alleviate their fears of being left behind.

Many firms feared that if they did not team up, they would lose their market positions to foreign competitors for whom cooperation was nothing new. Some firms—especially smaller, younger firms that specialized in information processing technologies—formed joint ventures for survival. Affiliations with larger telecommunications firms gave them access to much-needed management experience, as well as to sales and service capabilities they could not afford on their own.

Cable Equipment. In 1973 Oak Industries and L.E. Myers Co. formed Myers-Oak Communications Construction Corporation, a 50%-50% joint venture, to provide construction services in the United States and Canada for overhead and underground trunk and feeder CATV systems. L.E. Myers was a Chicago-based electric utilities contractor that specialized in building transmission lines and distribution systems for utilities. The child's facilities were originally Myers', and thus the venture may have been a way for it to divest its interest in a business that was becoming highly uncertain.

Demand for cable services developed on a city-by-city basis, and as cities became increasingly aware of their bargaining power in awarding cable contracts, they sought better prices. Cable service companies tried to pass these pressures for lower prices on to cable construction firms. Myers-Oak was sold to another cable construction company in 1975, due to a lack of economic construction activity in the CATV market.

Satellites. In 1973 Fairchild Industries and TRW set up a joint venture to design and manufacture three-axis body stabilized satellites with multichannel communications capability. Their child was to supply domestic satellites to RCA Global Communications. American Satellite, a joint venture of Continental Telecom and Fairchild (discussed in chapter 9), formed an agreement in 1982 with Tandem Computers to develop, market, and implement INFOSAT, the first fail-safe satellite data transmission system for continuous on-line transaction processing, distributed data processing, and information systems management.

In the 1980s, cable TV was challenged by a new delivery channel, direct-broadcast satellite (DBS). The new technology offered enhanced picture quality through a time multiplex component (TMC) transmission system. In 1983 ALCOA and NEC Communications formed a joint venture, ANCOM, to make and market direct-broadcast satellite subscriber equipment (dish-shaped receivers, priced between $750 and $1,000, to receive programming transmitted by satellite signals). ALCOA produced the offset-feed dish antennas, and NEC manufactured the addressable receivers/descramblers in Japan. By using parents' facilities, ANCOM expected to realize significant scale economies. Its first customer was to have been a joint venture of CBS and Satellite Television Corp., but the CBS-STC venture never materialized, due to the vast excess satellite transmission capacity in place by 1984 (see chapter 9).

Olympia & York and United Telecommunications Inc. formed a joint venture, OlympiaNet, in 1984 to install shared communications facilities in forty Olympia & York buildings nationwide. The $100 million venture linked the building by satellites provided by United Telecommunications. Shared systems used common switching equipment, making them less costly than the cost of buying a private system.

Communications Networks. In 1977 Corning Glass Works and Siemens A.G. formed a joint venture, Siecor Optical Cables, to offer fiber optic systems. Corning contributed the wherewithal to make optical fiber, and Siemens provided the electronic components necessary to make and market a system of optical fiber communications. Insilco Corp. and Fiber Communications Inc. formed a joint venture, Times Fiber Communications, in 1977 to make fiber optics for communications uses. Times Fiber Communications also offered fiber optics communications *systems*, in a bundled strategy similar to that of Siecor. M/A-COM (a manufacturer of microwave radio and other communications devices) and Philips Optical Communications Corp. (of Philips N.V.) formed a joint venture, Valtec, to supply optical fiber cable and components for the telephone and defense markets. By 1981 the funding requirements of Valtec had become difficult to satisfy. (Optical fiber was being increasingly used by telephone companies across the United States as it became competitive with traditional copper cable. This rapid growth was expensive, and it resulted in substantial excess capacity, as chapter 9 explained.)

In 1980 M/A-COM and Aetna Life & Casualty formed a 50%-50% joint venture, Local Digital Distribution Co. (LDD), to provide digital transmission and network access control equipment for local distribution of voice, high-speed data, and image communications. LDD supplied local network equipment to the common carrier and specialized common carrier industry, as well as to other authorized entities. (Aetna was also a partner in Satellite Business Systems, discussed in chapter 9.)

In 1980 Atlantic Richfield's Anaconda unit and LM Ericsson Telephone Co. (of Sweden) formed a 50%-50% joint venture, Anaconda Ericsson, to make wire and cable products and telecommunications equipment in the U.S. and abroad. The child operated Anaconda's power and telecommunications cable units and the electronics facilities of Anaconda's wire and cable division. The joint venture also involved other Anaconda products such as PBXs, subscriber carrier equipment, and concentrators. Ericsson contributed capabilities in electronics and telecommunications, as well as LM Ericsson's telecommunications equipment marketing operations in the United States, Canada, and other interests. (Ericsson's sales and service outlets distributed private automatic telephone exchanges, transmission equipment, and components, including PBXs, key systems, intercoms, radio, paging equipment, and transmission equipment.) The child was operated as a separate, wholly owned subsidiary of its parents, and it set up a separate, wholly owned subsidiary, called A-E Telecommunications Inc., to handle its nonwire and cable telecommunications activities. When the joint ventures lost more than $50 million on revenues of $480 million in 1982, its parents changed the child's name from Anaconda-Ericsson to Ericsson Inc. and shuffled ownership shares.

In 1983 CSX Corporation formed a joint venture with Southern New England Telephone called LightNet to lay cables for a fiber optical network for long distance communications services along CSX's right of way. LightNet planned to sell access to this network to commercial customers, including other common carriers, large users of communications services (such as banks, insurance companies), and government agencies. LightNet's estimated cost was between $300 million and $600 million, and its scope included twenty-four states east of the Mississippi and 4,000 system miles. Financing was planned by selling customers an interest in LightNet—at least $10,000 for each mile of the system they used, but the two partners (CSX and Southern New England Telephone)—retained equal shares for the remainder of the operation. Firms that purchased an interest could resell or lease their rights to the high-speed data transmission service firms that were emerging in 1983. (CSX and Southern New England Telephone did not plan to lease their share of capacity, however. Southern New England Telephone, for example, planned to use its capacity to offer its own long-distance telephone services.)

Similar joint ventures were planned by other railroads, such as (1) Electra Communications, a joint venture planned by Cable & Wireless and the Missouri-Kansas-Texas Railroad; (2) Fibertrak, a joint venture of Norfolk Southern Corp. and Sante Fe Southern Pacific (forming an 8,100 fiber optic network); (3) Microtel, a joint venture of Norfolk Southern, M/A-COM, Centel, and E.F. Hutton; and (4) Litel Communications, a joint venture of Centel, Alltel, and Pirelli, among others. In addition to these joint ventures, AT&T had announced fiber-optic expansions totaling 10,000 miles, Satellite Business Systems (SBS) was negotiating for access to fiber transmission facilities for part of its voice traffic services. MCI and GTE Sprint each planned fiber-optic networks that together would exceed 22,000 miles, and a 23,000-mile system was announced by United Telecommunications. Substantial excess communications capacity was anticipated if all of the satellite services and fiber-optic networks planned by railroads and private corporations were indeed constructed (see chapter 9).

Private Branch Exchanges (PBXs). PBXs are computerized switchboards that route telephone calls within an office and provide services such as transferring calls and conference calling. Advanced PBXs can also switch nonvoice data to allow users of computer terminals, for example, to share information with each other or larger computers. PBXs can handle fewer than thirty to tens of thousands of telephone lines and can cost from several thousand to millions of dollars. Since PBXs used ordinary telephone wires to send information, they were cheaper than other types of data networks for most applications. The combination of voice and data handling abilities made the PBX a prime candidate to serve as the information hub in the electronic office. Incompatible designs, however, had created technical barriers to linking various computers and PBXs to make them work together.

By the 1980s, data processing firms recognized that building the PBX was not a trivial matter—the technologies were quite different from that of building computers. But because modern office and factory automation systems relied on a combination of computer and communications technologies, information processing companies were expected to be conversant in an increasing number of diverse technologies. Several computer companies found that they could not master data, text, voice, images, and graphics communications—in addition to data processing—alone. They were forced to take partners.

Meanwhile, the telephone industry was in turmoil in the 1980s due to rapidly changing technology and deregulation, including the AT&T divestitures. As boundary lines blurred between telecommunications and data processing, success in the telephone business was becoming more dependent on software. Two diverse competitor groups were converging in their pursuit of market share in the office-of-the-future markets: (1) computer makers moving into communications to link their machines and (2) communications equipment producers making products, such as computer terminals, to sell their switches. (By the late 1980s as much as 40 percent of PBX sales was expected to be generated by extra features and add-ons, including terminals and software.)

In 1976 Fujitsu Ltd. and American Telecommunications had formed an 82%-18% joint venture, American Telecommunications Systems Inc., to make and sell electronic private branch exchanges. The PBXs, which were assembled in California, did not exceed a capacity of 500 telephone lines. (One year earlier, American Telecommunications Corp. had formed a joint venture with Telephonax Inc. to make and sell telephone answering machines.)

In 1981 Anaconda-Ericsson (a joint venture of Atlantic-Richfield's Anaconda and LM Ericsson of Sweden) had purchased Axxa, Citicorp's office automation subsidiary (also called Lexar Business Communications, Inc. or LBCI), maker of the Lexar automated workstation that had been developed internally. The acquired unit became part of the Anaconda-Ericsson Information Systems unit (described above).

Seeing that deregulation would open opportunities, Continental Telecom and Thomson-CSF (of France) had formed a joint venture in 1981 to design, manufacture, and market business communications equipment and systems in the United States. This was a reversal of Continental Telecom's earlier PBX strategy. (During the 1970s, Continental Telecom had divested itself of PBX manufacturing operations to focus on voice and data telecommunications services.) Their venture was cancelled due to uncertainties regarding French government policies one year later.

In 1982 Northern Telecom (of Canada) entered a cooperative agreement for equipment standards with Sperry Corp. It forged similar agreements with twenty-nine other computer makers. Eventually every data processing and PBX manufacturer was expected to have technology standard agreements, or they would find it difficult to compete. The agreements were nonexclusive (or spider's webs) in 1982 and did not involve huge fees. In 1982 IBM and Mitel (a Canadian PBX maker) formed a joint effort to develop an advanced PBX that IBM could market under its own name. Its introduction was delayed by software development problems, and by 1983 IBM was "examining" its Mitel arrangement. (IBM had sold its own PBX in Europe for years but did not consider that device as being suitable for U.S. markets.)

Every manufacturer of computer or communications equipment did not *want* to sign joint venture agreements in 1982. In particular, firms that had (or intended to offer) both computer and communications products were not anxious to team up with potential competitors. Thus Wang promoted its own Wangnet, and AT&T was waiting and watching in 1982. But competition was becoming intensified in 1983, and companies were finding it harder to keep up on their own. Technology was moving faster and product lives were shortening. As a result, firms could not take their established long periods of time to develop new products. The entire process of innovation was moving too fast for many of them, especially when the 1983 PBX market became so competitive that manufacturers underbid their own distributors.

Despite vendors' frenzied marketing efforts, large customers were delaying their purchases of major electronic office equipment in 1983 because office equipment from different vendors was still not compatible in a single system. (Each vendor used a different type of cable, and corporate customers did not want to lock themselves into dependence on a single supplier.) A potential market of $3 billion in equipment and $3.4 million in telephone lines awaited firms that could solve the compatibility problem. So some data processing firms endorsed the PBXs of particular vendors as a standard for interconnecting their respective office equipment. They hoped to surmount the problem of customer reticence by endorsing each other's equipment and by entering into joint product development agreements and felt pressed to cooperate because demand for office systems had not grown as rapidly as they had thought it would. Other firms dropped out in 1983. For example, computer maker Datapoint Corp. sold its communications division after an unsuccessful attempt to crack the market for telephone private branch exchanges (PBXs). AT&T had a market share of 29.1 percent in 1983; Northern Telecom had 17.9 percent, Rolm had a 16.7 percent share, Mitel had 12.8 percent. GTE had a 4.6 percent share, NEC had 5.4 percent, and others carried the remaining 13.5 percent.

IBM set the competitive tone for 1983 when it invested in Rolm, a PBX maker (a 15 percent interest initially), and then acquired the rest of Rolm in 1984. Although Rolm was the acknowledged leader in digital, computer-controlled PBXs (with 85 percent of its 1983 sales in PBX systems), it was small (with sales of $400 million in 1982) when compared with AT&T, IT&T, or Siemens. Nevertheless, Rolm had built a reputation for excellent software that permitted customers to upgrade their systems on an ongoing basis, thereby enabling them to have the most up-to-date office functions and high quality. The digital equipment Rolm sold allowed IBM to meet the premier challenge of the office automation market—how to integrate the transmission of voice and data. Rolm was expected to set standards in the interface area to solve problems affecting the connectability of computers with communications equipment. Satellite Business Systems (see chapter 9) and Rolm were bound closer to IBM in 1984 through an integrating organization, Telecommunications Products.

IBM's alliance with Rolm did not contain exclusivity provisions. Thus IBM presumably could reach technical accords with other PBX makers, and Rolm could continue its work with other computer vendors. The Rolm-IBM agreement jeopardized the earlier agreement between IBM and Mitel Corp., however, and this occurred at a time when Mitel had other problems. In 1983 Mitel had formed a joint venture with Britain's ICL PLC, but by year end the agreement to sell telephone gear went into limbo due to delays on Mitel's end. Mitel also joined with satellite equipment maker Scientific-Atlanta Inc., to design, make, and sell private communications networks.

AT&T's American Bell entered the data communications field with plans to market a wide range of communications equipment, much of which integrated telephones and computer equipment. AT&T was by far the world's largest PBX maker, although it had entered late with an advanced model to handle both voice and data. AT&T announced numerous computer-based devices for the office that would be compatible with its PBXs. AT&T used its 25 percent stake in Olivetti, the Italian office products and information processing conglomerate, to offer advanced products. AT&T technology—microprocessors, large-scale mini-computers, and data communications networks—was utilized in several of Olivetti's products for sale on both continents.

AT&T and Wang announced a joint research effort toward interfacing their product lines in 1983. (AT&T became the first licensee of Wang's Document Communications specifications, which AT&T had once proposed as an industry standard. Wang had used AT&T's AIS/NET 1000 as a bridge between IBM and Wang products.) By 1984 Wang was mentioned in connection with Sonecor and BBN for network development in the PBX business. Wang obtained laser printers for resale from Xerox and developed its communications interface with Quotron Computer in 1983. Wang made minority investments in Tymshare (acquired by McDonnell-Douglas) for network access and in VLSI Technology Inc. for technology access.

AT&T was offering computer-phones with Convergent Technologies in 1983. AT&T and Convergent Technologies designed and built a family of office work stations to rival IBM's MS/DOS base (and to champion Unix products like AT&T's thirty-eight series). AT&T pragmatically introduced its new personal computer with capabilities to use *both* DOS and Unix, however. In 1983 AT&T and Philips N.V. formed a joint venture, AT&T/Philips Telecommunications Systems, to (1) manufacture and sell network switching equipment in Europe, (2) manufacture and sell digital exchanges for public telephone networks outside the United States, and (3) offer cable and microwave transmission networks that carried phone messages. The joint venture between AT&T and Philips N.V. won a contract from British Telecom in 1985 for specialized switching equipment. AT&T/Philips Telecommunications Systems expanded its domain to provide turnkey telecommunications systems for newly industrialized countries and cable systems and microwave technology. AT&T/Philips Telecommunications Systems sought to be the preferred second source vendor in sales to European governments.

The difficulty of learning telephone technology motivated several other cooperative strategies. To ensure survival in the competitive environment of office automation/computerization, the less dominant computer manufacturers entered joint ventures and other alliances to strengthen their product lines. Rolm and Northern Telecom Inc. had each formed technical pacts with Digital Equipment, Hewlett-Packard Co., and Data General, for example. Datapoint, Xerox, and Wang had promoted heavily the idea of using higher-speed local area networks as another way of linking different brands of equipment. NCR bought a 19 percent interest in Ztel Inc., a start-up PBX firm. Western Union purchased 25 percent of Vitalink's shares. Control Data invested in a 35 percent share of Centronic's equity and a 30 to 40 percent interest in Source Telecomputing. Fujitsu purchased its telecommunications equipment for resale from GTE.

In 1983 LM Ericsson, the fastest-growing information processing company in Europe, formed a joint venture with Honeywell, Inc. The move was very important to LM Ericsson, which had to penetrate the world's largest market for telecommunications equipment and information processing gear or lose its market position in the emerging global battle for technological leadership. Powerful corporations such as AT&T, Rolm, and Northern Telecom were competing in the United States with Ericsson's data terminals, automated bank tellers, and office automation products in 1983. Rivalry was most fierce in the market for products that formed the centerpiece of Ericsson's strategy: computerized telephone switches. The child was expected to "Americanize" LM Ericsson's product line and help it to develop new products specifically for the U.S. market.

In 1984 Wang Laboratories terminated its in-house efforts to develop a PBX product line. Instead, it purchased a 20 percent interest in InteCom Inc. (of Dallas), a firm controlled by Exxon in 1982, and jointly developed a PBX with it. InteCom had developed a product similar to installing an Ethernet and PBX, an integrated switching device (IBX) system for digital data as well as voice communications. Wang also made its personal computer compatible with IBM's, making it easier to connect machines from both vendors into an office system where they must communicate.

Demand for PBXs was slowing in 1984, however, and firms scrambled for market share, even selling at a loss to get into customers' premises. Only four firms approached the critical mass representing 15 percent U.S. market share in 1984: AT&T, Rolm, Mitel, and Northern Telecom. (Other vendors would have to sell overseas in order to attain the scale economies needed to break even.) A shakeout seemed to be imminent—as in personal computers, where the structure had become IBM, Apple, and "all the others."

Local Area Networks (LAN). Local area networking, in its simplest form, was a cable that operated like an electronic highway for transporting information to and from different computers within the same office area. Network sales generated between $250 and $350 million in 1984 and were expected to grow to as much as $1.5 billion by 1988. There was great uncertainty concerning how the LAN industry would develop because different transfer speeds were appropriate for transferring various classes of data. One scenario suggested that hierarchies of different capacity communications links representing different network speeds might develop; thus customers would use lower-capacity links for slow-speed PBXs and data transfer, and larger-capacity links for higher-speed computer-to-computer transfers. Another scenario suggested that LANs would eventually *replace* the PBXs because they could transmit voice as well as data.

The first local area networking approach to become an industry standard was the Ethernet, developed by Xerox, Digital Equipment Corp., and Intel Corp. after seven years of joint research. The partners jointly published the technical details of their LAN approach and invited vendors to wire up accordingly. More than 5,000 Ethernet systems were in operation in 1984, and over 200 vendors (including AT&T) sold it.

In 1981 Honeywell and SESA (of France) had formed a joint venture to offer a packet-switching network in the United States. The system's architecture fit Honeywell's information technology strategy and appeared to be a way to enter the communications industry as well. But after the partners had devoted considerable efforts to developing second-generation software for the network, they concluded that it was not appropriate for the market, neither as a stand-alone product nor imbedded in Honeywell equipment.

Over 16,000 LAN networks were in operation to link computers within offices in 1984, but their hardware had to be compatible to use LANs. If incompatible computers could be linked, 100,000 local networks could be in operation by 1988. Networks to link different vendors' computers had been available from firms such as Datapoint, Systek, Ungermann-Bass, and other small firms prior to this time, but many office equipment users were waiting for IBM's product announcement before committing to a particular LAN configuration. In 1984 IBM announced local area network products that linked previously incompatible personal computers. But the long-awaited "token-ring" network (to tie together many kinds and sizes of IBM computers that were not originally meant to work together) would not be available until 1986.

Cellular Mobile Telephones. Cellular mobile telephones were car telephones that operated through radio connections to networks (or cells) of broadcast towers located throughout a city. General Electric formed an alliance with Northern Telecom in 1982 to acquire cellular telephone technology. Until 1984 costs for cellular mobile telephone units ranged between $1,500 and $2,500. In 1984 Tandy/Radio Shack and Mobira Oy (a subsidiary of Helsinki-based telecommunications firm, Oy Nokia A.B.) created a joint venture to make and sell cellular mobile telephones that would be sold through its 1,100 Radio Shack stores for around $1,000. Tandy also agreed to make and sell mobile phones for Bell Atlantic Mobile Systems, Inc. (a subsidiary of Bell Atlantic Corp.) and for Gencom Inc. (a subsidiary of Dallas-based Communications Industries Inc.).

In 1984 Airfone Inc., a joint venture of Western Union Corp. and Goeken Communications, launched its public air-to-ground telephone service that was offered on major U.S. airlines. Assuming the offering proved to be economic, its principal barrier to expansion in 1984 was access to radio channels assigned by the FCC.

Child Activities. Joint ventures were formed where tasks were sufficiently different from parents' core activities that they were willing to let their child have autonomy in developing the necessary technology and products. Joint activities were used by firms that entered a market late as a means of catching up, particularly where they were not familiar with the technologies needed to attain success. This situation also increased the child's autonomy in operations.

The rapid pace of technological change and the complexity of communications equipment products necessitated close coordination between the joint-venture child and its technology parents. Moreover, the relatedness of communications equipment to the product lines of parents explained why many joint-venture children did not have their own distribution channels and marketing organizations. Diverse firms that were not competitors previously pooled their resources in a joint venture that developed and made equipment that parents sold under their own respective brand names in competition with each other. For them, the joint venture's lifespan depended on its ability to keep abreast of the latest technological developments in its equipment. Because scale economics were realized by pooling production requirements in their child, cost advantages were gained through cooperation. But parents were free to purchase from outsiders if their prices or features were superior to that of their child.

Summary

The electronic components, computers and computer peripherals, office equipment, and communications equipment industries illustrate environments where technology changed rapidly and cooperative strategies were commonplace. OEM arrangements were very transient. Firms obtained products from outside vendors that fit their needs for features or low costs until another OEM vendor offered better features, prices, or the old products' technology was superseded. The old OEM arrangement ended and firms switched to a new vendor. Thus, unless joint ventures were between firms that both contributed technology and personnel to keep up with the industry, they would be considered inferior to OEM arrangements, cross-licensing relationships or other alliances that did not create a child. Unless partners were prepared to permit their joint-venture child to develop into stand-alone entities, *few* joint ventures were formed (or if formed were not permitted to endure beyond one technological generation). Patterns regarding autonomy varied substantially where joint ventures were formed. The child's products filled out parents' product lines, and parents ultimately shared in the knowledge their child created. But relationships were not always amicable.

The best use of joint ventures in these environments was where scale economies were substantial when partners let their child produce for them. In cases where scale economies were not significant (because few firms produced the product in question in significant quantities or it was obsolesced before they progressed far down the experience curve), the creation of joint ventures did not make sense. Moreover, parents seemed to enjoy the spider's web nature of their informal alliances that were buttressed by legal exchanges of patents, knowledge, and computer tapes. Effective management of minority investments and joint ventures was an enigma that engineering-based managers did not wish to ponder. One often-expressed sentiment was that because high technology industries changed so quickly, it did not make sense to let the child continue beyond the time when the venture has completed its purpose. Managers did not want to consider how to dissolve a "dodo-bird" organization.

Defining the scope of joint ventures (as lawyers did) inhibited the flexibility of partners in their innovative activities, but giving the child an open lifespan (to develop a line of products) was not regarded as an adequate solution either. Decision making was regarded as cumbersome within a joint venture because it required a different mentality to make them work than if the business unit were fully owned. Managers became frustrated when they found it difficult to tell the child's management that something must be done quickly.

The child needed to coordinate its activities closely with parents when it shared facilities, personnel, or resources with them, when it was captive in its parents' vertical chains of processing, or when competitive needs for parents' advice, services, and resources were great. The child's needs to coordinate with its parents were greatest when technology changed rapidly and prices changed erratically, requiring parents' help in modifying products or technologies.

The competitive needs of industries where knowledge obsolesced rapidly required that the child control its key facilities. Having such control gave the child more autonomy than some parents were willing to accept. It was difficult for parents to accept that employees had to be loyal to the joint venture (not its parents) to seek its success. But only if the child did so would parents thrive from joint activity as suppliers, distributors, or owners.

The Microelectronics & Computer Technology (MCC) consortium offered an interesting counterpoint to parents' adversities to the suggestion that their child be allowed to develop into an entity in its own right. Funded by membership fees collected from its parents, MCC had no manufacturing facilities of its own or distribution channels or marketing organization. It controlled patent rights on the technology it had developed. Its parents were free to use that knowledge (or not). After a period of exclusivity, licenses were available to outsiders. Parents were free to develop mechanisms for coordinating with MCC (or not). They could send personnel to work in MCC (or not). But the large number of nonaffiliated engineers within the child made it likely that MCC would develop into a "boisterous" child, one in which managers want to move faster and more aggressively than its parents are prepared to sanction.

Designing ways to repatriate and communciate technology to parent organizations effectively was of greater concern than worries about bleed-through. In settings where technologies could rapidly become obsolete, advantages had to be exploited quickly to recover their development costs before they were obsolesced. Thus many licenses, joint development projects, and joint ventures were found where the pace of technological change was rapid; crucial knowledge was shared with the child *faster* under such circumstances. Because knowledge was so highly appropriable as well as perishable, parents had to rethink their attitudes regarding the control of technology in their use of joint ventures.

11
Joint Ventures and the Evolution of Industry Structure

The 181 joint ventures and other forms of cooperative strategy that form the industries of this chapter illustrate long histories of using joint ventures to share costs, risks, and outputs of large upstream facilities. Managers in these industries have used joint ventures to consolidate excess capacity and, more recently, to revitalize their industry structures. These industries have been challenged by mature demand, excess capacity, and the specter of global competition. Because it is possible to track many decades of joint-venture practice within them, it also is possible to test hypotheses concerning the changing use of joint ventures as industries have evolved. Analyses concerning evolutionary cycles and joint ventures should be of interest to managers who seek to maximize their firms' strategic flexibility by adjusting their cooperative strategies to changing competitive conditions.

The structural changes documented in this chapter were driven by changes in demand and in technology. Joint-venture strategies in embryonic industries are contrasted with those where industry structures are well established. The examples suggest that as differentiated products become less distinguishable from those of competitors, joint ventures are used for different purposes.

Motives

Two change forces are examined in this chapter—changes in demand and changes in ways of satisfying demand. Changes in market traits must be considered first, then changes in the most effective competitive strategies. Both market and industry change forces drove firms to embrace joint-venture strategies.

I am indebted to John G. Michel (Ph.D. candidate, Columbia University) for industry background documents as well as his analyses of joint-venture patterns in the petrochemicals, genetic engineering, and steel industries for use in this chapter. Thanks also to Paul A. Gelburd and Stanley W. Herman (both M.B.A., 1982) for earlier research assistance in petrochemicals and genetic engineering, respectively.

Changes in Demand Traits

Vertical joint ventures built infrastructures in settings where demand was uncertain and product standards not yet established. Horizontally related competitors in this study were often partners in the rearing of their vertically related child within embryonic industries, especially if the costs of creating distribution channels, transportation systems, or other supporting activities were substantial. Vertical joint ventures, whereby parents shared their child's outputs (or used their child to absorb their respective outputs), were particularly useful within settings where demand grew rapidly—to utilize large plants economically—perhaps initially by sharing a supplying plant with a customer or a competitor.

Joint ventures were particularly appropriate in slow-growth settings if significant scale-economy advantages were available at large production volumes (particularly if cost reduction was becoming the key to effective competition). Joint ventures allowed firms who were former rivals to retain the most efficient parts of their assets in building new, world-scale competitive entities. (Joint ventures also permitted firms to divest their assets incrementally in situations where they faced such high exit barriers that no buyer could afford to purchase them outright.) Short-term joint ventures were used more frequently where demand was uncertain or business risks were high, particularly when demand grew rapidly. Joint ventures enabled firms to be more responsive to variations in customer demands, provided parents designed their alliances effectively.

Changes in Industry Structures

Joint ventures were found to be an important structural trait of industries where firms embraced them to explore technologies they could never afford to use alone. Cooperative strategies introduced new vigor into lethargic industries as well as helped embryonic industries to develop useful products faster. Joint ventures were used when industries were embryonic to gain "first-mover" advantages, and spider's webs of joint ventures were used to test many technologies when the "best" technology was yet unknown.

As projects grew larger and more risky, as technologies became too expensive to afford alone, and as the challenges of global competition increased, joint ventures enabled firms to survive together where they could not do so independently. Horizontally related children rationalized overbuilt industry capacity and accommodated new players in slow-growth settings. As customers became more similar across the globe, the need for joint ventures fell unless partners were willing to give their child full autonomy and assets to pursue global strategies.

Finally, the more volatile the competitive environment, the less attractive joint ventures became over time. Short-term alliances replaced longer-term partnerships. Firms continued to forge joint ventures and other arrangements for pooling skills, intelligence, and resources, but they became more fickle in their alliances. The more experienced a firm became in the use of cooperative strategies, the greater its competitive advantage because it understood better when shared ownership ventures no longer met the requirements of an industry better than going it alone.

Industries

Petrochemicals

Petrochemicals are derived from petroleum or natural gas that has been fractionally distilled or "cracked" (to break down heavier hydrocarbons by heat, pressure, or catalysts) into hydrocarbon feedstocks of lighter molecular weights. Petrochemical feedstocks—acetylene, benzene, ethane, propane, toluene, and xylene—are used in many synthetic rubbers, fibers, and plastics.

Joint ventures were used to develop the U.S. petrochemical industry. When the Federal Trade Commission reported in the mid-1950s that 15 of the 1,000 largest U.S. corporations were joint ventures, petrochemical firms comprised the bulk of these children. Although partners were often horizontally related to each other, parents were often *vertically related* to their joint-venture child. This pattern may be explained by the minimum efficient scale (MES) differences of upstream and downstream stages of processing in the petrochemicals industry. Outputs from supplying plants were so large that they had to be shared by partners. Risk and cost sharing also motivated firms to use joint ventures.

Need for Joint Ventures. There were many similarities between the need for joint ventures in the oil exploration industry and the petrochemical industry. Productive capacities in petrochemical processing plants were huge, capital requirements to build them were vast, and long lead times were needed to bring petrochemical plants onstream. Because joint ventures could be managed on a project basis (like a successful oil well), partners could share petrochemical plant outputs according to their proportions of ownership. Given the vast productive capacities involved in basic petrochemical processing, partners' willingness to take their share of the child's outputs made the venture economic. Take-or-pay contracts often secured the child's financing arrangements.

Since bulk chemicals were commodity-like, profitability was increased through operating cost reductions. To attain them, firms competed to develop superior processes for making petrochemicals. But doing so was risky because expected yields were often not attained. Sometimes new technologies could be obtained through licensing arrangements with overseas firms that were not direct competitors (although the promised yields of their processes were often not realized). In other cases, technology licenses were not available because firms would not share their knowledge with outsiders. In such cases, firms had to develop their own processes in-house. When this was necessary, diverse approaches to lowering costs could best be tested at lower risks by taking partners.

Intermediate and finished petrochemical products were more differentiated and subject to smaller-scale technologies. Product innovations dominated process innovations as a means of competing. Motivations for cooperative strategies were similar to those covered in chapter 8; product differentiation skills were often close to firms' strategic cores and of great importance to them. Joint ventures enabled firms to expand product lines and customize their products to suit diverse markets. But since the attributes of petrochemicals changed less frequently than those of other products examined in this study, joint ventures lasted longer and partners were less likely to become mismatched in this industry.

Petrochemical firms frequently developed new products and tested new processes through joint ventures in order to minimize individual firms' losses. Frequently the feedstocks for the venture were provided by the refineries of one partner, while the chemical processes of the other partner were used in production. Such cooperative arrangements accelerated innovation and facilitated the testing of new materials and methods. The shared risks of these ventures enabled petrochemical firms to participate in larger write-offs if these ventures failed.

The oil shocks of the 1970s modified the historical pattern of partners' relationships. Chemical firms seeking stable access to petrochemical feedstocks integrated vertically or formed joint ventures with oil firms seeking higher value-added margins through further processing of their feedstocks. When the oil firms brought their knowledge of joint ventures to bear on the petrochemicals industry, joint ventures became larger and more global in their scope.

Choosing Partners.

Petrochemicals. In 1924 General Motors and Exxon formed a joint venture, Ethyl Corp., to make and sell tetraethyl lead catalysts. Ethyl Corp. operated at arm's length from its parents because Exxon's competitors were reluctant to purchase catalysts (a source of product differentiation) directly from Exxon. In 1937 PPG Industries and Corning Glass Works formed a joint venture, Pittsburgh Corning Corp., to manufacture hollow glass building blocks and cellular glass products. In 1947 PPG Industries and Koppers Co. formed a joint venture, Koppers Pittsburgh Co., to produce materials for resins in paint manufacturing. Early synthetic rubber joint ventures included Copolymer Corp. (seven parents) and American Synthetic Rubber Corp. (twenty-nine parents).

National Chemstrand began as a joint venture to produce nylon, as did Beaunit-El Paso Natural Gas and Nylon Industries. Fiber Industries began as a joint venture to produce Fortrel polyester. H. Maurice Chemicals (a child of Heyden Chemical and Shawinigan Chemicals Ltd.) made formaldehyde. Monsanto-Heyden produced methanol. A child of Pure Oil and Atlantic Refining made benzene, and Texas-U.S. Chemicals made styrene and butadiene in the 1960s. American Viscose obtained raw materials for rayon production from its child, Ketichikan Pulp Co., which was owned with Puget Sound Timber & Pulp. Enjay and J.P. Stevens formed a joint venture, National Plastics Products, to make polypropylene fiber.

Other early chemical joint ventures included: (1) Ethyl-Dow Chemical Corp. (a child of Ethyl Corp. and Dow Chemical created to ensure that Ethyl Corp. would continue to buy its bromine requirements from Dow); (2) Owens Corning Fiberglass Co. (child of Owens-Illinois and Corning Glass), which was engaged in the development and manufacture of fibrous glass products; (3) Dow Corning Corp. (the very successful child of Corning Glass Works and Dow Chemical), which made electrical insulating resins, greases, fluids, and elastomers resembling natural or artificial rubber called silicones; and (4) South Minerals Corp. and (5) Southern Petroleum Corp. (both children of PPG Industries and American Cyanamid). Cities Service and Sinclair Oil (later a part of ARCO) formed (6) Sinclair Delaware Corp., and then Sinclair Delware Corp. joined with Empire Gas and Fuel Co. to form (7) Richfield Oil. Cities Service (often working through its jointly owned child, Empire Gas and Fuel) joined with Conoco to create both (8) Petroleum Chemicals Inc. (to operate a petrochemical complex at Lake Charles, Louisiana, including a butadiene plant, an ethylene plant, and an ammonia plant) and (9) Mid South Chemical (to make ammonia for direct application fertilizer). Cities Service and Conoco also formed (10) Calcasieu Chemical Corp., which owned an ethylene glycol plant in Lake Charles that was operated by (11) Petroleum Chemicals (one of their other joint-venture children). Richfield Oil and Stauffer Chemical formed (12) American Chemical, a vinyl chloride and ethylene products producer. Sinclair Oil and Koppers Co. formed (13) Sinclair Koppers Chemical Co. to construct a styrene monomer plant in Houston. Monsanto and Fabenfabriken Bayer Farben formed (14) Mobay Chemical Co.; (15) Jefferson Chemical was formed by American Cyanamid and Texaco; Swift & Co. and Skelly Oil formed (16) Des Plaines Chemical (to turn Swift's large phosphate deposits into agricultural chemicals), and Swift & Co. with Stauffer Chemical formed (17) Hawkeye Chemical (to produce ammonia). Conoco and Ansul formed (18) Ancon Chemicals to make methyl chloride; Sun Oil and Olin Corp. formed (19) Sun Olin to make urea and ethylene; El Paso Natural Gas and Rexall Chemical formed (20) El Paso-Rexall to make ethylene; and Richfield Oil and Witco Chemical formed (21) Witfield Chemical to make detergent alkylates. Most of these joint ventures were not in operation in 1984.

In the early 1950s B.F. Goodrich and Gulf formed a joint venture, Goodrich-Gulf, to make synthetic rubber. Gulf's refinery sent butadiene to the child to make the raw materials used in Goodrich's rubber fabrication plants to make tires. (Some tires were sold in Gulf Oil service stations.) The petroleum and synthetic rubber industries were in a state of flux at that time, and neither company was certain how much it wanted to risk in synthetic rubber. In 1965 B.F. Goodrich was negotiating to buy Gulf's share in Goodrich-Gulf. The joint venture was thirteen years old and was the largest synthetic rubber producer in the United States. By 1965 Gulf wanted to move into more finished products through its 100 percent owned Spencer Chemical Co. subsidiary, but doing so brought it into competition with its joint venture, Goodrich-Gulf. Thus, despite its dominance of the synthetic rubber industry, Goodrich-Gulf's future was limited because its mission was bounded. If Goodrich-Gulf expanded forward into fabrication of rubber products, it would infringe on Goodrich's territory. If Goodrich-Gulf expanded upstream into refining, it would infringe on Gulf's territory.

Also in the early 1950s, Goodyear Tire & Rubber, National Lead Co., and Bird & Son formed Rubarite Inc., a joint venture that made rubberized baryites for use in highway asphalt mixtures. Goodyear supplied rubber and National Lead supplied baryites to their child, which sold the mixture to Bird & Son, an asphalt mixing firm.

In 1959 American Viscose and Sun Company formed a joint venture, AviSun Inc., to make and sell polypropylene film and fibers. American Viscose was the major U.S. producer of rayon fibers; AviSun was a major diversification for it into synthetic fibers. Sun sold its interest in the joint-venture child to Amoco (Standard Oil of Indiana) after a few years, since it had no close strategic link to the child.

In 1960 Hercules and Stauffer Chemical formed Texas Alkyes, one of the most profitable joint ventures in the U.S. petrochemical industry's history. The child exploited Hercules's alkylation patents and Stauffer's production skills.

In 1960 El Paso Natural Gas Co. and Dart Industries formed a 50%-50% joint venture, Rexene Polyolefins, to make polyethylene plastics. In 1974 Rexene Polymers Co. (a division of Dart Industries) and El Paso Products formed another joint venture, Consolidated Thermoplastics, to make polyethylene films. Dart and El Paso had several joint operations together, including polypropylene, polyethylene, and polyethylene film resin facilities, and Rexene Polymers operated plants for them. Although Rexene Polyolefins Co. announced an expansion of its polyethylene film production capacity in 1978, its parent, Dart, sold its many joint ventures with El Paso to its partner in 1979, stating that the divestiture was part of its continuing strategic plan to move out of plastics raw materials businesses to concentrate on its chemical specialties activities, instead. Because El Paso possessed an assured supply of the basic hydrocarbon feedstocks needed for its plastics operations in a market where hydrocarbon feedstocks were scarce, it was logical that El Paso continued in the polyethylene and polypropylene businesses instead of Dart.

In 1961 National Distillers & Chemical and Owens-Illinois formed a 50%-50% joint venture, National Petro Chemicals Corp., to make high-density polyethylene (HDPE), which was used to make garbage bags and plastic containers. The Deer Park, Texas, plant had a capacity of 500 million pounds per year of HDPE, and Owens-Illinois had been a customer of its child. National Distillers had operated the child's plant. In 1983 National Distillers & Chemical acquired its partner's 50 percent interest in National Petro, but its former partner continued to be a customer after the buy-out. Philip Petroleum and National Distillers & Chemical had formed Alamo Polymers to make polypropylene for internal consumption (and outside sales), and formed A-B Chemical to make polyethylene for similar uses.

In 1963 the Antitrust Division of the U.S. Justice Department sued to break up Petroleum Chemicals (the joint-venture child of Cities Service and Conoco). Cities Service sold its 50 percent interest in the child, so no precedents regarding unlawful combinations were established. The next major antitrust challenge was against Penn-Olin, the joint-venture child of Olin Corp. and Pennsalt Chemicals Corp., and it established a rule of "potential entry," which said in effect that joint ventures were permissible only where partners would not enter a business activity alone. (By 1984 this policy had been changed due to economic necessity when competing in global industries.)

In 1966 Atlantic-Richfield (ARCO) and Halcon formed a joint venture, Oxirane Corp., to build a propylene oxide plant. Atlantic Refining had merged in 1965 with Richfield Oil Corporation, which was partially owned (60 percent) by Cities Service and Sinclair Oil (30 percent each), to create ARCO. Sinclair Oil was merged into Atlantic-Richfield in 1969.

In 1967 Dow Chemical and Olson Brothers formed a joint venture, Dolco Packaging Co., to produce apple trays formed from extruded polystyrene foam. Olson was a large California distributor of egg products and was an early experimenter in the development of foamed egg trays from extruded polystyrene. Dow left the polystyrene packaging business after the experiment was completed and Olson Brothers purchased its interest.

Petrofina (Belgium) used joint ventures to further its vertical integration strategies, especially in the United States. It had long been Petrofina's explicit strategy in petroleum to (1) seek out strong joint-venture partners; (2) seek the lowest production costs possible; (3) leverage the company heavily for new ventures; and (4) plow earnings back into exploration and downstream operations. Petrofina's managers saw joint ventures as a way to boost production and spread costs. Competitors credited Petrofina's successes to its ability to choose strong partners. Furthermore, Petrofina gave its joint ventures a great deal of leeway and the resources needed to operate autonomously. Petrofina's wholly owned U.S. subsidiary, Cosden Oil & Chemical, was helping its parent to pursue its petrochemicals mission with three large joint ventures—with Borg-Warner, with Hercules, and with B.F. Goodrich, respectively.

In 1968 Cosden Oil & Chemical and Borg-Warner formed a 50%-50% joint venture, Cos-Mar, to build a 500 million pounds per year styrene monomer plant in Louisiana. Cosden Oil took 600 million pounds of the styrene monomer output for its own uses. (Styrene monomer was a basic raw material for synthetic rubber, polystyrene, and ABS thermal plastics. The ethylbenzene step in producing styrene monomer was energy-intensive.) In 1976 Cos-Mar added a 700 million pounds per year plant adjacent to the old one, and Cos-Mar became a 69%-31% joint venture to reflect Cosden Oil's relatively greater investments in their child.

In 1980 Borg-Warner (which was partially owned by Robert Bosch GmbH) and Cosden Oil expanded Cos-Mar's styrene monomer plant from 1,300 million pounds per year to 2,200 million pounds per year. They replaced the energy-intensive ethylbenzene alkylation equipment with more efficient styrene equivalency unit and expanded manufacturing capacity. Borg-Warner increased its share of the Cos-Mar joint venture to 50 percent by contributing additional capital. Their offtake shares were similarly adjusted to 50 percent each, giving each partner 650 million pounds per year of styrene monomer.

In 1976 Petrofina and Montedison formed a joint venture to build a 150 thousand-ton polyester plant in Belgium. That same year Petrofina (through Cosden Oil & Chemical) and Hercules formed a 25%-75% joint venture, Hercofina, to produce and market dimethyl terephthalate (DMT) a raw material for polyesters in the United States. Through the joint venture, Hercules integrated backward to feedstocks in 1976, and Petrofina integrated forward, into the part of the petrochemicals industry with higher value-added margins.

Hercofina began with assets of $362 million. Petrofina's interest in the joint venture was permitted to grow to 50 percent as it invested in capital improvements for the child's expansion. Meanwhile, Hercules was trying to sell its interest in the terephthalates business. In return for its initial 75 percent in the joint venture, Hercules contributed all assets, business contacts, and technology for the production and sale of terephthalates, including three terephthalate facilities, two para-xylene producers, and one methanol plant. Because of worldwide overcapacity and growing competition from PTA suppliers (a superior substitute), demand for DMT became cyclical. Hercules had already closed a small (200 million pounds per year) DMT plant in 1974 when the market had deteriorated, and it had stopped construction on another DMT plant (800 million pounds per year) in 1975 before its joint venture. In 1979 Hercofina was the leading producer of DMT for the polyester fibers industry and was wallowing in excess capacity.

In 1979 Hercofina agreed to license its technology for the production of dimethyl terephthalate to Bombay Dyeing and Manufacturing Co. Moreover, it sold its mothballed DMT plant at Burlington, New Jersey, for $51 million to Bombay Dyeing for reassembly in India. Hercofina sold its 100 million gallon methanol plant to Allemania Chemical Corp., a 50%-50% joint venture of Ashland Chemical Co. and International Minerals and Chemicals Corp., because (1) it felt that a sizable investment was required to modernize the plant to compete effectively and (2) Hercofina was unwilling to make that investment.

In 1977 B.F. Goodrich and Cosden Oil & Chemical (Petrofina) formed a 50%-50% joint venture, Abtec Chemical, to make and market Abson ABS (acrylonitrile-butadiene-styrene) thermoplastics. Cosden was a major producer of the styrene monomers and polymers that were the basic raw materials in ABS production, but ABS was not a major part of its forward integration strategy. The ABS business seemed to be booming in 1977, and Abtec intended to move aggressively, by using the materials and experience of its parents. But U.S. producers of styrene-acrylonitrile resins (SAN), a thermoplastic material of the ABS family, were leaving the market at that time. By 1978 only Dow, Monsanto, and the newly formed Abtec Chemical remained in the industry.

In 1979 Abtec Chemical Co. agreed to sell technology, trademarks, and other necessary information to Mobay Chemical to permit it to enter the ABS business. Mobay, a subsidiary of Bayer A.G. (which had purchased its former partner, Monsanto's interest in the child) had been seeking a means of entering the U.S. ABS market for some time. (Bayer was already a major producer of ABS in West Germany.) Mobay purchased Abtec's line of Abson resins from its parents later in 1979 when Goodrich and Cosden Oil decided to exit. Mobay exited in 1982 and offered the ABS assets for sale to outsiders.

Some firms had short-lived experiences with joint ventures. For example, in 1970 Air Products & Chemicals and North American Rockwell formed a 50%-50% joint venture, TekTran, for the development and production of advanced equipment for the welding and nondestructive testing market. As an outgrowth of the TekTran joint venture, a patented rapid welding system suitable for the automobile industry was developed for commercial use. But in 1973 Air Products & Chemicals bought out Rockwell's interest in TekTran.

In 1971 the Howdry Division of Air Products & Chemicals and Haldor-Topsoe of Denmark formed a joint venture, Howdry-Topsoe, to manufacture and market catalysts for production of chemicals. The venture ended one year later when Haldor-Topsoe defaulted.

In 1974 Amoco Production Co. (a subsidiary of Standard Oil of Indiana) and Houston Chemical (a subsidiary of PPG Industries) formed a 51%-49% joint venture to extract and market iodine from brinewater that Amoco found while exploring for hydrocarbons in Oklahoma. PPG had experience in fluorine and bromine production and was seeking higher-margin products, such as iodine. Although prices for iodine fluctuated severely over the next decade, the venture continued to operate and earn satisfactory returns for its parents. A similar Oklahoma-based joint venture was formed by Beard Oil Co., Godoe (USA) Inc. (a subsidiary of United Resources Industry Co. Ltd. of Japan) and Inorgchem Developments Inc. (a subsidiary of Mitsui & Co.) in 1981. Godoe represented a leader in the extraction and manufacturing of iodine. (Most iodine was imported into the United States from Japan or Chile.)

In 1973 Robintech and Shin-Etsu Chemical Co. (Tokyo) formed a 50%-50% joint venture, Shintech, to produce polyvinyl chloride (PVC), a material used in plastics. In 1976 Shin-Etsu Chemical purchased Robintech's 50 percent interest in Shintech Inc. The venture was successful, but it was dissolved due to differences in opinion concerning future expansion of Shintech. Robintech wanted the child to expand upstream, to make vinyl chloride monomers and chloralkai products. Shin-Etsu wanted the child to expand PVC production and expand downstream into related chemical products.

In 1974 PVO International and Anchor Chemical Co. (United Kingdom) formed a 50%-50% joint venture, Pacific Anchor Chemical, to make and sell the Anchor range of epoxide curing agents in North America. Curing agents were used in combination with epoxide resins in the manufacture of plastics.

In 1974 Rohm & Haas and Teijin formed a 50%-50% joint venture, Carodel, to manufacture polyethylene terephthalate. The child built a 350 ton per day polyester chip plant in North Carolina that began operating in 1977 using Teijin's technology and manufacturing know-how. Rohm & Haas was to have taken 70 percent of the child's output for use in its polyester fiber operations, but in 1977 Rohm & Haas notified Teijin that it wanted to get out of the fiber business due to the worldwide fiber recession. Rohm & Haas closed its fiber plants adjacent to the Carodel chip plant and liquidated its interest in Carodel, pending its sale to a third party.

In 1974 ethylene production was based primarily on light feedstocks (20 percent) because light crude oil was readily available. But leading petrochemical firms envisioned that by 1985 as much as 55 percent of ethylene production would rely on heavy crude oil as a raw material. Accordingly, they formed joint ventures to anticipate this processing change.

In 1975 Atlantic-Richfield (ARCO) and E.I. DuPont de Nemours planned to form a 50%-50% joint venture, Centennial Hydrocarbons Co., to design, construct, and operate a facility to produce petrochemical raw materials from heavy crude oil. With a planned capacity of 100,000 barrels of feedstock per day (mostly to be supplied by ARCO) the plant would cost $500 million and would provide DuPont with backward integration to the raw materials from which 70 percent of its products were made. Late in 1977 ARCO withdrew from the Centennial Hydrocarbons partnership because of its dismal forecasts of low demand for ethylene and other hydrocarbons that the child would have produced. ARCO was planning to sell its share of Centennial's output on the open market where severe excess capacity was anticipated.

In 1975 E.I. DuPont de Nemours and National Distillers & Chemical Corp. formed a joint venture, Syngas Co., to produce carbon monoxide and a mixture of carbon monoxide hydrogen (synthesis gas) that was converted into ammonia, alcohol, and other organic compounds. Both partners used the gases as raw materials for their products. DuPont needed synthesis gas to make acetic acid for di-methyl terephthalate as well as for vinyl acetate. National Distillers & Chemical needed acetic acid to make vinyl acetate. The partners also planned a venture whereby DuPont built and operated an acetic acid plant. In 1979 Syngas Co. began operations at its new 200 million gallon per year methanol plant, which used residuum (the residue from crude oil refining) rather than natural gas. It continued to operate in 1984.

In 1975 Robintech and Armosig (France's largest pipemaker) formed a joint venture, Armotech, to make PVC foam pipe products for nonpressure plumbing applications where weight savings were important. (Robintech filed for protection under bankruptcy laws in 1984, and the venture has been shut down.)

In 1976 Champlin Petroleum Co. (a subsidiary of Union Pacific Corporation), ICI Americas (a subsidiary of Imperial Chemical Industries, of London), and Soltex Polymer (a subsidiary of Solvay et Cie, of Belgium) formed a joint venture, Corpus Christi Petrochemical, to build a 1.2 billion pounds per year ethylene plant. The joint venture began operations in 1980, and it produced propylene, benzene, crude butadiene, and ethylene from heavy crude oil. Champlin (37.5 percent ownership) supplied the needed liquid feedstocks from its nearby refinery. ICI (37.5 percent) took ethylene from its child to supply the 450 million pounds per year ethylene oxide-ethylene glycol facility it was building. Soltex Polymer (25 percent) took ethylene from its child for its 440 million pounds per year high-density polyethylene plant. Champlin was the joint venture's operator, and ICI was marketing contractor for surplus ethylene output.

The ethylene plant cost $600 million and was the means for its parents to pursue their respective expansion strategies in petrochemicals. Champlin made a $210 million expansion in its crude oil refinery to bring its capacity to 125,000 barrels per day. Soltex Polymer purchased a polyethylene plant from Celanese to enter the U.S. petrochemicals market, and it planned to make polypropylene, as well. The joint venture was ICI's entrée into the U.S. petrochemicals industry, and it allowed ICI to expand into specialty chemicals by making its own vinyl chloride monomer (VCM). Ethylene feedstocks were provided for ICI by Corpus Christi Petrochemical, which continued to operate in 1984.

In 1976 Union Carbide (UCC) financed its ethylene expansions in Louisiana, as well as its ethylene pipeline system, by forming a 50%-50% joint venture, Gulf Coast Olefins, with a Luxembourg-based consortium of banks, Société Fiancière Europēene. Gulf Coast Olefins supplied ethylene to UCC's high-density polyethylene (HDPE) and ethylene oxide plants under a long-term contract. The joint venture enabled Union Carbide to obtain a secure source of ethylene while also engaging in an ambitious expansion program in other markets. But in 1978 Union Carbide Corp. was required to purchase Société Financière Europēene's 50 percent share of Gulf Coast Olefins because the market price for ethylene was 30 percent lower than UCC had predicted and the price was too low for Gulf Coast Olefins to show any profits toward purchasing its parents' interests. Under the terms of their agreement, UCC took over its partner's interest in their joint venture when this occurred.

In 1976 Hercules Chemical and Tate & Lyle (a major U.K. sugar producer) formed a joint venture to make xanthan, a material produced by a fermentation process from sugar. Hercules was the world's largest manufacturer of water-soluble polymers (substances that thicken water), and it had well-established marketing channels to sell gels and other thickening agents. Tate & Lyle provided the fermentation technology needed to make xanthan, a premium product that had only one other manufacturer, Merck. After numerous unsuccessful efforts, the joint venture finally collapsed in 1981 when its parents concluded that it could not bring xanthan beyond the pilot plant stage.

In 1976 Fallek Chemical and Lankro Chemicals (a subsidiary of Diamond Shamrock Europe) formed a 50%-50% joint venture, Fallek-Lankro Corp., to manufacture in the United States a line of phenoxy acid herbicides then produced by Burts & Harvey, Lankro's Agrochemical Division. Fallek provided distribution facilities, and Lankro provided technology to make phenoxy acid. Until its own output came onstream, Fallek-Landro marketed the Burts & Harvey line of herbicides in the United States and Canada. Fallek-Landro's plant added excess capacity in an industry where prices were already depressed and where Dow Chemical dominated the phenoxy herbicides market. In 1978 Diamond Shamrock Europe wrote down the value of its phenoxy herbicide joint venture in the United States by 1 million pounds after heavy losses in the first year of operation. (Its original interest had been 3.5 million pounds.) Because it expected that the phenoxy herbicide plant would eventually prove to be profitable, Diamond Shamrock acquired in 1980 Fallek Chemical Corp., a privately held international trading and manufacturing firm, and the remaining 50 percent of Fallek-Lankro, the herbicide joint venture.

In 1976 Arrow Group Industries (a subsidiary of Chromalloy) and Contico International formed a joint venture, Arrow-Contico, to develop a line of consumer products in the plastics field to include garbage cans, sprayers, barrels, and outdoor furniture. Arrow was a manufacturer of metal storage sheds and garages, and Contico was a plastics firm. The joint venture expanded Arrow's product line.

As earlier chapters have noted, Oak Industries used many joint ventures to diversify into many domains simultaneously. In 1976 Oak Technology and Fothergill & Harvey Ltd. (United Kingdom) formed a joint venture, Oak-Fothergill, to make products from advanced composite materials, primarily graphite fiber materials. In 1979 Oak-Fothergill produced a line of radiolucent tops for medical X-ray equipment. By 1980 its line included cassette fronts for X-ray changers, tops for orthopedic and surgical tables, and X-ray coverplates. Fothergill & Harvey purchased Oak's interest in the child after it had become well established in the U.S. market because Oak's cable TV operations made it hungry for cash.

In 1980 Oak-Mitsui, the joint-venture child of Oak Industries and Mitsui Mining, provided copper foil for Oak's laminate products. Asia Pacific Resin Corp., the 25%-75% joint venture child of Oak Industries and Ciba-Geigy manufactured resins, another raw material for laminates, and provided sources of new business for Oak's other products through sales of glass fabric and resin to outside customers. In 1982 Oak Industries and Dow Corning formed a joint venture, ODC Inc., to produce silicone-coated glass fabric to be used as roofing materials. ODC Inc. utilized Dow Corning silicone technology and Oak Industries technology for coating fiberglass fabrics with resins.

In 1977 B.F. Goodrich and Bechtel Corp. formed a joint venture, H.C.C. Chemical Co., to build an 800 tons per day chlorine plant, which also produced 880 tons per day of caustic soda and an 800 million pounds per year plant to make ethylene dichloride (EDC), an intermediate chemical for the production of vinyl chloride and PVC. Although Goodrich produced EDC at its Calvert City plant, it still purchased most of its EDC needs to produce vinyl chloride monomer from outsiders prior to this joint venture. Construction of the jointly owned facilities would have assured Goodrich of an adequate supply of EDC for the near future, but in 1978, B.F. Goodrich sought alternative plant sites for its H.C.C. Chemical chlorine-caustic joint venture with Bechtel. Delays and threats of lengthy litigation in Texas prevented the joint venture from breaking ground. (The joint venture was vigorously opposed by citizens' groups concerned with the Bayport plant's effect on property values and the environment of Galveston Bay.)

In 1977 International Minerals and Chemicals (IMC) and Air Products & Chemicals formed a joint venture to build the world's largest methanol plant (1,306 tons per day). The plant's process was based on ICI's technology and included the world's largest reformer. IMC possessed abundant reserves of natural gas in Louisiana that served as feedstocks for the joint venture. Some of the child's output was marketed to outsiders because the partners could not consume their child's full output through their business units that made methylamines.

In 1977 Monsanto and Conoco formed a $450 million joint venture to manufacture ethylene and related products and to process heavier crude oils into feedstock. Outputs were shared on a 50%-50% basis. Monsanto made a major expansion of its existing petrochemical complex at Chocolate Bayou that more than doubled the facility's capacity to 8 billion pounds of petrochemicals a year, including 1.5 billion pounds of ethylene. (Monsanto operated the ethylene complex for the partnership.) Conoco built a complementary feedstock manufacturing unit at its Lake Charles refinery with a capacity of 100,000 barrels of crude oil per day. (Conoco operated the feedstock unit for the partnership.) Monsanto retained ownership of its existing plant at Chocolate Bayou, but the expansion was owned by the child. Both plants were used by the joint venture that brought together the crude oil position of Conoco with the chemicals position of Monsanto and doubled Conoco's chemical production volume.

By 1980 the jointly owned petrochemicals complex at Chocolate Bayou, Texas, was successfully on stream and operating at 80 percent capacity. The joint venture consumed 75 percent of the Lake Charles facility's output, but the economics of the new plant were not quite as favorable as expected due to unexpected regulatory price differences for feedstocks. In 1981 Conoco acquired Monsanto's share of their child because Conoco was merging with DuPont and the U.S. Department of Justice saw antitrust violations in its joint venture with DuPont's major competitor.

In 1978 Hercules and Philips Petroleum formed a joint venture, Custom Oil Recovery Technology (CORT), to develop a tertiary oil field flooding product. Based on Hercules's water soluble polymer products, Philips and Hercules developed a product that they decided was not economically feasible when oil prices receded. The joint venture was sold to American Cyanamid, the firm that was strongest at producing the water-soluble chemical that eventually proved to work best for oil field recovery.

In 1978 Air Products & Chemicals and Degussa Corp. formed a joint venture in automotive catalysts to supply emission control catalysts to North American automakers. Air products had manufactured catalysts at its Calvert City plant for sale by Degussa in the past. Under their joint venture, the partners developed new generations of catalysts to supplement Air Product's existing product line.

In 1978 Borden Inc. entered into a licensing agreement with Toyobo Co. of Japan to obtain exclusive use of Toyobo technology in the manufacture of biaxially oriented polypropylene film in the United States. Borden also became U.S. sales agent for certain Toyobo oriented polypropylene (OPP) films. (OPP was less dense than cellophane and yielded up to 33 percent more material per pound of raw materials, resulting in savings of up to 30 percent to packagers over the cost of cellophane.) The licensing agreement followed a two-year search by Borden for OPP film technologies acquisition, and Toyobo sent a five-man team to offer technical advice during the installation of equipment and general start-up of Borden's North Andover plant.

In 1978 Hercules Chemical and Boots Co. Ltd. (United Kingdom) formed a 40%-60% joint venture, Boots-Hercules Agrochemicals Co., to manufacture and sell agricultural chemicals in North America. Hercules contributed its existing agricultural chemicals plants to their child and operated them on a fee basis for the joint venture. Boots used the joint venture as a way to market its Mitak and Taktic insecticides after gaining EPA labeling registration. Neither Hercules nor Boots were major forces in the world agricultural chemicals market, and Hercules had been losing sales because the worldwide agricultural chemicals industry was depressed in the mid-1970s and highly competitive. Apart from its two new products, Boots' agricultural chemicals product line consisted mainly of phenoxy hormone herbicides, a highly competitive and oversupplied sector of the market. In 1981 FBC Chemicals was formed to market and distribute products formerly marketed by Fissons, Inc. and Boots-Hercules Agrochemicals Co.

In 1978 PVO International and Scott Bader Co. (United Kingdom) formed a 50%-50% joint venture, Pacific Scott Bader Inc., to manufacture and market aqueous polymers used to improve gloss, flow, and leveling of latex paints in the United States. PVO had been the sole U.S. distributor of Scott Bader's line of acrylic emulsion and solution polymers since early 1977. Their joint venture was short-lived because Scott Bader Co. overestimated the value of its partner's contribution. When PVO International was acquired by another firm, Scott Bader bought its interest in their joint venture and continued to operate it alone.

In 1978 U.S. Steel began a search for a joint-venture partner to build a $500 million ethylene and petrochemicals complex. Although U.S. Steel already had assets of $550 million in its chemical division, it saw a need to be in plastics because automakers were replacing steel with plastic. U.S. Steel and National Distillers & Chemical jointly owned RMI Co., the second-largest U.S. manufacturer of titanium.

In 1979 Tenneco Chemicals (of Tenneco Corp.) approached USS Chemicals (a subsidiary of U.S. Steel) to form a joint venture, TENN/USS Chemicals, to make and sell petrochemicals, including phthalic anhydride and other synthetic resins, in a world-scale plant. The plant came onstream in 1983. At the time of the venture's formation, both partners used and sold the products of the joint venture. But during the plant's construction, Tenneco Corp. decided to deemphasize its petrochemicals business. USS Chemicals was left to absorb the entire production output internally or on a merchant basis.

In 1981 Texaco Chemical Co. and the USS Chemicals Division of U.S. Steel formed a joint venture, TEX/USS Polyolefins Corp., to make high-density polyethylene (HDPE). TEX/USS Polyolefins Corp. built a light olefins plant to provide ethylene feedstock for the HDPE facility, as well as for other purposes. But the TEX/USS Polyolefins venture had become inactive in 1984 and was in the process of being dissolved.

In 1979 the 50%-50% joint venture of Ashland Chemical and International Minerals and Chemicals, Allemania Chemical Corp., which purchased the Louisiana methanol plant of Hercofina (the joint venture of Hercules and Petrofina), made modernizing investments to make the methanol plant competitive. Allemania's parents consumed a portion of the child's output and it marketed the remainder to outsiders. IMC was a large consumer of methanol, using it as a raw material in the manufacture of formaldehyde and methylamines. The joint venture continued to operate in 1984.

In 1979 Cetus Corp. and Standard Oil of California (Chevron Corp.) formed a joint venture to produce alkene oxides and furfural (fructose) through catalysts of various biomass materials with enzymes. In the process of converting ethylene and propylene to their oxides and glycols, fructose was produced as a by-product. In 1980 efforts to develop the alkene oxide step were dropped in favor of moving the fructose by-product process closer to commercialization. But in 1981 Chevron withdrew from the fructose joint venture with Cetus. It had spent $7 to $8 million up to that point and balked when it was time to fund a pilot plant. Under terms of their agreement, Cetus was entitled to all the technology it had developed.

Corn wet milling plants often took oil companies as partners in ethanol joint ventures. Oil companies' interests in their child's performance depended on the demand they faced for their oil and gas products. In 1980 CPC International (the world's largest corn wet milling firm) and Texaco formed a joint venture to produce fuel-grade ethyl alcohol. CPC built facilities at its corn wet milling plant in Pekin, Illinois, and it supplied feedstocks to Texaco that were fermented and distilled into alcohol. The alcohol was blended with unleaded gasoline to make gasohol. Other gasohol projects announced in 1980 included a 60 million gallon per year fuel-grade ethanol plant built by Ashland Oil and Publicker Industries and a 12.5 million gallon per year ethanol plant by Diamond Shamrock and Amstar Corp. The Diamond Shamrock venture never came together. Publicker filed for protection under the U.S. bankruptcy laws.

In 1980 the Saudi Arabian government formed joint ventures to move downstream from oil production. Its joint ventures gave it the capacity to produce large quantities of refined oil products and basic petrochemical commodities. Its partners included Mobil, Royal Dutch/Shell, Exxon, Ashland Oil, Mitsubishi, Dow Chemical, plus a partnership (Celanese and Texas Eastern). Although firms that were crude-short, like Mobil, were logical participants for these joint ventures, even crude-surplus oil companies, like Exxon, participated in these joint ventures because of the importance of the Saudi Arabian industries.

In 1980 Great Lakes Chemical and Merichem Co. formed a joint venture to supply key intermediates to the synthetic pyrethroid industry. Great Lakes held majority interest in the joint venture, and the child consummated a contract with Shell Oil Chemical Co. to supply a key intermediate for its synthetic pyrethroid insecticide, Pychin. Synthetic pyrethroids were a new generation of pesticides known for their efficacy in killing a broad spectrum of insects at extremely low dosages, with low toxicity to humans and animals. (Natural pyrethrum was obtained from flowers cultivated mainly in Africa.)

In 1980 Pacer Technology & Resources, Inc. and the Sumitomo Group (Japan) formed a joint venture to build an adhesive technical center and a facility to manufacture cyanoacrylate and other advanced adhesives in the United States. Pacer made adhesives and container systems for chemical and adhesive companies. It had been involved primarily in the consumer market for adhesives but hoped to move into the industrial market, where prices were more stable and margins were greater, through the joint venture. Sumitomo was a diversified firm (with sales of over $28 billion) that produced adhesives in Japan and marketed them in the United States through packagers and distributors. The joint venture gave Sumitomo a means to increase its U.S. market share by winning customers that wanted their supplier to be close by.

In 1980 Quaker Chemical and Alkaril Chemicals (Canada) formed a 50%-50% joint venture to manufacture specialty surfactants and textile chemicals. Quaker Chemical was seeking diversification because 60 percent of its sales were to the steel and auto industries, which had been hit by rough economic times. By becoming a surfactants producer, Quaker gained entry into numerous new end-markets. Virtually every product Quaker made contained surfactants in some form or other.

In 1981 Union Carbide Corp. and Henkel (West Germany) formed a joint enture in the United States to produce fatty alcohols based on natural fats and oils. Henkel, the world's largest producer of natural alcohols, provided technology for the joint venture. Union Carbide operated their jointly constructed plant, which had a capacity of 110 million pounds per year of fatty alcohols. A major portion of the new plant's detergent-range alcohols output were used by UCC's Ethylene Oxide Derivatives Division.

In 1981 Dow Chemical Co. and Production Operators Corp. formed a joint venture, Cynara Co., to provide gas separation services to the oil and gas industry. In 1984 the child continued to develop and commercialize processes using hollow fiber membranes for separation of gases such as carbon dioxide from hydrocarbon gases, which Dow Chemical had been using in a variety of applications.

In 1981 Celanese Plastics and Specialties Co. formed a joint venture to build a carbon fibers production facility with a capacity of 300,000 pounds per year. The joint venture was Celanese's first entry into production of carbon fibers, but it had been marketing Celion carbon fibers in the United States and abroad since 1976 under exclusive agreement with Tong Berlon Co. of Japan. Celanese also formed a joint venture with Osmonics in 1983 to develop membrane products.

In 1981 PPG Industries and DuPont formed a joint venture, PD Glycol, to manufacture ethylene glycol. A new plant with a capacity of 420 million pounds per year was built near an existing PPG ethylene glycol unit (which had a capacity of 200 million pounds per year) that PPG contributed to the joint venture. PD Glycol obtained equipment from an inactive PPG ethylene glycol plant in Puerto Rico that had previously taken its feedstock from Puerto Rico Olefins Co., a defunct joint venture of PPG and Commonwealth Oil Refining. PPG Industries and DuPont made investments in PD Glycol to improve its facilities and processes.

PPG was a merchant supplier of ethylene glycol. DuPont did not produce ethylene glycol in 1981 but used it to make polyester fibers (Dacron) and plastics. DuPont had worked with PPG Industries in the past and was engaged in other petrochemical joint ventures. Its need to consume the child's outputs for in-house production made the venture of a size that was larger than most others. The venture enjoyed scale economies that few other firms could match, and as the venture proceeded, its economics improved.

In 1981 Occidental Petroleum (Oxy) and ENI formed a joint venture, Enoxy, to run petrochemical and coal facilities and sell outputs worldwide. Enoxy's plants were acquired from ISR, a synthetic rubber firm that was formed in 1956 by eight rubber firms, including Dunlop, Goodyear, and Michelin, to provide a secure source of raw materials. The joint venture gave Oxy a customer for its coal output and moved it downstream from refining to petrochemicals where products enjoyed higher value-added margins.

In 1982 Diamond Shamrock and Showa-Denka formed a 50%-50% joint venture, SDS Biotech, to give the Japanese parent a means of entering the U.S. agricultural chemicals market. Diamond Shamrock sold Showa-Denka half of its interest in an ongoing agricultural and animal health business unit.

In 1974 Hercules and Montedison had formed a 50%-50% joint venture, Meroc, which was highly successful. In 1983 Hercules and Montedison restructured their joint venture in petrochemicals (Meroc) to form a new joint venture, Himont, and their joint venture in pharmaceuticals (Adria Laboratories) to form Erbamont. (See chapter 12 for a discussion of the pharmaceuticals joint venture.) The 50%-50% joint venture in plastics had assets in excess of $1 billion, and it combined Montedison's technology with Hercules's marketing strengths. The assets of Meroc (the joint venture that was formed in 1974) were folded into Himont, which had a combined capacity in excess of 2.5 billion pounds of polypropylene. Hercules contributed (1) polypropylene-resin plants in six locations, as well as (2) pilot plants, (3) supporting facilities, and (4) pipelines. Montedison contributed (1) polypropylene-resin plants in five locations, as well as (2) pilot plants, (3) supporting facilities, and a (4) key catalyst, developed jointly by Montedison and Mitsui Petrochemical that was capable of reducing the production costs of certain plastics sharply. Himont acquired Montedison's interests in joint ventures with Mitsui and with Petrofina. It purchased polypropylene and services from Montedison and sold polypropylene resins to Hercules and Montedison.

Hercules had been emphasizing specialty chemicals and other high-margin businesses (including pharmaceuticals) because it believed that commodity petrochemical businesses had become overcrowded and too cyclical to justify major new capital investment by the 1980s. The joint ventures with Montedison solved several problems for Hercules. Although it dominated the world polypropylene resin market, Hercules needed to invest heavily to keep costs down. The joint venture gave Hercules access to lower costs through the catalyst and process Montedison had co-developed. Moreover, it lessened Hercules's vulnerability to competitors' activities in polypropylene because the business represented 12 percent of sales after 1983, compared with 16 percent before the joint venture's formation.

In 1983 Northern Petrochemical and Kuraray formed a 50%-50% joint venture, Evalca, to make and sell EVOH plastic resins for the food and other packaging customers in the United States. Kuraray provided the child's technology. (All other EVOH resins were made in Japan.) Northern Petrochemical provided market access. The market was still growing in 1985 and new competitors were expected to enter.

In 1983 Air Products & Chemicals and Dynalectron Corp. formed a joint venture to gain a license from M.W. Kellogg, a subsidiary of Wheelabrator-Frye (which was acquired by Signal Company) for a process used for converting heavy oils and petroleum residuals to gasoline. The partners worked jointly to develop commercial uses for the process.

In 1983 Fuji Photo and Philip A. Hunt Chemical (which was 63 percent owned by Olin Corp.) formed a joint venture, Fuji-Hunt, to penetrate the fast growing Japanese market for electronic chemicals. Their child made and sold photoresists—sensitive coatings used in the semiconductor and microelectronics industries. Fuji had developed some photoresist technology on its own, but it preferred to exploit it through the joint venture with Hunt, by sharing resources, technologies, and risks, because Fuji's main corporate priorities were elsewhere. Hunt was a major photoresist manufacturer in Europe and the United States with minimal sales in Japan. In exchange for market access, Fuji gained access to Hunt's technology. Fuji-Hunt was based in Japan, and it wanted to supply materials to the winners of the semiconductor battles, whether they were U.S. or Japanese. Philip A. Hunt Chemical expected to serve non-Japanese semiconductor firms, while Fuji-Hunt served Japanese semiconductor firms.

Forming a venture with Fuji rather than going it alone allowed Hunt to move quickly to gain market share before too many other firms entered the business. Other firms, such as Allied Corp. and DuPont, were poised in 1983 to launch major efforts in electronic chemicals because it was one of the few niches of the chemicals industry that was expected to be highly profitable.

Table 11–1
Joint Ventures in the Petrochemical Industry, 1983

There were fifteen joint ventures in olefins, rubbers, resins, and derivatives in operation in 1983.

Child	Partner	%	Partner	%	Products
Allied Ethylene Plant	Allied Corp.	42	BASF Wyandotte	42	Ethylene
American Synthetic Rubber	25 members of the rubber industry				Polybutadiene and other rubbers
Calcasieu	Cities Service	28.4	Conoco	28.3	Ethylene oxide and glycol
	Sears	28.3	Northern Petro-chemical	15	
Chemplex	Getty Oil	50	American Can	50	Olefins, LDPE, HDPE
Copolymer Rubbers & Chemical	Armstrong Rubber	50	Gates Rubber	25	Butadiene, rubbers
	Sears	25			
Corpus Christi Petrochemicals	Champlin Oil	37.5	ICI	37.5	Ethylene, propylene
	Soltex	25			
Cos-Mar	Petrofina	50	Borg-Warner	50	Styrene
Enterprise Chemical	Enterprise Products	50	Hercules	50	Propylene
Monochem Inc.	Borden	50	Uniroyal	50	Acetylene, vinyl chloride
Neches Butane	Texaco	50	Goodrich	50	Butadiene
National Petro-chemicals	National Distill-ers & Chemicals	50	Owens Illinois	50	HDPE
PD Glycol	PPG Industries	50	DuPont	50	Ethylene oxide and glycol
Polybutadiene plant	Philips Petroleum	33.3	Armstrong	33.3	Polybutadiene
	General Tire	33.3			
Sun Olin	Sun Oil	50	Olin Corp.	50	Ethylene oxide and glycol
Propylene plant	Agway	66.7	Southern States	33.3	Propylene

There were six joint ventures in aromatics and derivatives in operation in 1983.

Child	Partner	%	Partner	%	Products
American Petrofina of Texas	Petrofina	50	Union Oil	50	Toluene, xylene
Hercofina	Petrofina	50	Hercules	50	Terephalate and esters
Resins					
Hercor Chemical	Hercofina	50	Commonwealth	50	Paraxylene
Quintana-Howell	Quintana Refinery	50	Howell	50	Benzene, tolu-ene, xylene
TENN/USS Olefins	USS Chemicals	50	Tenneco Co.	50	Phtalic anhy-dride, plas-ticizers
Rubicon	ICI	50	Uniroyal	50	Aniline, isocyanates

Table 11–1 continued

There were eight other petrochemical joint ventures, primarily in fertilizers in operation in 1983.

Child	Partner	%	Partner	%	Products
Allemania	Ashland Chemicals	50	IMC Co.	50	Methanol
Benson Nitrogen Products	W.R. Grace	50	Terra Chemicals	50	Urea and nitrogen
Napthalene Plant	Getty Oil	50	Union Oil	50	Napthalene
Melamine Chemicals	Ashland Chemicals	50	First Mississippi	50	Melamine
National Helium Corp.	National Distillers & Chemicals	50	Panhandle Eastern	50	Natural gas liquids
Oklahoma Nitrogen	Gulf Oil Terra Chemicals	37.5 25	W.R. Grace	50	Ammonium
Syngas Co.	DuPont	66.7	National Distillers & Chemicals	33.3	Carbon monoxide, methanol
Triad Chemicals	First Mississippi	50	Mississippi Chemicals	50	Ammonia, urea

In 1983 there was substantial excess capacity in the declining Japanese petrochemicals industry. Cutbacks were being coordinated by Japanese Parliament under its antimonopoly law, which encouraged cartels and joint ventures to eliminate an industry's excess capacity and make it more competitive. Twelve Japanese ethylene producers and six ethylene derivate makers were grouped into three consortia, each with its own joint marketing company. Although the agreements were voluntary, each Japanese consortium was required to trim production capacity by 36 percent.

The Japanese industrial policies reflected a major transformation that was occurring throughout the petrochemicals industry in 1984, as oil-producing nations—like Mexico, Saudi Arabia, and Canada, which once had flared the natural gas that occurred in nature with crude oil—began using it to make ammonia or methanol. Similarly, their excess crude oil was used to make ethylene or other petrochemicals.

In the United States, firms responded to these conditions of excess capacity by forming horizontal joint ventures to divest petrochemical businesses or shut in plants to bring supply in line with demand. Table 11–1 indicates which petrochemical joint ventures were still in operation in 1983. During an earlier era, when feedstocks had been cheap and abundant, joint ventures had been vertically related to their parents. Since U.S. feedstocks were no longer the lowest in cost, joint-ventures for backward integration were no longer justified. By 1985 the need to reduce industrywide excess capacity had forced antitrust policies concerning horizontal combinations to be amended. The realities of global competition motivated the use of joint ventures in a manner similar to that of the U.S. steel industry.

Genetic Engineering. Recombinant-DNA technology (genetic engineering) was a generic technology that could be applied to the development of many chemical products.[1] Its structure was still undeveloped or embryonic in 1984, and many joint ventures were used to help pioneering firms launch their products because the capital investment needed to scale up to commercial volumes was high and the technology of recovering commercial product after fermentation was complex. Although commercialization of genetic engineering techniques would occur first in the ethical pharmaceuticals field, the greatest long-term economc impact of genetic engineering was expected to be in the chemical and energy industries, and these included (1) ethanol, (2) crude oil recovery, and reduced needs for (3) petroleum-based chemicals used on crops and in chemical reactions. Fungicides, insecticides, and herbicides are included in the discussion below (as well as genetically engineered seeds). Chapter 12 considers the use of joint ventures to exploit genetic engineering technology in the ethical pharmaceuticals industry.

Parent firms with experience in large-scale fermentation activities were the most desirable joint-venture partners in 1984, as were firms with strong distribution channels because fledgling, stand-alone genetic engineering firms initially lacked access to commercial scale facilities and distribution channels to develop and sell their products. Stand-alone genetic engineering firms hoped to progress from (1) contract research (to earn revenues for funding of their own research and for future product development) to (2) licensure or outright sale of genetically engineered products that were developed (again, selling outputs to outsiders as an OEM vendor to fund future projects) to (3) joint ventures with outsiders where they retained control, captured more value-added, and brought products to marketplace in their own right), and finally to (4) stand-alone plants that marketed their own products through their own sales forces. In 1984 few genetic engineering firms, including Cetus and Genentech, could function alone (without outsiders' cash or marketing or production skills). Consequently, there were many joint ventures and other cooperative agreements in genetic engineering.

Cetus's major shareholders included Standard Oil of California (Chevron Corp.), Standard Oil of Indiana (AMOCO), and National Distillers & Chemical. In 1978 Chevron began a joint research venture to develop ways of enhancing production of alcohol for use in gasohol, cost-saving methods for producing large-scale industrial chemicals, and microorganisms for improved oil recovery from heavy-oil fields. Its cancelled project Cetus has been described above.

In 1984 Cetus Corp. and Nabisco Brands Inc. formed a joint venture, Nabisco/Cetus Food Biotechnology Research Partnership, to conduct research and development activities using recombinant-DNA technology and other biochemical skills that could be applied to the processing of food and food ingredients. Their child carried on programs of research for third parties as well as for its partners. Nabisco possessed market access to distribute any products developed by the child on its behalf. W.R. Grace and Cetus formed a 51%-49% joint venture, Agricetus, to apply biotechnology techniques to the development of higher-yield, disease-resistant crops in 1984 when Grace purchased an interest in Cetus's agricultural operations in Madison, Wisconsin (Cetus Madison).

In 1979 Lubrizol (through its venture-capital arm) purchased a 20 percent interest in Genentech. Alfa-Laval purchased a 6.4 percent stake in Genentech in 1983. Because Genentech was positioning itself as a pharmaceutical firm, most of its joint ventures and licensing agreements were in hormones and ethical pharmaceutical applications. Corning and Genentech formed Genencor to develop enzymes for food processing and chemical industries.

Dow Chemical entered a $5 million agreement with Collaborative Genetics to generate fundamental genetic-engineering techniques and purchased a 5 percent interest in its parent, Collaborative Research Corning Glass Works also engaged in joint research with Collaborative Research.

In 1980 Flow Laboratories (a subsidiary of Flow General) and Contract-Holding B.V. (the parent company of Contract Roestvrijstaal B.V., a Dutch fermentation equipment maker) formed a 50%-50% joint venture to make fermentation equipment in the Netherlands. The joint venture focused its attentions on applications in biotechnology.

In 1980 Allied Corporation acquired an equity interest in BioLogicals and funded research involving the use of biotechnology to diversify into high technology products. Allied did not have an in-house genetic-engineering-research effort at that time. Allied purchased a 6 percent interest in Genetics Institute to obtain rights of first refusal to findings from its research program in DNA probes.

Many corporations purchased minority interests in genetic engineering firms to gain access to research for a particular line of applications. Ethyl Research Laboratories purchased a 2 percent interest in Biotech, a firm that specialized in hybridoma and genetic engineering technology. W.R. Grace granted Synergen an R&D contract to develop microorganisms for producing flavoring and fragrance agents. Koppers held a 30 percent interest in Genex, had a right of first refusal on projects it was funding, and held a 5.8 interest in Engenics, a firm that was researching continuous processes for mass-producing genetically engineered organisms. (Mead also purchased a 5.8 interest in Engenics.) Koppers formed a joint venture with DNA Plants Technology to develop diagnostic kits for plant diseases.

Eli Lilly had a research contract with Phytogen to improve the photosynthetic capabilities of plants. Martin-Marietta formed R&D joint ventures with Chiron Corp., Native Plants, and Molecular Genetics, respectively, to develop crops with increased resistance to pests and diseases, improved yields, and reduced dependency on fertilizers. Monsanto formed an agreement with Bio Technica to develop agricultural chemicals using its proprietary recombinant DNA technology.

Heinz granted Bio Technica an R&D contract to develop techniques for manufacturing an amino acid used in aspartame, an artificial sweetener. Genex also made one of the amino acids used to produce aspartame.

In 1983 Alfa-Laval and Cardo (Swedish fermentation expert) formed a 50%-50% joint venture, AC Biotechnics. Cardo held a 19 percent interest in Advanced Genetic Sciences and formed a joint research venture in plant genetics and agricultural products. Rohm & Haas purchased a minority interest in Advanced Genetic Sciences and invested in its research projects with agricultural applications.

Tosco and Upjohn each invested in research programs with Applied Molecular Genetics (AMGen). Tosco sought an enhanced oil recovery process using microbes. Upjohn and AMGen formed a joint marketing agreement for bovine hormone.

Child Activities. The changing purpose of the joint-venture child can be traced to the changing relationships among partners which occurred over time. Prior to the 1970s, petrochemical joint ventures had linked horizontally related parents upstream to a vertically related child. The energy crisis created feedstock scarcities and skimpy profit margins. Supply uncertainty made their child play a critical role in parents' value-added chains. Firms' desires to participate in markets that offered them higher value-added margins brought together vertically related partners, which performed upstream and downstream processing activities. They became linked in the vertical chain of processing through their joint ventures.

Parents controlled market access for their child's outputs. Chemicals were sold by the carload or by pipeline, and one sales force could handle a wide range of chemical products. Outputs were usually consumed internally by parents or marketed on a merchant basis by parents' sales representatives. Thus, petrochemical joint ventures were often operated in close coordination with one or more of their parents due to their physical proximity and the highly interconnected nature of a technology. Linkages between parent and child were simply a matter of laying a pipeline from one plant to another. Some partners transferred all relevant assets for a line of petrochemicals to their joint venture child and gave it complete autonomy to manufacture them for in-house consumption, but parents usually marketed the outputs they did not consume themselves.

Even where the child was given full authority to operate a complex and interrelated facility of several plants and had secured its feedstock with twenty-year supply contracts, parent firms often dissolved their joint ventures with ease by selling their shares to each other or to a third party. The child's personnel were employees of the child and were tied to its fate.

Petrochemical joint ventures were often of long duration and involved assets in excess of $500 million. Compared with them, the futures of genetic engineering joint ventures were uncertain because it was not yet clear what roles parents would play in commercializing their child's products. Parents controlled market access for the outputs of genetic engineering joint ventures, should any commercializable products be produced.

Steel

Vertically integrated producers of steel often engaged in the following stages of activity: operating coke ovens, blast furnaces, steelmaking furnaces, rolling and finishing facilities. Technological improvements were devoted to increasing efficiencies, alleviating steps in production, and substituting scarce raw materials with more abundant ones. Continuous casting steelmaking technology offered energy savings, lower costs per ton, higher labor productivity, decreased pollution, and higher quality. Direct reduction technology used relatively abundant natural gas as a raw material rather than scarce coking coal.

It was not necessary to be an integrated steel producer in order to prosper in the steel industry. Raw virgin steel slabs could be purchased from offshore steel firms if firms did not make their own. Some steel producers (such as specialty and alloy steel makers) did not have furnace facilities; they started with semifinished products and specialized in the finishing process. Minimills were not vertically integrated, for example, because they did not make their own pig iron. Instead of incurring the costs of pig iron, mini mills often relied on the use of scrap or pre-reduced ores to make a limited range of products. (Mills that did *not* use virgin iron ore for steelmaking could not serve customers like the automotive and appliance industries, which used flat-rolled steel made from pig iron in 1984.)

Many U.S. steel firms were still backward integrated in 1984. During the 1950s and 1960s, U.S. steel firms had formed joint ventures to mine iron ore and to build processing plants for low-grade taconite ore from the Mesabi Range (to supplement their dwindling pure iron-ore reserves). Forty iron ore joint ventures were identified by researchers in 1957, and take-or-pay contracts secured the financial viability of these joint ventures, as in the chemicals industry. Take-or-pay contracts also bound steelmakers to cover ore production expenses, even if they could not use their child's outputs. When steel plant capacity was retired, during the 1970s, steel makers' iron ore mines should have reduced capacity as well. But writing off these investments required steelmakers to recognize debts from joint-venture obligations that often did not appear on their consolidated balance sheets. Unlike the chemicals industry where large write-offs occurred whenever processes were deemed uneconomic or outputs too low, steel firms did *not* face the exit barriers of ore mines in a timely fashion. They let the costs of shutdowns become substantial deterrents to retiring their excess capacity.

By contrast, Japanese steel firms were located on deep sea harbors and were less vertically integrated than U.S. firms. They purchased raw materials from outsiders and sold 80 percent or more of their outputs to Japanese trading companies that marketed those outputs to outsiders. (U.S. steel makers owned iron ore mines and marketed the largest portion of their outputs through their own distribution networks.) Not surprisingly, the Japanese trading companies developed superior marketing capabilities in the global arena when compared with U.S. steel firms, and by 1985 the steel industry was a global one.

Need for Joint Activities. Prior to 1940, U.S. firms produced 33 percent of the world's steel, but they became net importers of steel in 1959 and produced only 15 percent of the world's steel in 1980. Nations with lower labor costs, such as South Korea and Brazil, rose to prominence in steel making in the 1980s when even Japanese steel firms suffered from the effects of excess capacity brought about by their enthusiastic overexpansion in the previous decade. Joint ventures were needed in the United States in the 1980s to transfer cost-effective technology and to rationalize outmoded and inefficient excess capacity in both steel making and iron ore mines.

Steel makers had expected that steel (and iron ore) demand would rise from the 1950s to the 1980s. As recently as 1974, the U.S. steel industry was prosperous and operated at full capacity. But stagnant consumption and a shift to electric furnace steel making—a process where scrap steel was recycled, thereby eliminating the need for iron ore—left the industry with overcapacity in iron ore mining that greatly exceeded the demand of steel mills. Moreover, U.S. steel-making plants were not as modern as those of overseas competitors. As U.S. protectionism intensified to include steel product quotas and other restrictions, laws to protect environmental quality undermined domestic plant efficiencies. Outsiders used joint ventures as a means to enter the large U.S. steel market with new technologies at a time when domestic producers seemed most sickly.

Choosing Partners. In 1974 U.S. steel capacity was fully utilized, and steel makers were very profitable. Scarcely anyone was building new capacity because it was widely recognized that the U.S. steel industry was facing a mature market. Nevertheless, in 1974 Texas Industries (a Dallas-based building materials firm) and Co-Steel International (of Toronto) formed a 50%-50% joint venture, Chaparral Steel Co., to build a 220,000 ton steel plant south of Dallas because southwest U.S. markets faced a steel product shortage. Chaparral's plant was equipped with an electric arc furnace, continuous casting facilities, and high-speed rolling mill equipment and used a market mill, a specialized steel mill that utilized scrap as its raw material. Chaparral's facility was substantially smaller than an integrated mill and had lower production costs. (Co-Steel had substantial experience with market mills.)

By 1979 Chaparral Steel had added a $180 million melt shop and rolling mill, thereby doubling its annual production to 1 million tons of billets. Its mill was unlike any other North American facility, with a 130 ton electric arc furnace and a continuous rolling mill, because Chaparral's plant was designed to be highly efficient. Its workers continued to innovate process improvements year after year, giving Chaparral a productivity rate of 2.4 man-hours per ton of output in 1982, which compared very favorably with the U.S. steel industry's average rate of 8.0 man-hours per tons. (In 1984 its productivity was 1.4 man-hours per ton of steel; the fastest mill in Japan produced at 2.8 man-hours per ton at that time.)

Chaparral's unique policies concerning worker involvement contributed heavily to its enduring success and its ability to set world records for output. When other U.S. steel makers were purchasing technology from Japanese competitors, Chaparral was *selling* licenses to its processes to Nippon Kokan. Although the future of the U.S. steel industry looked troubled in 1984, the long-term outlook for Chaparral Steel seemed favorable. Chaparral Steel earned $15 million in net income for 1982 and contributed most of these profits to its parents. Texas Industries and Co-Steel considered Chaparral to be quite successful, and they permitted Chaparral to go to the capital markets in its own right to finance its $180 million expansion.

In 1973 subsidiaries of Hoover Bearings and Pechiney-Ugine-Kuhlman (discussed in chapter 7) formed Hoover-Ugine, a 50%-50% joint venture for the direct conversion of scrap steel into wire rod. The venture used wire rod technology provided by its parents and constructed a $15 million plant in Michigan. Pechiney contributed its process improvements, which were similar to those of other 1973 market mills.

In 1975 Ishikawajima-Harima Heavy Industries Co. (IHI), Armco Steel and Foster Wheeler Corp. cooperated to use the Armco method in building direct reduction steel plants. Under their agreement, IHI and Foster Wheeler supplied equipment to companies using Armco's direct reduction technology. (Foster Wheeler also allied with IHI through technical agreements on chemical plants and heating furnaces. Armco later expanded its licensing agreement with Foster Wheeler to include Voest-Alpine A.G. in a three-way technology alliance.)

Similar alliances developed in 1975 between Kawasaki Heavy Industries and Swindell-Dressler (to license, make, and sell plants using the Hill process developed by Swindell) and between Kobe Steel, Mitsui & Co., and Midrex Corp. (to produce, sell, and install direct reduction plants using the Midrex method). Each coalition hoped that their technology would become the industry standard. In 1976 Kawasaki Heavy Industries provided Pullman Inc.

with iron ore reduction technology for use in its plants. By 1984 Kobe Steel owned Midrex Corp. and Kawasaki Steel owned a 25 percent interest in California Steel Industries.

In 1975 International Minerals & Chemical Corp. (IMC), and Allegheny Ludlum Steel Corp. formed a 75%–25% joint venture, ALS Metals Co., to build a $31 million 40 megawatt electric furnace to produce both 50 percent and 75 percent ferrosilicon furnace facility in Alabama. The child was located adjacent to a plant owned by the Tennessee Alloys Corp. (TAC) Division of IMC, which operated the venture's facility. ALS Metals' parents took its output in proportion to their ownership shares.

In 1976 Quebec Cartier Mining Co. (a subsidiary of U.S. Steel Corp.) and Sidbec of Quebec formed a joint venture with British Steel to build an iron ore pelletizing plant in Canada. Ownership shares were Sidbec (50.1 percent), British Steel (41.67 percent), and U.S. Steel (8.23 percent). The venture continued in 1984, but it needed renegotiation of its terms to make it economic.

In 1978 Midland-Ross Corp. was granted a license by Nippon-Kokan to produce furnaces to make high-strength steel using a continuous annealing process called NKK-CAL. Midland-Ross planned to sell the furnaces in the U.S. and Europe, when the depressed steel market improved. The continuous annealing process facilitated the production of high-strength steel without expensive alloying agents.

In 1978 Nippon Steel Corp. and Brown & Root (a subsidiary of Halliburton) signed a ten-year agreement whereby the partners jointly received orders for coke oven plants. Nippon Steel provided engineering and designing skills for the ordered plant; Brown & Root constructed it. The partners manufactured plant equipment themselves or procured it from outside vendors, depending on customer specifications. In 1977 Nippon Steel had provided Wean United Inc., a producer of rolling mill machinery, with a license to manufacture Nippon Steel's continuous annealing and processing lines in the United States. Wean United obtained other technology licenses in 1981 from Ishikawajima-Harima Heavy Industries.

In 1976 Bliss & Laughlin and Kyodo Shaft Co. Ltd. formed a joint venture, BLK Steel Inc., to build a new plant in Illinois for coil to bar stock cold finishing. In 1978 Leggett Wire (a subsidiary of Leggett & Platt) and Armco Wire (a subsidiary of Armco Inc.) formed a 50%-50% joint venture, Adcom Wire Co., to operate Leggett's wire-drawing plants in Florida and Kentucky. The partnership provided an additional internal source of wire for Armco while strengthening Leggett & Platt's position.

In 1979 Sumitomo Metal Industries agreed to supply Lone Star Steel, a subsidiary of Northwest Industries, Inc., with steelmaking technology. The agreement covered know-how for basic design and operation of converters and a continuous casting system to be adapted to U.S. mills, but not construction or equipment. In 1980 Bethlehem Steel obtained a technology agreement to acquire Sumitomo's continuous casting technology and know-how for use at its Steelton works in Pennsylvania. Sumitomo helped to determine the machine's scale and place of installation and offered other related know-how.

In 1980 Wheeling-Pittsburgh Steel Corp. obtained equipment know-how and financing for $140 million worth of continuous casting installations from a major creditor, Mitsubishi. In 1981 Kawasaki Steel Corp. agreed to provide Bethlehem Steel with knowledge concerning productivity improvements attained by using Kawasaki's computerized blast furnace operating system. The Kawasaki system detected infra-furnace reactions and prevented furnace deterioration through the use of various types of installed sensors that measured gas ingredients, temperatures, pressures, and raw materials distribution. Deviations from the ideal figures stored in the computer were adjusted by process controls according to sensor feedback.

When McLouth Steel filed for protection under bankruptcy laws in 1982, Cleveland-Cliffs Iron Co., its joint-venture partner in Empire Iron Mining Partnership, was forced to take over its partner's share of the child's iron ore output under the take-or-pay contract that bound them. If Cleveland-Cliffs had not done so, Empire would have defaulted on $264 million in debt. (Cleveland-Cliff's other partner in Empire Iron Mining, International Harvester, was in no condition to assume its share of the joint venture burden in 1982, as the discussion of the farm and industrial equipment industry below explains.) Cleveland-Cliffs traded a 35 percent interest in the Empire mines to Jones & Laughlin (a subsidiary of LTV Corp.) in exchange for interests in two of LTV's mine holdings. Cleveland-Cliffs was a joint venture partner with LTV in another iron ore mine that carried $122 million in debts in 1982.

By 1982 the threat of quotas and other trade barriers made Japanese steelmakers seek ownership stakes in the U.S. steel industry. The United States was their largest market for steel. Owning part of a steel mill there allowed them to maintain or increase their market shares without violating U.S. trade laws. To that end, Kobe Steel Ltd. studied an equity investment in and joint venture with Wheeling-Pittsburgh Steel Corp., the eighth largest U.S. steel firm. Kobe was also studying an investment in ailing McLouth Steel Corp. Sumitomo Industries Ltd. had already rejected several proposals from U.S. steel firms in 1982, but it continued to study equity investments in and joint ventures with U.S. steel makers. In 1983 Nippon Kokan and Ford Motor Co. planned a fadeout joint venture whereby Ford would sell it a 75 percent interest in its River Rouge steel mill. The venture fell through because workers' unions opposed the concessions that they would have been asked to make if ownership had changed hands. British Steel and U.S. Steel proposed a joint venture in 1983 that would combine supplying operations at Ravensburg, Scotland, with finishing operations at Fairless Hills, near Philadelphia. Unions were also opposed to this joint venture, fearing perhaps that a chain reaction of joint ventures would occur throughout the industry. U.S. Steel reduced its productive capacity by 20 percent by the end of 1983, taking a $1.2 billion writedown, since it had no other means of improving its situation.

Several U.S. steel makers formed global partnerships to purchase raw steel slabs from firms that operated more economical plants. Ford Motor Co.'s River Rouge steel unit obtained 120,000 tons of steel slabs allegedly shipped from Thyssen A.G. of West Germany. Republic Steel Corp., Sharon Steel Corp., McClouth Steel Products Corp., and Lukens Inc. purchased raw steel from producers in locations that ranged from Brazil to South Korea. Brazil's Siderbras (owned by Kawasaki Steel Corp. and Finsider of Italy, among others) constructed a $3.3 billion steel plant to produce semifinished steel for export to foreign steel companies.

Early in 1984 Bethlehem Steel and Inland Steel announced plans to produce galvanized steel jointly at Bethlehem's Burns Harbor plant in Indiana. Rust resistant steel was one of the few U.S. markets that was growing in 1984. Ford Motor Co. solicited a joint-venture partner for an electrogalvanizing steel operation in order to obtain corrosion-resistant steel for use in automobile production. U.S. Steel was chosen as Ford's 50%-50% partner.

In 1984 Wheeling-Pittsburgh Steel Corp. and Nisshin Steel Co. formed a joint venture to make rust-resistant steels at one of Wheeling-Pittsburgh's existing plants. Nisshin Steel was Japan's sixth-largest steel firm and its largest producer of stainless steels. Nisshin also purchased a 10 percent interest in Wheeling-Pittsburgh in 1984. But when Wheeling-Pittsburgh filed for protection under U.S. bankruptcy law in 1985 after the United Steelworkers union refused to approve a debt restructuring plan that affected their pension funds, the future of Wheeling-Pittsburgh's joint venture with Nisshin Steel became uncertain.

Jones & Laughlin Steel was merged with Republic Steel in 1984 to form LTV Steel. The resulting company planned to shut down redundant and inefecient facilities and to divest ownership of those facilities that the U.S. Justice Department considered to be in violation of antitrust laws. (But a proposed merger between U.S. Steel and National Steel was disallowed by the Antitrust Division because divestitures were not explicitly planned as part of the combination.) Republic Steel owned a 50 percent stake with Armco Steel in Reserve Mining Co., a taconite ore producer that was idled during 1982 and 1983. Jones & Laughlin took little more than one-third of its take-or-pay entitlements from various iron ore interests that it shared with Cleveland-Cliffs during this period.

LTV Steel Co. and Sumitomo Metal Industries Ltd. formed a 60%-40% joint venture in 1984 to make rust-resistant steel in the United States. Sumitomo was a leading producer of steel pipe. The LTV-Sumitomo joint venture was the fifth partnership in the area of electrogalvanized steel that was announced in 1984, and leading U.S. automobile manufacturers agreed informally to purchase the outputs of the joint ventures in order to encourage these investments.

In 1984 National Intergroup Inc., parent of National Steel (the only domestic steel maker to show a profit in 1983), and Nippon Kokan (NKK) formed a 50%-50% joint venture to acquire National Steel. The two firms had been exchanging technology for over twenty years, and NKK wanted to acquire a U.S. firm that made sheet steels such as were made for the U.S. automobile and appliance industries. Nippon Kokan, Japan's second largest steel maker, was suffering in 1984 because the world's largest integrated steel mill (which NKK owned) was operating below 50 percent of capacity and the company as a whole was using less than 65 percent of its steel-making capacity.

In 1984 Nippon Kokan acquired a 40 percent interest in International Light Metals Corp., an aluminum extrusions subsidiary of Martin-Marietta Corp. The subsidiary was created especially for this transaction and was a fade-out joint venture for Martin-Marietta of its Torrance plant in California. International Light Metals held 85 percent of the U.S. market for titanium extrusions and produced a variety of other aluminum and aluminum alloy extrusion products. Allegheny International and NL Industries jointly owned the largest U.S. producer of titanium, Titanium Metals Corp. of America, and wanted to sell it. The second-largest titanium firm, RMI Co. (which was jointly owned by U.S. Steel and National Distillers & Chemical) had been for sale since 1982 with no acceptable offers.

Child Activities. The steel industry's experiences with joint ventures also illustrate how the child's role changed over time. In the early years of development, horizontally related parents formed vertically related joint ventures in iron ore mining to develop their industry by procuring stable sources of raw materials. When cheaper sources of ore and pig iron developed overseas, steel firms' obligations to their joint ventures encumbered their strategic flexibbility. Unlike the petrochemicals firms, which shut down their joint ventures when they no longer served their needs, steel firms delayed disentangling their iron ore coalitions until they loomed as significant exit barriers, and their tardiness in retiring capacity hurt them later.

By 1984 steel joint ventures linked horizontally related partners in horizontal fade-outs. This pattern was consistent with the behavior expected of firms in mature (or declining) industries with high exit barriers. The rules of steel competition had changed radically and required drastic actions to amend its problems.

The child in steel joint ventures was usually managed by the partner possessing the best technology and knowledge of how to produce steel most economically. Because the parents and child were so closely related, proportional output agreements and other practices that treated the child like an extension of its parent organization were commonplace. On this point, the steel industry joint ventures differed from those of the petrochemicals industry where children were given greater operating autonomy.

Farm and Industrial Equipment

Farm equipment included tractors, combines (threshing machines) cultivators, plows, mowers, harrows, discs, seeders, balers, corn pickers and wagons, feed grinders and wood splitters, seed corn dryers, seeders and fertilizer spreaders, among others. Distribution of worldwide 1984 market shares for the farm equipment industry was estimated to be as follows: Deere (32.4 percent), International Harvester (15.2 percent), Massey-Ferguson (11.1 percent), Kubota (9.0 percent), Fiat (8.7 percent), Ford (8.6 percent), Sperry-New Holland (6.4 percent), J.I. Case (4.6 percent), and Allis-Chalmers (4 percent).

Construction equipment included bulldozers, excavators, earth movers, graters, dredges, dump trucks, finishers, cement mixers, cranes and drilling rigs, among others. The construction equipment market suffered from excess capacity and stagnant demand in 1984. For example, forklift trucks were used in manufacturing plants to move pallets of product or raw material from place to place. Factory automation systems had reduced the need for forklift trucks and demand was expected to decline. Forklift trucks had become a commodity-like business, and the lowest-cost producers of them were Japanese firms.

Need for Joint Activities. Joint ventures in the farm and industrial equipment industries were needed to rationalize excess capacity, consolidate product lines and widen product offerings, transfer manufacturing technology, provide sources of lower-cost production, and forge global distribution channels. Many cooperative agreements were used to obtain products (to fill out firms' lines after they shut in their underutilized plants). The joint-venture patterns in farm and industrial equipment paralleled those in the automotive industry (which are discussed in chapter 12). Prior to the conditions that depressed U.S. demand for farm and industrial equipment, joint ventures were formed by U.S. firms primarily overseas as a means of entering protected markets.

Choosing Partners. In 1977 Allis-Chalmers agreed to market agricultural tractors made by Toyosha Co. Ltd. (a medium-size agricultural tractor maker). The marketing agreement permitted Toyosha to expand its tractor sales network overseas. Allis-Chalmers marketed the Toyosha Co. products as a way to obtain small tractors to fill out its product line. In 1978 FMC Corp. obtained marketing rights to sell a medium horsepower, water-cooled agricultural tractor made by Iseki Agricultural Machinery. Eaton Corp. formed a joint venture in its forklift truck business with Sumitomo Heavy Industries of Japan to spin off its holdings. Under this arrangement, Sumitomo forklift trucks were sold through Eaton's distribution channels under Eaton's name. (Eaton took a low equity interest in this venture as a way of fading out of this business area.)

In 1984 Caterpillar Tractor Co. relied on South Korea's Daewoo Heavy Industries Ltd. To make its forklift trucks. (Daewoo also made small automobiles for General Motors in a joint venture discussed in chapter 12.) In the interests of survival, firms were making products for each other for each to sell under their respective brand names. Caterpillar's joint venture with Mitsubishi provided it with small crawler tractors and wheel loaders. Komatsu, Japan's leading construction machinery maker, was establishing its first U.S. assembly plant in 1984, in a move calculated to strengthen its position in that market after the relative yen-to-dollar price advantage of its bulldozers, hydraulic excavators, and other construction equipment exports had faded. Komatsu had licensing agreements with International Harvester and Bucyrus-Erie, but these expired in 1982 when Komatsu intensified its U.S. marketing efforts.

In 1979 Allis-Chalmers formed a joint venture, Fiat-Allis, with Fiat to make earthmoving and construction equipment. When the joint venture was founded Allis-Chalmers owned 35 percent, and Fiat was the operator. The venture did not go well, and Allis-Chalmers charged that Fiat operated Fiat-Allis to go further its own interest to Allis-Chalmers's detriment. As the venture progressed, Allis-Chalmers lost its equity position because it could not cover losses. By 1982 Fiat owned 85 percent in the venture, and Allis-Chalmers was trying to phase out the rest of its interest. Their joint venture had reported annual losses of nearly $50 million in both 1979 and 1980. In early 1985 Allis-Chalmers Corp. was talking with other farm equipment manufacturers to aid its ailing farm equipment division. Deutz, the U.S. subsidiary of West Germany's Kloeckner-Humboldt-Deutz A.G., was mentioned as a potential buyer or joint-venture partner.

In 1983 International Harvester (the second-largest farm machinery maker) and the French subsidiary of Massey-Ferguson were studying a variety of cooperative ventures to make farm equipment parts for each other. Both firms were troubled because demand within their industries was depressed due to higher farm productivity and farm consolidations, among others. Demand for farm and industrial equipment was so depressed that it was widely recognized that the industry would have to shrink or make marriages. At that time, Regie National des Usines Renault reported that it was discussing joint ventures to make tractors in Europe. The New Holland farm equipment division of Sperry Corp. also said that it received overtures from Harvester.

In 1983 Deere (the world's largest agricultural machinery maker) announced a tie-up in development, production, and sales of construction machinery with Hitachi Construction Machinery (Japan's second-largest agricultural machinery firm—after Komatsu Ltd.). Their alliance reflected the need for regrouping among world construction machinery makers who have been long in the doldrums amid worldwide recession. In their venture, Deere and Hitachi Construction Machinery (HCM) planned to develop jointly three models of small- and medium-sized hydraulic excavators. Major parts and components of the new models were produced by HCM in Japan to supply

Deere in the form of knock-down kits. Deere built a factory in the United States to produce engines for the assembly with HCM-made parts. Hitachi Construction Machinery and Deere also planned a comprehensive technological cooperation relationship to share expertise on bulldozers and cranes, as well as the mutual use of each other's after-sale service world networks.

By tying up with Deere, HCM aimed at advancing into the U.S. market without causing trade friction. Combined production of hydraulic excavators by HCM and Deere was estimated to reach more than 30 percent of total output or the biggest share in the U.S. market.

Caterpillar Tractor Co., the leading manufacturer of earth-moving equipment, acquired a 20 percent interest in Advanced Robotics Corp. (ARC) in 1984 and formed a joint-development agreement with ARC in the area of arc welding robots. (Additional minority interests in ARC were being offered to other big manufacturers of heavy machinery.) Caterpillar faced depressed demand and intense competition in 1984 from foreign competition, especially from Komatsu, which invested $80 million annually on its factory automation efforts. These included computer-driven flexible manufacturing systems and other cost-reduction investments. The interest in ARC was both a diversification and an effort to raise efficiencies in Caterpillar's manufacturing process.

After five years of industrywide depressed demand and labor problems, International Harvester could no longer sustain its losses. In 1984 the J.I. Case subsidiary of Tenneco Inc. acquired some of the assets of the farm equipment product line of International Harvester. J.I. Case had also suffered losses in its farm and construction equipment operations. It was difficult to find buyers for troubled units in these industries in the 1980s. J.I. Case was the second-biggest manufacturer of large tractors, and International Harvester was the second-biggest maker of farm equipment. Tenneco had tried to acquire all of International Harvester in 1983, but it could not satisfy International Harvester's unfunded pension obligations. In 1984 Tenneco acquired only the Harvester assets it wanted—primarily products to broaden its own line—leaving International Harvester to liquidate the remainder. The new arrangement with J.I. Case left the pension fund exit barrier for Harvester to manage. Approximately 40 percent of the industry's tractor-making capacity would be eliminated by Harvester's demise. Tenneco purchased tractor engines from its joint venture with Cummins Engine Co. (see chapter 12).

In early 1985 Clark Equipment Co. and A.B. Volvo of Sweden merged their respective business units (Clark Michigan Co. and Volvo B.M. A.B.) into one of the world's largest makers of construction and mining vehicles and machinery. Their child distributed both Clark and Volvo products in the United States. Clark products were added to Volvo dealer lines overseas. Volvo B.M. made off-road construction vehicles, including dump trucks. Clark made heavy construction machinery, including wheel loaders and trucks.

Child Activities. The activities joint ventures in farm and industrial equipment had to be closely coordinated with those of their parents because the industry had become a global one. The best economies were realized by pursuing a strategy of drawing on the outputs of plants that offered the most advantageous production costs, wherever they were located, and transshipping them to local markets. Successful implementation of such strategies did not allow the joint-venture child to enjoy much autonomy.

U.S. joint ventures in the farm and industrial equipment industry were formed to reduce excess capacity and to consolidate the strongest parts of remaining productive facilities. Successful implementation of such downsizing did not allow for much autonomy in the child's activities unless the management system of the child rewarded its managers for achieving performance objectives related to rationalization of facilities, cost reductions, productivity improvements on a fixed asset base or other behaviors consistent with competition in mature markets.

Summary

The patterns of joint ventures used in the chemicals and steel industries illustrate that partners combined initially to obtain feedstocks or raw materials, to share economic assets with large outputs, to spread costs, and to pioneer new processes or products. The petrochemicals, steel, and farm and industrial equipment industries enjoyed substantial scale economies when their facilities were fully utilized. As plant scales increased, the unit sales volume needed to attain these scale economies were larger than the U.S. market alone. Technology was complex and subject to continual improvements. The capital requirements to keep abreast of these changes were immense. Hence, it was not surprising that firms engaged in joint ventures with overseas firms to broaden their product lines and increase their sales volumes. Close coordination with parents in such ventures was important because the child's markets can be standardized and because excess capacity prevented them from realizing scale economies if they did not coordinate activities closely.

The patterns of joint ventures used in these industries illustrate how partners combine under adversity to consolidate their assets to bring supply in line with demand. Horizontally related competitors joined forces to create vertically related children early in the chemicals and steel industries; they formed horizontally related joint ventures to realize the significant scale economies available at large production volumes, especially as cost reduction became the key to effective competition in all three industries, for they allowed rivals to pool the most efficient parts of their respective facilities when rationalizing capacity. When demand grew slowly (or was declining), close coordination between parent and child was needed to serve the most promising customers while closing the most appropriate facilities. In this manner, parent and child were both most profitable while keeping capacity in line with demand. Because the child was often physically interconnected with its parents in a vertical relationship, its activities had to be coordinated closely with its parents' activities.

Future liaisons in these industries may give way to acquisitions, particularly as global partners find their relationships with local partners to be unwieldy. Depending on local policies regarding foreign ownership, joint ventures could be a transitory or more enduring form of organizational arrangement. Joint ventures prospered in the petrochemicals industry historically because the partners were homogeneous in their expectations for the joint venture and in their outlooks concerning competition. But in the future, partners that seek to coordinate the disparate pieces of global systems may find themselves at odds with each other more frequently. The more volatile the competitive environment, the less attractive joint ventures will become over time unless they can be used to absorb excess capacity and reduce firms' propensities to engage in destructive price competition.

In petrochemicals, where the scope of a joint-venture child could encompass several plants, supporting facilities, and pipelines, partners frequently operated those parts of the jointly owned enterprise that were most closely related to their ongoing business activities. Selling tasks were usually performed by parent's sales forces if there was any output to sell on a merchant basis.

Substantial day-to-day autonomy in manufacturing activities was granted to the managers of petrochemical ventures because their business units were better equipped to function as stand-alone entities. Yet close coordination was needed on some decisions because the child was captive in its parents' vertical chains of processing. In steel and the farm and industrial equipment industry, where firms were less likely to consume great proportions of their joint venture's outputs in their own processing activities, access to distribution channels were more important and the joint-venture child often marketed the products of its parents as well as its own outputs.

Note

1. This section is condensed from chapter 9 of K.R. Harrigan, 1983, *Strategies for Vertical Integration* (Lexington, Mass.: Lexington Books), pp. 209–241.

12
Joint Ventures and Global Industries

Many of the eighteen joint ventures and other cooperative agreements in the industries of this chapter faced global competition, and firms within them pursued global strategies. They offered standardized products in diverse geographic markets where customers needs were similar. They gained logistical scale economies in doing so. Accordingly, analyses of how firms used joint ventures where market access was *not* the source of competitive advantage should be of interest in addressing questions of joint venture duration and parent–child coordination in global competition.

Motives

Global strategies were most attractive where customers' tastes were similar across markets and firms could use the same (or very similar) products to satisfy demand in these many markets. Substantial scale economies accrued to firms that could coordinate their activities closely across international markets. Such firms had little need for partners (except to penetrate protected markets) unless their opportunities to exploit competitive advantages faded rapidly. Thus when global firms took local firms as partners, they often maintained close controls over their many plant locations, assembly plants, warehouses, and distribution facilities within their global systems. They frequently treated their child as an extension of their corporate system of business units and integrated their partners' products into their global product lines.

Rather than form joint ventures—and cope with the unwieldiness of shared decision making—global firms sought licenses, cross-marketing agreements, and other informal ways to cooperate. Even where alliances were announced as being "joint ventures" in several examples from these industries,

Background research for the medical products, ethical pharmaceuticals, and genetic engineering industries was provided by John G. Michel (Ph.D. candidate) and Stanley W. Herman (M.B.A. 1982). Background research for the engines and automotive industries was provided by John R. Thomas (M.B.A. 1983).

their arrangements proved merely to be agreements to work together in bidding for a contract, sharing research findings, or serving as OEM vendors. Where joint-venture children were formed to satisfy local governmental requirements, these units were rarely given tasks that created competitive advantage for the rest of the global system. They were a means of implementing part of a global strategy that had been forged for other parts of parents' global systems. The ideas, innovations, and suggestions of the joint-venture child diffused infrequently through that system. Instead the flow of information tended to be one way, reflecting the lack of autonomy that global strategies afforded local business units.

Industries

Medical Products and Ethical Pharmaceuticals

Medical products included artificial organs, blood products, filtration and collection systems, self-diagnostic products, and other equipment or devices that often required Federal Drug Administration (FDA) approval for commercial sale. Medical products also included instruments and equipment used by manufacturers of ethical pharmaceuticals (and other health-care products), industries like ethical pharmaceuticals and by hospitals and other health-care delivery channels.

Ethical pharmaceuticals were available only on prescription, and their efficacy for a particular use (indication) was substantiated only after meticulous clinical testing. The FDA permitted ethical pharmaceuticals to be marketed only for those uses that had been properly validated. The high value-added per ounce economics of pharmaceutical production made multisite plant strategies feasible. The proprietary nature of R&D activities made centralization necessary. The major barriers to entering the pharmaceutical industry were local ones: penetration of local regulatory requirements and access to distribution channels.

Need for Joint Activities. The medical products industry enjoyed a vigorous pace of technological innovation in which products were created that never existed previously. Joint ventures were used to develop promising discoveries, to shepherd them through the FDA certification stage, and to introduce them to physicians. Joint ventures were used to share the risks of new technologies and to establish technological standards (as well as to establish credibility for the use of new medical products among customers).

Joint ventures were frequently used in the medical products industry to finance the efforts of small but creative enterprises with promising ideas. Larger, more experienced partners often sold their child's outputs through their existing marketing channels. As with the example of the fledgling genetic engineering firms, originating partners often needed more than just money. They needed the start up assistance of partners with larger laboratory facilities and scientific staffs in order to commercialize their discoveries.

Many joint ventures in the medical products industry were vertically related to their parents. This pattern reflected the importance of access to distribution channels in global industries. Since customers' health needs were the same throughout the globe, joint ventures between partners seeking geographical expansion and access to worldwide distribution channels occurred frequently.

Competition in ethical pharmaceuticals centered on R&D and new product innovation. Joint ventures and licensing agreements were used to fill out firms' product lines as the costs of bringing new drugs to market skyrocketed. Successful inventors of new medical products needed the aid of established marketers' distribution networks because selling costs were substantial and knowledgable sales representatives were scarce. Few firms pursued joint R&D ventures (except in the area of genetic engineering) because patents were a strong source of competitive advantage in these industries.

Choosing Partners.
Medical Products. In 1969 Cordis Corporation and Dow Chemical formed a 50%-50% joint venture, Cordis-Dow Corp., to provide products, systems, and services in hemodialysis and blood oxygenation. The venture was based on Dow's patent covering technology for spinning microndimension hollow fibers of plastic and on Cordis's ability to sell medical devices. Its first product was a small disposable artificial kidney developed by Dow's research laboratories, which used the hollow fiber technology. Successful competition in artificial kidney systems initially required a sophisticated membrane and other fabrication technology (which Dow contributed). During the first six or seven years of the venture, Cordis-Dow was dramatically successful. But as competition intensified, the partners disagreed concerning the need to recapitalize their joint-venture child. Dow purchased its partner's share in 1983 when their interests were no longer compatible.

Dow Chemical held minority investments in several chemicals and pharmaceuticals firms, including 9.5 percent of Rorer Group (pharmaceuticals), 9 percent of Millipore (separation technology), and 8 percent of Morton Thiokol (chemicals). In 1984 Dow increased its stake in Morton Thiokol to 15 percent.

In 1970 Alcon Laboratories and FMC Corp. formed a 50%-50% joint venture, AviCon Inc., to develop FMC's patented microcrystalline collagen material for medical uses. FMC licensed the technology to the relatively small Alcon Laboratories, initially. It proposed a joint venture later, thinking that it had relinquished control over a very promising biomedical technology to Alcon. The partners had different expectations concerning the product's market potential by 1980, and when Alcon's progress in launching the Avitene antibleeding agent became unacceptable to its partner, the product was given to an outside marketing agent for distribution (American Hospital Supply). When the product did not grow as fast as FMC had hoped it would under the outsider's attentions either, Alcon offered to sell its interest to FMC. Instead, Alcon Laboratories acquired its partner's interest in the joint venture in 1983 and introduced a second-generation product. Demand for the clotting agent continued to grow (but not at the rate FMC had expected), and it performed satisfactorily for its new parent. In 1984 Alcon Laboratories negotiated an 80%-20% joint venture with a Japanese partner for the clinical testing and market penetration of its Avitene product in Japan.

In 1972 Owens Illinois Inc. and Jintan Terumo Co. Ltd. formed a joint venture, Kimble-Terumo, to manufacture and market its Japanese parent's Venojet blood collection system in the United States. The Venojet system consisted of a sterile double-ended needle, a glass collection tube, with a color coded rubber stopper and a reusable plastic tube holder. Jintan offered technical know-how, and Owens offered manufacturing and distribution expertise.

In 1973 Milton Roy Co. (a manufacturer of industrial ophthalmic and medical equipment) and Extracorporeal Medical Specialties Inc. formed a joint venture, MilRoy-Extracorporeal Inc., to develop, engineer, and service artificial kidney systems. Milton Roy maintained parallel manufacturing facilities in Europe, and it provided the technology and manufacturing for the U.S. joint venture. Extracorporeal Medical Specialties did the marketing. Milton Roy sold its interest in the joint venture to its partner in 1976 when changes in the medicare reimbursement schedule made the venture less attractive. Johnson & Johnson acquired Extracorporeal Medical Specialties in 1979, and it sold the artificial kidney systems business to Delmed Inc. in 1984.

In 1974 Ampak Ltd. and Owens-Kimball Ltd., a subsidiary of Owens-Illinois, formed a 50%-50% joint venture, Plant-Kimble Ltd., to manufacture glass products for the drug and pharmaceutical industries, utilizing Owens-Illinois patents and technology.

In 1974 Purolator Inc. (a manufacturer of auto filters) and Johnson & Johnson agreed to work together to develop and make certain medical products to filter blood. Purolator made the products at its aerospace division plant in California; Johnson & Johnson marketed the blood filtration products under its Intercept trademark name. A manufacturing license was subsequently issued to Johnson & Johnson because it wanted to bring this activity in-house.

In 1975 Avon Medicals (a part of the Avon Rubber Group in the United Kingdom) and Drake Willock Co. formed a U.S. joint venture, Dravon Medical Inc., to manufacture and sell the Avon range of sterile packed disposable medical products, particularly those associated with treatment of kidney disease. Dravon Medical had a twelve-acre site two miles from the Drake Willock headquarters at Oregon. Some Avon products were also manufactured in Drake Willock's factory.

In 1976 Allergan Pharmaceuticals and Santen Pharmaceuticals (Japan) formed a joint venture, Santen-Allergen, to market products for the care of both hard and soft contact lenses. Allergan made ethical ophthalmic preparations for the treatment of eye diseases. Allergan's Soflens tablet for cleaning contact lenses was marketed worldwide by Bausch & Lomb under a marketing agreement formed in 1974.

In 1977 Narco Scientific Industries and Asahi Optical Co. formed an agreement for U.S. distribution rights to a fiber-bronchioscope based on fiber optics. The medical instrument enabled physicians to view patients' lungs from the inside.

In 1977 Union Carbide and Xonics Inc. formed an agreement to create Union Carbide Imaging Systems Inc. to distribute several devices for blood analysis and processing. Xonics made a low radiation breast X-ray machine that Union Carbide intended to market it aggressively, particularly at hospitals and clinics that performed a large number of breast cancer examinations. Xonics had orders worth $15 million for its low radiation cameras, but it was unable to produce them. It needed Union Carbide's assistance to cure its design and manufacturing problems. (Picture quality was often erratic due to the inconsistency of the toner, a formula Union Carbide had tried to improve.)

Xonics had claimed that its new technology produced sharper chest and breast X-rays, but its designers were still working on a way to produce sharp pictures when the venture ended. There was some doubt concerning whether Xonics could obtain the production facilities needed to manufacture the new machines once the picture problem was solved. Xonics had tried to solve that problem by acquiring control of Baird-Atomic, a firm that Xonics believed possessed the technical facilities and marketing reputation to exploit the new cameras' X-ray technology, but Baird-Atomic had rebuffed Xonics twice.

In 1977 Abbott Laboratories and Millipore Corp. formed an agreement whereby Abbott marketed Millipore's intravenous membrane filter products in conjunction with Abbott's line of human health-care products. Both partners had other cooperative agreements in the medical products industry, and this arrangement was quite successful for them.

In 1978 EMI Medical Inc. (a subsidiary of EMI Ltd.) and Nuclear Medico Services Inc. formed a joint venture to make and sell mobile neuro-scanning systems. EMI Ltd. sought a means of selling a CT scanner that it had developed in the U.S. market.

In 1978 Baird Corp. signed a sales representative agreement with Cordis Corp. to market Baird's System 77 gamma camera for nuclear cardiology use. Baird's existing sales force became Cordis employees, and Cordis became the sole sales agency for Baird's products. (Cordis had a sales force of eighty-five that served hospitals in the United States and abroad.) Had the sales arrangement proven successful, the partners might have entered a joint venture agreement. But Cordis devoted only eight sales representatives to the Baird products, despite an increasing emphasis in nuclear medicine on cardiology products. The relationship dissolved.

In 1978 the American Red Cross and Baxter Travenol Laboratories formed a joint venture to build, own, and operate a $45 million blood plasma fractionation facility. The Red Cross had depended on five companies to fractionate plasma in the past, including Baxter. In 1979, however, American Red Cross and Baxter Travenol cancelled their joint venture to construct and operate a facility for fractionation of blood plasma and its components. Facilities costs for the venture had risen substantially above those anticipated when the venture was formed.

Baxter Travenol Laboratories had formed many cooperative ventures with ethical pharmaceutical firms to package their products in Baxter's intravenous (IV) solution containers. Under these arrangements, Baxter performed the admixture step of combining partners' drugs with a sterile solution, filtering it, and labeling the IV package for delivery to hospitals in a ready-to-use form.

In 1979 Cobe Laboratories Inc. agreed to distribute the water filtration membranes of Osmonics Inc. in connection with Cobe's artificial kidney system. Osmonics also formed joint ventures with Tri-Clover to market its membranes in cheese processing equipment and with Celanese to develop additional membrane products. Cobe Laboratories purchased proprietary Osmonics membranes, which it resold as part of a complete dialysis system.

In 1979 Physio-Control Corp. and Valleylab Inc. formed a 50%-50% joint venture to develop and market pacemakers. Valleylab contributed assets and technology developed during its research efforts. Physio-Control financed the development project already under way and provided additional technical resources because it saw the pacemaker as a way to diversify into other implantable devices.

Akzona (formerly American Enka), a U.S. firm, was 66 percent owned by Akzo N.V., a Dutch firm, in 1980. Enka A.G. was also an Akzo affiliate. In 1980 Akzona Inc. and Enka A.G. formed reciprocal joint ventures—Membrana Inc. and Membrana GmbH. Membrana Inc. (which was based in Chicago and was 52 percent owned by Akzona) sold Accurel membranes and membrane systems in the United States and Canada. Membrana GmbH (which was based in Wappertal, West Germany, and 52 percent controlled by Enka A.G.) sold Accurel membranes and membrane systems outside the United States and Canada. Furthermore, Membrana GmbH had worldwide responsibility for blood detoxification membranes and acted as sales agent for Cuprophan (which Enka A.G. produced), a widely used artificial kidney dialysis membrane.

The parallel joint ventures tried to commercialize their parents' microfiltration membranes by developing new markets for their use. For example, Membrana GmbH developed applications for Accurel polypropylene hollow fibers (which were developed by Akzona) in blood separation. Membrana Inc. introduced a nylon cartridge membrane that was very well received by the electronics and pure water equipment industries. But the joint ventures' successes were limited somewhat by their parents' difficulties in coordinating activities. Despite their many experiences in working together, the rival business units maintained a stubbornness in accepting each other's suggestions that delayed their children's progress in innovation activities.

In 1980 Fabergé Inc. and BCSI Laboratories Inc. agreed to develop a patented home-use device for early detection of breast cancer. Fabergé acquired rights to purchase as much as 80 percent of BCSI's common stock, with rights of first refusal to acquire the remaining stake. (BCSI Laboratories was privately held, and the cancer detection device was its only product.) Fabergé Inc. increased its 41 percent stake in BCSI to 60 percent in 1981.

In 1980 Pfizer Medical Systems (a subsidiary of Pfizer Inc.) formed a marketing agreement with Aloka Co. Ltd. (a Japanese medical equipment maker and subsidiary of Japan Radio) to market Aloka's ultrasound products throughout the United States and Canada. Ultrasound used sound waves to produce cross-sectional images of the body. Pfizer Medical Systems made computerized tomographic (CT) scanners, microfocus X-ray, and mammography systems.

Pfizer had obtained permission to market American Scientific & Engineering Inc.'s CT scanners in 1978. During that same year, Aloka Co. had granted Narco Scientific the exclusive right to market its diagnostic ultrasound imaging system in the United States. The exclusivity provision was rescinded when Pfizer was also recruited to market Aloka's systems.

In 1981 National Patent Development Corp. and Pilkington Brothers Ltd. formed a joint venture to develop National Patent's soft contact lens business worldwide. Pilkington loaned National Patent $10 million, which was convertible into the optical group's equity.

In 1981 Birtcher Corp. and Medical Monitors Inc. formed a joint venture, Bir-Med Inc., to develop and sell a line of patient care products. The invention Medical Monitors contributed proved to be noncompetitive, and the joint venture was never fully consummated.

In 1981 Intermedics Inc. and Infusaid Corp. (a subsidiary of Metal Bellows) formed a joint venture to develop and introduce a family of implantable infusion devices for distribution of medication inside the human body. Both partners made medical devices, but Intermedics had superior skills in obtaining FDA approval of implantable devices.

In 1983 Custom Application Systems and Flow Laboratories formed a joint venture, Flow Laboratories/CASI, to make automated medical laboratory equipment. Genentech and Hewlett-Packard formed a joint venture, HP Genenchem, to develop biotechnology instruments. BMC Industries and Walman Optical formed a joint venture to make polycarbonate eyeglass lenses.

In 1984 Abbott Laboratories invested in minority positions in Boston Scientific Corp. and in Fuller Research Corp. to bolster its health-care position. Boston Scientific developed special catheter products, and Fuller Research developed fibers for laser beam surgery.

In 1985 Polaroid and Hoechst A.G. formed a joint venture to develop rapid access medical diagnostic devices. The $10 million investment was one of several ventures with other firms that Polaroid was backing to develop another winning product as growth in sales of its instant photography products slowed.

Ethical Pharmaceuticals. Because drugs were a necessity and most competition among patented drugs was on the basis of innovation, new patentable drugs were needed at a rate faster than most firms' laboratories could satisfy; hence, cross-licensing arrangements and joint ventures were undertaken to increase the rate of technological change. Few of the joint-venture children possessed basic R&D facilities. Rather, they provided toxicology tests and other research to register their parents' ethical pharmaceutical products, and they marketed approved products in the United States. Because these marketing agreements and other means of attaining vertical integration have been covered elsewhere, they are merely sketched below.[1]

The ethical pharmaceutical industry provides an exception to the argument that control of market access is more important than control of technology because patent protection was strong and gave patent holders an irreplicable competitive advantage. The ethical pharmaceuticals industry had been prolific in the number of new chemical entities discovered and certified during the 1960s. But the 1970s and early 1980s were characterized by a period of low R&D productivity. Genetic engineering technologies and other innovations were expected to increase the number of new chemical entities entering the U.S. pharmaceuticals market in the 1990s. Until then, U.S. pharmaceutical firms pursued licensing agreements, marketing ventures, and other cooperative strategies to fill out the gaps in their product lines. But because control of patents (and the knowledge surrounding them) was so important in the ethical pharmaceuticals industry, technology partners frequently disclosed proprietary information concerning their products directly to the FDA in a manner that protected their knowledge from access under the Freedom of Information Act.

In 1966 Farbenfabriken Bayer A.G. and Schering-Plough formed a 50%-50% joint venture to register and market Bayer's products in the United States. The arrangement provided a large outlet for products other than Bayer aspirin, which was purchased by Sterling Drug from the Alien Property Custodian shortly after World War I.

Hoechst A.G. and Roussel-Uclaf formed a joint venture, Hoechst-Roussel European, in which Hoechst held majority ownership control. But since their joint venture operated in France, Hoechst-Roussel European was managed by Roussel-Uclaf. Through their joint venture, Hoechst and Roussel-Uclaf established a jointly owned U.S. subsidiary, Hoechst-Roussel Pharmaceuticals in 1970, which operated independently from American Hoechst, a wholly owned subsidiary that served as marketing arm for its West German parent. Hoechst-Roussel Pharmaceuticals possessed the autonomy to reject pharmaceutical products from its parents, and it exercised that freedom by declining to develop, test, and market some Roussel-Uclaf drugs. In 1984 Roussel-Uclaf sought U.S. partners to form a joint venture that would develop and market its products in the United States.

Japanese pharmaceutical firms formed marketing joint ventures with U.S. drug makers instead of marketing agreements if possible to gain a toehold into the U.S. market. Joint ventures were the first step in a sequence of exporting drugs from Japanese laboratories to eventually producing the drugs in the United States. Japanese firms relied on their U.S. partners in licensing agreements and joint ventures to ease their products through the maze of U.S. regulations.

In 1975 Marion Laboratories and Chugai Pharmaceutical Co. Ltd. formed a marketing agreement to sell an antiulcer drug in the United States. Marion Laboratories was particularly skilled at performing the R&D work necessary to shepherd pharmaceutical substances through the process of obtaining FDA approval. In exchange for these services, Marion received U.S. marketing rights for these products. In 1976 Marion Laboratories and Daiichi Seiyaku Co. Ltd. formed an agreement giving Marion the rights to develop and sell an anti-inflammatory drug used in the treatment of swellings, as for sprains, fractures, and postsurgical trauma. In 1977 Marion Laboratories and Les Laboratoires Servier S.A. formed a U.S. development and marketing agreement for a drug used to control cholesterol levels in the blood.

In 1976 Merck & Co. Inc. and Alza Corp. agreed to develop pharmaceutical products jointly in the cardiovascular and anti-inflammatory fields of therapy. The resulting products were to be marketed by Merck under worldwide royalty licenses from Alza. The arrangement also provided for Merck to purchase 3.5 percent of Alza's common stock.

Alza licensed A.H. Robins Co. to make and sell its membrane controlled drug delivery system in 1975. Alza formed a joint research agreement with C.H. Boehringer Sohn in 1976 to develop pharmaceutical products based on Alza's transdermal system for providing continuous, controlled administration of drugs directly through the skin into the bloodstream. (In 1981 C.H. Boehringer Sohn and Bio-Science Laboratories (a subsidiary of Dow) established a jointly owned medical diagnostic referral laboratory in West Germany.) In 1977 Alza formed a joint research venture with Sandoz Inc. to incorporate Sandoz's compounds into Alza's delivery systems. In 1981 Alza Corp. and SmithKline Beckman Corp. extended their joint research venture whereby SmithKline made and sold Alza's rate-controlled drug administration systems, including both implants and an osmotic pill that delivered a timed drug dosage.

In 1977 Ciba-Geigy acquired Alza Corp., and the two firms formed product development and marketing agreements. Alza had limited penetration of its products in the United States, and Ciba-Geigy agreed to market drugs for it there. Alza had developed two drug-delivery systems that could be used under the terms of the acquisition to place many Ciba-Geigy products in the market. One such delivery system was a flexible-membrane unit placed under the eyelid and programmed to continuously release a precise dose of medication for the treatment of glaucoma. The other delivery system was a similar unit placed in the uterus for birth-control purposes.

In November 1976 SmithKline's Tagamet ulcer medicine was introduced. Tagamet was so successful that SmithKline's manufacturing capacity was inadequate initially to accommodate demand. Manufacturing services were obtained under short-term contract from other pharmaceutical companies. In 1981 SmithKline had joint ventures with Fujisawa Pharmaceutical (to manufacture and market Tagamet in Japan) and with Alza to develop systems of drug administration that were rate controlled. SmithKline funded Alza's research and marketed their venture's output. In a reciprocal venture, Fujisawa Pharmaceutical Corp. and SmithKline Beckman Corp. formed a joint venture in 1981 to market Fujisawa's antibiotic products in the U.S. (In early 1985 Fujisawa Pharmaceutical Co. Ltd. acquired a 22.5 percent interest in LyphoMed, Inc.) Also in 1981 SmithKline formed (1) a licensing-and-supply agreement with Key Pharmaceuticals for nitroglycerine products, it obtained (2) worldwide marketing rights for an Italian drug from Simes to treat congestive heart problems, and it acquired (3) a license from Toyama Chemical to produce and sell an antispasmodic drug. SmithKline's 1981 research venture with an Allergan subsidiary included a project to apply histamine blocker knowledge, gained from Tagamet's development, to applications in eye disease. Its research venture with Immunex to develop macrophase activating factor gave it worldwide marketing rights to resulting biotechnology products.

In 1977 Abbott and Takeda Chemical Industries of Japan formed a joint venture, Takeda-Abbott Products, to develop new pharmaceuticals to market in the United States and Canada and to register and market antibiotics, sedatives, antihypertensives, and other products that had been already introduced in Japan and other markets. The joint venture was designed to be a fade-out, giving ownership to Takeda. But it had an undefined horizon regarding when the fade-out was to occur. As long as Abbott provided services that Abbott-Takeda could not perform adequately itself, Takeda needed a partner in the U.S. market.

In 1977 Norwich Pharmaceutical (a division of Morton-Norwich Products Inc. and Merz & Co. (of Chemische Fabrik) formed a 50%-50% joint venture, Eaton-Merz Laboratories Inc., to market a new contraceptive in the United States that was manufactured by Norwich Pharmaceutical. The new product had been developed by Merz & Co. after eight years of research. Sales of the product in West Germany exceeded $2 million in 1976, and Merz was hoping to preempt competitors, such as Whitehall Laboratories and Jordan-Simmer Inc., which were also moving rapidly to enter the U.S. market in 1977. Morton-Norwich Products and Reckett & Coleman Ltd. formed a joint marketing agreement to introduce antiarthritic pharmaceuticals in the United States in 1977. In 1982, Procter & Gamble acquired the Norwich-Eaton pharmaceuticals and proprietary drugs business unit.

In 1977 Cutter Laboratories (a subsidiary of Bayer A.G.) and KabiVitrum A.B. formed a 60%-40% joint venture, Cutter-Vitrum Inc., to build a North American plant to produce and sell Intralipid (a fat emulsion used in total parenteral nutrition products). Cutter was serving as distributor for the product when the joint venture was created, and it operated the child's plant on a lease basis.

In 1979 Miles Laboratories (a subsidiary of Bayer A.G.) and Scripps Clinic & Research formed a joint venture to provide testing services in immunology and endocrinology. In addition to providing toxicology services, their laboratory prepared immunochemical materials.

In 1981 Astra A.B. and Merck & Co. Inc. formed an agreement to develop and market drugs made by Astra (Sweden's largest pharmaceutical firm) as for cardiac arrhythmia in the United States. Under this agreement, Merck invested $60 million in programs to develop several drugs discovered by Astra for the U.S. market. Although Merck marketed these drugs exclusively initially, Astra and Merck formed a 50%-50% joint venture in 1982. Astra licensed its child to make and sell its pharmaceutical lines in the United States. Merck provided production services and use of its sales force. (The partners intended to build a separate sales organization for their child when volumes were high enough for their cardiac, antidepressant, and steroidal products.) The new joint venture operated independently of Astra's U.S. subsidiary, which concentrated on anesthetic, hospital, and dental products.

In Japan, Merck and Banyu had cooperated overseas in licensing and distribution for over thirty years. Their joint-venture child, Nippon Merck-Banyu had manufactured and marketed Merck pharmaceutical products since the 1950s. About 40 percent of Banyu's product line was Merck items. After starting with a low ownership percentage in Merck-Banyu, Merck finally worked its equity up to 100 percent by 1984. (Pfizer had worked its equity up to 95 percent of its Japanese affiliate in 1984.) In 1983 Merck acquired a 51 percent interest in its partner, Banyu Pharmaceutical, and in 1982 Merck purchased a 30 percent interest in Troii Pharmaceuticals, another Japanese company.

In 1981 G.D. Searle & Co. and Synthelabo S.A. (a subsidiary of Nestlé) formed a 51%-49% joint venture to develop, register, and market pharmaceutical products in the United States. Because pharmaceutical products were constantly threatened by obsolescence from other firms' discoveries, the joint venture engaged in substantial R&D activities to develop Synthelabo's discoveries for the U.S. market. Synthelabo and Lederle Laboratories formed a 50%-50% joint venture in 1973 (in France, where Synthelabo's market presence was strong) to market American Cyanamid's suture products, and it had formed several others throughout the globe.

Searle and Knoll Pharmaceutical Co. (a joint venture of Schering A.G. and BASF) formed a marketing agreement to market cardiovascular drugs. In 1978 Searle and Pennwalt had formed a marketing agreement to sell hypertension drugs and anti-inflammatories. Faced with a ten-year gap until its own products came onstream, Searle sought marketing agreements to sell other firms' drugs to fill out its product line, and it sought arrangements to leverage its aspartame sweetener product (discussed in another section below).

In 1982 Glaxo Holdings (United Kingdom) and Hoffman-LaRoche formed a marketing agreement for Glaxo's Zantac, an ulcer medicine that rivaled SmithKline's Tagamet. Glaxo was a 100-year-old pharmaceutical firm with strengths in science and weaknesses in global marketing. Although Glaxo had gained a U.S. foothold by acquiring Meyer Laboratories in 1978, it had too few sales representatives to launch an effective campaign to introduce Zantac against Tagamet.

The Hoffman-LaRoche sales force, by contrast, was a very effective, very aggressive U.S. marketing organization. Under Glaxo's arrangement with Hoffman-LaRoche Inc., Zantac was sold under the Glaxo name and Hoffman-LaRoche received a royalty on sales. The royalties from selling Zantac eased Roche's transition to dependence on products still in the R&D and FDA certification pipeline. (Its patent protection on Valium expired in 1985.) The arrangement was unusual, however, because U.S. pharmaceutical firms did not usually market outsiders' products under outsiders' labels. (Doing so created value for outsiders that might want to enter the U.S. market on their own in the future.)

In 1981 American Home Products Co. and Sanofi (a subsidiary of Société National Elf Equitane) formed a 49%-51% joint venture to develop and make cardiovascular pharmaceuticals created by Sanofi in the United States. The venture also covered psychotropic and anticancer areas. In 1982 Merrell-Dow and Otsuka Pharmaceutical Co. Ltd. formed a set of reciprocal joint ventures to market each other's product in the United States and Japan, but their plans fell through as a result of significant changes in the assumptions underlying the partners' letter of intent.

In 1982 Pfizer and Lederle Laboratories (a subsidiary of American Cyanamid Co.) teamed with Toyama Chemical, and Eli Lilly joined Shionogi &

Co., to sell cephalosporin products in the United States. Lederle Laboratories and Toyama had formed a worldwide marketing agreement covering Toyama's semi-synthetic penicillins in 1976. Pfizer and Key Pharmaceuticals had formed a co-marketing agreement to sell sustained medical release medications made under Key's patent in 1977.

In 1983 Eli Lilly & Co. and Yamanouchi Pharmaceutical Co. Ltd. formed a long-term cooperative agreement in pharmaceuticals. If the terms of their agreement were fulfilled, it would progress from a licensing relationship, to a joint venture to an independent U.S. company owned by Yamanouchi. (It was not clear whether the stand-alone child would manufacture active bulk pharmaceuticals or perform basic R&D activities.)

The Yamanouchi-Lilly joint venture was of such dramatic magnitude in Japan that many other Japanese firms were reviewing their policies to assess whether they too should seek joint ventures to manufacture or perform research in the United States. Although some U.S. pharmaceutical firms were interested in partners to gain reciprocal joint ventures in Japan, others were interested in them as protection against the coming shake-out in the U.S. pharmaceuticals industry. The pressures of global competition required firms to invest larger sums in R&D, activities to attain higher levels of R&D success, and to attain critical mass (to exploit global scale economies) at a larger size. Without such levels of effort, U.S. pharmaceutical firms would lack the horsepower needed to fill their product lines with significant products in the future.

In 1974 Hercules and Montedison had formed a small pharmaceuticals 50%-50% joint venture, Adria Laboratories, which gave Hercules access to Montedison's drug products for registration in the United States. Adria was primarily a marketing arm for a global pharmaceutical firm. It did not do much research. In 1983 Hercules and Montedison updated their joint ventures in a new deal whereby Hercules traded its 50 percent interest in Adria for 15 percent stake in Montedison's drug and health-care operations, which were spun off as a new company, Erbamont N.V., a global pharmaceuticals firm. The new firm produced bulk and intermediate pharmaceuticals primarily, but also made diagnostic test kits, reagents, and laboratory materials, analytical instruments, and biomedical equipment. The restructuring gave Hercules participation in an international, vertically integrated pharmaceutical firm. Its most important product was Adriamycin, an anticancer (chemotherapy) drug that accounted for 33 percent of its prescription pharmaceutical sales in 1982. Erbamont N.V. also produced diagnostic test kits, reagents, and laboratory materials, analytical instruments, and biomedical equipment.

In 1984 pressures on foreign drug companies in some markets had become so unattractive that global pharmaceutical firms were evaluating joint ventures as a way to phase out of those markets. For example, non-Canadian drug companies received only two years of patent protection for their products in Canada.

Genetic Engineering. As chapter 11 noted, recombinant-DNA technology (genetic engineering) was applied first to the development of pharmaceutical products (where products were more expensive per ounce of processing). Fledgling, stand-alone genetic engineering firms lacked access to commercial scale facilities and distribution channels to develop and sell their products. They used joint ventures to overcome the barriers of entering the ethical pharmaceuticals business on their own.[2]

Established pharmaceutical firms took minority interests in genetic engineering firms and formed research joint ventures in order to develop products to fill out their product lines. Frequently they also invested in a spider's web of minority investments and joint ventures to hedge their bets concerning which products would prove to be commercially successful.

Monsanto held a 30 percent interest in Collagen and formed a joint-research venture to study the use of collagen from animal sources for the replacement of lost human tissue. Monsanto held a 2 percent interest in Genentech and formed a joint research venture to develop animal growth hormones with Genentech. Monsanto held an 8 percent interest in Genex through InnoVen, a venture-capital program operated jointly with Emerson Electric.

In 1978 Genentech and Eli Lilly formed a joint venture for the production of human insulin. Genentech was moving to become a vertically integrated pharmaceutical house. Hence its Genencor venture (with Corning) to produce enzymes, its use of KabiGen and Hoffman-LaRoche as its agents, and the licensing arrangement with Eli Lilly were all decisions intended to maximize the success of its projects. Genentech was using joint ventures because it lacked the capital and wherewithal to satisfy all of its needs internally.

In 1979 Genentech arranged for KabiGen A.B. of Sweden, then the world's largest supplier of human growth hormone, to manufacture a genetically engineered growth hormone it had developed. Both KabiGen and Genentech intended to market the product. Sumitomo Chemical Co. began clinical testing of Genentech's new biologically engineered growth hormone in 1981.

Fermentation capability was a strength of Hoffman-LaRoche, and it formed a joint venture with Genentech to exploit that strength. Under their joint venture's terms, both Genentech and Roche could manufacture the interferon they had jointly developed, but Hoffman-LaRoche was responsible for marketing the product. In 1981 Hoffman-LaRoche, which was licensing its interferon technology to Takeda Chemical Industries Ltd. and Mochida Pharmaceutical Co., planned to produce interferon using G.D. Searle's cell fusion method. Hoffman-LaRoche also held equity in Agrigenetics, as did Kellogg Co. (In 1984 Lubrizol—Genentech's early backer and owner of a 25 percent interest—purchased Agrigenetics. It also took a 28 percent interest in Sungene Technologies Inc. and purchased two seed companies. Agrigenetics also purchased a dozen seed companies.)

In 1984 Genentech and Baxter-Travenol Laboratories formed a joint venture, Travenol-Genentech, to develop radioimmunoassay products for the diagnostics market. Baxter-Travenol was the majority owner and it contributed to the child the assets of its Clinical Assays Division, which included production facilities, its own U.S. sales force, and access to worldwide marketing organizations, making the child a stand-alone unit. One of their first products was a test for the acquired immune deficiency syndrome (AIDS) virus, which was produced under a license from the Department of Health and Human Services (HHS).

Since all of Baxter-Travenol's relevant assets were placed into the joint venture, there were fewer concerns about unauthorized bleedthrough of technological information than in many other joint ventures in the medical products and ethical pharmaceuticals industry. This arrangement gave the joint-venture child more autonomy to act quickly and enabled it to focus its objectives with greater clarity, since it did not have to manage conflicts of interest between parent and child organizations. (Baxter-Travenol Laboratories also had a marketing agreement with Genetics Institute to distribute recombinant-DNA–derived factor VII.)

In 1979 Schering-Plough's markets were plateauing, and the firm was seeking investment opportunities close to its core business that offered promises of high paybacks. Schering-Plough acquired a 13 percent interest in Biogen N.V. for $8 million, giving it right of first refusal for any health-care products Biogen might develop. Biogen S.A. brought together ten top university scientists and INCO. Its major U.S. support came from INCO (a venture capital arm of International Minerals & Chemical) and Monsanto, and one of its first discoveries was a formulation of interferon. Together, Biogen and its partners were studying the production of interferon. (Schering-Plough maintained a parallel, biotechnology research facility in-house, and in 1982 it began building a plant to ferment and purify interferon.) INCO held the marketing rights for Biogen's animal growth hormone products. It also held equity in ImmunoGen, a monoclonal antibody research firm.

Alza held a 20 percent interest in DNAX and licensed its partner to use Alza's technology for drug delivery systems using enzymes. Schering-Plough later acquired a 100 percent interest in DNAX.

Cetus undertook a series of research contracts for royalties and joint ventures, in order to obtain security in financing its products, but one of its first research contracts was with Schering A.G. (It studied the use of microorganisms to enhance antibiotic yields.) A similar arrangement with Roussel-Uclaf (to improve the productivity of vitamin B-12 processes) also provided Cetus with royalty revenues. Major Cetus shareholders included SOCAL, AMOCO, and National Distillers & Chemical. SOCAL maintained its investment in Cetus even after it canceled the fructose joint venture (described in chapter 11). National Distillers & Chemical and Cetus were jointly researching the use of recombinant-DNA techniques in improving microorganisms used in the fermentation of alcohol.

In 1981 Cetus formed a joint venture with Shell Oil to produce human interferon. The funding for the Shell/Cetus research-and-development agreement was used to begin construction of a large-scale, $10-million facility in Emeryville, California, to produce the interferon. The Norden Laboratories of SmithKline Beckman marketed Cetus's animal vaccine products. Triton Biosciences (a subsidiary of Shell Oil) funded Collaborative Research's clinical trials of interleukin-2, an anticancer drug. In 1984 Cetus formed a research venture with Nabisco Brands. It was also receiving research funding from Weyerhauser Co., National Distillers & Chemicals, and Shell Oil.

In 1980 Dow Chemical purchased 5 percent of the common stock of Collaborative Genetics (an affiliate of Collaborative Research) and entered into a joint research agreement concerning fundamental genetic-engineering techniques. Collaborative Research made human fibroblast interferon and human urokinase for clinical use, nucleotides and enzymes for genetic engineering and molecular genetics research, and growth factors for tissue cell culture and cell biology research. Fermentation capability was a strength of Dow Chemical, which expected to double its pharmaceutical sales volume by 1987.

In 1981 Flow General Inc. and Schwar-Mann (a subsidiary of Mediscience Inc.) formed a 50%-50% joint venture to develop human interferon using genetic engineering technologies. The agreement contained a sunset clause that limited its duration to five years, with an option to renew the partnership.

In 1983 Syntex and Genetic Systems Corp. formed a joint venture, Oncogen, to develop, certify, and market serum assays, tissue (biopsy) assays, and in vivo imaging for diagnosis of human cancer, using diagnostic kits. In 1983 Syva (Syntex's diagnostic subsidiary) and Genetic Systems received FDA clearance to market a jointly developed diagnostic test for herpes simplex viruses (HSV). Earlier, the partners jointly developed a monoclonal antibody-based diagnostic test for chlamydia.

By 1983 Japanese firms had obtained over fifteen technology transfer agreements for gene-splicing from U.S. firms seeking royalties from its use in Japan. For example, Shionogi & Co. purchased gamma-type interferon technology from Biogen. Toray Industries Inc. and Daiichi Seiyaku Co. obtained similar licenses from Genentech. Biogen licensed rights to a pharmaceutical for destroying cancer tumor cells to Suntory Ltd. But Schering-Plough licensed gamma-type interferon technology from Suntory Ltd. AMGen formed a 50%-50% joint venture, Kirin-AMGen Inc., with Kirin Brewery Co. to manufacture, test, and sell a synthetic human hormone for treating anemia. Kirin's interest in the joint venture stemmed from its long-term interest in entering the pharmaceuticals industry.

In addition to a joint research venture, Abbott Laboratories held a 19 percent share in Applied Molecular Genetics and a co-marketing agreement for cancer products with Centocor. Warner-Lambert formed a marketing agreement with Centocor for its monoclonal antibody test kits. (In 1982 FMC Corp. and Centocor formed a joint venture to do research and commercialize monoclonal antibodies for cancer treatment.) In addition to joint research activities, American Cyanamid held a 15 pecent interest in Cytogen and a 20 percent interest in Molecular Genetics.

Merck funded Chiron's research on a genetically engineered hepatitis B vaccine and gained a worldwide license to use its technology for that purpose. Bayer A.G. and Cutter Laboratories funded Genetic Systems Corp. in exchange for marketing rights in 1984. Anheuser-Busch and Interferon Sciences formed a joint research venture to develop interferon and other products. Bristol-Myers formed a joint marketing agreement with Genex to distribute alpha and beta interferon developed through recombinant-DNA research.

Johnson & Johnson held a 7 percent equity interest in BioLogicals and a licensing agreement covering therapeutic agents. Ortho Pharmaceutical Corp. (a subsidiary of Johnson & Johnson) formed a co-marketing agreement with Hybritech for monoclonal antibody diagnostic tests that Hybritech was developing. Efforts to develop DNA probes linked Johnson & Johnson with Enzo Biochem (in which it held a minority interest), Abbott Laboratories with AMGen, Syntex with American BioNuclear, and Baxter Travenol Laboratories with Genentech. Collaborative Research and American Hospital Supply formed a joint venture to market Collaborative's diagnostic test kits using DNA probes.

Even as leading chemical and pharmaceutical firms unveiled their in-house biotechnology research facilities, they continued to make minority investments in small biotechnology firms. For example, DuPont purchased a 7 percent interest in Biotech Research Laboratories Inc. and obtained a license to make and sell a diagnostic kit for AIDS as it also dedicated a new $85 million biotechnology laboratory for in-house research.

Child Activities. The medical products and ethical pharmaceutical industries' use of joint ventures was primarily as a means to underwrite new ventures or to penetrate new markets. These ventures were autonomous when they were forms of venture-capital investments. Parallel research facilities and formal programs for technology transfer characterized relationships between parent and child in the genetic engineering ventures where small firms needed the help of larger established firms for funding, for scale-up technologies, and to gain market access to exploit their technological innovations.

But autonomy was rare where joint-venture children were part of global pharmaceutical firms. With the notable exception of the Hoechst-Roussel joint venture, children did not refuse to develop, test, and market their parents' products in the U.S. market. They were primarily *marketing arms* of their global parents, and this pattern was supported by the competitive advantage afforded by patents in the pharmaceutical industry. Few partners formed joint ventures for basic research. Instead, joint ventures (and other forms of cooperative strategy) enabled firms that were standardizing their products globally to overcome local variations in market conditions and customer preferences regarding dosage forms.

Engines

Jet engines and other large propulsion devices were very costly products that were demanded in small volumes. The development program for a medium-size engine exceeded $500 million in 1976.

Large engines (and other complex propulsion devices) were capital- and labor-intensive products. Although key engine features could be standardized, each customer wanted minor customizations. Joint ventures in this industry had cost-reduction motivations like those discussed in chapter 7, as well as global strategy motivations that caused vendors to centralize production in a few sites. Because a centralized facility could produce all but the finishing steps where customized features were added in order to exploit scale-economy advantages, the industry should have evolved into a concentrated structure of few firms operating centralized plants. Instead, the structure evolved into rival consortia with many subcontractors operating in many geographically dispersed locations, and this evolution was due to governmental requirements regarding local content.

Need for Joint Activities. The example of engines illustrates many of the themes of earlier chapters, for engines were capital-intensive but highly sensitive to the quality of labor inputs. Engine designs were complex to understand and hence were differentiated to varying degrees in customers' perceptions. Engine technology was highly complex and subject to rapid changes in component attributes.

There were few suppliers of engines and other large propulsion devices, and their products were sold primarily to governments or other large and sophisticated purchasers (such as airlines) that both realized *and exercised* their inherent bargaining power over their vendors. Most frequently, customer bargaining power was exerted in the form of demands for greater proportions of local labor content as a percentage of the total costs of the very expensive engines. This request aided governments' employment objectives and gave them more favorable balances of trade.

Vendors of large engines tried to satisfy governments' demands that local suppliers, artisans, and workers be employed, but because the components and skills needed to produce engines of high quality were not always available in customers' local economies, a complex system of credits awarded for purchases of *other* locally produced goods and services was developed to permit vendors of engines to offset the sales price of their products by their purchases from local manufacturers. Frequently, this practice resulted in a series of quasi-barter transactions that were orchestrated by the vendors themselves or by a trading company.

Unexpected combinations of partners occurred as customers' requirements grew to be more sophisticated. Satisfying their demands required firms to cooperate with partners that were previously tough competitors. Coalitions were formed on a project by project basis, and while firms cooperated on one project they competed intensely against each other on projects where they were not partners.

Choosing Partners. In 1968 Ford Motor Co. and Thermo Electron Corp. formed a joint venture to develop a small, low-power steam engine. Thermo Electron served as operator, taking responsibility for the project and for providing necessary personnel, equipment, and facilities. Ford provided technical aid in connection with the design, engineering, and manufacture of any products developed as well as funding. This was not a product sold to a network of global customers, and the joint venture's motivations were primarily cost-sharing and risk-reduction.

In 1974 Mack Trucks and Garrett Corp. (both subsidiaries of the Signal Cos. Inc.), Klöeckner-Humboldt-Deutz A.G., and Volvo formed a joint venture, Industrial Turbines International, to develop small gas turbines for use in trucks and buses. The partners were trying to meld gas turbine technology for aerospace applications (Garrett) with that for industrial applications. As the venture proceeded, the turbine it had developed became less economic than the standard diesel engine for trucks, and the project was dropped.

In 1975 J.I. Case and Mercedes-Benz formed a joint venture to market a diesel-powered tractor in North America. Baimler-Benz, the West German manufacturer of Mercedes-Benz passenger cars, commercial vehicles, and diesel engines, exported diesel engines and later knock-down kits from its home base. Their agreement provided for U.S. assembly operations if the venture proved to be successful. The tractor was built by Daimler-Benz, and Case (the local partner) took responsibility for sales, service, warranties, and parts inventory in North America.

In 1980 Cummins Engine Co. and the J.I. Case subsidiary of Tenneco Inc. formed a five-year, $900 million diesel joint venture, Consolidated Diesel Co. Case used the engines in its farm and industrial equipment. Cummins sold the remaining output to its customers.

In 1980 Westinghouse Electric Corp. and Sulzer Brothers Ltd. formed a licensing agreement to make, sell, and service the Swiss firm's slow-speed and medium-speed diesel engines in the United States. The diesel engines were used for commercial ship propulsion and noncombatant naval vessels.

In 1981 Allis-Chalmers and B&W Diesel formed a licensing agreement permitting Allis-Chalmers to build, sell, and service slow-speed diesels designed by B&W Diesel (formerly Burmeister & Wain) A/S, of Copenhagen, Denmark. B&W was an autonomous operation owned by Maschinenfabrik Augsburg-Nürnberg Aktiengesellschaft (M.A.N.) of Augsburg, West Germany. Allis-Chalmers formed a Marine Diesel Division to handle the B&W engine program.

In 1978 Cutler-Hammer, Raytheon, and Loral Corp. formed a joint research venture to develop an electronic countermeasures system to meet the self-protection requirements of military aircraft. General Motors and Schiller Industries had formed a similar agreement in 1976 to build precision components for the platform, gyro, and accelerometer of a navigational system designed for the USAF-Lockheed C-141 transports and the SAC Boeing KC-135 tankers. Teams of subcontractors were commonplace in military sales where it was efficient to set industrywide design standards and to delegate development work, much like the teams of semiconductor firms discussed in chapter 10.

In 1976 Anderson, Greenwood & Co. formed a joint venture with Bellanca Aircraft Corp. to make and sell the Aries T-250 single-engine, four-passenger aircraft that Anderson, Greenwood had been developing since 1970. Its subsidiary, Anderson, Greenwood Aviation Corp., granted Bellanca exclusive permission to market its aircraft, subject to Bellanca's obtaining sufficient financing to undertake its responsibilities in doing so. Bellanca and Anderson, Greenwood were locked in litigation in 1984 because they had not been able to fulfill promises to each other concerning this venture.

In 1976 Aeronautique Dessault-Bereguet Aviation S.A. and Société Nationale Aérospatiale (the government-owned aerospace firm) formed a joint venture to produce an eight-passenger tri-jet for sale in the United States. The French firms cooperated with McDonnell-Douglas Corp. to develop a medium-range jetliner.

In 1976 Rolls-Royce and Pratt & Whitney formed a set of reciprocal joint ventures to develop two jet engines. Each partner initiated a design for one of the engines and followed its partner's lead in standards for the other engine. When the U.S. Department of Justice balked at approving cooperation on both engines, progress within the joint venture halted because Rolls-Royce had no design participation on Pratt & Whitney's engine, the one for which the Justice Department approved collaboration. The Pratt & Whitney-initiated design was for the JT-10D jet engine of 20,000-30,000 pounds thrust for the next generation of medium-range airliners. The Rolls-Royce–initiated design was for the RB-401 small engine of 5,000-6,000 pounds of thrust, for use in business aircraft and small military jets.

This incident is noteworthy due to the U.S. antitrust agency's attitude regarding the proposed alliance. The engine designs were not for competing products, by virtue of their size differences. There were few producers of jet engines, and it was not unusual for them to wish to share the costs of development by working together. (For example, General Electric and Société Nationale d'Etudes & de Construction de Moteors d'Aviation—Snecma—of France formed a rival joint development venture for jet engines in 1976. Their CF6-6 was designed to compete directly with Rolls-Royce's RB211.) If the Rolls-Royce/Pratt & Whitney joint venture was halted, Rolls-Royce would need greater funding assistance from the U.K. government in order to make its design economic at the smaller sales volumes inherent in going it alone.

In 1977 the proposed joint venture of Pratt & Whitney and Rolls-Royce fell through. Some blame for the partnership's dissolution was placed on the airlines themselves, since their power requirements and engine specifications kept changing.

Although Rolls-Royce pursued its larger engine design independent of Pratt & Whitney for this project, the other members of the original consortium stayed with Pratt & Whitney (54.5 percent). They included Motoren und Turbinen-Union München GmbH (10 percent) and Fiat SpA and Alfa Romeo SpA (2 percent).

Many firms were forming joint ventures in 1978 to make jets. For example, the Airbus partners included Aérospatiale (47.9 percent) of France, Messerschmitt-Bolkow-Blohm or MBB (31.1 percent) of West Germany, VFW-Fokker (16.8 percent)—itself a Dutch and German joint venture, and Construcciones Aeronauticas (4.2 percent). Airbus Industrie was formed to compete against consortia of U.S. and European firms, including McDonnell-Douglas, Boeing, Dessault-Bereguet Aerospace, and teams of Japanese aerospace firms, including Mitsubishi, Fuji, and Kawasaki.

The Pratt & Whitney Division of United Technologies cooperated with the Airbus consortium by forming a joint venture to supply JT-9D jet engines for the Airbus. British Aerospace, MBB, VFW-Fokker, and Seritalia cooperated in their joint venture, Panavia, to build a Tornado fighter-bomber, multirole combat aircraft. (Grumman Corp. and British Aerospace Co. formed a joint venture to market the jets to the USAF for its tactical fighter program.) Aérospatiale and Westland Aircraft Ltd. (United Kingdom) jointly developed the Puma, Gazelle, and Lynx helicopters. MBB and Agusta (of Italy) were considered for future ventures with Aérospatiale. General Electric and Volvo A.B. exchanged technology to develop a jet aircraft engine. McDonnell-Douglas and MBB exchanged information concerning advanced fighter planes.

In 1980 Fairchild Industries Inc. and Saab-Scania A.B. formed a joint venture to develop a thirty-passenger plane for the U.S. market. Their alliance continued through 1984 when they competed against more than five other teams to supply turboprop jets to small U.S. airlines. Their joint venture was highly successful, and their child built a factory in Maryland as well as Linkoping. The first aircraft was delivered in 1983. Saab-Fairchild's rivals included the joint venture between Aérospatiale and Aeritalia, as well as DeHaviland and other manufacturers of small jet aircraft.

In 1980 Rolls-Royce Ltd. and Pratt & Whitney (a subsidiary of United Technologies Corp.) agreed jointly to develop an engine for jet fighters capable of vertical and short-run takeoffs. The British-designed Pegasus engines were chosen for the AV-8B Harrier aircraft, which was being developed by British Aerospace and McDonnell-Douglas Corp., for the Pentagon. In this joint venture, Pratt & Whitney manufactured approximately 25 percent of the value of the parts of the engines, with Rolls-Royce assuming the remaining portion. The Harrier program required for 450 engines, including spares, with a total value of about $1.5 billion. Under U.S. defense procurement rules, one partner on designs developed overseas had to be American. Rolls-Royce had been working informally with Pratt & Whitney on the Pegasus engine. The joint-venture agreement between Rolls-Royce and Pratt & Whitney put their private arrangement on a formal contractual basis.

Fearing that Japansese competitors would soon devote their efforts to aerospace, U.S. firms began to discuss joint venture among themselves in 1980. A consortium of American, European, and Japanese companies was formed to develop a jet engine for a new 150-passenger airplane. Japanese firms sought membership in such joint ventures because they feared that rising protectionism would restrict their access to the U.S. and European markets. For example, Rolls-Royce Japanese Aero-Engines was a consortium of Rolls-Royce, Ishikawajima-Harima Heavy Industries, Kawasaki Heavy Industries, and Mitsubishi Heavy Industries.

In 1981 Grumman Aerospace Corp. agreed to assist Arianespace S.A. in marketing its booster rockets to U.S. firms. Grumman proposed to sell aircraft in France and was required to bring business back to France to offset the business being taken out by selling aircraft there. Arianespace was a consortium of European firms that developed the Ariane missile launcher. Grumman also cooperated with General Dynamics on the F1-11A and F1-11B programs for the U.S. Navy and Air Force.

In 1983 the Link Flight Simulation Division of the Singer Company and Lockheed-Georgia Division of Lockheed formed a joint venture to provide a flight simulator for the C-130 Hercules cargo aircraft that was produced by Lockheed. The simulator facility was used to train operators having an insufficient number of aircraft to justify purchase of their own Hercules simulators.

In 1983 two teams battled for the U.S. shuttle contract. Rockwell's team included Boeing, United Airlines, and United Technologies. Lockheed's team included Morton Thiokol Inc. and Pan American World Airways.

In 1983 the engine for a new passenger plane was built by an international consortium in order to ameliorate federal concerns about local content (employment) and national security (local suppliers). The consortium included: Pratt & Whitney's team (50.1 percent)—United Technologies, Motoren und Turbinen-Union München GmbH, and Fiat Aviazione SpA—to make the combustor and turbine portions of the engine, and Rolls-Royce's team (49.9 percent)—a Japanese joint venture representing (1) Ishikawajima-Harima Heavy Industries; (2) Kawasaki Heavy Industries; and (3) Mitsubishi Heavy Industries—to build the fan and compressor. The new jet engine had 25,000 pounds thrust and was used in aircraft such as the 150-seat Airbus jetliner. General Electric and Snecma formed a joint venture, CFM International, to co-produce a 150-passenger aircraft engine.

In 1984 Boeing, Mitsubishi Heavy Industries Ltd., Kawasaki Heavy Industries Ltd., and Fuji Heavy Industries Ltd. formed a joint venture to develop jointly a medium-size, medium-range jetliner in competition with the Airbus consortium. Boeing held a 75 percent interest; its Japanese partners held the remaining 25 percent. General Electric competed against Pratt & Whitney for the engine orders. General Electric and Rolls-Royce had formed a 75%-25% joint venture in 1984 to co-produce aircraft engines. This alliance was a surprise since Pratt & Whitney usually cooperated with Rolls-Royce on jet engines.

Rolls-Royce took a 15 percent interest in General Electric's ongoing program to build engines of 53,000 pounds thrust in 1984. Such engines were used on the Airbus wide-body jets and Boeing's 747 jumbo jets. Correspondingly, General Electric took a 15 percent interest in Rolls-Royce's program to develop jet engines of 35,000 thrust. Such engines were used on smaller jets, such as the Boeing 757 airliner.

In 1984 joint ventures were also being used to sell helicopters. Bell Helicopter Textron Inc. and United Technologies' Sikorsky Aircraft Division each signed with Short Brothers (a Northern Ireland airframe builder) to sell helicopters to the Royal Air Force. Bell allied with Dornier to modify helicopters for use by the West German army and air force. Aérospatiale and Messerschmitt-Bolkow-Blohm (MBB) allied to create attack helicopters. Agusta and Westland Helicopters allied to build maritime models. History suggested that these alliance would be uneasy, at best. For example, Goodyear Tire & Rubber and Piasecki Aircraft Corp. had tried to cooperate to make helicopter powered heavy lifters in 1975. But their venture was terminated one year later due to differences in corporate culture.

Child Activities. Government policies concerning national security and need to sustain local employment level made manufacturers of diesel engines, jet engines, and aircraft include more local content. This pressure pulled against the forces that made the diesel engine, jet engine, and aircraft industries became global. Close coordination was needed between partners in order to design pieces of engines and other complex and capital intensive products. What were called joint ventures were often in fact loosely formed alliances that had been formed to coordinate projects when bidding teams were successful.

Almost every government required some form of offset arrangement when overseas vendors tried to sell them military products. Some governments required co-production arrangements as well as offsets. In those situations, pieces of military products were subcontracted to manufacturers in customer nations. Partnerships in military products were also necessary in cases where governments prohibited the resale of domestic technological products in products assembled overseas. Thus, a U.S. firm took a British firm as partner, for example, to provide engines when aircraft were to be sold to countries that were on the U.S. government's technology restriction list.

Automobiles

The automotive industry had evolved from one where firms preferred to export complete vehicles during the 1910s and 1920s to one that exploited the advantages of a global organization. By 1984 the automotive industry had gained access to improved computer power and computer-communications capabilities. This technology enabled the automobile manufacturers to track lower materials costs, labor productivities, and other sources of comparative advantage and exploit these opportunities in a program of worldwide sourcing. With this information, they could erect manufacturing plants in many geographic sites and coordinate their efforts through improved control systems.

As local governments increased their trade barriers against imports by demanding greater proportions of local content, automobile manufacturers built assembly plants and changed their logistics patterns. Often, they imported knock-down kits composed of parts manufactured in lower-cost environments. Whenever possible, automobile manufacturers procured only the cheap, easy-to-make components locally, unless governments intervened to prevent such practices. Since programs using local content for the expensive, difficult-to-make components were generally not economic unless large production volumes could be realized, governments generally had to protect the automotive firms that satisfied these investment requirements by treating them like national champions.

If local restrictions concerning imports of lower-cost components became too stringent, automobile manufacturers could not include those plants in their closely coordinated global strategies. Instead, local competitors banded together to make their respective plants economic in sourcing agreements to provide standardized designs for axles and other common components. The designs of major automobile manufacturers became more standardized throughout the world as major parts suppliers, like Dana and Rockwell, worked with major automobile manufacturers to design components that could be interchanged across companies.

As the pressures for fuel economy required the development of more sophisticated vehicles, the task of incorporating another firm's components into an automobile manufacturer's vehicles became an astronomical engineering feat. Long-term alliances became more attractive than loose cooperative agreements because technologically complex vehicles required close coordination on *all* aspects of automobile components. Yet automobile manufacturers were reluctant to bind themselves in relationships that limited their day-to-day operating autonomy. Consequently, firms participated in design consortiums, but they tolerated few cooperative strategies that required shared decision-making activities. Their intolerance for cooperation may have been born from their tradition of competition among divisions within multidivisional automobile manufacturers as well as among other automobile firms within a particular market, regardless of technology sharing agreements. The NUMMI joint venture—General Motors and Toyota—was a pioneering effort in an industry that needed more consolidation joint ventures (as in the steel industry) as well as innovation joint ventures (as in the electronics industry).

Need for Joint Activities

Designing and tooling a new car took three years or more, and the cost of creating an all-new car in 1984 exceeded $1.5 billion. Demand was slowing, and the European automobile firms were entering an era of consolidation to remain profitable, to increase productivity, and to market cars worldwide. U.S. firms were expected to follow, in order to bring capacity in line with demand, to fill out their product lines with the models that customers demanded, and to exploit cost advantages.

Choosing Partners

In 1971 Chrysler Corp. purchased 15 percent of Mitsubishi Motors. At that time, the Japanese firm welcomed the chance to sell automobiles through the Detroit firm. But when Chrysler had years of poor performance, Mitsubishi suffered by its affiliation with Chrysler. Nissan Motors and Toyota Motors were using other U.S. automobile firms' distribution channels to enter the U.S. market and erode Mitsubishi's position. When Mitsubishi could stand it no more, it created its own distribution channels and introduced its own sporty cars, sedans, and trucks through a newly organized Mitsubishi dealer network. (Mitsubishi continued to supply cars to Chrysler on an OEM vendor basis.) In 1981 Mitsubishi Motors began to distance itself from Chrysler because other healthy automobile manufacturers had formed joint ventures with each other at that time to capitalize on their *strengths* to cut costs and increase market share. Chrysler was not healthy in 1981. Later Mitsubishi Motors and Chrysler announced a $500 million agreement to build subcompact cars jointly in the United States beginning in 1988.

In 1980 Chrysler and Peugeot began talks on a wide range of possible marketing and production ventures, including the production in the United States of a new Peugeot car. Renault, Peugeot, and Volvo had pooled capital to develop and produce jointly a small engine to be used by all three companies. Chrysler began seeking similar alliances while Mitsubishi remained distant.

In 1983 Chrysler and Volkswagen discussed a joint production agreement to develop a new vehicle almost from scratch. Chrysler needed help in creating a replacement for its aging Omni and Horizon subcompacts. Chrysler's ties with Volkswagen went back several years. Volkswagen had supplied the engines for Chrysler's Omni and Horizon initially and had purchased a U.S. plant from Chrysler. In 1985 Chrysler was seeking joint-venture partners. It increased its equity interest in Mitsubishi to 24 percent. Chrysler announced a joint venture to build sports cars in Italy with Officine Alfieri Maserati SpA in 1985.

In 1978 American Motors (AMC) and Renault formed a marketing agreement for AMC to sell Renault cars in the United States. (Renault had imported AMC Nash-Ramblers to France during the 1950s.) Renault gained access to a vastly expanded U.S. dealer network and to U.S. manufacturing facilities for a fraction of the cost of foreign direct investment by cooperating with AMC. The partners also conducted joint engine design studies. The Renault-AMC cooperation agreement evolved from a minority investment to a position of majority ownership by Renault. Cooperation had enabled American Motors to enjoy substantial economies in launching its production of the Alliance, which was built by Renault, because its partner had already developed the car and a way to manufacture it cheaply. But as chapter 8 noted, Renault's large losses in 1984 limited the speed with which it could develop resistance welding robots and other cost-saving process improvements that might help American Motors to compete as a global player.

In 1979 Saab and Lancia were discussing a joint venture to make medium-sized sedans, as well as other arrangements to share technology. Honda and British Motors formed a joint marketing venture in 1979. Fiat joined Alfa Romeo and Renault truck division in a joint venture to build a diesel engine plant in Northern Italy, and Fiat discussed joining Daimler-Benz in a joint gearbox manufacturing facility in 1979. In 1980 Fiat and Peugot formed a joint venture to design and build electronically controlled, fuel-efficient, low-polluting engines. Volvo and Renault formed a joint subsidiary to handle Volvo production, and British-Leyland and Honda Motors had formed a joint venture to produce a midsize car with Honda production methods, engine, and transmission. (British-Leyland marketed the car in Europe, and Honda sold it in the rest of the world.) Alfa Romeo and Nissan Motors formed a joint venture to produce small cars in Italy in 1980. Nissan purchased a 36 percent share in Motor Iberica S.A., a Barcelona truckmaker, and increased its share to 65.5 percent later. Toyota acquired a minority interest in Lotus, the tiny British car-builder that was a world leader in developing sophisticated suspension systems. Toyota also owned a 14.7 percent interest in Daihatsu Motors, a small-car specialist.

Nissan Motors had become an aggressive builder of overseas alliances by 1980. Compared with Toyota, Nissan was an old-line firm in Japan. (Toyota was considered to be the upstart.) But Toyota was more cautious and conservative. Nissan had been the first Japanese automobile manufacturer to plunge heavily into automation, and its plants were considered to be showcases of robotic technology. Toyota, by contrast, had moved relatively slowly in factory automation techniques, relying instead on factory management techniques like just-in-time inventory control, which it had pioneered, to achieve superlative quality and high productivity.

In 1979 Ford Motor acquired a 24.4 percent interest in Mazda. Ford's alliance with Toyo Kogyo (Mazda) outside the U.S. market had allowed Ford to outsell General Motors there since the mid-1960s. Toyo Kogyo had supplied Ford with the right products (small cars like the GLC as well as small trucks) at the right cost because Toyo Kogyo's labor costs were substantially lower than Ford's costs in Europe. Ford had both made and sold Toyo Kogyo products under its own brand name overseas. Since their affiliation, Ford and Mazda had created a series of programs to supply components to their respective affiliates dealing at an arm's-length basis. In 1985 Mazda was seeking stronger ties with Ford Motor Co. because it had become difficult to do business alone in the global automobile industry. It was scheduled to begin building small cars at a Ford plant in Michigan in 1987.

In 1980 Toyota offered to form a joint venture with Ford Motor Co. and with Ford's 25 percent owned Japanese affiliate, Toyo Kogyo Co. to build automobiles in the United States. Toyota-Ford discussions did not progress far, however, because the potential partners had different products in mind. Moreover, they could not agree on the proportion of components that would be made in the U.S. child's plant. (Toyota allegedly wanted to obtain the most profitable components—engines and other drive train parts—from its plants in Japan for assembly in the United States. Moreover, Toyota wanted to be the operating manager.) Discussions of a potential partnership between Ford and Toyota ended in 1981.

In 1979 Isuzu Motors Ltd. had been negotiating with its U.S. partner, General Motors, to supply the latter with its recently developed small diesel engine, which was said to be the most efficient in the world in fuel economy. (General Motors owned 34.2 percent of Isuzu Motors.) General Motors hoped to use the Isuzu engine as a stopgap before devising a small fuel-economy diesel engine of its own. In 1981 General Motors and Suzuki had formed a manufacturing and marketing agreement to produce a minicar for resale in the United States. (General Motors owned a 5 percent stake in Suzuki Motor Co.) The tie-up with Suzuki solved several marketing and supply problems for General Motors because it allowed GM to offer a product that was a proven success, rather than risking the tooling costs for a product that might flop. Suzuki's minicar line dove-tailed nicely with the larger cars and trucks built by Isuzu Motors. The two-way sourcing base gave General Motors access to an array of vehicles for the U.S. market and enabled it to participate in the booming Asian-Pacific market, as well.

In 1980 General Motors and Toyota began discussions about a 50%-50% joint venture to manufacture a family of Toyota-designed cars in the United States. By 1983 their negotiating teams had created a twelve-year, jointly owned venture, called New United Motor Manufacturing Inc. (NUMMI), to produce a version of Toyota's subcompact Corolla model in a formerly shut-in General Motors plant in Fremont, California. Toyota was chosen as operating manager of the joint venture, and it used Japanese supplies for automotive components until Toyota could teach U.S. suppliers how to meet its quality standards. Initially, the cars were sold under the Chevrolet name. Partners split profits from the joint venture; but as the car's designer, Toyota received design and engineering royalties based on unit sales volumes. (Toyota's U.S. marketing and distribution activities were already adequate prior to its liaison with General Motors. It did *not* need its partner's market access to penetrate the U.S. automobile market.)

Toyota hoped to learn about the U.S. labor environment through the joint venture. Also, the venture was a response to U.S. critics (especially the UAW) that had called for federal action against the rising tide of Japanese imports. (The Japanese automobile industry's interest in a production base in the United States paralleled the Japanese response to informal quotas on steel exports to the United States. "Voluntary" quotas on cars were established in the face of mounting U.S. criticism of Japanese car imports. Under these pressures, Honda Motor Co. had built a plant in Ohio, and Nissan Motor Co. had done the same in Tennessee.)

General Motors was curious regarding whether Japanese management techniques could be applied successfully to a U.S. unionized labor force. Consequently, Toyota was given maximum freedom in the agreement to bring in their programs and their work methods. Toyota insisted on hiring autonomy and freedom to use its own work rules, including the flexibility to move employees from one task to another. (At most, Toyota wanted three work categories. The typical U.S. automobile manufacturer had twenty-five work categories and had enjoyed substantially less flexibility than Toyota to redeploy workers to even out work flows. The UAW union acquiesced in this matter.

In 1984 General Motors and Daewoo Corp. of South Korea agreed to produce cars for export to the United States from their joint venture, Daewoo Motor Co., beginning in 1986. Doing so required the partners to expand their child's production capacity from 80,000 to 200,000 cars per year. Observers noted the flurry of cooperative ventures in 1985 and suggested that the world automobile industry would consolidate to a few remaining firms by 1990.

Child Activities

There was great interest in 1984 concerning how General Motors and Toyota would integrate their child's activity with their own. Conflicts between partners were not expected to be substantial, due to the way in which the venture had been structured and due to similarities concerning their management styles. The partners' cultures were *more similar* than those of other U.S. automakers. Until 1982 Toyota had sold its automobiles in Japan through a separate company, Toyota Motor Sales, which was managed by Japanese who had learned their marketing techniques from General Motors Japan during the 1930s. Many of the principles of Toyota marketing and distribution were *more* similar to those of General Motors than they were to those of competitors like Ford or Nissan, for example.

NUMMI, the Toyota-GM joint venture, operated with substantial autonomy from one of its parents (General Motors) as it adopted the customs of the other (Toyota). For example, NUMMI ran preemployment training programs to teach potential employees Toyota's Japanese employment fundamentals (as did Nissan Motor Manufacturing Corp. in its U.S. operations). NUMMI planned to hire only those workers who could adapt to Japanese-style management practices. U.S. automobile firms watched this experiment with great interest in 1985.

Summary

Since the activities of joint ventures often shared facilities with those of their global parents, they had to be coordinated closely with those of wholly owned business units. The principal role for the local partner was to (1) cope with local regulations concerning product standards and efficacy, (2) represent the global firms' activities as those of a local firm within protected markets, and (3) provide products to round out partners' offerings to global customers. Close coordination with parents' activities was especially important when the child's products did not have to be differentiated in a special way for local customers—where the image of the product, its quality, and other attributes that customers valued were similar from market to market.

Many global firms used cross-licensing agreements to move quickly in exploiting new technologies within diverse geographic markets. They kept close control over R&D activities, using their child as a way of extending their reach into diverse markets. Licensing was a first step for some global firms in their efforts to gain a toehold into new markets, where they often imported products made in offshore facilities. In some cases, liaisons with local partners gave way to acquisitions, particularly as global partners found their relationships with local partners to be unwieldy.

Protectionism, trade balance offsets, and requirements for local co-production detracted from the implicit efficiencies of global strategy because they required firms to make investments in facilities that would not have been otherwise justified by the needs of the system. Implications of this government requirement are treated further in chapter 16 as part of the discussion of the implications of joint-venture strategies for public policy.

Notes

1. This section is condensed from chapter 10 of K.R. Harrigan, 1983, *Strategies for Vertical Integration,* Lexington, Mass.: Lexington Books.

2. This section is condensed from chapter 9 of K.R. Harrigan, 1983, *Strategies for Vertical Integration,* Lexington, Mass.: Lexington Books.

13
Summary: Joint Ventures and Adaptation to Change

T his chapter summarizes managers' comments concerning the usefulness of joint ventures as a means of adapting to changing competitive conditions. It also evaluates the robustness of the arguments presented in chapters 3, 4, and 5 concerning the creation of competitive advantage through joint-venture strategies. In particular, it compares findings concerning (1) partners' bargaining power; (2) parent–child relationships; and (3) the child's needs for autonomy with respect to its competitive environment with the framework presented in figure 3–2. The summary addresses how parents created synergies in their relationships with joint ventures, and it considers how much autonomy joint ventures enjoyed as stand-alone entities. It draws upon the chapter summaries and adds new information from the field interviews.

Chapter 14 summarizes findings concerning the use of joint ventures as technological change agents. Chapter 15 details how managers might best form and guide their joint-venture children. Chapter 16 notes that public policy changes may be needed in order for joint ventures to realize their full potential as managerial tools for improved economic performance.

Firms varied substantially in their uses of joint ventures both within industries and across them. Some firms, like Control Data Corp., used joint ventures because doing so was a part of their corporate culture. Other firms formed them because they faced too much risk in their competitive environments and possessed too few skills internally to cope with these challenges alone. Firms created joint ventures to pursue their own objectives. Usually these objectives were related to strategies to obtain resources and skills that firms lacked internally. Firms accommodated the objectives of their partners in joint ventures *only* where those objectives did not clash with their own. Therefore, the best joint ventures matched firms possessing strengths that complemented those of their partners.

Supplementing Resources and Capabilities

Managers were unanimous in noting that joint ventures were harder to manage than wholly owned business units but that joint ventures were undertaken when the need to do so was substantial. Since there was no need for firms to form joint ventures if they could do everything by themselves, and since firms would not use joint ventures without considerable incentives (since they were so unwieldy to manage), it is reasonable to assume that firms used joint ventures to expand their competitive capabilities and create new strengths.

Firms obtained relatively easy access to expertise and to distribution outlets through joint ventures and moved faster in securing market share than if they had had to develop these assets on their own. By pooling facilities, firms were able to keep their costs low until their internally generated sales volumes reached critical masses that justified investments in their own plant, equipment, sales force, and other facilities.

Accelerated Competitive Response

There were *limits* to the widespread efficacy of joint ventures, however, and firms had to adjust their cooperative strategies to the special problems of certain types of competitive environments. In embryonic industries, for example, where great uncertainty loomed concerning which marketing approach would prove to be most successful or which technological standards customers would embrace, *more liaisons of shorter durations* resulted from firms' unions. In order to avoid long entanglements in arrangements that could prove to be wrong later, firms adopted less binding partnership arrangements within embryonic settings. For example, firms concluded that alliances that lasted for shorter durations, such as when technology changed rapidly, should not bear children. Instead, firms created teams on a project-by-project basis for such environments. When partners' interests changed, ventures had to end in a nondisruptive fashion as firms moved on to their next dancing partners. To facilitate easy transitions, agreements were formed to last for only a few months at a time and proceeded on the basis of a handshake rather than a voluminous legal document. They terminated when one partner notified the other verbally.

Some market opportunities evaporated within months if they were not exploited quickly. High technology products, in particular, needed faster market penetration in order to place them into distribution channels and consumers' hands before products became obsolete or were copied by others. When it became important to maneuver faster, partnerships (which did not create a child) were used to accelerate firms' international product introductions. It was especially important to have access to international linkages as it became increasingly expensive to reach key markets within a global system quickly, particularly when the half-life of a technology was very short and firms could scarcely recapture their development costs alone. Loose partnerships were combined with licensing agreements and other ways of disseminating and exploiting whatever transitory competitive advantage firms possessed in recognition of the temporariness of such strengths. These informal alliances saved time and kept firms from being preempted by competitors. For many firms, these arrangements were a faster way to penetrate international markets and build up significant market shares than going it alone.

Children were more likely to result when partners joined forces in the early stages of industry maturity, when technology changed less rapidly and when product standards had at last been established. As demand uncertainty—concerning the nature of customer tastes, price sensitivities, product features, and other market traits—lessened and firms became more concerned with how to force effective strategies to satisfy demand—using lowest-cost technologies and other tactics to protect their turf—they began to seek the talents of accomplished partners and began to form joint ventures of greater durations.

Children were also more likely to be formed as industries matured and competitive advantage was gained through higher-scale economies. Joint ventures were used to rationalize smaller, inefficient plants and to replace them with more efficient ones without creating floods of excess capacity. Many joint ventures were actually *disguised divestitures* in cases where one partner no longer wished to invest in a particular market or in the industry.

In summary, different cooperative strategies—of differing durations and involving different types of progeny—were used in industries of different ages and infrastructure stability. Where there was still great uncertainty concerning the efficacy of technologies, customers' tastes and other structural traits that affected the attractiveness of profit-making opportunities within an industry, partners kept their joint activities informal and brief. When industries matured—as more competitors entered and technological standards were better accepted—fewer joint ventures per firm, each encompassing a larger investment or scope, were used within industries such as petrochemicals, communications equipment, and home video entertainment products.

Building Strengths

All cooperative strategies—joint ventures, minority investments, cross-licensing agreements, and so forth—were a means of extending firms' domains with relatively lower investment stakes than if they went into a venture alone. As such, they permitted firms to develop new competencies, gather more competitive intelligence, and engage in activities they could not justify economically otherwise. The ideal objective in choosing a joint-venture partner was to offset each other's strengths. Therefore marketing firms chose partners that offered technology, innovation, management experience, or funds, for example. Technology partners sought a means to penetrate markets quickly.

Joint ventures were an excellent way for firms to strengthen their competitive postures by expanding their product lines. In such cases, partners with good products (or manufacturing technology) but poor marketing skills, for example, could obtain better market coverage by sharing the benefits of their experience curve advantages in manufacturing with potential entrants possessing the strengths it lacked.

Whether these strengths were realized or not, the 1980s were a time for dazzling Wall Street with the illusion that firms were building strengths through cooperative strategies. Valuation problems were rampant as firms' stock prices enjoyed speculative gains when joint ventures were announced, especially in evaluating technology transfers. If firms overvalued their partners' technology contributions, their errors were *never* admitted to outsiders, due to the images that firms were projecting in the financial community during this era. If there were start-up problems or partners' technological contributions were not as promised, these realities were masked by speculative stock price increases that signaled investors' delight that small firms were bettering their technological positions (by allying with big firms) or that big firms, which had not been doing anything impressive in a particular line of research, had found a promising way to catch up.

The higher a product line or area of technology was in strategic importance, the more reluctant firms were to use cooperative strategies to leverage their competitive positions. Joint ventures were formed to supplement some existing strengths; but *other* forms of cooperation were used in those areas that constituted firms' strategic cores. One explanation for firms' reticence to trust partners in areas of great strategic importance may be that firms were reluctant to rely on the successes of others for survival. Joint ventures were considered to be appropriate to gain new and related strengths; but some knowledge was too sensitive for firms to share through joint ventures. They preferred to acquire it rather than share such knowledge. If firms cooperated at all in those areas, it was through exclusive arrangements in order to protect their competitive advantages.

In summary, results were somewhat contrary to the joint-venture framework that had predicted that joint ventures would be a middle ground—a compromise—for firms in need of assistance that valued their respective contributions highly. Industry experience thus far has not found most U.S. firms to be willing to compromise on the use of joint ventures in areas of great importance to them, and if they cooperate at all in these areas of high strategic importance, it is only through relationships of exclusivity where they are strongly in control.

Bargaining Power

Partners were most attractive when they possessed great bargaining power because firms did not want to form joint ventures with partners weaker than themselves. But joint ventures were most likely to be formed among *industry underdogs* because firms that were dissatisfied with their marketing skills or their product lines would have to accept equally hungry (but deficient) firms as partners. (Dissenting managers did not believe that joint ventures offered weak firms a way to improve their competitive positions. When two or three large companies—with vast resources of their own—combined to form joint ventures, they argued, their behavior signaled that the activity in question was highly risky. Otherwise, any one of the partners would have supported the activity with in-house funding to avoid sharing the proceeds with partners.) Together, the underdogs tried to create stronger competitive entities. But if one of the partners were stronger than the other with respect to assets, skills, resources, or other attributes that gave it greater bargaining power, that firm extracted compensation for those strengths from its partners. The alliances ended up more costly for the weaker firms.

This scenario of asymmetric strengths should not be a surprising one. Joint ventures were a way for firms to acquire strengths and resources that they lacked. In order for the bargain to work—for the other firm to desire a joint venture also—partners had to be *unable* to utilize their own strengths fully. In addition to pooling their assets, firms added the know-how that allowed partners to build on each other's basic strengths in a way that they could not do alone. Thus a firm's bargaining power was based on *what it knew and could do* as well as what it possessed.

Terms of some joint ventures agreements created bargaining power *for the child*. They were supported by parents that used joint ventures to provide a stable source of raw materials. Using this guaranteed demand (secured by parents' take-or-pay contracts), children penetrated new markets to dispose of excess outputs. Since they were not constrained by their parents in the markets they could serve (after satisfying supply commitments to their parents), enterprising children were able to prosper more than competitors that had no parents to absorb a base level of outputs and more than other joint-venture children that were *prohibited* by their parents from dealing with outsiders.

In sum, these children had the best of both worlds. Their contracts with parent firms gave children bargaining power to offset downside risks. Their stable base of parental demand also gave joint ventures bargaining power against customers in resisting their urgings to cut prices merely to fill their plants to break-even levels.

Even minority investments gave firms preemptive power because they blocked competitors from acquiring suppliers that could serve industrywide demand better by remaining independent. This has often been the case because competitors are suspicious of vertically integrated suppliers. The example of Ethyl Corp., the child of Exxon and General Motors, suggests that arm's-length distancing was necessary before Exxon's competitors would purchase its tetraethyl lead catalyst. Similarly, a passive linkage—like a minority investment by IBM in Intel—strengthened independent suppliers without capturing them by making them a part of a competitors' vertically integrated chain. (Antitrust regulations made fears concerning *downstream* blocking unfounded because the antitrust agencies were more sensitive to firms' attempts to capture distribution channels through acquisitions. In 1984 upstream blocking was sometimes done under the guise of an informal national industrial policy.)

In summary, findings suggest that joint ventures and other forms of cooperative strategy were used by weak firms to create stronger market positions. Despite skepticism by managers, a plethora of minority investments, joint R&D projects, and joint ventures were announced by firms that had never ventured jointly before. This pattern suggests that firms' searches for sources of competitive advantage had led them to consider even joint ventures as a way to build strengths from weaknesses.

Creating Synergies

If synergies were created through joint ventures, they accrued from vertical relationships or from shared resources. The coordination difficulties of joint ventures made it most likely that synergies would be enjoyed among *horizontally related partners* with horizontally or vertically related children. Homogeneous joint-venture partners enjoyed greater synergies because it was easier for them to agree on how to correct operating problems in their child, and how to coordinate its activities with theirs. Vertically-related joint ventures enabled parents to avert the jealousies that erupted between business units that competed for the same customers because such children were not competitors of their parents' business units. (Coordination problems associated with attaining joint-venture synergies should not be underrated. Synergies did not accrue unless relationships between business units were consciously managed, and doing so effectively required parents to make appropriate tradeoffs concerning the benefits of child autonomy and parent–child coordination. The struggle for control was frequently a difficult one.)

Vertical Relationships

A major hypothesis examined in this study concerned whether joint ventures could thrive without access to the means to function as a stand-alone entity. Based on results from field studies, it would seem that it was *not* necessary for the joint venture to have any downstream facilities, provided the child was not penalized for its failure to sell outputs that were not consumed by its parents. This amendment in the framework of chapters 3, 4, and 5 reflects firms' diverse motives for forming joint ventures, as well as the different missions parents gave to their children.

For example, if a joint venture was formed to be a supplier to horizontally related parents, as was the case with Magnetic Peripherals Inc. (MPI) and with Honeywell-Ericsson, parents would not want their child to sell its excess outputs to outsiders, especially not at prices reflecting their marginal costs of production. Parents restricted their joint venture's customer list because they had pooled their internal needs for components in order to exploit scale economies. If their resulting cost savings gave them a significant competitive advantage, it was unlikely that parents would share this cost advantage with outsiders. Vertical synergies were enjoyed in such cases. (As chapter 9 noted, MPI violated all of the theoretical rules about joint ventures and contradicted most of the managers' success rules as well. MPI was remarkably successful, however, despite its lack of a marketing and sales force of its own.)

Depending on the industry, creating an effective sales force could require fifteen to twenty years. Some U.S. customers still retained a bias against purchasing foreign products in 1984, as in the example of the electrical utility industry. In such settings, access to the established partners' sales forces was desired by firms in making joint-venture agreements. When joint ventures were restricted to manufacturing and development activities to make products for resale through parents' distribution channels, local parents withheld market access from foreign competitors. In effect, local partners acted as marketing agents for overseas firms to postpone their investments in U.S. sales offices, and this pattern was found frequently overseas when U.S. firms tried to reach customers in markets with alien distribution channel structures by selling through a local firm that acted as sales agent.

Except for the pharmaceuticals industry, managers concurred that market access was a very important (if not the single most important) competitive resource U.S. partners controlled in joint-venture negotiations (because technology changed so quickly that competitive advantages based on it were less durable than those based on market access). However, many firms described in the industry chapters valued access to partners' technologies more highly than they valued their sales organizations and accumulated goodwill with the trade. They helped foreign partners to learn how to market products effectively in the United States. In one case, the foreign partner sent its personnel on calls with the local partner's sales force in order to make customer contacts and observe marketing practices. In another example, ASEA continued to use its joint-venture partner's sales force after it purchased the remaining 50 percent interest in its child from RTE Corp. rather than establish its own U.S. marketing organization. Thus, ASEA extended its former partner's product line by using RTE as its U.S. sales agent.

Boisterous Children. When joint ventures marketed outputs using their own sales forces, frictions resulted unless the child's parents defined specific geographic sales territories that became the child's exclusive responsibility. Failure to circumscribe the joint venture's market domain resulted in boisterous children going into competition against their parents, and when this occurred, few vertical synergies were realized. U.S. antitrust laws (among others) discouraged marketing cooperation among upstream competitors, as the motion picture studios' experience with their Premiere programming packager venture (to reach cable television customers) has illustrated. Marketing territory allocations could also violate such laws if they were not carefully defined, as is noted in the section on shared facilities, below.

Joint ventures developed their own marketing and sales forces when their parents could not consume the child's outputs in quantities that would utilize their plant's capacity efficiently. For example, Texaco's need for ethanol declined as oil prices dropped, and it could no longer absorb the volumes it was obliged to purchase under the take-or-pay contract it gave its partner, CPC International, in their Pekin ethanol joint venture. Although it may not have been the intention of Pekin's parents to give it a sales force, the oil industry's reversal forced the child to sell ethanol on a merchant basis and it did so with great zest. Alternatively, joint ventures have been forced to develop their own marketing and sales forces in cases when business units within parent firms refused to market their products, as in the example of the motion picture industry.

Sheltered Children. Although they offered synergies, vertical joint ventures posed unique problems if the child was restricted from dealing with outsiders—by right-of-first-refusal arrangements or by outright parental prohibitions. These problems were similar to the problems that excessive vertical integration of the wrong type could create for wholly owned business units. For example, the child was more likely to become sickly if it was required to rely on its parents for more than 50 percent of its purchases. In consumer products, in particular, a similar caution could be extended to joint ventures that relied on parents to take more than 50 percent of children's outputs; without the discipline of outside markets to reflect consumer preferences, the child was more likely to make products that the market did not want and its parents were more likely to be locked into purchases that were out of fashion. Careful management of the buyer–supplier relationship between parents and child was needed in order for the benefits of vertical synergies to offset the *dangers of strategic inflexibility.*

Overreliance by the child on its parents as customers could injure firms' strategic flexibility as well as the child's longevity, as in situations where one parent wanted to change its historic supplier–buyer relationship with the child while its partners were content with their old allocations of the child's outputs (or purchases). Without that parent as customer, the child's plant became uneconomic. It had to go to the outside market. Many parents did not relish partial ownership of a vertically related merchant unit and instead terminated their child. Alternatively, some firms never fell into the strategic flexibility trap of giving long-term take-or-pay contracts to their joint-venture partners and never agreed to totally open-ended technology-sharing arrangements that could not be truncated without penalties.

Jealousies among Partners. Joint ventures among vertically related partners posed particular problems when firms knew each others' costs, especially when the payback cycles for various stages of processing were asynchronous. Thus, firms that finally enjoyed better economics after making large expenditures for several years (with no return) faced resentment from partners downstream that were on different cash flow cycles. For example, mining ventures required substantial rates of return to justify eight years of development expenditures, but steel companies forgot that their partners had starved for years to develop their mine. All they noticed was the high returns that were enjoyed once a mine came in and the low returns they faced in their own core businesses. *Corporate memories were short* in supplier–buyer relationships, and partners that believed they were on the short end of a joint venture wanted to renegotiate their agreements when they perceived that partners' profit margins were too wide or when other perceived inequities existed. Partners' displeasure at discovering suppliers' profit margins often made them forget that the child was earning a fortune for them as well as for the prospering partners.

Conscious efforts were required to exploit the potential for vertical synergies between parent and child when several partners had buyer–supplier relationships with their joint-venture child. All partners had to be treated equitably, and the child's future viability had to be protected in managing those synergies. Transfer pricing mechanisms were designed to ensure that no party benefited to the detriment of the others. Product development had to be coordinated to reduce internecine jealousies when parent and child could become competitors. The child needed autonomy to purchase inputs from outsider suppliers (or to sell to outside customers) when they were willing to better the prices offered by parents. When joint ventures were only development and manufacturing companies for their parents, it was more difficult to determine whether their outputs were cost-competitive with those of outsiders (since parent firms were their only customers). If the joint venture could not match the prices of outside suppliers, it was often terminated. But if parents were willing to tolerate periods of underutilized capacity, joint ventures provided them with helpful back-up sources of supply.

Horizontal Relationships

Synergies were best exploited in vertical joint ventures when parents agreed not to undermine their child's ability to attain break-even levels of capacity utilization by maintaining internal business units that paralleled the joint venture's activities. Managers agreed that activity duplications created conflicts of interest between parent and child when they possessed buyer–seller relationships, as well. Parents' purchases of components from in-house, wholly owned business units frequently undermined their child's economics to the detriment of other partners.

There were fewer horizontal synergies from R&D joint ventures. As the example of ethical pharmaceuticals has shown, no basic R&D was performed within jointly owned business units in that industry, with the exception of the genetic-engineering experiments. (Basic research activities were too close to pharmaceutical firms' strategic cores.) The Microelectronics and Computer Technology consortium in electronic components, software, and computers was unique in its focus on basic research, since its sponsors' survival also depended on successes in basic research.

As chapter 14 explains, innovation activities were especially difficult to manage successfully within joint ventures because parental jealousies were difficult to overcome in areas closest to firms' strategic cores. In consumer products, survival depended on firms' abilities to sustain differentiated images. Similarly, there were few successful joint ventures in consumer products industries for the purposes of creating new marketing activities and sales forces (unless these were to penetrate new markets such as cable television, home video, or other outlets where parents had no existing stakes). Parents were less likely to create a child for the purpose of replicating activities on which they depended for strategic survival.

Sharing Resources

Shared resources provided the potential for synergies between parent and child (or between partners) when a means was devised to ameliorate scheduling jealousies and other inevitable problems, such as learning how to cooperate where entities were accustomed to competing. Firms faced the same problem in-house among their wholly owned business units when their cultures had previously emphasized competition. When business units were accustomed to bargaining aggressively during intrafirm transfers of resources and competing for capital from the corporate funding sources, resource sharing posed a difficult challenge for affected business units.

In a well-coordinated joint venture, like Magnetic Peripherals Inc. (MPI), partners consciously shared their child's outputs and depended on their joint venture to satisfy their needs for as long as it continued to be a cost-competitive vendor of magnetic memory devices. Parents did not maintain parallel facilities in-house so as not to undermine the joint venture's success by creating rivalries or reduce the scale economies all partners shared in. When Sperry joined the MPI joint venture, it had its own magnetic peripherals business unit, ISI. The Sperry facilities, people, and talent were transferred to MPI. During the transition period, Sperry customers were serviced until non-compatible products could be phased out in favor of MPI common products.

Parents shared marketing and sales resources with their child when joint ventures were formed to supplement firms' product lines, as in the example of office equipment firms selling their child's private branch exchange (PBX) products. Parents shared processing facilities upstream with their child when joint ventures were formed to expand firms' market coverage, as in the example of motion picture firms diversifying into home video and cable television programming packaging.

The petrochemical industry was a literal web of interconnected processing units that shared feedstocks, intermediaries, and facilities regardless of ownership, and it had done so successfully for over twenty years. This structural trait had forced managers of petrochemical operations to address the problems of sharing selling facilities—as well as processing facilities and other resources—earlier than managers in most other industries. Historically, separate activities had been created primarily when there was no economic reason to combine operations therein. It is useful to review why this pattern of sharing facilities had evolved as it did.

When most joint ventures shared inputs, distribution facilities, or other resources with the business units of their parents, frictions resulted from their internal competition for suppliers' (or distributors') attentions for their respective plants (or products) if negotiations or selling activities were needed subsequent to the decision to build the initial plant. For many firms, the costs of arbitrating among business units that shared supplying or distributing facilities were not offset adequately by the synergies they realized. The coordination problems of interrelated business activities increased the use of arm's-length transactions and child autonomy in choosing suppliers (and distributors). Firms also avoided these conflicts by creating self-contained activity centers. Since there was only one place within parents' organizations where any particular activity was done, this arrangement reduced internecine warfare. Alternatively, firms reduced the problems of shared facilities by increasing the number of parallel activities employed where it was economic to do so. (Some of the side payments used to reduce the problems that shared resources created are recounted in chapter 15, which provides guidelines for forming and managing cooperative strategies.)

Two pressures accelerated the transition of the child into an autonomous business unit within industries where its activities were conducive to stand-alone facilities. First, the managers of joint ventures were as boisterous as those in charge of other internal venturing units. If the venture was successful, they pressed for more autonomy, often in the form of the child's own capabilities and facilities. Managers also pressed for a larger share of corporate funding in competition with wholly owned business units. (The latter source of intrafirm jealously accelerated some joint ventures' entries into the capital markets in their own right to obtain supplemental financing.) Second, as chapter 15 explains, loyalties to the child developed that led managers to advocate actions that were inimical to parents' interests.

Child Autonomy

This section summarizes additional findings concerning the boisterous child —the joint venture that evolved (sometimes too quickly to suit its parents) into an autonomous entity that was allowed to choose whether to purchase from (or sell to) outsiders. The preceding section summarized findings concerning whether joint ventures could thrive without the means to function as stand-alone entities. It concluded that parents may be satisfied with children that do not have their own sales capabilities (or development facilities), but parents could create problems for themselves by sheltering their child too much.

Autonomy created problems on the other end of the continuum. Too much autonomy often resulted in strong joint ventures that were terminated by (1) bringing children inside parents' organizations (one partner purchased the interests of the other); (2) spinning them off into a stand-alone corporation (like the Corning family of joint ventures); or (3) letting them vie for outside financing (like TriStar Pictures) in arrangements that converted parents' interests into minority investments. In this last example, less internal coordination between the organizations of the parents and their former child occurred over time as each entity pursued its respective business strategy. As the industry chapters have suggested, minority agreements strengthened other players without bringing them too closely into the investing firm's orbit. (As IBM's acquisition of Rolm suggests, more managerial control—as well as equity control—was needed when closer coordination of business activities was desired.)

When firms ventured into new arenas, they used implicit cut-off points in rationing their capital expenditures to decide when to cut off funding for start-up or entrepreneurial ventures. A similar discipline guided parents' decisions concerning when their joint ventures should evolve into autonomous units, be folded into parents' organizations, or be liquidated. If partners did not wean their child after its time for nourishment had passed or convert it to another organizational form, the joint venture became a drag on its parents' performance and on their morale.

Industry differences suggested how quickly joint ventures evolved from loose corporations to partnerships to stand-alone entities (if at all). Volatile competitive conditions required shorter-lived and more informal liaisons. Demand uncertainty required tentative affiliations, modest funding, and pilot plants or test situations. By 1984 few industries' structures were likely to remain unchanged for long. Some relationships retrogressed, as in the example of Xerox pulling Rank-Xerox more closely under its control as competition intensified and profit margins thinned.

Partners had to anticipate how their industry could evolve if they hoped to provide for all contingencies in their joint-venture agreements. As chapter 15 notes, even partners that preferred to negotiate decisions as conflicts developed (rather than setting out divorce settlements in great detail in a legal document) found it necessary to agree on the child's purpose. If the child was attaining its strategic mission successfully, managers conceded, partners had to put up the cash as it became necessary or give the joint venture authority to go elsewhere for funding. Recognition of this contingency required partners to establish ground rules for how their joint ventures were going to operate—concerning how much autonomy as well as cash the child could claim as it matured and as strategic milestones were attained. This contingency also suggested that the management system—the controls and other management policies for accountability to the joint venture's parents—had to be anticipated in advance of the child's birth.

Experienced parents gave their children more autonomy in operating decisions (where such autonomy was appropriate for the child's mission) than did first-time parents. The first joint-venture experiences seemed to be the most difficult ones. Moreover, as their joint ventures matured, experienced parents weaned their child from using corporate resources without sharing in their costs. Hence, control systems similar to those used in allocating overhead costs to internal start-up ventures (perhaps in the form of a corporate overhead or strategic-expenditures account) were maintained by experienced managers to track relevant shared costs until the child acquired dedicated facilities, personnel, and other resources of its own.

Joint ventures that were to become part of parents' integrated global systems posed a special problem with respect to autonomy (and joint-venture termination). Although the child's management system did not have to resemble that of its surviving parent initially, parents felt more comfortable about integrating the child into their global system if, with time, its control system became more similar to their own. If high coordination with parents' operations was not required of the joint venture, its management system did not have to evolve beyond what was needed to be helpful to the child's managers, and these problems were avoided.

Control of Whole Tasks

Unless the child was allowed to stand on its own—with its own assets, personnel, resources, and self-contained information reporting systems—it could not hope to operate autonomously. When joint ventures controlled everything—marketing, manufacturing, and even research—they made more informed decisions. Many parents found this level of control desirable because it provided a check and balance against their wholly owned organization's prowess. Autonomous joint ventures were able to focus on competitive issues and make decisions faster because they controlled (or could acquire) the resources they needed. Joint ventures could not respond to competitive conditions as quickly when there were interface problems between parents' business units and child. Moreover, if the joint venture operated in a highly volatile industry, its autonomy to form alliances with outsiders—to use outside manufacturers to get a product quickly, to make licensing and technology agreements, to buy marketing services—was necessary for its strategic survival.

Sometimes it was necessary to throw the child out of its nest for it to gain the competitive resiliency it needed to survive. Furthermore, parents sometimes understood their child's role more clearly after they cut it loose. In one case, a child was given autonomy when it did not want to be free. Its managers were terrified of being on their own. But when the child went out and found the resources it needed to make a good product (which it offered to sell through its parents' marketing organizations), it was rebuffed by jealousies inside parent business units (because its sister units had been told they had to market the child's products and they did not want to do so). Sadly, the child offered to sell its new products through a competitor's organization. When the child's parent realized that its products were good enough to interest rivals, the child was invited back into the nest. (In fact, it was *ordered* to deal only with family members thereafter.)

In another example, one partner pushed the other to put more aggressive managers into the child because its markets were becoming more competitive. Managers of the caliber that the parent wanted from its partner demanded more operating autonomy, and they received it. The child became a major supplier to both parents over time because it consistently out-performed its wholly owned sisters and other competitors.

Arm's-Length Dealings

When joint ventures have true arm's-length autonomy to buy and sell where the best margins can be earned, they maximize their parents' earnings as well as their own. In one example where a seasoned manager had been placed in charge of a joint venture and given operating autonomy, he reported back to its parent firms that his team was making decisions that were best for the child. Obligations to supply its parents with raw materials were satisfied at competitive prices, and surplus outputs were sold at market prices as well. Had parent firms restrained the child's management team when they moved away from their captive role, parents would not have enjoyed the profits their child went on to win. Indeed, with time, the child's operations would likely have become uneconomic without the sales volumes generated by sales to outsiders, and its plant probably would have been shut in. (Giving the child its own marketing capability had not been a part of the original scheme in this example, and parent firms had not been aware that the child's managers had researched outside market opportunities until they were *advised* of the management team's decision.)

In order for joint ventures to make informed operating decisions that would increase their parents' returns, vertical relationships with parent firms' wholly owned business units were encouraged but not required. Experienced managers concluded that the sacrifices made by trying to tie together synergies between parent and child operations were so debilitating to the child's management, in terms of their abilities to run their own businesses on a profit-and-loss basis, that their attentions to such issues were scarcely justified. If their child's managers were smart, they reasoned, they would realize that it helped parent firms to purchase from their divisions. Such managers expected that wholly owned divisions would be given a chance to sell to the child. Beyond that, parents obtained better performances from their joint ventures when they did not force their business units to trade with each other.

Finally, better results were obtained when arm's-length operating autonomy was combined with policies that did not sap the child's abilities to compete. The entrepreneurial spirit that allowed joint ventures to thrive was fragile. In one large and notable failed joint venture, managers were told that they had operating autonomy to build up a large market share position for the child. When the child's sales force responded to its parents' mission with great enthusiasm (and success), jealousies within one parent's organization led it to curb the child's autonomy and to reserve certain accounts for in-house development. Many of the child's best sales representatives resigned. Then the other parent decided that the instructions that had been given to the child's sales force had resulted in the wrong customer mix. The sales force compensation plan was changed, and a new policy of parental review of contracts was instituted. Slowly the parent firms pulled their child closer to their in-house operations. Although parents talked about making their child more entrepreneurial and about giving personnel opportunities to compete locally as best they could, the good customers were divided between parents' wholly owned units. The child failed.

In summary, joint ventures could be an attractive response to risky environments, competitors' incursions, and other challenges firms confronted if they were used in an informed manner. Parents needed realistic expectations for their child and a clear understanding of the shortfalls arising from confusion. Partners needed to agree on their child's mission and how the child would relate to each of them. Partners had to maintain clear understandings with each other—as well as good relationships among managerial counterparts—to keep their joint ventures under strategic control.

14
Summary: Joint Ventures as Technological Change Agents

T his chapter summarizes findings from field interviews concerning the use of joint ventures in areas of technology transfer and innovation. It contrasts competitive environments where joint ventures are appropriate with those settings where licensing or other loose partnership arrangements were more appropriate. It also summarizes findings concerning how firms transferred technology and surmounted the not-invented-here biases that prevented them from exploiting opportunities to supplement their organization's internal capabilities. Finally, it sketches findings concerning the use of parallel facilities and spider's webs of cooperative agreements within settings where exclusive agreements may have been more appropriate.

As chapter 13 noted, few joint R&D partnerships thrived in the area of basic research because that activity was too close to firms' strategic cores. Furthermore, technological advantage was becoming increasingly difficult to protect, and firms were reluctant to expose this activity to appropriation. Accordingly, a discussion of findings concerning technology joint ventures must include some assessment of how firms coped with the threat of obsolescence, piracy, bleedthrough, and other negative forces that reduced the value of firms' competitive advantages, and these threats are treated below.

Solving Technological Problems

Although firms engaged in few basic R&D partnerships, joint ventures to exploit knowledge in new applications or markets thrived. Development joint ventures enabled firms to enter new fields, and assignment of scientific personnel to such challenges revitalized them by letting them concentrate on novel technology areas. Although there were few basic research joint ventures, there were several ways that joint activities helped firms to solve technological problems that they could not cope with alone.

Technological Leapfrogging

Joint ventures were a way to bring some uniformity to a stream of products that were developed through highly uncertain R&D expenditures (with a success rate analogous to striking oil, for example). R&D discoveries came in bunches followed by long dry spells, if they came at all. Firms recognized that their dependence on in-house R&D efforts alone were often inadequate to remain competitive in some industries, especially as competition within them intensified.

Firms entered cooperative arrangements in technological areas in order to avoid having to buy assets, replicate laboratories and testing periods, and build up a marketing presence in industries that were subject to rapid rates of obsolescence. Firms sought licenses as a means to offer new products more rapidly or offered them as a means of getting their products into new markets faster without having to build up a special sales force.

Increasing Value-Added Margins

Even firms with vast R&D and technological capabilities used joint ventures and other cooperative strategies to supplement their in-house capabilities where partners offered (1) the ability to manufacture equivalent products at a reasonable price or (2) credibility among customers, as was needed to promulgate technological standards.

Joint ventures enabled firms to exploit technologies that their own organizations had underutilized. By sharing access to promising materials with entrepreneurial firms, for example, it was possible to develop new applications for them, new product formulations, or other ways to recover value on products that in-house research personnel had viewed as ugly ducklings.

Retail access was a formidable bargaining chip that enabled firms with distribution strengths to choose partners with the best technology (or the most promising technological approach). Firms that controlled retail access sometimes formed joint ventures to gain technological innovations for their product lines. The joint-venture decision was like a make-or-buy decision for them because they could satisfy their needs for innovative products by purchasing them from outside vendors for resale, if they wished to do so. Margins were better for such firms on products manufactured internally, but since their strategic core was retailing—not R&D or manufacturing—they preferred to take partners, especially in areas of very difficult, high technology products where they lacked in-house design capabilities.

Learning about State-of-the-Art Technologies

Joint-venture opportunities were often missed because (1) managers were unwilling to defer to differences in corporate cultures and (2) partners would not be open. Some U.S. firms tended to believe that their partner was trying to take their market away from them. Because they feared that they were creating a competitor, some firms tended not to share information freely. If partners did not bargain in an open and flexible way, the strain that the negotiating team placed on the partnership reduced the joint venture's progress in forming a good working relationship as well. A right-of-first-refusal licensing agreement or other loosely formalized liaison was often a preliminary step for firms that desired a more formal relationship but did not know each other very well.

It was necessary for partners to be well informed on the value of technologies *before* discussing joint ventures. Woe be unto managers who skimped on their homework in this area, a manager of several joint ventures noted, because it was easy to become misled and confused in discussions of risky and unproven technological approaches. Some of the best technological joint ventures were formed by partners that had each done considerable R&D work on the problem in question prior to their collaboration. Since partners had done the market research and product development work before discussing a venture, they knew from a technical and marketing standpoint whether the approaches proposed in a joint venture would yield commercializable results in the near future.

Technological problems were solved best when partners sustained an amiable relationship. When firms became upset with the course of cooperative agreements to share technology or to market products locally, they began to drag their feet on the next generation of technology transfer. Legally, it was difficult to assess whether a partner was really holding back on technology that was not covered by a carefully worded document. Sometimes renegotiations were necessary. For example, if a partner believed that its bargaining position had changed with respect to its partners—making its cooperation *more* important to the joint venture's success—it seized management control over the child's operations (often without changing the equity arrangement) by taking control of distribution or by holding back on the next generation of technology.

In order for partners to work together productively, a trust relationship had to be developed in which partners admitted that they shared information with their parents, learned from each other, and were planning to capitalize on their partners' strengths. Open relationships between partners reduced dissatisfactions later when the agreement was renewed, renegotiated, or terminated.

Protecting Technological Assets

Many U.S. joint ventures in 1984 linked horizontally related firms in horizontally related activities. Because such cooperative strategies linked potential (if not actual) competitors, special care had to be given to protecting partners' strategic cores when they formed joint ventures.

The closer activities were to firms' strategic cores—the higher their importance for firms' survival—the less likely firms were to rely on the research success of joint ventures or other arrangements with outsiders. The closer the research area was to parents' strategic cores, the more concerned they were with losing control of knowledge pertaining to those technological applications. In areas of high strategic importance, parents would make deals—licensing, cross-marketing, or other arrangements that they could control tightly—but they would *not* create a joint venture.

Firms could be as crafty as they pleased in writing clauses to protect technology rights, but the joint venture's success depended on trust. Patents were nearly useless in many industries, and technology (which was embodied in firms' personnel) grew legs and walked into competitors' laboratories looking for better compensation despite employment contracts prohibiting its use for two years or more after termination. There was really no way to ensure that a particular trade secret would not be lost. But if a trusted partner chose to betray its partner by pirating intellectual property, word went out in the industry. Reputation was valued among scientists and engineers who took pride in their own solutions to problems. A conscientious scientific community protected some of their firms' technological assets.

Intellectual Property Rights and Patents

In research ventures, partners often cooperated in developing technology and patents that were applied to different end uses. If the joint venture developed a novel patentable technology that created an asset base that was not put in by its parents, the child owned it. As the partners moved off in diverse directions to develop technology, their joint venture sometimes became a licensing repository to keep track of royalties. In some cases, the child survived as a paper corporation—solely for the purpose of protecting its technology and licensing it for the benefit of its parents—long after other business activities within the joint venture had ceased and its scientists had moved on to other projects, perhaps within other firms.

If firms were concerned about control of their proprietary knowledge, they might use exclusive licensing provisions, right-of-first-refusal provisions, noncompetition agreements, and other contractual provisions to protect knowledge from disseminating to unauthorized third parties. But these provisions protected knowledge only to a limited extent because patent transgressions had to be litigated to recover damages. Moreover, the harm will already have been done. Instead, managers suggested that certain proprietary parts of firms' core technologies should be withheld from their child and transferred only under stringent licensing provisions (as in the case of a computer operating system's source code) or sold on an OEM vendor basis (as in the example of the 256K RAM chip that made a particular piece of equipment work).

Copyright laws protected some software products, and licenses that were based on control of patents provided that certain information could not be passed on or used in another application (or for another purpose) without the owner's explicit permission. But it was also difficult to litigate violations of these property rights. Software, in particular, was such a complicated phenomenon that courts were not adequately equipped to deal with infringements of these rights in 1984. Good faith at the top of an organization did not mean that some employee within a firm would not try to steal information concerning software.

Therefore, firms became cautious concerning which customers they would license. They preferred to deal with firms on the basis of personal trust. They relied on their abilities to innovate generation after generation of improved technology to keep them ahead of blatant thieves. They retained design control of crucial components and prohibited licensees from making certain kinds of changes in their products without explicit permission (which they frequently withheld). Consequently, pirated knowledge became increasingly obsolete as firms introduced enhancements of their original technology. Above all, managers emphasized that they did not deal with potential partners when they felt uncomfortable with them because so much of their joint venture's success depended on activities that could not be covered adequately by legal documents.

Joint-venture contracts often specified that if the partnership was ended, the surviving partner (the one that purchased its partner's interest) retained rights to use its partner's technology on a royalty basis if it was not the owner of the technology. Ownership was a nettlesome problem because all of the child's technology originally came from its parents. Parents differed in how they controlled technology developed within their child. Many firms let their child be the royalty-collecting intermediary when partners wanted permission to license technology that may have been contributed by another parent. Other firms prohibited any ownership of technology by their child. Some parents insisted only on a licensing right-of-first-access for technology developed by their child and allowed their child to license technology to others, as well. Other parents did not allow their child to license its knowledge to outsiders.

Licensing and Control of Technology

Licensing strategies used to promulgate a technological standard (like the Ethernet standard for connecting business machines or the Interpress standard for exchanges among document-creation devices, like personal computers and electronic printers) required inventing firms to (1) license all applications and to (2) find partners (like Intel and Digital Equipment) to endorse these standards in their technical specifications. Royalties were usually minimal for standard-setting licenses because firms were encouraging others to use their designs. By contrast, licensing strategies to exploit patents were usually on an exclusive or narrowly shared basis because the firms that took licenses sought competitive advantages over others.

Licensing was rarely more attractive than a joint venture as a means of *acquiring knowledge,* unless, by granting a license, firms gained access to another license that they desired. Except in unique cases, like the pharmaceuticals industry (sketched below), simple licensing fees offered lower returns than taking a piece of the action in a joint venture. Licenses enabled entrepreneurial firms and inventors to receive advances against royalties with no risk participation, but joint ventures could teach fledgling firms how to exploit a technology, enter a new market, or learn how to market their discoveries appropriately.

Often pharmaceutical firms were not motivated to enter joint ventures if their products were good because the economics of licensing *their* products were superior to those of joint ventures. Royalties ran in a range between 7 percent and 12 percent for a mere granting of rights; some royalties were as low as 1 percent (or as high as 15 percent for a new chemical entity in a significant pharmaceutical therapeutic area that could exploit first-mover advantages). Similarly, when a non-U.S. company licensed a product to a U.S. partner under that scenario, an 8 percent to 12 percent profit went right to the licensors' bottom line with no risk and no investment if it chose the right licensees.

The top end of the royalty scale made the licensing option more attractive than a joint-venture arrangement *for exploiting assets* for all except the most spectacular products. If a product were in that category, its inventor would recover higher returns with a joint venture than a license. First-mover advantages were very important in the ethical pharmaceutical industry, and the first new drug in a therapeutic category to hurdle the Federal Drug Administration (FDA) barriers captured the largest market share, regardless of where it was invented. (Sales forces did not suffer as severely from the not-invented-here (NIH) syndrome that discouraged scientists from championing outsiders' products enthusiastically. They sold anything in their line that paid well.) Therefore, if the new product was efficacious (and the first of its kind), it received more attention than "me-too" products. Unless the U.S. partner was shepherding a direct competitor product through the regulatory maze in ethical pharmaceuticals, it was often interested in expanding its product line with a license from outsiders. Even 15 percent licensing royalties on pharmaceutical products left adequate margins for firms that bore toxicological and other testing costs to make their venture economic.

Technology, market knowledge, and other sensitive information transferred to joint ventures was frequently protected from unauthorized exposure to partners that could become competitors (or to unauthorized parties) by confidentiality agreements and explicit, formal agreements signed at very senior levels within partners' organizations. Some managers were skeptical concerning their lawyers' abilities to prevent bleedthrough from occurring, however, especially within the electronics industry, where patents were virtually useless.

Technological Bleedthrough

Bleedthrough was knowledge (not covered by formal agreements) that was gained by working with partners on joint ventures. Some firms formed joint ventures to gain knowledge, skills, and technology, and they hoped to transmit this knowledge back to their parent organizations. It was difficult to avoid knowledge bleedthrough when a joint venture composed of personnel from different research laboratories came together. Successful firms—which knew how to exploit *positive bleedthrough*—had developed a science for engineering arrangements between the parent and the child in their day-to-day communications and in everything else. This was done to ensure that knowledge was returned to the parent. It was necessary for managers to design this bleedthrough process carefully, since knowledge of joint ventures' work methods, managerial practices, and technologies was not accepted readily by firms' in-house research organizations.

When parents' scientists worked together in a joint venture to develop products for the U.S. marketplace, partners frequently devoted space to parallel research experiments in their wholly owned laboratories to learn more about their partner's technological approaches. Sometimes, they even moved scientists and other technical people through the joint venture and back to their wholly owned laboratories to disseminate information. Doing so was consistent with the principles of science—results from experiments had to be replicable—and sometimes yielded the additional bonus of new insights obtained from scientists that tried to extend their partners' approaches. As long as intellectual property rights were not abused, partners were not very much concerned by such practices.

Special care was given to designing management systems for the special tensions of joint ventures formed with partners that would otherwise be the firm's competitors. For example, the organizational configuration and management systems that a parent firm might prefer to use within its child may have provided too much information about how the firm looked at markets and competition that it would not want to pass through to partners. Accordingly, firms often designed management systems that gathered information for in-house laboratories and selling organizations but did not allow much information to flow back to their children.

Many managers noted that they did not explicitly consider how to manage positive technological bleedthrough, but there were many informal ways that information could be collected for that purpose. For example, one electronics firm formed a vertical agreement with a semiconductor house for the purpose of keeping up to date on state-of-the-art developments in chip-making technology. In exchange for this information, the electronics firm used the semiconductor firm as a second-source vendor on its products.

Some firms concluded that any knowledge developed in their child was usable by all partners. Their position permitted partners to pool ideas and information without the need for the many protective mechanisms that ordinarily impeded collegiality. Many firms expected their joint venture to receive a monthly entourage of visitors from its parents; they also sent research teams to study their child's procedures and progress regularly. In this manner, firms reduced the tensions caused by technology bleedthrough by discussing the problem openly with their partners and recognizing that collegiality was a two-way street.

Managers with several joint ventures to their credit also concluded that some partners will do almost anything to learn if they want information badly enough. Recognizing this, managers initiated discussions with partners on these points and negotiated training fees as compensation where they were taking partners' personnel on sales calls or teaching them other skills that were highly appropriable.

Finally, when all else failed, concerns about the bleedthrough of shared information to unauthorized third parties motivated firms to segregate their research operations and to exchange information between them carefully. Firms protected information from getting into the hands of potential competitors (which also had joint ventures with their partners) by keeping their child physically removed from contact with other parts of the parent and by ensuring that proprietary information was not disseminated easily through the parent organization to the child. Such precautions required tight legal definitions of what technology was licensed to the child and of how information developed by the child was returned to its parents. (It also discouraged the creation of synergies.) Such procedures were necessary—tedious as they were to implement—because if firms could not define their technology tightly, they lacked a proper basis for joint ventures. Managers discouraged firms from forming technology agreements without such precautions unless they wanted to encourage their technology to be disseminated to the rest of their industry.

Transferring Knowledge

One of the side benefits of working together in joint ventures was the cross-pollination process whereby ideas were shared among research, manufacturing, or marketing personnel and transferred to parents' organizations. If firms tried consciously to do so, it was almost always possible to learn something useful from partners when facilities could be shared. (Such suggestions were heretical to some U.S. firms because they already believed that outsiders' ideas were inferior or because they already had filed patents on these ideas but never thought to apply them.)

Concerns regarding negative technological bleedthrough were often unfounded where partners had not learned to cope with the not-invented-here syndrome. As one manager noted, bleedthrough was not a problem because its partner's scientists were too jealous to recognize when knowledge should have been shared with its parent's laboratories.

One of the problems with technology transfer was that nobody wanted to let anything go, yet some knowledge or assets had to be traded in order to transfer technology. Solving this problem required that firms assess the value of partners' contributions. Scientists and engineers complained that partners' technology was rarely as good as either side said it was and raised other objections concerning why ventures would not work.

Experienced managers put scientists, engineers, and plant managers on their negotiating teams, as well as their operating teams. They took an open position regarding their desire to acquire technology and manufacturing know-how and wrote strong technological protection contracts to protect the intellectual property rights of all partners. Finally, they formed joint ventures in an incremental approach that permitted them to see the technology and test it for a right-of-first refusal fee before they formed arrangements that committed them more deeply. If partners' products or processes proved to be as good as had been represented, experienced managers ensured that knowledge flowed back to their wholly owned divisions through a variety of management systems and integrating mechanisms.

Not-Invented-Here Syndrome and Parallel Facilities

Rapid technological change and customer diversity forced firms in the electronics, pharmaceutical, factory automation, office equipment, communications, and financial services industries to be polygamous. Competition required them to form a spider's web of cooperative agreements—often of short durations. But implementing such strategies was difficult until firms had worked through how to accept outsiders' products as readily as they accepted their own inventions. Managers cited their firms' not-invented-here problems as being a major impediment to making timely responses to competitive pressures. Many managers cited IBM's success in launching its Personal Computer—which was assembled by IBM using parts made primarily by outsiders (not as a joint venture)—as an example of how their firms would have to adapt to technological changes in the future, including learning to accept innovations pioneered by joint ventures as if they were in-house products.

Jealousies between partners—as well as between parent and child—based on the NIH syndrome resulted in firms' performing some suboptimal activities.

For example, one child had to develop its own sales force and cultivate its own customer contacts because it could not get its products to commercialization through *either* of its parent's laboratories. In both cases, the child's products had created conflict of interest problems because they competed with parents' wholly owned products.

Foreign partners found joint ventures with U.S. firms to be frustrating because their products were orphaned by the child's technical personnel. Their products did not receive proper attention from the child's engineering staff or were dismissed as being too difficult to adapt to U.S. customer tastes. U.S. firms reported similar complaints when working with European partners overseas, especially if the U.S. firm held many patents in an area but had not been able to commercialize its products successfully. (Sometimes the foreign partner's concerns about NIH inertia barriers were unfounded, but in at least one major firm top management declined to be involved in any more joint ventures that committed their firm to bringing another company's products into their internal portfolio of products.)

The principal alternative to rewarding engineers and scientists for accepting technology across business unit—or parent–child boundaries—was to build duplicate facilities to permit each group to create its own products. Few managers viewed that alternative to the NIH problem as an attractive solution. In many cases, firms could not afford to duplicate research facilities in several sites. Even when firms erected small pilot plants, they encountered difficulties in persuading their research groups to accept its results if they had not performed the tests themselves or blessed them beforehand. For example, by the 1980s many local governments required multinational firms that developed products overseas to form joint ventures to establish local research activities (because the highest value-added margins were frequently given to R&D activities that yielded patentable products). Such investments duplicated existing facilities, and their scope had to be small since they were not cost-justified. Managers with experience in these facilities reported that the fragmented research units were not as productive as a large, centralized research laboratory and that their products were not as well accepted as those developed by in-house units.

Many managers were wrestling with the NIH problem in 1984—both within their firms and across joint-venture boundaries. Managers combatted the NIH problem by giving business units—including their joint ventures—missions to develop products for a particular specification or application and prohibiting other business units within the firm from duplicating that research mission. Products were shared across the firm, and business units were required to accept each other's components under the umbrella of strategic missions.

Other firms required partners to maintain duplicate facilities to replicate research findings and verify their child's information; alternatively, some firms solved the NIH problem by transferring *all* of their research facilities to the child and by requiring their business units to use the child as their research arm. Incentive programs were created in some firms to reward *both* the technical personnel that caused information, patents, and products to flow from one division (or child) to another and the receiving division (or child).

To combat NIH, technical personnel, which had been permitted to disapprove proposals for cooperative arrangements in the past, were being disabused of their long-held opinions that their laboratories (and internally developed technology) were always the best. Top management intervened in the process to review rejected proposals for joint ventures and asked second teams to study the most promising partnerships again. By elevating such questions to the corporate level within firms where top executives also possessed technical skills—and by giving these issues corporate attentions—managers attempted to overcome organizational tendencies to reject outsiders' ideas without careful study.

Knowledge Repatriation and Management Systems

Highly diversified firms tried to ensure that knowledge gained through exposure to partners within joint ventures was diffused back to parent laboratories through meticulous programs of repatriation. At the group level, for example, firms held annual technical meetings where engineering managers and leading R&D scientists gathered divisional engineering and R&D personnel for an interchange of information and ideas. Projects were coordinated through divisional reports concerning who was doing what in technology with which partner.

At the corporate level, highly diversified firms appointed officers—such as vice presidents in charge of technology—to track major technological changes beyond the corporate sphere of activity and track which potential partners were working in those areas of science. Top technical officers also coordinated transfers of technology that was created within the company where it might be useful in a joint venture with other divisions or with outsiders, as well as technology that was received from others—through licenses or joint ventures—that might be useful in some other part of the company. Managers confessed that their attempts to control and coordinate flows of technical information within highly diversified firms were, as yet, imperfect because top technical officers sometimes discovered that in-house technical efforts—or technological joint ventures—that other divisions could have benefited from had existed inside the firm for years without their knowledge. Corporate technical offices were frequently unaware of bootstrapped technical projects, especially where divisions possessed the authority to enter joint ventures and other cooperative agreements without involving their corporate legal staff.

Managers repatriated knowledge from their joint ventures to the mother corporation, and between business units of the same corporation, using matrix organizations, integrated sales forces, and internal cross-usage agreements. An integrated sales force and marketing organization sold products from *all* divisions—regardless of the ownership of their originator—to a particular customer. For example, all products intended for consumption by the paper industry would be sold through a sales force with experience in serving paper mills, and the cost of selling was shared by client business units (including joint ventures) that used this service. (Parallel sales forces were prohibited.) Internal cross-use agreements permitted firms to apply knowledge developed for one application to all other markets where it possessed strengths.

Managers confessed that it was difficult but necessary to repatriate technical personnel if the joint venture failed to retain the knowledge that had been created. This process was more painful for the engineers than for parent firms because they had become accustomed to making their own decisions, running interesting projects, and enjoying more autonomy than their parent firm could tolerate. This problem is developed further in chapter 15.

Personnel Rotation and Collegiality

Information was shared by creating fellowship among technical personnel. Firms tried to transfer knowledge by rotating personnel between their joint ventures and wholly owned laboratories. Returning scientists and engineers presented seminars to their colleagues to share research findings or to explain the new approaches taken by the research team in the child's laboratories, for example.

When firms purchased technology, they sent a platoon of engineers and scientists through plants using the patents, machinery, and other assets they were buying to learn how to use it. Personnel rotations became increasingly commonplace as, for example, technical personnel lived at partners' plants for a month, then returned to parents' plants for a month, then returned to partners' plants for another month, and so on. Because there were many ways that technical personnel transferred information, partners' employees were encouraged to develop relationships of collegiality, and joint-venture team members were chosen for their abilities to work together. Partners had to be indefatigable in their quest to understand everything possible about a technological approach—both to make it work and to pass it on within their parent firm. (For this latter objective, technical personnel with communication skills were chosen for joint-venture team membership.)

Creativity was encouraged by the intellectual curiosity of the collegial process. It was healthy for partners to provoke discussions concerning how product designs, management procedures, and plant set-ups could be changed in joint ventures, even if doing so irritated partners for a time, because managers found that they reconsidered their points after the argument and gained new insights about their problems. In academia, collegial (and uninhibited) professors sometimes argued ideas for hours and covered blackboards (and themselves) with chalk before they had pushed through a problem to their satisfaction. If the child's research team could achieve that level of comfort and collegiality in working together, a productive research joint venture was feasible. In many cases, however, R&D joint ventures were not successful ways to develop knowledge, especially not on a long-term basis, because parents preferred to control the research activity in-house.

In one collaboration, partners exchanged engineers for a short, on-site development effort that was followed by extensive consultation by telephone and computer links. One partner possessed design strengths; it supplied creative genius—the type of "mad artists" that invented ideal ways to solve technological problems. The other partner supplied pragmatic engineers who sorted through the pros and cons of the artists' dreams to select projects appropriate for commercialization. The engineering team modified and finished the artists' designs, made plans for automated factory assembly, and installed the manufacturing systems in both partners' plants. The collaboration was satisfactory until the artistic partner's viability was threatened by substantial losses in its main line of business.

Some firms were more interested in advancing knowledge than in obtaining a quid pro quo when they showed their technological files to partners. They tended to be very open in sharing information to encourage a similar openness among partners. In this manner, they hoped to enhance their child's creativity and success rate. Joint-venture partners candidly admitted that they used personnel rotation as a means of transferring technology to parent organizations. Moreover, they asserted that they picked the brains of the partners' personnel as they were rotated through the child and expected that their partners would be as meticulous in exploiting the knowledge of their technical personnel. They sent their very best technical personnel to the joint venture—on the theory that to make it work, they should hold back nothing.

This ease in sharing personnel stood in marked contrast with that of some partners. Japanese managers and engineers, for example, allegedly had an inferiority complex about working for a child organization. Although U.S. managers asserted that money cured that malady, many firms treated their joint ventures like stepchildren, and they pulled their best technical personnel out of the child when it was time to spin it off or sell their interest in it to partners. In fact, many parent firms "loaned" their best technological personnel to joint ventures. Although their salaries were paid by the child during their tenure there, the revolving door back to the parent firm was open, and personnel retained their benefits in parent company personnel programs. Despite findings that suggested it was necessary to close the revolving door and make the management team (as well as the research team) employees of the child with an interest in improving the child's well-being, many firms used personnel rotation as a way to transmit knowledge back to parent research facilities. (This point is developed further in chapter 15.)

Spider's Webs versus Exclusive Partnership Relationships

Some firms required exclusivity when they entered joint ventures in areas that were of high strategic importance to them, like Xerox in xerography. Other firms preferred exclusivity because they wanted to keep the management of their joint activities simple, preferring one joint venture per product or concept basis. (Such firms did not rule out the possibility that they would create second-generation joint ventures with the *same partners* for new projects that had not been perceived when the first joint venture was formed.)

Firms created a spider's web of agreements with themselves at the hub when they examined several technological approaches simultaneously with different partners. Spider's webs of agreements were becoming increasingly necessary by 1984, and firms created cooperative strategies with many different firms (which were sometimes partners of each other in other joint ventures) to exploit diverse therapeutic areas of product applications, different markets, or even various geographic territories. In genetic engineering, established firms created a spider's web of joint arrangements with small research firms—by therapeutic area to gain a "first look" at technology or by right-of-first-refusal to use their partners' research findings. The small genetic engineering firms, in turn, each formed a spider's web of alliances to gain financing and potential customers for their particular technology. (Small genetic engineering firms also wanted to form a spider's web of joint ventures with established pharmaceutical houses and chemical firms to impress the capital markets and venture capitalists. Listing major multinational firms with strong in-house research facilities as their partners somehow made smaller firms' financial reports look stronger.)

If the gestation period needed to move a product from the workbench through development and pilot plant testing to the marketplace was a long time, longer duration relationships were more acceptable than where a technology's half-life rarely exceeded eighteen months. Where technology changed rapidly, firms moved on from partner to partner, and sometimes formed a spider's web of parallel arrangements to test several technological alternatives and approaches simultaneously.

Some market opportunities were so transitory that firms formed many joint ventures (with many partners) quickly in order to snatch a portion of the market. In cable television, for example, spider's webs of joint ventures proliferated because they were one means for competitors to enter more regional markets and share the high capital costs of doing so. The technological risks of entering the communications services industry were tremendous, which might explain why spider's webs of joint ventures were used by so many players to enter that market. The window of opportunity in communications equipment—especially private branch exchange (PBX) systems—would not open until firms had created technological standards to reassure their customers against obsolescence. Spider's webs of technical standards agreements were necessary in the PBX market to launch firms' products.

Other market opportunities were transitory because they were projects with predefined sunsets, such as military defense contracts, for example. For such markets, firms formed teams until a project was over. Then relationships were dissolved normally. Firms formed partnerships for one project with companies that were competitors for another contract. Because subcontracting was commonplace in defense contracts, other members of the industry served as suppliers to a prime contractor for a particular project while they competed aggressively on opposing teams for other contracts.

As technologies changed with increasing speed, one of the difficulties that firms encountered in negotiating rights to use other firms' technologies was their desire for exclusive use of patents or other technology. Partners frequently reserved the right to sell products using their technology themselves in firms' home markets. Initially U.S. firms balked on this point because they had wanted total control and exclusivity. But as this request was made more frequently, and as U.S. firms lost more licensing deals to smaller, more accommodating competitors, they became more pragmatic concerning their demands for exclusive rights. They developed a cost–benefit argument that evaluated (1) the likelihood that a licensor would enter the U.S. market later in its own right, (2) how much market share the firm expected to lose to such late entrants, and (3) how much benefit was gained by exploiting the license now. To their surprise, some managers concluded that their firm could concede the question of marketing rights for the patent-holder and sell consulting services to the licensor later to help it to formulate products to suit U.S. tastes without harm. Firms even prospered in some cases by letting them seek new marketing agents when licensors overestimated their products' market potential. Such changes were grounds to renegotiate their arrangements—on better terms—when partners returned sheepishly after their own marketing analyses.

Firms learned with experience that exclusive agreements with sluggish partners tied their hands from being able to respond to rapidly changing competitive conditions. With hindsight, managers suggested that it was sometimes wiser to *break* an exclusive agreement and pay their legal costs rather than stand by helplessly while competitors captured their market share.

If firms understood what their true competitive advantage was, they were in a better position to recognize when granting an exclusive relationship (or accepting one) was better for them than associating with several firms that competed with each other. In one successful partnership, a take-or-pay contract to buy components was given to a partner that was especially strong in making certain components in exchange for an exclusive relationship with it to build turnkey equipment. Later, the partner decided it wanted to build machines on its own and paid the firm to learn how to do so. The partner's renegotiations came at a time when other competitors were entering the machinery market and machinery margins were failing. The firm had been building machines originally as a way of selling its components and elements (which used proprietary knowledge and were difficult to make). It was delighted to release its partner in exchange for another take-or-pay contract covering its elements as well as its components.

In summary, joint ventures that created children were not the only forms of cooperative activity firms used to cope with technological problems. Many types of joint activity of varying durations were used to leapfrog technologies, to increase value-added margins, and to keep abreast of state-of-the-art developments in their fields.

Managers recognized that bleedthrough problems were created by pooling information, but they regarded this phenomenon as being more helpful to collegiality than harmful for its damage to competitive advantage. Indeed, managers found more problems in *encouraging* bleedthrough than in discouraging it. For them, joint ventures were a particularly vexing way to adapt to technological changes where in-house personnel harbored not-invented-here biases against the child's innovations. Where NIH was a problem, firms found it easier to transfer knowledge by using in-house facilities in loosely formed joint research efforts, rather than by forming a child that might be horizontally related to the parent organization.

15
Summary: Guidelines for Forming and Managing Joint Ventures

Competitive stakes increased in the 1980s as U.S. firms tried to assimilate information-processing, telecommunications, and other competitive skills. No firm could hope to develop the many technologies they needed in-house; they could not afford to fund all of the projects needed to remain competitive on several fronts. Well-structured joint ventures offered them one way to supplement the shortfalls even large companies faced in coping with these challenges. Accordingly, findings concerning how firms managed cooperative strategies should be of interest to managers for the insights they offer concerning joint-venture success.

This chapter reflects managers' observations (gathered from field interviews) concerning their experiences in structuring and operating joint ventures. There seems to be an experience curve in using joint ventures in the sense that the more managers understood what worked in joint-venture strategies, the more they wanted to replicate their successes. Some managers—representing both parent and child viewpoints—were unabashedly pleased with their arrangements. Moreover, those partners *and their children* often concurred, when interviewed separately, in identifying how firms might alleviate the stumbling blocks that accompany cooperative strategies.

This chapter also reflects other managers' suggestions concerning what *not* to do when forming and running such ventures. It reflects their experiences in suggesting how joint ventures can go awry.

Finding Partners

Successful firms were inundated with proposals to form joint ventures in the 1980s. But they often preferred to find their own projects and to dance with partners of their own choosing. Sometimes firms were successful in getting the partners of their first choice, but they did not always get their selection of allies. Firms' expectations and attitudes concerning their partners determined whether they believed they had entered a shotgun wedding or allied with a prince. If managers wanted the venture to succeed badly enough, they found a way to agree on their child's activities. They made the venture work.

Successful and experienced firms preferred to work with experienced partners. The ideal objective in choosing a joint-venture partner was to offset the firm's strengths. Accordingly, attractive partners offered market access, experience, or technology in addition to cash. Although it was often easier to find silent partners that put up only cash, experienced managers welcomed the stimulation of partners' questions in risky ventures. Nobody possessed all of the knowledge, managers noted. (Exceptions were found where firms clearly wanted to operate the venture and were looking for a "sugar daddy." These ventures were usually of limited durations because such partnerships became a drag on management creativity.) Adverse reputations also influenced partner selections. Desirable partners had established track records concerning their abilities to work together with partners.

Find a Way to Agree

If a joint venture was a good idea, it would not seem that partners needed to be coaxed into an alliance. Managers' experiences suggest that selling *was* necessary, however, to overcome partners' fears and objections concerning this strategy option. For example, a successful joint venture that lasted over ten years almost did not happen. The target partner had rejected the proposal, but the leading partner's chairman called his counterpart and suggested that there must be a way to make the alliance work. Staff rejected the idea, but the top executives sat down to explore what could make the venture work. Adopting the attitude that the market opportunity sounded too good to reject, they persuaded their operating managers that no problems were too great to overcome. The agreement was very different by the time it had been worked through the two organizations from the original plan, but the deal was eventually done with great enthusiasm on both sides.

Asymmetries among partners were both a strength and a weakness in joint ventures. Resource differences could give partners strengths when they combined. But differences in management styles and outlooks were disruptive. Individuals with hidden agendas, in particular, made some joint ventures fail. The structure of the agreement, the distribution of ownership shares and board composition were less likely to trip up a child than were individuals who did not disclose their lack of commitment to the venture (or other hidden axes they wished to grind). Many executives commented that joint ventures were a marriage where compatible partners were needed and that running joint ventures where partners did not value the child as being of equal importance was difficult.

Having experience with previous joint ventures made firms more formidable when negotiating deals with naive firms because the experienced managers understood what joint ventures could (and could not) do better. Joint-venture experience made managers more relaxed in supervising joint-venture children, too. The more relaxed partners became about the idea of doing joint ventures, the more willing they were for a little give and take to occur in their efforts to hammer out a satisfactory joint-venture compromise.

Shotgun Wedding

The enthusiasm of top managers caused joint ventures to be formed, but the enthusiasm of operating managers made joint ventures work. Operating managers were not universally enthusiastic about them. Some experienced managers remained uncomfortable about joint ventures even after running several of them. They used joint ventures *only* where they saw no other way to attain their firms' objectives. Characterizing joint ventures as "shotgun marriages" that they entered without enthusiasm, these managers viewed joint ventures as unholy alliances with partners that would never be their first choices for business associates. In retrospect, they suggested that a match had been made poorly because their negotiating teams had devoted too much attention to questions of who would control technology produced by their child and what the financial arrangements would be. Too little attention had been devoted to questions of *how their relationships would be managed.* The child's managers could not roll up their sleeves and find a way to get the job done because their authority and positions within their respective parent firms had been poorly defined.

This finding is not offered to suggest that attention should not be directed also to details concerning financial arrangements, technology transfer, or other issues concerning assets. It suggests that firms that were fat, dumb, and happy made poor partners because they were not hungry enough to think through operating details. Such joint ventures were troublesome to manage because partners lacked the strong authority and incentives needed to make them succeed.

When managers were just thrown together without the advance opportunity to work out details concerning how their firms' respective cultures would mesh, they were especially likely to feel that their hands had been forced. Frequently partners became frustrated by what they perceived as a lack of aggressiveness in their partners. Moreover, since corporate memories were often short and managers moved on to other assignments, partners sometimes lost sight of their original objectives in forming the joint venture— particularly where the child's activities required years of subsidization before it could stand on its own. Poor performance always exacerbated tensions between partners and increased managers' frustrations with their counterparts.

But when partners were upset with each other, they rarely confronted their differing expectations. Instead, they criticized *the child's managers.* They balked in making additional investments or quibbled about how the child should make a decision. Sometimes they took over the reins of management. In brief, managers in charge of joint ventures suffered because parents drew the child closer when they were upset, thereby robbing managers of the autonomy and flexibility needed to compete effectively.

Someday a Prince Will Come

Partners' expectations were sometimes unrealistic. They wanted a prince and would not settle for partners that looked like frogs. Rather than discuss a joint venture with available (and eager) partners, some firms held out for the ideal mate. They did not recognize that leading firms needed joint ventures *less* than followers did.

One successful firm with several joint ventures to its credit took a very deliberate approach toward the formation of its joint ventures. It identified the need for a partnership. It developed a list of potential partners and screened them. It approached *several* dancing partners simultaneously to discuss the venture and decide which of them would be the best partner for the venture in question. They had a long engagement period where managers on both sides moved slowly to a consensus concerning how to operate their child. When the marriage was finally consummated, the child received everything needed to run as a stand-alone entity. Subsequent intervention by parents in their child's operating decisions was minimal because the resulting management team closely reflected the values of its parents. (This approach would not work as well in a highly changeable environment or in situations where competitive advantages must be exploited quickly.)

Even in joint ventures that shared facilities with one parent, the search pattern among successful firms was a careful one. For example, firms often proceeded methodically to search the globe for the best possible partners. First, they interviewed the customers they hoped their joint venture would serve. Then they interviewed research institutes and any other experts with knowledge concerning where the technologies they sought might be observed or obtained. Finally, when managers finally found the technology and chose their target firms, they learned enough of the potential partners' languages to converse with top executives (if their potential partners did not speak English) and courted these partners by offering them access to the U.S. market.

Some frogs turned into princes later, especially when child managers from each parent firm were allowed to learn how to work together. One successful joint venture exploited the pressures the child's managers felt from their respective parents to form great camaraderie *within the child*. When the child matured, it created some difficulties at headquarters (because the child's management team had become so successful in working together that they outperformed jealous wholly owned units). After the child's success had buoyed its parents through hard times in their respective industries, the child's management team finally won respect as the prince it really was.

Managers were rewarded for using their intuitive skills. If they were uncomfortable with potential partners' managers during the negotiation period, they did not consummate an agreement. They justified this rule by noting that because so much must be done within a joint venture on faith and good feelings, that parents should give priority to the abilities of the operating managers to cooperate and to the good feelings those managers generated in them. After all, one manager counseled, "Staff is not running this business; I am."

Operating managers also suggested to their parents that the best way to make a successful joint venture was to choose skilled managers, trust them on operating decisions, and focus on the common interest that brought partners together in dealings with the other firms. Firms must learn to make the best of their alliances, managers suggested. Advance the common interest, stop worrying about what might have been, and if parents are worried about whether partners bring more to the party than the firm does, develop a means for readjusting partners' interests as conditions change.

Silent Partners

The best partners were horizontally related to each other and understood the business activities of their child. Partners that contributed only cash and could not act as operators became a source of irritation as some joint ventures proceeded. Schisms occurred because if a passive partner's managers did not understand a business activity, doubt existed in their minds concerning whether they had been told the truth by their partners' managers, especially when they did not like the results of those facts. If the joint venture was in trouble, such managers were more likely to think that the true condition of the business could not possibly be as bad as it was represented to be by partners' managers.

If the venture thrived, the child's managers began to look on the passive or unknowledgeable parent as a drag on their efforts because, although passive firms might have been "silent" with respect to their partners, they often asked detailed questions of their child. In the worst case, the active partner and the child (which was often managed by the active partner's personnel) came to resent sharing the fruits of their successful labors with firms that had been little more than bankers or venture capitalists. Even if the passive partner insisted on being actively involved in decision making, managers from active partners did not consult the ineffective managers from the passive partner regularly in some cases. Active partners even began to think they need not bother explaining facts to managers who did not know what they were talking about (or who challenged everything they said). Eventually a schism developed between the "insiders" and the "outsiders" unless the outside partners' managers found a way to become insiders themselves without being a drag on their partners. A program of educating these managers (and of supplementing industry knowledge within the rest of the outsiders' organizations) was needed to make partners' outlooks more homogeneous.

One Step at a Time

Cautious managers suggested that a step-by-step relationship was prudent when forming a joint venture with new partners. They suggested giving potential partners a proposal and some issues to study. If the partner came back with suggestions and could negotiate on the critical points of the venture, a small project was warranted. If that worked out, another joint venture was formed.

Firms that believed in long engagement periods or trial marriages formed study teams composed of managers from each partner. The managers on these teams then suggested how the child—representing the combined assets of its parents—should change its sourcing arrangements, its resource deployments, and the mix of products made at each plant, among other details. The management team also suggested whether some plants should be closed as they worked through the most economical way to run the new child. (Their objective was to bring down the cost of operations significantly. Valuation questions were left to the negotiators.) No joint venture was formed (1) if the management team could not develop a useful set of suggestions concerning how to rationalize the two companies' capacities or (2) if the management team (which was, in fact, understudying for the role of managing the child) could not work together.

Managers that took a cautious approach—a little project, then another one if the first experience was a good one—seemed to be more satisfied with the use of joint ventures than those that moved too fast or not carefully enough in forming alliances. The incremental approach enabled managers to keep adding to the complexity (or breadth) of things that they trusted a partner to do, on the basis of their previous experiences together. The incremental approach kept their expectations for a particular partner lower and enabled managers to be more analytical in assessing why a particular venture did not work out. (In this manner, firms did not have to give up hope of working with a particular partner if one venture floundered due to uncontrollable factors—such as product obsolescence, rabid competitors, or economic recession—that had made it more costly than expected.)

It was important to be ready for a successful child. Managers suggested that funding must be provided to exploit opportunities that developed for their joint venture. If parents could not provide the cash when it was needed for new opportunities, they had to be prepared to let their child approach the capital markets in its own right to obtain funding.

Many Dancing Partners

Success within some industries required partners to be promiscuous. It was advantageous for them to take several partners in a spider's web of cooperative strategies in these settings. For example, liaisons among military contractors (and subcontractors) demonstrated political expediency. One day firms competed neck and neck on one project; the next day they were on the same team for a different project. When firms had to move quickly to exploit a transitory advantage, partners were selected for their ability to offer attractive solutions to particular customer problems. Few stand-alone children resulted from these marriages, and like the musical-chairs pairings of the electronic components industry, no firm was expected to solve all of its problems alone.

Joint ventures were just another contractual form, as far as the motion picture firms were concerned. Joint ventures were not individually large deals for them, and they permitted firms to lock up talent for the duration of a project while allowing competitors to have similar alliances with their partners for other projects.

A willingness to dance for a short time with several partners allowed firms to move faster in responding to changes in market demands than exclusive arrangements of longer durations did. Part of their flexibility in using a spider's web of agreements arose from the informality of these alliances. (When firms were accustomed to forming coalitions in this manner, they were also frequently adept at internal venturing arrangements.) But dissimilarities in the ease with which firms made joint ventures and reached decisions when operating within them was sometimes an irritation in partnership relationships. It was unwise to use loose arrangements in businesses where intellectual property rights were poorly protected or where the child's activity would be closely meshed with the assets of its parents.

Loose alliances—personal service contracts, OEM vendor agreements, or other arm's-length arrangements—were preferred by managers when dealing with highly dissimilar partners, entrepreneurs, and other situations where managers felt uncomfortable about forming joint ventures. An example of where this approach was preferred included many types of creative people who wanted an equity participation in their creations but did not want a salary or to be part of a corporate monolith. Astute managers suggested that large firms should help such entrepreneurs to incorporate and deal with them on a contractual basis. Some managers went so far as to suggest that joint ventures were a bad idea when the partners were trying to achieve incompatible objectives. Their comments reflected the difficulties they envisioned in overcoming the exit barriers associated with joint-venture agreements. The multiple–partner projects approach was also suggested when jointly developed products would be sold to one partner's competitors. Expressing motivations like those that caused Exxon and General Motors to form Ethyl Corp., several managers suggested that vertically integrated customers would be reluctant to purchase products that were too closely associated with their rivals. (This fear was analogous to the problem faced in oil well drilling when no partner would buy drilling services from a firm that was too closely allied to an oil exploration firm, to avoid revealing the location of good oil prospects to rivals.)

Whose Turn Is It to Lead?

Successful joint ventures enabled partners to see each other's viewpoints. Sometimes, offsetting joint ventures were formed in which partners took turns being the operator. In the Alaska Pipeline agreement, for example, partners' ownership percentages were readjusted to reflect the percentages of crude oil they shipped as customers. In this manner partners balanced the perspectives of buyer and seller in making decisions.

Many managers cautioned that their joint venture died when managers started thinking about how they could shortchange their partner. (Many announced joint ventures fell through because potential partners could never see each other's needs in the second round of bargaining.) The name of the game was cooperation, one manager suggested, not rape.

Ventures with Entrepreneurs

Joint ventures between large and small firms (or entrepreneurs) posed difficulties because of their differences in evaluating each firm's contributions. Joint ventures were necessary because if firms tried to acquire small firms' interests in products or devices, they found that inventors wanted outrageous sums of money.

Inventors were, more often than not, overly optimistic concerning their product's success. Moreover, because inventors saw only the rosy side of things, they often wanted compensation for their discoveries based on the enormous market potential they were certain existed for their products. Inventors did not see the risk and expenses of launching their discovery that corporate partners would have to bear, expenses that could include more engineering and substantially more testing. In medical products, for example, there were regulatory uncertainties and toxic pitfalls that the inventor could not imagine that had to be hurdled before the concept became a practical device. A joint venture enabled an entrepreneur to share in the risks that its cautious partners envisioned in order to realize the higher rewards the entrepreneur anticipated. Moreover, offering an inventor a piece of the action was a way of hedging an investing firm's bets concerning the new technology without bursting the inventor's balloon. (The inventor's enthusiasm was needed to work out bugs when bringing some products to commercialization.)

Since entrepreneurs and inventors were more informal than corporate partners, the incremental approach to joint-venture formation worked well with them. A joint venture could initially proceed on the basis of a handshake and some inventors looking at a product. If their demonstrations projects were successful, a formal agreement could follow. But prudent managers realized there were limitations to what could be written into a contract to ensure joint-venture success. *Alliances failed because managers did not make them work, not because contracts were poorly written.*

Writing Contracts

When partners reached a meeting of minds, it was time to negotiate a contract. The most frequent answer explaining why announced joint ventures never went beyond the discussion stage was that ventures were sunk by lawyers. This explanation suggests that managers were homogeneous in their outlooks; lawyers were too adversarial. A more likely explanation for joint-venture deaths at the contract-writing stage was that partners did not think through their arrangements adequately before they reached the altar. The probing questions the lawyers asked exposed these shortfalls in partners' agreements, and the venture fell apart.

Joint ventures usually encompassed a particular technology or line of products. Lawyers were very good at spelling out the legal scope of joint ventures, but in doing so they often limited the life of the child to a particular undertaking. Although they were merely doing their jobs in renegotiating joint-venture agreements at the end of a project, lawyers often seemed to accentuate the fact that partners had grievances with each other. When lawyers convened to renegotiate joint ventures, they revealed areas of discontent within partners that had been borne without comment previously. By calling attention to inequities, lawyers made it more difficult for partners to agree to work together thereafter.

Lawyers preferred to write explicit agreements that specified performances for every contingency. In particular, they suggested that a divorce settlement be negotiated before the marriage was consummated. Many managers found the act of writing contracts unpleasant; they were *not* actively involved in contract negotiations, and they suggested that the only time they consulted their contracts was when their joint ventures failed. (Then they hoped that their lawyers had written a good divorce settlement for them.)

Prenuptial Agreements

Prenuptial agreements were necessary to record the intentions of the parties when the joint venture was formed. The major reason to write contracts as carefully as possible (and within legally accepted guidelines) was to capture the understandings that were so firmly in everyone's minds and so beautifully understood by everybody at the original negotiations. The managers that built joint ventures did not continue to run them as their careers progressed.

In order for a joint venture to succeed, partners had to agree on (1) their child's mission, (2) the markets it would serve, (3) the products it could offer, (4) the obligations of each partner in assisting their child, and (5) the process by which the venture would be dissolved when it had outlived its usefulness. More difficult to write were details concerning (6) how managers from diverse cultures would blend their parents' management styles to work together within the child. Contracts for (7) supplies and (8) purchasing relationships, (9) horizon points for reviewing their child's progress, and (10) renegotiation thresholds were often in the document that recorded the original meeting of minds.

Sometimes partners raced ahead in a joint venture with great euphoria. In their interest to get the project done, they formed a ragged agreement that they intended to amend and refine later. If they missed a key point in their agreements, managers confided, such haste often came back to haunt them.

Despite the temptation to forge ahead in a joint venture, great care had to be given to anticipating every possible change in partners' business relationships and to develop a means of handling any events negotiating teams could not foresee. As negotiating teams worked through this process (which could take from five months to three years), managers learned about their counterparts (assuming managers were a part of the negotiating team). With time, partners came to rely on the word of their partners in such situations, and a manager's word became the bond that contributed to some joint ventures's successes.

Thus, it was important to have not only talented lawyers but also experienced managers involved in joint-venture negotiations. Because the integrity of managers was important for the venture's success and because firms would undoubtedly have to "go to the well" several times in the future, the clever, dishonest, or devious manager would be recognized over time as one who "spits in the community well." Whatever was fair for one firm had to be fair for its partner, and firms that did not bargain for equitable treatment for all partners had less joint-venture success.

Protecting Property Rights

As chapter 14 noted, knowledge shared with the joint-venture child could be protected on paper through proprietary nondisclosure agreements. Knowledge could be protected by assigning partners' property rights to the joint venture (indeed, managers suggested that their children were even more aggressive in protecting their patents—even against infringements by parents—than they themselves might have been). But where technological bleedthrough was a recurring problem, managers offered few suggestions. Lawyers suggested that parents could license their child to use their knowledge or withhold the information altogether. The latter suggestion often defeated the purpose of cooperative venture strategies, however.

As was the case in any highly competitive industry, firms had to understand the nature of their competitive advantage when writing joint-venture contracts if they hoped to protect those advantages. In one service joint venture, astute lawyers inserted a clause that made key personnel of the child become employees of the surviving parent in the event of venture termination. Operating managers had not consciously set out to structure the deal in that manner (although it surely was a sensible provision to protect the value of the child's business interests because personnel were the principal assets of the business activity). In this case, the partner that wanted to sell its interest had contributed the services of its top producers without realizing that they stayed with the venture when the other firm acquired its interest. Thus, having a savvy lawyer write the contract paid off for the firm that had delegated this task, much to the chagrin of its partner (which had also delegated this task to its lawyers).

Demanding Fidelity

Managers agreed that it was unwise to restrict partners' activities in another field. (Lawyers advised that it was illegal.) That meant, for example, that a pharmaceutical joint venture making products for care of gastrointestinal problems would not want to restrict a parent from doing research in psychotherapeutics. The joint-venture partner would be a stronger parent to its child if it developed expertise in related fields, and the joint venture could benefit from its parent's suggestions concerning analogous approaches in its own sphere of responsibility.

With experience came a more relaxed position from managers on questions of exclusivity. One manager suggested that all the firm wanted from its partners was a telephone call to advise them when the relationship ceased to be an exclusive one. Recriminations were fruitless in his industry because technologies changed too rapidly. Penalties were too difficult to extract from unfaithful partners because patents were virtually worthless.

Divorce Settlements

Termination clauses were treated as very important by lawyers. In a typical agreement document, approximately 80 percent of the joint-venture agreement's content was devoted to questions of who would buy out whom, at what price, and who would act as source to whom after the venture terminated. The divorce settlement clauses also determined who would get which assets when the venture folded and what would happen to the people, to the trade secrets generated, to the patents generated, and to everything else associated with the child's activities.

Most joint ventures contained divorce settlements because lawyers became worried about parent firms' obligations during the joint-venture negotiation phase. Creditors (especially banks) also demanded divorce settlement clauses in joint-venture agreements in order to know what their rights would be when the venture went bad. The child's managers, by contrast, did not believe that divorce settlements needed to be specified in advance because nobody could foresee accurately what events might arise. They preferred to sail along, operating the joint venture and negotiating problems on a day-to-day basis with parents until the alliance broke down. (Successful joint ventures never reached deadlocks, apparently. Their managers always found a way to resolve conflicts among partners until parents mutually agreed that a change was needed because the child had achieved its original purpose.)

Some joint ventures did fail because (1) partners could not get along; (2) their markets disappeared; (3) managers within the child could not work together; (4) what was thought to be good technology from one partner (or whatever the contribution was to be) did not prove to be as good as was expected; (5) partners that were to contribute information could not get their personnel down the line to deliver what had been promised; or (6) partners simply reneged on their promises to deliver on their part of the agreement, among other reasons. Even good joint ventures endured for ten years at best in many cases because the necessity that spurred their creation could not survive forever in evolving competitive markets. In some ventures, management assignments within parent firms changed so dramatically that the new personnel could no longer recall the logic that had stimulated a joint venture's creation. For the new managers (who were not involved in the child's birth), maintaining the firm's relationship with its partners became a nuisance. Without the attentions of the managers that gave birth to joint ventures, interest in their well-being waned. If the child became ill after its godfather had moved on, the new generation of managers was more likely to terminate it than to nurture the child.

Paradoxically, joint ventures between large and little partners were most difficult to maintain if the venture proved to be successful because satisfying the child's working capital requirements (not to mention its capital requirements) could stretch the small partner beyond its capacity. If a small company had neither the cash nor the credit to supply its fair share of funding, ownership shares were reallocated. Doing so was a painful process for entrepreneurial, high technology firms that felt as though they were selling their birthrights when they could not afford the capital demands placed on them. Yet these same firms could not afford to buy out their large partners (because they had been undercapitalized and were often operating on slim margins in their primary business activities even before the joint venture had been formed).

Some firms used the Russian roulette system in 50%-50% joint ventures to value partners' interests when joint ventures were terminated. (This was a system whereby two children sharing a piece of pie ensured equity by letting one child cut the pie in half while the other child distributed the pieces between them.) One firm with many successful joint ventures to its credit did not believe that joint ventures should necessarily terminate after a certain number of years, arguing that managers could have no idea when they formed their joint-venture agreements how their child would fare at their first horizon date. To ensure stability during the first phase of its joint-venture agreements, this firm insisted that no partner could sell its interest in the child. Partners were locked into the first round of funding obligations to give the child a chance to develop. For the second phase of its joint-venture agreements, this firm stipulated that disgruntled partners could sell their interests—but only after offering it to other partners first and only by selling it in *a block*. (Departing partners could not bring in many new partners.) For the third phase of its joint-venture agreements, this firm insisted that the child be transformed into a corporation with the opportunity to sell shares to the public if it survived the first two phases of development. (Making the child a public company terminated the partnership—but not the child's business activity or any vertical relationships that may have existed). Phase three was a way for joint-venture partners to liquidate their investments.

Other managers eschewed such arrangements because they did not believe that the child should be allowed to have a life of its own. (In many cases, letting the child issue its own securities would create horizontally related *competitors,* they noted.)

Ownership versus Control

Most firms preferred to hold majority control in their joint ventures, but many managers made a distinction between ownership control for the purposes of accounting and consolidation of interests, as compared with control for running a joint venture. Several managers were comfortable with asymmetric profit splits or with management splits that did not mirror the breakdown of ownership interests for the purposes of accounting, as long as *they* were the child's operators. Experienced firms formed hybrid teams from partners' management ranks (as well as from outside recruiting), or they simply chose one partner to be the joint venture's leader.

If a minority partner wanted to invest no more than a 75%-25% ownership split, the partner was considered to be a financial investor by many firms and not entitled to much in the way of management rights. It was necessary to consult such partners if the size of the joint-venture investment were doubled or another major change were contemplated. But minority (25 percent) partners were usually expected to be passive. There were exceptions, such as where a 24 percent partner was asked to supply managers for a joint venture. A comparison of the skills each partner controlled occasionally determined which firm would be the joint venture's operator.

Debates concerning the proper division of ownership shares among actively involved parents have been recounted in many earlier studies of joint-venture strategies. Managers continued to debate which pattern of ownership best ensured joint-venture success in this study. Operating control was more important than equity control, they agreed, but finding ways to overcome impasses among partners was considered to be most important to joint-venture success.

Division of Ownership Shares

Parent managers that favored asymmetric ownership shares believed that it was desirable to have one partner in charge and that ownership shares should reflect this power structure. Too many failed joint ventures, they argued, had 50%-50% ownership splits where partners could not agree on the child's direction. All that a 50%-50% ownership interest really guaranteed partners was the right to fight. Even parent managers within excellent 50%-50% joint ventures said they distrusted equal ownership splits in general because when the child was established as a 50%-50% joint venture, it was presumed that partners would be able to work out everything along the way. Managers often found that such a presumption was not realistic. They insisted that one of the partners be identified as having primary responsibility for running the child in their subsequent joint ventures. The other partners, they suggested, should hold the operator accountable.

Some parent managers suggested that three partners were more desirable than two partners when a means of governing and resolving conflict within joint ventures was sought because there would be less chance that the partners would fall into a deadlock. The experiences of Satellite Business Systems and others suggest, however, that running a triparty joint venture was extremely difficult, especially with respect to its direction and control. *Joint venture managers, by contrast, expressed a preference for two (not more) parents and for 50%-50% joint ventures rather than uneven equity splits.*

Managers that favored equal ownership shares believed that 50%-50% ownership splits ensured that partners interests (and parents' opinions) would not be quashed. Such managers feared minority partners' interests would be shortchanged in asymmetric ownership structures (such as 51%-49% or 75%-25%) where majority owners might ride roughshod over the needs of partners. (In one of the most extreme cases, a 46 percent partner awoke one morning to discover that another firm had purchased the other 54 percent interest in its child.) Many managers noted that there must be a consensus because a joint venture cannot be managed against any partner's interest for long. For these managers equal ownership shares were the outward symbol of partners' equality inside their joint ventures.

Although 50%-50% joint ventures were widely acclaimed as being difficult to manage, such arrangements seemed best to capture the spirit of partnerships. They were desirable in high technology joint ventures (especially with entrepreneurial firms) to ensure that such partners remained interested in and involved with the child's technological development activities. Equally distributed ownership was the only way, some managers argued, that top management stayed interested enough in a child's activities to avert problems before it was too late.

At the basis of a successful 50%-50% joint venture, most managers conceded, was personal trust—usually between the managers who formed the joint venture originally. The spirit of that founding relationship must keep working in order for a joint venture to run successfully. Although examples from the oil industry have suggested that ownership shares should be renegotiated whenever partners' interests change, some managers disagreed with this practice, suggesting that if firms had to *renegotiate* ownership terms, they probably had made a poor deal in the first place and should back out. If a joint venture was not right on a 50%-50% basis, it was not likely to be right on a 90%-10% basis (or any other split) either.

Managerial Control

Ownership share distribution mattered less than how operating control (and participation in decision making) was actually apportioned. It was often necessary to spell out responsibilities carefully and to keep the lines of authority clear in order for a joint venture to succeed. Otherwise, squabbles ensued. Firms were pragmatic concerning control over joint ventures where project leadership could be determined by parents' skills and experiences, as in the example of a lead partner with navy experience to lead a navy contract team. They found it easier to work together where each partner respected the other's knowledge and personnel well enough to send in their engineers, go through the facts, and reach agreements concerning what should be done.

Clear leadership authority was needed in volatile businesses like the financial services industry where communications were very important. It was difficult to operate a successful financial services company using a bureaucratic decision-making process, for example, where it was necessary to be able to move fast. In such settings, there could not be any management by committee, unless the committees could be convened immediately and possessed the power to bind the corporation in making difficult decisions. Although partners could use their veto power and the joint venture's voting structure to protect their ownership interests, somebody had to be contractually obligated as its leader.

Although one of the biggest problems in running joint ventures occurred where neither partner was clearly in control, the experiences of some minority partners suggested that firms that refused to form joint ventures unless they were the operators did not make very good "partners." One such source of frustration occurred where an operator, which controlled market access that its partners desired, wanted its minority partners to make presentations to convince it that various actions should be taken before it would consider their opinions.

Using Managers Effectively

Managers sometimes believed erroneously that they could set up joint ventures and let them run themselves. Most joint ventures required much more management time than many parents had expected. Choices concerning who to appoint to the child's management board and which managers to place in charge of the child's operations were crucial to the child's success. Without tremendous management attentions from parents as well as from the child's top executives, the child was often in danger of failing.

Some managers criticized this notion, explaining that joint ventures took twice as much time to manage as wholly owned business units because parents were unwilling to delegate some decisions to their children. It is clear that being able to cope with the many possible conflicts that could arise concerning parents' egos, child motivation, and other problems required somebody to devote significant amounts of time, negotiation skills, people skills, and selling skills to managing conflicts. But it was not clear whether that executive had to be within the child's organization or in one of the partners' organizations. One central coordinator was all that was needed to bring partners to rational agreements.

Joint-Venture Management Style

Several managers blamed joint-venture failure on the wrong choice of managers to lead them. Joint-venture managers must be State Department–trained in diplomacy, one executive noted, because they must be able to approach the chief executives of *all* parents and explain the child's activities. Working through management board members alone was not a sufficient way to gain the trust and sponsorship of parent firms. Unless the child's managers could capture the support of its parents, it was treated like a stepchild.

The best joint-venture managers were those who would do well within a matrix organization (because they could deal with the political differences of parents in a diplomatic fashion while satisfying their diverse needs). In managing points of obvious controversy between partners, it was important for the child's manager to gather the opinions of the experts (the managers whose opinions on a particular topic were most likely to be asked when a child's proposal was evaluated) within each *parent* (whether the parent knew the child's busines or not) before making a recommendation to the joint venture's management board. If the child's manager had incorporated each parent's viewpoint in the proposal, the manager's recommendation became the plan that parents' own experts had recommended.

One sure way for a joint-venture relationship to fail was for its managers—wherever they were recruited—not to consult all of the partners on decision alternatives, planned expenditures, and other proposals. Giving managers more of a free rein than perhaps was the original intention could improve the joint venture's return to both parents, but partners wanted to share in that success, especially if founding managers' egos were closely tied to the child's success. (As one manager noted, not bringing partners along on a joint venture's decisions was like excluding biological parents from their child's wedding.)

A Serpent in Our Bosom

Parent firms missed an opportunity to tap their manager's entrepreneurial tendencies when they let their joint ventures be used as personnel dumping grounds. Rather than correct this management failure, parents recognized that burnt-out, low-potential, or politically embarrassing managers staffed their children and treated them accordingly. Alternatively, parent firm managers removed high performers from their joint-venture assignments soon after the first honeymoon was over and denied their child the high-level attentions reserved for wholly owned business units. When this occurred managers assigned to the joint-venture child became jaundiced because running the joint venture was no great honor within parents' organizations. Rather than making the joint venture a convenient parking place for senior executives awaiting retirement, firms could have made them a *reward* for enterprising managers and rewarded innovative behavior.

It was not surprising that the strategies of partners would be different or that they had different corporate cultures that their managers carried with them into the child. Problems arose, however, when the joint venture was treated as a stepchild or was left to fail. Because they kept thinking of the revolving door that would bring them back to their respective parents, managers identified with the parent's interests rather than with the child's needs. Managers could not think of themselves as employees of the child, and their decisions reflected this schism (as did the joint venture's failure).

The child's manager had to be detached from loyalties from either parent in decision making, even if that meant the manager was recruited from outside.

(The manager could come from one of the partners if a very neutral attitude could be taken and the confidence of the other partner could be gained. But since it was difficult to persuade the other parent to trust this manager, a more radical solution was often needed.) To combat the problems of split loyalties, some firms *closed the revolving door* and hired talented outsiders—with loyalties to neither parent—to lead the child and hold its critical jobs. With time and success, joint ventures developed their own teams and asserted their independence. Employees from each parent were still needed if the child's activities were to be coordinated with those of its parents' because it was helpful for the child to have someone on hand who knew the corporate people, who knew where to go to get things done, who knew where the closets were and what was behind the closet doors in getting the job done. It was helpful to have employees on hand who could call in old favors—as when the child needed something pushed through its parent's organization—to make day-to-day operations of the venture run smoothly. But the message-carrier did not have to be the president of the child.

When managers became loyal to the child, conflicts with their parents were inevitable, especially when parent managers had encouraged the development of a guerilla mentality by the child's managers through their own treatment of them. In many cases, the child was an underdog. Its managers were two groups of rag-tag people who were trying to make the child succeed. The child's management team developed a closeness because they were the black sheep of their respective parent firms and received little respect. The child may have operated for a decade, for example, but the parents' managers still misspelled the child's name and mispronounced it. The child's organization may have been kept lean (or understaffed), and large decisions were made at very low-grade levels. Going back to a parent firm that resembled a paramilitary organization after a decade of autonomy rarely appealed to the child's managers.

When managers within parent organizations finally realized that their child had grown into an independently minded entity with its own markets and its own priorities, their feelings of alienation were scarcely surprising. After all, the child had occupied a corner on one floor of its parent's sixty-story office complex for years, and its revenues were a pittance when compared with those of its parent. Suddenly the child was stealing top management talent from its parent and competing for resources.

As it matured, the child often wanted freedoms—such as freedom to enter joint ventures in its own right. (If the child was allowed to forge its own joint ventures, its experienced managers made excellent parents of the child's child because they knew what worked and which parentally imposed policies made a child's manager impotent.) Whether parent firms permitted their child to go to the stock market in its own right, develop competing facilities, or form their own joint ventures depended very much on what parents wanted from their liaisons. Some managers asserted that the child should be terminated when the venture was over (project-by-project basis). Others favored cascades of joint ventures (if appropriate) and let their children develop into autonomous entities.

Overcoming Impasses

Managers noted that many mistakes common to starting new businesses were made as joint ventures were started—underfinancing the child, choosing the wrong management team or defective technology, and other mistakes that would affect any business unit adversely. But joint ventures offered a unique problem due to their shared parentage: disagreements among the partners. Such conflicts were natural and were part of daily life because the interests of parents in joint ventures were rarely identical.

Decision making was cumbersome within a joint venture: It required a different mentality on the part of *parents* to make them work than if the business unit were fully owned. Managers within parent firms became frustrated when they found it more and more difficult to get something done quickly. No longer could management simply call down to tell the business unit that another 10 percent of a certain output was needed, for example, or to do this or do that when the business unit in question was a joint venture. An arm's-length agreement meant that negotiation with the other decision makers was needed, especially if both parents drew outputs from their child.

Such restraints on autonomy were especially difficult for parent firms that instinctively overmanaged their subsidiaries and for managers that were unaccustomed to techniques for managing cooperation. Even where such parents did not have management responsibility for the joint venture, a regular flow of requests from their managers to the child's managers for figures, status reports, and other information fairly overwhelmed it, especially if the joint venture was small and the inquiring parent was large. When frustrated parent managers slammed against the constraints of the matrix organization they had once created for a particular task, they layered in more and more people and procedures to solve their personality conflicts with the child or their partner by *buffering them*. As the situation grew more hidebound, parents lost track of the original relationships that motivated the child's formation. Little thought was given to how the management system between parent and child (and between partners) should have been modified to reflect the changing status of the joint venture.

How did managers break out of this quagmire? Some firms preferred to negotiate as they transacted business together. Since they could not foresee everything and the success requirements of their industry would make their products obsolete before the lawyers could write a contract to cover all contingencies, partners simply trusted each other. Others gave the child's manager more authority and autonomy, or they pulled the child even closer to them and ran it as a part of their regular management responsibilities. Some partners relied on the close personal friendships of their respective chief executive officers to resolve disputes. Others simply trashed the child.

Parents that drew their child closer often believed that partners should not expect to set up joint ventures, walk away from them, and expect everything to run without a hitch. These managers believed the child needed constant supervision and parental intervention to ensure that joint-venture managers knew what the parent wanted and to ensure that the technology partner, for example, was spending time, money, and effort to find the technology that the child needed or that the marketing partner was doing the right jobs. The roles remaining for their representatives within the child were primarily those of caretakers.

Parents that gave their child more authority and autonomy often believed that the fatal flaw in many joint ventures was that partners were not prepared to let the child live its own life. They tended to believe that if the child was run on a day-to-day basis by its parents, it was doomed to failure. Moreover, they argued that joint ventures must have control of the whole business and all of its assets. Successful joint ventures can stand on their own, they argued, and parents that would not transfer salient assets to the child were creating their own nightmare of interface problems.

If managers acknowledged that the child must eventually evolve into a stand-alone, independent entity with a life of its own, that was not grounds to abandon the child or deprive it of the sustenance that any fledgling needed. In order for joint ventures to survive (even if that meant they would become competitors of their parents), high-level attentions were needed from the chief executive officer of its parents, from board members, from financial officers with the parent, and from other functional heads to manage a seamless transition in the child's status. Unless this final step was done with statesman-like, nonparochial skills, another source of conflict could erupt.

Parents on both sides of the question of child autonomy recognized that partners' interests regarding their child would diverge with time—particularly if industry conditions (and thus profitability) deteriorated. Some firms negotiated management control buy-out arrangements, whereby one partner maintained operating control until the products of their partner had generated enough income (using a prespecified formula) to purchase most of the venture's equity. When the minority partner's equity position reached 80 percent (or a similarly high plateau), it also gained operating control from its partner. Such arrangements helped to ease the transition problems associated with joint-venture termination because they ensured that the surviving operator was committed to the joint venture's success.

Joint ventures that relied on the personal friendships of top executives to resolve partner disputes were in the most unstable positions if succession problems in one parent changed the relative importance of the child for that parent. When partners reached a cross-roads where decisions could not be made unanimously by the partners—where they reached a deadlock—it was time to unearth the legal documents and see what the lawyers had agreed on.

Board of Directors

It was important to select the right managers to serve on the child's board of directors to oversee its activities. In addition to competent managers and diplomatic skills, directors needed time to follow up on the activities of the child. Although there were a few joint ventures that attributed their success to their parents' willingness to leave them alone, these were the exceptions. Most joint-venture children needed more than just cash to succeed, and the closer their activities were to those of their parents, the more they needed day-to-day contact with parents' representatives. (Excessive coordination sheltered children, of course. During one interview, a management director responded to five telephone questions from the president of his firm's joint venture. The child had little or no autonomy concerning operating decisions, and at least one parent expected its life span to be short.)

As chapter 13 noted, parent organizations became jealous of joint ventures that they regarded as their horizontal competitors. Successful firms tried to identify pressure points in product development activities that would require close coordination between parent and child in advance. Then they set up the child's board of directors structure to avert those potential conflicts by their choices of appointments to the management board. Most joint-venture board members should be function-related to ensure that they have the knowledge needed to coordinate parent and child, managers suggested, and they should not be too highly placed within the parent firm's hierarchy. Executives within overseas firms even suggested that it was necessary to establish a small office near the child because the child's managers payed more attention to the viewpoints that they encountered most frequently and understood most clearly when making policy decisions.

Evaluating Joint-Venture Performance

Managers recognized that joint ventures were very complex to manage, that the probability of success was pretty low, and that the U.S. track record of joint ventures was not good. Moreover, every joint venture was unique because of the many possible ways in which partners might combine as well as the diversity of the partners themselves. Thus, trying to make two of them work under almost identical constraints in time, size, profitability, and so on was virtually impossible. Nevertheless, many managers realized that joint ventures were becoming increasingly important as a strategy option.

When the child became of increasing strategic importance, its information-reporting systems had to be separated from that of its parents to facilitate better measures of its activity, free and clear of other parts of parent-firm activities. Without such information, it was impossible to ascertain whether the child was in good health. Allocation of costs, such as those of shared personnel salaries or other shared assets was frustrating, but these practices had to change over time as the child's relationship with its parents evolved.

Were joint ventures overrated in their usefulness? Managers suggested that judgment depended on the joint venture's purpose. If firms could do everything themselves equally well as outsiders and were blessed with infinite cash resources, there was no need for joint ventures. The problems of coordination were formidable, and they were rarely outweighed by the benefits managers *expected* to receive. It would appear that a more realistic vision of joint ventures was needed in order for them to be used effectively. For example, joint ventures were formed to permit partners to make smaller investments in risky projects that they would otherwise have to tackle on their own. Managers hoped that the rate of return would be the same as if their firms had invested alone. If they were lucky, their returns on investment were higher. But since their ticket to entry was smaller (due to their pooled resources), they were exposed to less risk. The net effect of the risk–return trade off made joint-venture partners better off than if they had to go it alone.

Joint ventures were a transitional form of management—an intermediate step on the way to something else. Firms needed to create an incentive among their respective managers—both as partners and as parents—to cooperate with their child. Acquisition was a zero-sum game, but joint venture could be a non–zero-sum game if firms were cooperating, not trying to coopt their partners. The fact that the knowledge, products, or other resources were obtained through a joint venture (rather than through an outright acquisition) mattered less in determining success than the relationships among the people who operated the venture. The U.S. joint venture success rate has been improving as more firms apply creative solutions to their old ideas concerning how long ventures must last, who must be the operator, and what each player should bring to the party. There is more profit because of scale economies, because of integration economies from better balance between adjacent stages of production, and because of other cost savings from pooled resources that reduce the total cost of doing business. From a wealth-creating parent's perspective, the joint venture always offers an opportunity to improve on what firms can do alone. When managers had cracked the secret of how to maneuver within them, they were sold on the idea of joint-venture strategies as a means to attain successful performances.

16
Summary: Joint Ventures as Change Agents and Public Policy Implications

F irms' experiences in using joint ventures within the United States suggest that some changes in public policy regarding innovation, economic regulation, and international trade may be needed. This summary chapter suggests some implications of patterns concerning U.S. joint-venture formation for antitrust and national industrial policy. In particular, it discusses the roles of parents and child within closely coordinated management systems and contrasts management practices with antitrust policies. It suggests the need for U.S. trading companies or systems integrators to assist firms that are hamstrung by local government requirements for offsets and co-production as a condition of international trade.

Future Trends

There will be more U.S. joint ventures and other forms of cooperative strategies in the future as firms are harder pressed to manage their existing assets efficiently and invest in new assets more frequently. Cooperation will be inevitable given the increasingly demanding nature of competition. As product lives shorten, industries become global, and capital entry fees grow higher, more firms will consolidate their ongoing facilities and work together in developing new ones to respond to this challenge.

Joint ventures will be used to reduce harmful effects on the environment, as in the example of the Alaska Pipeline joint venture formed in 1977, where it would have been undesirable to have several companies tromping across the fragile tundra to build parallel pipelines. Moreover, since scale economies increased geometrically as the diameter of a pipeline increases, a joint effort was the least costly way to bring crude oil to the mainland United States for processing.

Early in an industry's development, firms used joint ventures to create products and to penetrate markets. When new technologies were tested, as in the petrochemicals industry, firms often used joint ventures to share risks and pool outputs. This trend will continue and become more commonplace as the pace of innovation accelerates and as firms cannot recover their capital expenditures on a generation of assets by going it alone.

When demand slowed and firms expired many other competitive approaches to sustaining profit levels, they used joint ventures to retrench and consolidate in order to make more efficient use of facilities. Where firms are reluctant to form such joint ventures in the future on their own, due to the high exit barriers associated with plant closings, government assistance may be appropriate in order to rationalize excess capacity in a nondisruptive fashion.

The experiences of U.S. firms in forming domestic joint ventures can be compared readily with those of firms within other mature economies, as in the United Kingdom where joint ventures have included Royal Dutch/Shell, Rank-Xerox, British Aircraft Corp. (Vickers and General Electric Ltd.), Mardon Packaging (Imperial and B.A.T.), Bakelite Xylonite (DCL and Union Carbide Corp.), United Glass (Distillers and Owens-Illinois), and British Titan (ICI and Lead Industries). In particular, the experiences of firms within mature and failing industries hold lessons for U.S. public policy.

Consolidating Excess Capacity

Industrywide capacity rationalizations were needed in the United Kingdom when demand for locally produced products declined unexpectedly. These included fibers (1978–80), bulk steel (1977–85), petrochemicals (1982), and steel castings (1983). Government coordination in cartel schemes was needed to coax inefficient capacity out of these industries. Without the incentives provided by participating firms (which assisted those firms that retired excess capacity), high exit barriers would have created a problem of lags in shutdowns and disincentives (in the form of the least efficient plants remaining in operation while the efficient ones departed).

In the United States the 1984 Jones & Laughlin Steel merger with Republic Steel was approved because ownership in certain facilities (which the U.S. Justice Department considered to be in violation of antitrust laws) was divested. By contrast, the merger proposed between U.S. Steel and National Steel was disallowed by the Antitrust Division because *divestitures* were not explicitly planned for as part of their combination. This result seems to fly in the face of the steel industry's need for autonomy to close plants *as needed* to reduce excess capacity. Keeping obsolete plants in operation erodes industrywide price levels, thereby robbing firms of profits to invest in new processes and crippling them further in their efforts to cope with declining demand. A revision of U.S. policies regarding combinations in failing industries may be needed.

Shorter Product Lives

The rigors of shorter product lives, global competition, enhanced technological productivity, and other change forces translate into greater pressures on management to devise new ways to improve their products while sustaining competitive advantage. The challenge of cooperating productively with wholly owned sister business units has been difficult enough for operating managers when performance targets have directed their attentions to an adversarial posture instead. It will be even more difficult for them to sustain a cooperative spirit in dealing with partially owned entities. Yet they must overcome their not-invented-here prejudices because as product lives become shorter, firms must be ready faster with the next increment of improved productivity and product innovation. For firms within many industries, cooperation will be their best means of exploiting profitable opportunities before they go stale. Autonomy to form joint ventures for innovation purposes may require modifications of public policy.

Patents and Innovation

Joint ventures are necessary when a research task is of sufficiently high cost or risk that parents would not undertake the research individually. Most frequently these ventures will be in scientific areas where firms have not previously conducted research. Because of the importance of such activities to their strategic cores, few firms will engage in pioneering R&D joint ventures readily. To encourage knowledge sharing, special protection of proprietary knowledge is needed. In many cases, parents in this study maintained control of proprietary knowledge and would not allow their child to develop parallel facilities. If pharmaceutical firms pooled knowledge, for example, their disclosures to the Food & Drug Administration (FDA) were protected from such access by competitors (as well as local partners) as would be available under freedom of information acts or would be required by stringent licensing requirements. Federal pressures to reduce patent lives or make knowledge common among competitors destroyed partners' willingness to introduce their newest products and thereby harmed consumer welfare.

From an antitrust policy perspective, the level of secrecy required in R&D joint ventures may be unacceptable because outsiders are denied access to technology developed by partners (except perhaps after a reasonable time lag) or access into the R&D joint venture itself. The MCC and SRC research consortia in microelectronics provide examples of exceptional behaviors on these points because (1) outsiders will be permitted licenses for the child's technology and (2) membership is open (subject to reasonable entry fees). Many firms (including IBM) chose not to expose their secrets to competitors under the operating policies of these ventures, however. And their reluctance to join these joint ventures provides an interesting contrast to the behavior patterns antitrust laws had assumed would prevail. These R&D joint ventures are interesting also because of their similarity to the spirit of Japanese cooperation in research.

A principal difference between U.S. and Japanese R&D joint ventures pertains to their sources of funding. The Japanese government has typically subsidized up to 50 percent of the costs of R&D on designated projects (as in the example of a series of Laws of Extraordinary Measures for Promotion of Electronics Industry that were enacted beginning in 1957 to modernize Japanese industries and technologies by promoting its electronics industry). The Japanese government has routinely transferred the new technology it sponsored to all firms. (This practice also understates the amount of R&D actually spent to develop a new technology because the government money does not appear on the financial statements of Japanese firms.) Although Japanese firms may have cooperated during the "umbrella period" of federal support, they became vigorous competitors among themselves since the protected period has ended. The MCC and SRC partners may also be expected to compete vigorously in applying the knowledge they have developed jointly after their respective umbrella period for a particular patent has ended.

Antitrust

Antitrust policies regarding cooperative strategies have proceeded as though joint ventures were tantamount to mergers. Although some harm to competitive markets may occur if joint-venture partners pool their marketing facilities, less harm is likely to occur the closer the joint venture's activities are to the basic research end of the spectrum, as has been argued above. Fleeting competitive advantages necessitate joint research activities.

Much has been written since 1950 by learned scholars of antitrust law concerning the collusive effects of output joint ventures that obligate horizontally related partners to market their respective shares of the child's outputs exclusively through their child's marketing organization. *Few such joint ventures were observed in this study.* (Indeed, parents were highly *unlikely* to allow their horizontally related children to develop their own marketing organizations.) And those that created vertically related children did not seem to create much harm to competition. Ventures to provide access to downstream markets *helped* underdog firms to penetrate new markets more frequently than they created bottlenecks that harmed ongoing competitors. The major exception (the Premiere programming packaging service that would have combined the programming of four motion picture films) was disallowed.

Preemption

Interpretations of antitrust laws concerning joint ventures have generally held them to be anticompetitive if they have bottleneck properties that foreclose others from essential facilities or requirements. Preemption motives for joint ventures (where they were found in this study) were concerned with timing advantages, *not* with locking up competitors or shutting out the strongest firms in adjacent industries. Firms often found it advantageous to have joint ventures with a variety of competitors as well as with vertically related partners. Indeed, the latter interpretation of preemption motives is *unrealistic*, given the dynamic nature of partners' bargaining power.

It would be expensive for a firm to lock up the strongest potential partner to prevent it from forming an alliance with the firm's competitors because the strongest potential partner will possess the greatest bargaining power by virtue of its leadership position. The price of a joint venture will likely be staggering if partners are that good, that strong, and that successful. Joint ventures are more likely to be formed among firms that are not dominant in their industry. By pooling their marketing strengths and weak products (or technologies) with partners that offer what weak firms lack, the partners can do better than either could have done alone.

Exclusivity versus Spider's Webs Joint Ventures

In the motion picture industry, signing an actor to a film project for a finite time span prevented him from working on another project. But signing talent to a contract was a voluntary act that benefited both parties, and it did not violate antitrust laws. When a joint venture explored new technologies, its partnership often excluded partners' rivals. But firms make such decisions in light of the ease with which their competitive advantage could be appropriated. For example, in communications equipment, both IBM and Rolm wrote joint-venture agreements to ensure that they could form a spider's web of joint ventures with a variety of dancing partners. This flexibility is to their mutual advantage even after IBM purchased Rolm because (1) it enabled them to suggest equipment and interface standards and (2) it exposed them to technological improvements of their products. These benefits were enhanced by IBM's policy of relying on outsiders for pieces of its complex and interconnected system of computers and communications equipment. Neither firm's knowledge was easily appropriated.

Firms often formed joint ventures on a project-by-project basis when no harm to their distinctive competence was created by spider's webs of agreements. But they sought rights of first refusal for subsequent coalitions in areas where they did not want their competitors to link up with their partners. Such provisions were used when follow up opportunities that may not have been perceived at the time of the initial alliance later became apparent—as in the example of genetic engineering, where the venture's attractiveness is not known until pilot projects are proven.

The Long Arm of Antitrust

U.S. firms are bound by the provisions of U.S. antitrust laws as sketched above even when they operate overseas. Their freedom to deploy their child's assets everywhere within their global network is subject to these antitrust policies. Rules concerning market divisions (or other common provisions for allocating responsibility) pose public policy problems when interpreted through the lens of traditional antitrust laws. For example, agreements that protected parents' markets (domestic or foreign) from the child *or from foreign partners* would probably raise eyebrows within the Department of Justice. Yet such strategic missions concerning market coverage are a critical part of how firms pursuing global strategies coordinated the many parts of their organizations to maximize the economies of global networks. Arguably, global competitors can achieve allocative efficiencies superior even to those of local sovereigns. Thus impediments placed on firms' freedoms to shift resources to locations of comparative advantage often served political objectives better than economic ones.

International Competition

This section contrasts national trade practices with firms' autonomy needs in pursuing global strategies. Sometimes firms formed joint ventures voluntarily to adjust to customer trends such as growing component convergence (following product standardization). For example, automotive components suppliers—Bendix, Cummins, Eaton, and TRW in the United States and Lucas, GKN, and Bosch in Europe—formed their own worldwide networks of production facilities in order to remain competitive in the 1980s in anticipation of worldwide alliances formed among their automobile firm customers. Or firms formed joint ventures to overcome the advantages of local competitors that received protection.

The Need for Local Partners

Because governments often supported local firms to the detriment of outsiders, U.S. firms operating overseas were often at a disadvantage when compared with firms that promoted local federal objectives. To overcome disadvantages associated with local trade restrictions, outsiders often took local partners to acquire the image of being a national champion, even when they were not required to do so by local laws. For example, U.S. firms took local partners when they entered the Japanese markets in chemicals (Asahi Dow Chemical and Mitsubishi Monsanto, for example), pharmaceuticals (Banyu-Merck and Taito Sugar Refinery-Pfizer), and cosmetics (Taito Sugar Refinery-Bristol-Myers), as well as in precision controls (Yamatake-Honeywell) and electronic data processing (Honeywell-Nippon Electric Co.). Matsushita and Philips N.V. formed Matsushita Electronics. Even after Japanese requirements for local ownership were reduced, entering firms sought partners to penetrate unfamiliar distribution channels.

Except in cases of blatant graft, entering firms were free to choose their local partners in cases where proportions of foreign ownership in local firms were restricted. Thus, U.S. oil companies developing tar sands and other geological formations in Canada enjoyed substantial latitude in choosing their partners. Where governments required investments in local R&D facilities or purchases of locally produced goods to offset their purchases of imported goods, foreign firms have enjoyed choices concerning how to satisfy the spirit of these laws to date.

Offsets and Co-Production

Joint ventures do not always mean jobs for U.S. suppliers when, as in the example of the aerospace consortia, components must be made in West Germany, the United Kingdom, Italy, the Netherlands, France, Spain, as well as in the United States in order to be acceptable to government customers. Global firms are beginning to have fewer choices in the 1980s regarding *where* to locate their manufacturing operations due to laws regarding local content of imported goods and the need for offsetting purchases of local goods. The implications for firms' strategic flexibility of offset and co-production requirements patterns are especially clear in the area of any military product or military-related products. Firms form bidding consortia to offer products to powerful government customers. Ensuring that local content and offset rules will be satisfied are becoming a cost of winning contracts. For example, a $1.1 billion sale by the McDonnell-Douglas team of F-18 fighter planes may require a $1.4 billion offset, requiring the team to bring products out of Canada (for example) valued higher than the amounts sold to Canada. Sales of Harpoon missiles to the United Kingdom, for example, may carry an offset ratio of about 1.5 to 1. Israeli purchases of the LAVI fighter plane, for example, may require offsets, co-production, and OEM vendor arrangements that permit for the resale of the LAVI in the international arena by Israeli firms.

Trading Companies and Systems Integrators

Operations within a system of offsets and co-production agreements may require U.S. firms to establish entities to act as systems integrators. Like the trading companies that maintained access to global markets to dispose of goods taken in offset, firms that competed for the same government customers may wish to form joint ventures to coordinate the offset levels they are offering in competition with each other. (Without access to such information, U.S. firms often bid up the level of offsets they will take from overseas nations to win contracts from another U.S. vendor. Although such coordination could reduce the number of U.S. jobs bid away in offset agreements, under current interpretations of U.S. antitrust laws, such coordination by vendors of military products would be prohibited.)

In summary, there are numerous business practices involving joint ventures and other forms of cooperative strategy that reflect the realities of eroding competitive advantage and the need for rapid rates of innovation and heightened customer bargaining power in international trade more accurately than U.S. policies concerning economic regulation. Results from this study have suggested areas where reexamination of the premises underlying such policies may be in order.

Bibliography

Abell, Derek F., 1978. "Strategic Marketing," *Journal of Marketing*. 42(3):21–26.

Abernathy, William J., and Utterback, James M., 1978. "Patterns of Industrial Innovation," *Technology Review*. 80(7).

Aharoni, Yair, 1966. *The Foreign Investment Decision Process*. Boston: Division of Research, Graduate School of Business Administration, Harvard University.

Aiken, M., and Hage, J., 1968. "Organizational Interdependence and Intraorganizational Structure," *American Sociological Review*. 33:912–930.

Akerloff, G.A., 1970. "The Market for 'Lemons': Qualitative Uncertainty and the Market Mechanism," *Quarterly Journal of Economics*. 84:488–500.

"Allis Teams Up with Siemens," 1977. *Business Week*. August 1: 48G.

"Alumax—Turning Aluminum Capacity Upside Down," 1978. *Business Week*. March 6: 72–74.

"Antitrust Guide for Joint Research Programs," 1981. *Research Management*. 24(2): 30–37.

"Are Foreign Partners Good for U.S. Companies?," 1984. *Business Week*. May 28: 58–60.

Arpan, J.S., and Ricks, D.A., 1975. *Directory of Foreign Manufacturers in the United States*. Atlanta: Georgia State University School of Business Administration.

Asch, Peter, 1970. *Economic Theory and the Antitrust Dilemma*. New York: Wiley.

"ASEA: Swedish Robots Chase the American Market," 1981. *World Business Weekly* (United Kingdom). 4(20):32.

Asher, Joe, 1976. "Agbanking—New Twist on Joint-Venture," *Banking*. 68(9):70–180.

Augustine, W.D., 1982. "Utilities in Joint Ownership of Generating Facilities," *Public Utilities Fortnightly*. 109(9):31–34.

"Auto Makers Remodel Their Troubled Industry," 1980. *Business Week*. November 10: 48–49.

"Avoid Antitrust Charges on Joint Ventures," 1979. *Boardroom Reports*. May 15: 4.

"Ayer/Banker/Hegemann International Deal Linked," 1974. *Advertising Age*. 45(19): 2, 94.

Bacharach, Samuel B., and Lawler, Edward J., 1980. *Power and Politics in Organizations*. San Francisco: Jossey-Bass.

Bachman, Jules, 1965a. "Joint Ventures and the Antitrust Laws," *New York University Law Review*. 40:651–671.

Bachman, Jules, 1965b. "Joint Ventures in the Light of Recent Antitrust Developments," *Antitrust Bulletin*. 10:7–23.

Bain, Joe S., 1956. *Barriers to New Competition*. Cambridge, Mass.: Harvard University Press.

Baldridge, Malcolm, 1983. "Testimoney: On Government Policies to Promote High Growth Industries," U.S. Senate Committee on Finance: January 19, 1983.

Ball, Robert, 1981. "Renault Takes Its Hit Show on the Road," *Fortune*. 103(9): 274–284.

Ballon, Robert J., 1967. *Joint Ventures and Japan*. Tokyo: Sophia University Press.

——— , 1979. "A Lesson from Japan: Contract, Control, and Authority," *Journal of Contemporary Business*. 8(2):27–35.

"Bank Proposes Joint Effort to Develop New Software," 1980. *ABA Banking Journal*. 72(11):132–134.

Banks, Howard., 1981. "Partners of Necessity," *Europe*. 228:31–33.

"BASF and Dow Have Dropped Talks on a Takeover by One of the Other's Share in Dow Badische," 1977. *European Chemical News*. March 4: 4.

Beamish, Paul, and Lane, Henry W., 1982. "Need, Commitment and the Performance of Joint Ventures in Developing Countries." Toronto: University of Western Ontario.

Bell, D.E., Keeney, R.L., and Raiffa, H., 1977. *Conflicting Objectives and Decisions*. New York: Wiley.

Beresford, M., 1974. "And Now, Le Defi Japonais," *European Business*. 42:17–27.

Berg, Sanford V., Duncan, Jerome, and Friedman, Philip, 1982. *Joint Venture Strategies and Corporate Innovation*. Cambridge, Mass.: Oelgeschlager, Gunn & Hain.

Berg, Sanford V., and Friedman, Philip, 1977. "Joint Ventures, Competition, and Technological Complementarities," *Southern Economic Journal*. 43(3):1330–1337.

——— , 1978a. "Joint Ventures in American Industry: An Overview," *Mergers and Acquisitions*. 13:28–41.

——— , 1978b. "Joint Ventures in American Industry Part II: Case Studies of Managerial Policy," *Mergers and Acquisitions*. 13(3):9–17.

——— , 1978c. "Technological Complementarities and Industrial Patterns of JV Activity, 1964–1965," *Industrial Organization Review*. 6(2):110–116.

——— , 1979a. "Government Policy Towards Joint Ventures as a Mechanism Affecting R&D." U.S. National Science Foundation (Report RDA 75-19064).

——— , 1979b. "Joint Ventures in American Industry Part III: Public Policy Issues," *Mergers and Acquisitions*. 13(4):18–29.

——— , 1980a. "Causes and Effects of Joint Venture Activity," *Antitrust Bulletin*. 25(1):143–168.

——— , 1980b. "Corporate Courtship and Successful Joint Ventures," *California Management Review*. 22(3):85–91.

——— , 1981a. "Impacts of Domestic Joint Ventures on Industrial Rates of Return," *Review of Economics and Statistics*. 63(2):293–298.

——— , 1981b. "Impacts of a Pooled Cross-Section Analysis, Domestic Joint Ventures on Industrial Rates of Return," *Review of Economics and Statistics*. 63(2).

Berghoff, John C., 1964. "Antitrust Aspects of Joint Ventures," *Antitrust Bulletin*. 9(2):231–254.

Bergman, Michael, 1962. "Corporate Joint Venture under the Antitrust Laws," *New York University Law Review.* 37:712–734.

Berkman, Harold W., and Vernon, Ivan R., 1979. *Contemporary Perspectives in International Business.* Chicago: Rand-McNally.

Berlew, F. Kingston, 1984. "The Joint Venture—A Way into Foreign Markets," *Harvard Business Review.* 62(4):49–50, 54.

Bernstein, Lewis, 1965. "Joint Ventures in the Light of Recent Antitrust Developments," *Antitrust Bulletin.* 10:25–29.

"Billion Dollar Farm Co-Ops Nobody Knows," 1977. *Business Week.* February 7: 54–64.

Bing, Gordon, 1978. *Corporate Divestment.* Houston: Gulf.

"Biotechnology—Seeking the Right Corporate Combinations," 1981. *Chemical Week.* 129(14):36–40.

Bivens, Karen Kraus, and Lovell, Enid Baird, 1966. *Joint Ventures with Foreign Partners.* New York: National Industrial Conference Board.

Black, I.G., 1972. "Japan Renews Push into U.S. Plants, Hitachi Is Latest," *Iron Age.* 210:39.

Blair, John M., 1975. "The Implementation of Oligopolistic Interdependence—International Oil," *Journal of Economic Issues.* 9(2):297–318.

Blanden, Michael, 1981. "Why Banks Choose to Work Together," *Banker* (United Kingdom). 131:93, 95, 97, 99.

Block, Zenas, and Matsumoto, Hide, 1972. "Joint Venturing in Japan," *Conference Board Record.* 9(4):32–36.

Blois, K.J., 1972. "Vertical Quasi-Integration," *Journal of Industrial Economics.* 20:253–272.

———, 1980. "Quasi-Integration as a Mechanism for Controlling External Dependencies," *Management Decision* (United Kingdom). 18(1):55–63.

"Boots May Buy Its Way into U.S.," 1977. *Euromoney.* November, p. 160.

Borowitz, Albert I., 1970. "Joint Business Actions by Competitors: Are Any Permissible?," *Ohio State Law Journal.* 32:683–700.

Bourgeois, L.J., III., 1981. "On the Measurement of Organizational Slack," *Academy of Management Review.* 6(1):29–39.

Bourgeois, L.J., III, and Singh, Jitendra, 1983. "Organizational Slack and Political Behavior within Top Management Teams." Paper presented at National Academy of Management, Dallas.

Boyle, S.E., 1963. "The Joint Subsidiary: An Economic Appraisal," *Antitrust Bulletin.* 5(3):303–318.

———, 1968. "Estimate of the Number and Size Distribution of Domestic Joint Subsidiaries," *Antitrust Law and Economics Review.* 1:81–92.

Bradley, David G., 1977. "Managing against Expropriation," *Harvard Business Review.* 55(4):75–83.

Brady, G.J., 1958. "Many Tax Advantages Found in Joint Venture of Corporate Partners: How It Works," *Journal of Taxation.* 261:34–40.

Broden, Thomas F., and Scanlon, Alfred L., 1958. "The Legal Status of Joint Venture Corporations," *Vanderbilt Law Review.* 11:689.

Brodley, Joseph F., 1967. "Oligopoly Power under the Sherman and Clayton Acts," *Stanford Law Review.* 19:329.

Brodley, Joseph F., 1976. "The Legal Status of Joint Ventures under the Antitrust Laws," *Antitrust Bulletin.* 21(3):453–483.

——— , 1979. "Joint Ventures and the Justice Department Antitrust Guide for International Operation," *Antitrust Bulletin.* 24(2):337–356.

——— , 1982. "Joint Ventures and Antitrust Policy," *Harvard Law Review.* 95(7): 1523–1590.

Business International, 1965. *Ownership Policies at Work Abroad.* New York: Business International.

——— , 1971. *European Business Strategies in the United States: Meeting the Challenge of the World's Largest Market.* Geneva: Business International.

——— , 1972. *Recent Experience in Establishing Joint Ventures.* Geneva: Business International.

"A Busy Year at Philips," 1981. *World Business Weekly* (United Kingdom). 4(32): 24, 26.

Bylinsky, Gene, 1984. "Can Smokestack America Rise Again?," *Fortune.* February 6: 74–82.

Carter, Charles, and Williams, Bruce, 1957. *Industry and Technical Progress.* London: Oxford University Press.

Cascino, E., 1979. "How One Company 'Adapted' Matrix Management in a Crisis," *Management Review.* 68(11):57–61.

Caves, Richard E., and Porter, Michael E., 1978. "Market Structure, Oligopoly and Stability of Market Shares," *Journal of Industrial Economics.* 26:289–313.

Caves, Richard E., Porter, Michael E., and Spence, A. Michael, 1980. *Competition in the Open Economy.* Cambridge, Mass.: Harvard University Press.

Cleland, D.I., 1981. "Matrix Management (Part II): A Kaleidoscope of Organizational Systems," *Management Review.* 70(12):48–56.

Cohen, Laurie, 1984. "Failed Marriages," *Wall Street Journal.* September 10: 1, 18.

Coleman, J.S., 1966. "In Defense of Games," *American Behavioral Scientist.* 10:3–4.

"A Collision over Japan's 'European' Automobile," 1982. *Business Week.* May 10: 48–49.

Comanor, W.S., and Wilson, T.A., 1979. "Advertising and Competition: A Survey," *Journal of Economic Literature.* 17:453–476.

"Competitors Team Up to Stop AT&T," 1976. *Business Week.* June 7: 31–34.

"Computers—Teaming Up to Build Military Minicomputers," 1976. *Business Week.* December 20: 50.

Connolly, Seamus G., 1984. "Joint Ventures with Third World Multinationals: A New Form of Entry to International Markets," *Columbia Journal of World Business.* 19(2):18–22.

Conrads, Robert J., and Mahini, Amir, 1984. "The Risks and Advantages of Cooperative Ventures," *Wall Street Journal.* January 20: 36.

Contractor, Farok J., 1984. "Strategies for Structuring Joint Ventures: A Negotiations Planning Paradigm," *Columbia Journal of World Business.* 19(2):30–39.

Cook, Daniel D., 1981. "Unlikely Duo Tries to Hike U.S. Auto Spirits," *Industry Week.* 209(4):21–22.

"Cooperation Agreements Roster," 1977. *Mergers and Acquisitions.* 11(4):48–50.

Cozzolino, John M., 1981. "Joint Venture Risk: How to Determine Your Share," *Mergers and Acquisitions.* 16(3):35–39.

Crawford, F.O., 1978. "The Toils and Techniques of Sharing the Risk," *Euromoney.* August: 49–57.

Curtis, Carol E., 1982. "And Then There Were None," *Forbes.* 129(12):41–42.

Cyert, R.M., and March, J.G., 1963. *A Behavioral Theory of the Firm.* Englewood Cliffs, N.J.: Prentice-Hall.

Daniels, John D., 1971. *Recent Foreign Direct Manufacturing Investment in the United States.* New York: Praeger.

Davidow, Joel, 1977. "International Joint Ventures and the U.S. Antitrust Laws," *Akron Law Review.* 10:120–125.

Davidson, William Harley, 1980. "Corporation Experience Factors in International Investment and Licensing Activities: Study of International Business," Ph.D. diss., Boston, Harvard Business School.

Davidson, W.H., and McFetridge, D.G., 1984. "Recent Directions in International Strategies: Product Rationalization or Portfolio Adjustment," *Columbia Journal of World Business.* 19(2):95–101.

Davies, Howard, 1977. "Technology Transfer through Commercial Transactions," *Journal of Industrial Economics.* 26(2):161–175.

Davis, Stanley M., 1976. "Trends in the Organization of Multinational Organizations," *Columbia Journal of World Business.* 11(2):59–71.

Davis, S., and Lawrence, P.R., 1978. "Problems of Matrix Organizations," *Harvard Business Review.* 56(3):131–142.

De Houghton, C., 1967. *Crosschannel Collaboration.* London: PEP.

Delaney, Douglas W., 1982. "A Canadian Experience in Joint Ventures," *Canadian Business Review.* 9(2):27–29.

"Detroit's Latest Foreign Flirtation," 1980. *Business Week.* July 28: 48–50.

Dixon, Paul Rand, 1962. "Joint Ventures: What Is Their Impact on Competition?," *Antitrust Bulletin.* 7(3):397–410.

Dolan, Carrie, 1984. "Tektronix New-Venture Subsidiary Bring Benefits to Parents, Spinoffs," *Wall Street Journal.* September 18: 37.

Dovey, B.H., 1975. "Open Marriage—Corporate Style," *Proceedings*, American Marketing Association. 37:23–26.

"Dow Jones & Co. and Extel Corp. Have Increased Their Ownership in Teleprinter Leasing Corp. to 50% Each," 1976. *Wall Street Journal.* September 9: 4.

Drazin, Robert, and Kazanjian, Robert, 1983. "Strategy Implementation: Organizing for Internal Diversification." Paper presented at Business Policy and Planning Division, Dallas, National Academy of Management.

"Dropouts Rock Energy Ventures," 1982. *Chemical Week.* 130(9):16–17.

Drucker, Peter, 1974. *Management: Tasks, Responsibilities, Promises.* New York: Harper & Row.

"A Drug Giant Catapults into the U.S. Market," 1979. *Business Week.* October 22: 86.

Duncan, Jerome L., Jr., 1980. "The Causes and Effects of Domestic Joint Venture Activity," Ph.D. diss., University of Florida.

———, 1982. "Impacts of New Entry and Horizontal Joint Ventures on Industrial Rates of Return," *Review of Economics and Statistics.* 64:120–125.

Dunning, J.H., 1958. *American Investment in British Manufacturing.* London: Allen & Unwin.

Dymsza, William A., 1972. *Multinational Business Strategy.* New York: McGraw-Hill.

"Easing the Antitrust to R&D Alliances," 1983. *Business Week.* June 4: 29.

Eaton, B.C., and Lipsey, R.G., 1979. "Theory of Marketing Preemption: Barriers to Entry in a Growing Spatial Market," *Economica.* 46:149–158.

Eaton, Frederick M., 1952. "Joint Ventures," *Antitrust Law Symposium*, 4th Annual Meeting, Antitrust Law Division, New York, New York State Bar Association.

Edstrom, Anders, 1975a. "Acquisition and Joint Venture Behavior of Swedish Manufacturing Firms." Working paper, University of Gothenburg.

——— , 1975b. "The Stability of Joint Ventures." Working paper, University of Gothenburg.

Egelhoff, W.G., 1980. "Matrix Strategies and Structures in Multinational Corporations." Paper presented at Academy of International Business and Management, New Orleans.

Emmett, Ralph, 1977. "U.K. Software Group Aims at U.S. Market," *Datamation.* 23(9):273–275.

"An Era of International Expansion for the Banks," 1977. *The Banker* (United Kingdom). 127(612):36–38.

Erdahl, L.O., 1974. "Economic Aspects of Joint Ventures," *Mining Congress Journal.* 60:24–261.

Ethyl Gasoline Corp. v. United States, 309 U.S. 436, 453 (1940).

"Europe: A Challenge to the U.S. in Aerospace," 1978. *Business Week.* June 5: 64.

"Europe: A Helicopter Quartet Takes On the U.S.," 1975. *Business Week.* October 6: 41–42.

Evan, William M., 1965. "Toward a Theory of Inter-Organizational Relations," *Management Science.* 11:B217–B230.

Evan, William M., and Klemm, R. Christopher, 1980. "Interorganizational Relations among Hospitals," *Human Relations.* 33(5):315–337.

Ewing, K.P., Jr., 1981. "Joint Research, Antitrust, and Innovation." *Research Management.* 24(2):25–29.

"Executives Support Large Mergers to Counter Foreign Competition," 1984. *Wall Street Journal.* March 9: 36.

Fellner, W.J., 1949. *Competitive among the Few.* New York: Knopf.

Ferguson, Roger W., Jr., 1981. "The Nature of Joint Ventures in the American Manufacturing Sector," Ph.D. diss., Harvard University.

Festetics, P., 1974. "Strategic Considerations for Foreign Bank Expansion," *Columbia Journal of World Business.* 9(4):81.

"Fiat-Allis, the Joint Venture of Fiat (Italy) and Allis-Chalmers (US), Has Thus Far Not Been Successful," 1980. *Financial Times.* October 30: 33.

"Fiat SPA (Turin, Italy) and Kloeckner-Humboldt-Deutz AG (Cologne, W. Germany) Have Agreed to Unite Their Commercial Vehicle Production in a New Unit," *Wall Street Journal.* July 12: 14.

Field, P., and Reimnitz, J., 1978. "Foreign Banks in New York. Biting into the Big Apple," *Euromoney.* June: 49.

Filley, A.C., House, R.J., and Kerre, S., 1976. *Managerial Process and Organizational Behavior.* Glenview, Ill.: Scott, Foresman.

"Financing Joint Ventures and Making Everyone Happy," 1980. *World Business Weekly* (United Kingdom). 3(27):20–21.

Flaim, Theresa Ann, 1977. "Structure of the U.S. Petroleum Industry: Concentration, Vertical Integration and Joint Ventures," Ph.D. diss., Cornell University.

—— , 1979. "The Structure of the U.S. Petroleum Industry: Joint Activities and Affiliations," *Antitrust Bulletin*. 24(3):555–572.

Flick, Sol E., 1972. "The Human Side of Overseas Joint Ventures," *Management Review*. 61(1):29.

"Foreign Equity, Technical Fee and Royalty Pattern," 1982. *Economic Review*. 13(2):14–24.

Foster, Richard N., 1983. "To Exploit New Technology, Know When to Junk the Old," *Wall Street Journal*. May 2: 36.

Fouraker, Lawrence E., and Siegal, Sidney, 1963. *Bargaining Behavior*. New York: McGraw-Hill.

"Four JVs: Dow Corning, Titanium Metals Corp., Georgia Kraft and Ketchikan Pulp," 1975. *Fortune*. 91(6):120–141.

Foster, Geoffrey, 1973. "The Joint-Venture Gambit." *Management Today*. February: 75.

Franko, L.G., 1971a. "Joint Venture Divorce in the Multinational Company," *Columbia Journal of World Business*. 6(2):13–22.

—— , 1971b. *Joint Venture Survival in Multinational Corporations*. New York: Praeger.

—— , 1976. *The European Multinationals*. London: Harper & Row.

"Free-World Partners Plan Jets for the 1980's," 1976. *Business Week*. August 30: 64, 66.

Friedman, P., Berg, S.V., and Duncan, J., 1979. "External vs. Internal Knowledge Acquisition: JV Activity and R&D Intensity," *Journal of Economics and Business*. 31(2):103–110.

Friedman, Wolfgang, 1972. "The Contractual Joint-Venture," *Columbia Journal of World Business*. 7(1):57.

Friedman, W., and Beguin, W., 1971. *Joint Ventures in Developing Countries*. New York: Columbia University Press.

Friedman, W., and Kalmanoff, G., 1961. *Joint International Business Ventures*. New York: Columbia University Press.

Fusfeld, Daniel R., 1958. "Joint Subsidiaries in the Iron and Steel Industry," *American Economic Review* 48:578–587.

Gabriel, Peter P., 1967. *International Transfer of Corporate Skills*. Boston: Harvard Business School, Division of Research.

Galbraith, J.R., 1971. "Matrix Organization Designs—How to Combine Functional and Project Form," *Business Horizons*. 14(1):29–40.

Gesell, Gerhard A., 1965. "Joint Ventures in Light of Recent Antitrust Developments," *Antitrust Bulletin*. 10(1&2):31–40.

Ghemawat, Pankaj, 1982. "The Experience Curve and Corporate Strategy," Ph.D. diss., Harvard Business School.

Gilpin, Robert, 1975. "An Alternative Strategy to Foreign Investment," *Challenge*. 18(5):12–19.

Ginsburg, Douglas H., 1979. "Antitrust, Uncertainty, and Technological Innovation," *Antitrust Bulletin*. 24(4):635–686.

Gold, B., 1975. "Alternate Strategies for Advancing a Company's Technology," *Research Management.* 18:24–29.

Goldberg, Ray A., 1972. "Profitable Partnerships—Industry and Farmer Co-Ops," *Harvard Business Review.* 50(2):108.

Gottschalk, Earl C., Jr., 1984. "Allied Unit, Free of Red Tape, Seeks to Develop Orphan Technologies," *Wall Street Journal.* September 13: 36.

Grau, F.C., 1975. "Accounting for Real Estate Joint Ventures," *Management Accounting.* 6(57):15–20.

Greer, D.F., 1971. "Product Differentiation and Concentration in the Brewing Industry," *Journal of Industrial Economics.* 19:201–219.

Gregory, G., 1976. "Japan's New Multinationalism: The Canon Giessen Experience," *Columbia Journal of World Business.* 11(1):122–129.

"Ground Rules for Joint R&D Efforts Outlined," 1975. *Chemical and Engineering News.* 53(1):11.

Guetzkow, Harold, 1966. "Relations among Organizations." In Bowers, R., *Studies on Behavior in Organizations.* Athens, Ga.: University of Georgia Press.

Gullander, Stefan, O.O., 1975. "An Exploratory Study of Inter-Firm Cooperation of Swedish Firms," Ph.D. diss., Columbia University.

———, 1976a. "Joint-Ventures and Corporate-Strategy," *Columbia Journal of World Business.* 11(1):104–114.

———, 1976b. "Joint-Ventures in Europe—Determinants of Entry," *International Studies of Management and Organization.* 6(1&2):85–111.

Hale, G.E., 1956. "Joint Ventures: Collaborative Subsidiaries and the Antitrust Laws," *Virginia Law Review.* 142:927–938.

Hall, William, 1981. "Consortium Banks Adapt to a New Environment," *The Banker* (United Kingdom). 131(669):135–139, 197–205.

Halverson, James T., 1984. "Transnational Joint Ventures and Mergers under U.S. Antitrust Law," in *Proceedings: Fordham Corporate Law Institute.* New York: Bender.

Hambrick, Donald C., and Mason, Phyllis A., 1982. "Upper Echelons: The Organization as a Reflection of Its Top Managers," *Academy of Management Review.* 9(2):193–206.

Handler, Milton, 1982. "Reforming the Antitrust Laws," *Columbia Law Review.* 82(7):1288–1364.

Hardman, R., 1976. "Cross-Border Mergers Don't Make Sense—Yet," *Vision.* 72: 47–48.

Harrigan, Kathryn Rudie, 1980a. *Strategies for Declining Businesses.* Lexington, Mass.: Lexington Books.

———, 1980b. "The Effect of Exit Barriers upon Strategic Flexibility," *Strategic Management Journal.* 1(2):165–176.

———, 1981. "Deterrents to Divestiture," *Academy of Management Journal.* 24(2): 306–323.

———, 1982. "Exit Decisions in Mature Industries," *Academy of Management Journal.* 25(4):707–732.

———, 1983a. "Exit Barriers and Vertical Integration," in Chung, Kae, ed., *Proceedings*, Dallas, Academy of Management National Conference.

———, 1983b. "Research Methodologies for Contingency Approaches to Business Strategy," *Academy of Management Review.* 8(3):399–405.

———, 1983c. *Strategies for Vertical Integration.* Lexington, Mass.: Lexington Books.

———, 1984a. "Coalition Strategies: A Framework for Joint Ventures," working paper, Columbia University.

———, 1984b. "Innovations by Overseas Subsidiaries," *Journal of Business Strategy.* 5:7–16.

———, 1984c. "Integrating Parent and Child: Successful Joint Ventures," working paper, Columbia University.

———, 1984d. "Joint Ventures and Competitive Strategy," working paper, Columbia University.

———, 1984e. "Joint Ventures and Global Strategies," *Columbia Journal of World Business.* 19(2):7–17.

———, 1985a. "Exit Barriers and Vertical Integration," *Academy of Management Journal.* 28(4): forthcoming.

———, 1985b. *Strategic Flexibility: A Management Guide for Changing Times.* Lexington, Mass.: Lexington Books.

———, 1985c. "Vertical Integration and Corporate Strategy," *Academy of Management Journal.* 28(2): forthcoming.

———, 1986. *Managing for Joint Venture Success.* Lexington, Mass. Lexington Books.

Hartx, C.D., 1974. "A Business Trip to Eastern Europe: Joint Ventures and Practical Lessons," *Business Economics.* 9(4):34–40.

Harvard, Robert E., 1982. "Is Industry's R&D Effort Handcuffed by Antitrust?," *Iron Age.* 225(5):45–49.

Hayashi, K., 1975. "Japanese Ownership Policies in Multinational Business," *Proceedings*, National Academy of Management Conference, 261–263.

Henshaw, P.C., 1970. "Joint Venture Exploration," *Mining Congress Journal.* 56: 57–59.

"Here Come Foreign Banks Again," 1978. *Business Week.* June 26: 78.

Hergert, Michael L., 1983. "The Incidence and Implications of Strategy Grouping in U.S. Manufacturing Industries," Ph.D. diss., Harvard Business School.

Hills, S.M., 1978. "The Search for Joint Venture Partners," *Proceedings*, San Francisco, National Academy of Management Conference, 277–281.

Hlavacek, J.D., 1974. "Alternatives in Venture Management," *Combined Proceedings*, American Marketing Association. 36:481–482.

———, 1975. "Experiences from Domestic Joint Venturing," *Combined Proceedings*, American Marketing Association. 37:19.

Hlavacek, J.D., Dovey, B.H., and Biondo, J.J., 1977. "Tie Small Business Technology to Marketing Power," *Harvard Business Review.* 55(1):106–116.

Hlavacek, James D., and Thompson, Victor A., 1976. "The Joint-Venture Approach to Technology Utilization," *IEEE Transactions on Engineering Management.* VEM-23(1):35–41.

Hout, Thomas M., 1984. "Trade Barriers Won't Keep Out Japan," *New York Times.* April 29:B2.

Hout, Thomas, Porter, Michael E., and Rudden, Eileen, 1982. "How Global Companies Win Out," *Harvard Business Review.* 60(5):98–108.

"How Overseas Investors Are Helping to Reindustrialize America," 1984. *Business Week*. May 10: 103–104.

Hughey, Ann, and Kanabayashi, Masayoshi, 1983. "More U.S. and Japanese Companies Decide to Operate Joint Ventures," *Wall Street Journal*. May 10: 33.

Hunker, Jeffrey Allen, 1982. "Structural Change in the U.S. Automobile Industry, 1980–1995," Ph.D. diss., Harvard Business School.

Hunt, Michael S., 1972. "Competition in the Home Appliance Industry, 1960–1970," Ph.D. diss., Harvard University.

Hunter, Robert N., and Page, James G., 1974. "Joint Ventures—A Three-Way Marriage," *Mortgage Banker*. 34(8):38–41.

Hymer, Stephan H., 1960. "The International Operations of National Firms," Ph.D. diss., Massachusetts Institute of Technology.

Hymer, Stephan, and Pashigian, Peter, 1962. "Firm Size and Rate of Growth," *Journal of Political Economy*. 70:556–569.

"ICL Turns to Fujitsu for Help," 1981. *Business Week*. October 26: 130.

Ijiri, Y., and Simon, H.A., 1964. "Business Growth and Firm Size," *American Economic Review*. 54:77–89.

Inbar, M., 1972. *Simulation and Gaming in Social Science*. New York: Free Press.

"Industry Sources Foresee a Shakeup at CML Satellite Corp. between Cash-Rich Comsat and Its Domsat Partners, MCI and Lockheed," *Electronics*. March 7: 26.

"Industry's Problem Children," 1964. *Business Week*. October 24: 51–55.

"Investment Vehicle for Mortgage Banker—Joint Ventures," 1972. *National Real Estate Investor*. 14(10):55.

Jaeger, Walter H.E, 1960. "Joint Ventures: Membership, Types, and Termination," *American University Law Review*. 9(2):111–129.

———, 1960. "Joint Ventures: Origin, Nature and Development." *American University Law Review*. 9(1):1–23.

"Japan Is Buying Its Way into U.S. University Labs," 1984. *Business Week*. September 24: 72–77.

Johnson, Bob, and Batt, Robert, 1981. "The Japanese-American Connection." *Computerworld*. 15(32):59–60, 62.

Johnson, R.T., 1977. "Success and Failure of Japanese Subsidiaries in America," *Columbia Journal of World Business*. 12(1):30.

Johnson, Richard T., and Ouchi, William G., 1974. "Made in America (under Japanese Management)," *Harvard Business Review*. 52(5):108–125.

Johnson, Steven, 1973. "An Accounting System for Joint Ventures," *Management Accounting*. 10(54):37–38.

"Joint Banking Ventures Flourish," 1975. *Banker*. 125(589):291–295.

"A Joint VCR Venture to Deter the Japanese," 1981. *Business Week*. June 1: 45–46.

"Joint Venture Corporations: Drafting the Corporate Papers," 1964. *Harvard Law Review*. 393:130.

"Joint Venture Problems in Japan," 1979. *Columbia Journal of World Business*. 14(1):25–31.

"Joint Ventures: A Matrix for Beginners," 1978. *Institutional Investor*. 8(2):31.

"Joint Ventures and Cooperation Agreements, 1966–1984," *Mergers and Acquisitions*. Listings 1–18.

"Joint Ventures and Section 7 of the Clayton Act," 1962. *Stanford Law Review*. 14:777–799.

"Joint Ventures: How to Make Them Work (Panel Discussion)," 1972. *DE Journal*. 219:B27–B28.

"Joint Ventures: Justice Becomes a Cheerleader," 1984. *Business Week*. November 19: 48–49.

"Joint Ventures Likely in Chemicals," 1976. *Purchasing*. 80:24.

"Joint Ventures with Foreign Companies Can Preserve Market Position in Import-Plagued Areas," 1980. *Industry Week*. April 28: 69–72.

Justman, Moshe, 1982. "Dynamic Demand Functions: Some Implications for the Theory of Firm and Industry Organization," Ph.D. diss., Harvard Business School.

Kaczynski, Vladimir, and Levieil, Dominique, 1981. "International Joint Ventures in World Fisheries," *Journal of Contemporary Business*. 10(1):75–89.

Kahn, Alfred E., 1971. *The Economics of Regulation: Principles and Institutions*. New York: Wiley.

Karlin, Beth, and Anders, George, 1983. "Europe Looks Abroad for High Technology It Lags in Developing," *Wall Street Journal*. October 5: 1, 25.

Keller, R.T., Slocum, John W., Jr., and Susman, Gerald I., 1974. "Uncertainty and Type of Management System in Continuous Process Organizations," *Academy of Management Journal*. 17(1):56–68.

Kelly, Joseph, 1980. "The Japanese Challenge," *Dun's Review*. 116(2):80, 86.

Killing, J. Peter, 1980. "Technology Acquisition: License Agreement or Joint Venture," *Columbia Journal of World Business*. 15(3):38–46.

——— , 1982. "How to Make a Global Joint Venture Work," *Harvard Business Review*. 60(3):120–127.

——— , 1983. *Strategies for Joint Venture Success*. New York: Praeger.

Knight, K.E., 1967. "Descriptive Model of the Intra-Firm Innovation Process," *Journal of Business*. 40:478–496.

Kocan, P., 1962. "Reporting the Operation of Jointly Owned Companies," *Journal of Accounting* 7:3–24.

"Korean Surge Heightens Interest in Capital Goods, Joint-Ventures," 1976. *Commerce Today*. 1(73):29–30.

Kraar, L., 1977. "General Dynamics Struggles to Build a Plane for All Nations," *Fortune*. 95(3):180–192.

Krause, Kenneth R., 1973. "Joint Ventures and Family Labor Sized Farms," *American Journal of Agricultural Economics*. 11:35.

Krosin, Kenneth E., 1971. "Joint Research Ventures under the Antitrust Laws," *George Washington Law Review*. 39(5):1112–1140.

Kydland, F.E., 1977. "Equilibrium Solutions in Dynamic Dominant Player Models," *Journal of Economic Theory*. 15(2):130–136.

Leff, N.H., 1974. "International Sourcing Strategy," *Columbia Journal of World Business*. 9(3):71.

Leonard, William N., 1976. "Mergers, Industrial Concentration, and Antitrust Policy," *Journal of Economic Issues*. 10(2):354–381.

Levine, S., and White, Paul B., 1963. "Community Interorganizational Problems in Providing Medical Care," *American Journal of Public Health*. 53:1183–1195.

Levine, S., and White, P.E., 1961. "Exchange as a Conceptual Framework for the Study of Interorganizational Relationships," *Administrative Science Quarterly.* 5:583–601.

"Limit on Liability of Research Ventures Cleared by Congress," 1984. *Wall Street Journal.* October 3: 47.

Litwak, Eugene, and Hylton, Lydia F., 1962. "Interorganizational Analysis: A Hypothesis on Coordinating Agencies," *Administrative Science Quarterly.* 6:395–420.

Litwak, Eugene, and Rothman, Jack, 1970. "Towards the Theory and Practice of Coordination between Formal Organizations," in Rosengren, B., *Organizations and Clients.* Columbus, Ohio: Merrill.

Lockwood, R., 1975. "One Approach to Affiliation of U.S./Japanese Enterprise," *American Chamber of Commerce in Japan.* 12(3):7.

Lohr, Steve, 1983. "A Second Look at 'Kanban,' " *New York Times.* February 27: 14.

——— , 1984. "The Japanese Challenge: Can They Achieve Technological Supremacy?," *New York Times.* July 8: 18–23, 39, 41.

"Lotus Links Up with Toyota," 1981. *World Business.* 4(26):25.

Louis, Martin B., 1980. "Restraints Ancillary to Joint Ventures and Licensing Agreements," *Virginia Law Review.* 66(5):879–916.

Luce, R.D., 1957. *Games and Decisions.* New York: Wiley.

"Lucky-Goldstar: Using Joint Ventures to Sprint Ahead in the High-Tech Race," *Business Week.* July 9: 102–103.

McCarthy, J.E., 1976. "The Germans, The Dutch, The Japanese, The French, The Swiss, The Canadians, The British Are Coming," *Across the Board.* 13(12): 21.

"McDonnell-Douglas and Fokker Take Off on a Mid-Size Jet Project," 1981. *World Business Weekly* (United Kingdom). 4(20):23–24.

McKie, J.W., 1955. "The Decline of Monopoly in the Metal Container Industry," *American Economic Review.* 45:499–508.

McLellan, Vin, 1979. "SBS Partnership May Be Doomed," *Datamation.* 25(1):90, 101, 104.

MacMillan, Ian C., 1980. "How Business Strategies Can Use Guerilla Warfare Tactics," *Journal of Business Strategy.* 1(2):63–85.

——— , 1982. "Seizing Competitive Initiative," *Journal of Business Strategy.* 2(4): 43–57.

——— , 1983. "Preemptive Strategies," *Journal of Business Strategy.* 4(2):16–26.

"Made in USA or Japan?," 1970. *Industry Week.* December 21:26–31.

Mandarino, Ralph J., 1977. "Joint Venture Accounting," *Financial Executive.* 11(45): 24–31.

Mann, Richard A., and Roberts, Barry S., 1979. "When the Corporate Form Doesn't Make Cents," *Journal of Small Business Management.* 17(2):47–52.

Mansfield, E., 1962. "Entry, Gibrat's Law, Innovation and the Growth of Firms," *American Economic Review.* 52:1023–1051.

——— , 1968. *Industrial Research and Technological Innovation.* New York: Norton.

March, J.G., 1962. "The Business Firm as a Political Coalition," *Journal of Politics.* 24:662–678.

March, J.G., and Simon, H.S., 1958. *Organizations.* New York: Wiley.

Mariti, P., and Smiley, R.H., 1983. "Cooperative Agreements and the Organization of Industry," *Journal of Industrial Economics*. 21(4):437–452.

Markham, Jesse W., 1970. "Competitive Effects of Joint Bidding by Oil Co.'s for Offshore Oil Leases," in Markham, J., *Industrial Organization and Economic Development*. Boston: Houghton Mifflin.

Marquis, Harold L., 1964. "Compatibility of Industrial Joint Research Ventures and Antitrust Policy," *Temple Law Quarterly*. 38(1):1–37.

Martini, T., and Berman, J., 1957. "Expansion via Joint Subsidiaries," *Mergers and Acquisitions*. 83, 86–87.

Mead, W.J., 1967. "Competitive Significance of Joint Ventures," *Antitrust Bulletin*. 12:819–849.

Meehan, James W., 1970. "Joint Venture Entry in Perspective," *Antitrust Bulletin*. 15:693–711.

Meeker, Guy B., 1971. "Fade Out Joint Venture: Can It Work for Latin America?," *Inter-American Economic Affairs*. 24:25–42.

Menge, J.A., 1962. "Style Change Costs as a Market Weapon," *Quarterly Journal of Economics*. 76:632–647.

Merrifield, D. Bruce, 1983. "Forces of Change Affecting High Technology Industries," *National Journal*. January 29: 253–256.

Miller, Lawrence E., 1974. "Multinational Intercompany Agreements," *Business Lawyer*. 29(2):431–441.

"More U.S. and Japanese Companies Decide to Operate Joint Ventures," 1983. *Wall Street Journal*. May 10: 33.

Moskowitz, Daniel B., 1984. "Antitrusters Are Updating the 'Failing Company' Doctrine," *Business Week*. April 9: 31.

Myers, Summer, and Marquis, Donald G., 1969. *Successful Industrial Innovation*. Washington, D.C.: National Science.

Nash, J.F., 1950. "The Bargaining Problem," *Econometrica*. 18:155–162.

Nelson, R., and Winter, S., 1975. "Factor Price Changes and Factor Substitution in an Evolutionary Model," *Bell Journal of Economics*. 6(2):466–486.

"The New Economics of World Steelmaking," 1974. *Business Week*. August 3: 34–39.

"A New Era in Aerospace Joint Ventures. American Scorn Turns into an Urge to Join," *Multinational Business*. 2:1.

Newman, H.H., 1973. "Strategic Groups and Structure-Performance Relationship: Study with Respect to the Chemical Processing Industry," Ph.D. diss., Harvard University.

"A New Weapon against Japan: R&D Partnerships," 1983. *Business Week*, August 8: 42.

Nichols, Henry W., 1950. "Joint Ventures," *Virginia Law Review*. 36:425–459.

Nielson, C.C., 1965. "Reporting Joint Venture Corporation," *Accounting Review*. October: 795–804.

Nierenberg, Gerard I., 1968. *The Art of Negotiating*. New York: Hawthorne.

"Nord Strikes It Rich on Other People's Money," 1978. *Business Week*. June 12: 100.

Norris, William C., 1983. "How to Expand R&D Cooperation," *Business Week*. April 14: 21.

Ornstein, S.I., Weston, J.F, Intriligator, M.D., and Shrieves, R.E., 1973. "Determinant of Market Structure," *Southern Economic Journal*. 39:612–625.

Orski, C. Kenneth, 1980. "The World Automotive Industry at a Crossroads: Co-operative Alliances," *Vital Speeches*. 47(3):89–93.

Osborne, D.K., 1976. "Cartel Problems," *American Economic Review*. 66:835–844.

Ostrow, Joseph, 1977. "Marketing—Why Ad Agencies Should Enter into More Joint Ventures," *Media Decisions*. 12(5):80–82.

Palmer, Bruce, 1974. "Successful Data-Processing Co-ops Is Founded in Progressive Management," *Magazine of Bank Administration*. 51(4):37–39.

Pate, J.L., 1969. "Joint Venture Activity, 1960–1968," *Economic Review*. Federal Research Bank of Cleveland: 16–23.

Paul, Lois, 1981. "Joint Venture Tests Home Banking Waters," *Computerworld*. 15(11):34, 36.

Pavlista, S., 1981. "Turning 18 Firms into One That Works," *Venture*. 3(5):62–63.

Pearce, John A., and DeNisi, Angelo S., 1984. "Attribution Theory and Strategic Decision Making: An Application to Coalition Formation," *Academy of Management Journal*. 26(1):119–128.

Pennings, Johannes, 1981a. "Strategically Interdependent Organizations," in Nystrom, P.C. and Starbuck, W.H., *Handbook of Organizational Design* (vol. 1). New York: Oxford University Press.

———, 1981b. "Interlocking Directorates and Interfirm Coordination: Some Unresolved Issues and Answers," working paper, Columbia University.

"The Perils of Joint Ventures Have Not Deterred Their Growth," 1982. *Business Week*. April 26: 100.

Peterson, R.B., and Shimada, J.Y., 1978. "Sources of Management Problems in Japanese-American Joint Ventures," *Academy of Management Review*. 3(4): 796–804.

Peterson, Richard B., and Schwind, Hermann F., 1975. "Personnel Problems in International Companies and Joint Ventures in Japan," *Proceedings*, National Academy of Management Conference, 282–284.

Pfeffer, Jeffrey, 1972. "Merger as a Response to Organizational Interdependence," *Administrative Science Quarterly*. 17:382–394.

Pfeffer, Jeffrey, and Nowak, Phillip, 1976a. "Joint Ventures and Interorganizational Interdependence," *Administrative Science Quarterly*. 21(3):398–418.

———, 1976b. "Patterns of Joint-Venture Activity—Implications for Antitrust Policy," *Antitrust Bulletin*. 21(2):315–339.

Pfeffer, Jeffrey, and Salancik, Gerald, R., 1978. *External Control of Organizations: A Resource Dependence Perspective*. New York: Harper & Row.

Phillips, C.F., 1963. *Competition in the Synthetic Rubber Industry*. Winston-Salem: University of North Carolina Press.

Pitofsky, Robert, 1969. "Joint Ventures under the Antitrust Laws: Some Reflections on the Significance of Interfirm Cooperation," *Harvard Law Review*. 82:1007.

Pitts, Robert A., and Daniels, John D., 1984. "Aftermath of the Matrix Mania," *Columbia Journal of World Business*. 29(2):48–55.

Porter, Michael E., 1976a. *Interbrand Choice, Strategy, and Bilateral Market Power*. Cambridge, Mass.: Harvard University Press.

———, 1976b. "Please Note Location of Nearest Exit: Exit Barriers and Strategic and Organizational Planning," *California Management Review*. 19(2):21–33.

———, 1979. "The Structure within Industries and Companies' Performance," *Review of Economics and Statistics.* 61:214–227.

———, 1980. *Competitive Strategy: Techniques for Analyzing Industries and Competitors.* New York: Free Press.

———, 1985a. *Competitive Advantage: Creating and Sustaining Superior Performance.* New York: Free Press.

——— (ed.), 1985b. *Competition in Global Industries.* Cambridge, Mass.: Harvard Graduate School of Business Administration.

Porter, Michael E., and Spence, A. Michael, 1982. "The Capacity Expansion Process and Oligopoly: The Case of Corn Wet Milling," in McCall, J.J. (ed.), 1982, *The Economics of Information and Uncertainty* (Chicago: University of Chicago Press).

"Public Policy Issues Involved in Joint Venture in American Industry," 1979. *Mergers and Acquisitions.* 13(4):18–29.

Rand Corporation, 1984. "Management of Large, Joint and Remote Projects: Research Prospectus," Santa Monica, Calif.: Rand Corporation.

Raser, J., 1969. *Simulation and Society: An Exploration for Scientific Gaming.* Boston: Allyn & Bacon.

Reid, W., 1964. "Interagency Coordination in Delinquency Prevention and Control," *Social Service Review.* 38:418–428.

———, 1971. *Interorganizational Coordination: A Review and Critique of Current Theory.* Washington, D.C.: U.S. Department of Health, Education & Welfare.

Reklau, David L., 1977. "Accounting for Investments in Joint Ventures—A Reexamination," *Journal of Accountancy.* 3(144):96–103.

"Renault: Why the French Carmaker Needs the Linkup as Much as AMC," 1978. *Business Week.* June 19: 114–115.

Renforth, W., 1975. "International Joint Venture Operating and Performance Characteristics." *Proceedings*, National Academy of Management Conference, 249–251.

"Revising Laws to Encourage Investment," 1981. *World Business.* 4(26):7–8.

Reynolds, John I., 1984. "The 'Pinched Shoe' Effect of International Joint Ventures," *Columbia Journal of World Business.* 19(2):23–29.

Rhoades, Stephen A., 1977. "Sharing Arrangements in an Electronic Funds Transfer System," *Journal of Bank Research.* 8(1):8–15.

Roberts, Edward B., 1980. "New Ventures for Corporate Growth," *Harvard Business Review.* 58(4):134–142.

Robinson, Richard D., 1969. "Ownership across National Frontiers," *Industrial Management Review.* Fall: 41–62.

Rockwood, Alan, 1983. "The Impact of Joint Ventures on the Market for OCS Oil," *Journal of Industrial Economics.* 21(4):452–468.

Rosenthal, Edmond M., 1982. "Risk-Sharing Key Factor as Joint Ventures Multiply," *Cable Age.* March 18: 21–29.

Rothwell, R., 1975. "From Invention to New Business via the New Venture Approach," *Management Decision.* 13(1):10–21.

Roulac, S.E., 1980. "Structuring the Joint Venture," *Mergers and Acquisitions.* 15(1):4–14.

Rowe, Frederick M., 1980. "Antitrust Aspects of European Acquisitions and Joint Ventures in the U.S.," *Law and Policy in International Business.* 2(2):335–368.

Sayles, Leonard R., and Chandler, Margaret K., 1971. *Managing Large Systems.* New York: Harper & Row.

Schelling, Thomas C., 1956. "An Essay on Bargaining," *American Economic Review.* 46:281–306.

——— , 1960. *Strategy of Conflict.* Cambridge, Mass.: Harvard University Press.

Scherer, F.M., 1965. "Firm Size, Market Structure, Opportunity, and the Output of Patented Inventions," *American Economic Review.* 55:1097–1125.

——— , 1967. "Research and Development Resource under Rivalry," *Quarterly Journal of Economics.* 81:359–394.

——— , 1979. "The Causes and Consequences of Rising Industrial Concentration: A Comment," *Journal of Law and Economics.* 22:191–208.

Scherer, F.M., Beckenstein, A., Kaufer, E., and Murphy, R.D., 1975. *The Economics of Multi-Plant Operation: An International Comparisons Study.* Cambridge, Mass.: Harvard University Press.

Schermerhorn, John R., Jr., 1974. "Determinants of Cooperative Interorganizational Relations: Notes Toward a Framework for Interfirm Cooperation," in Grun, T.B., and Roy, D.F. (eds.) *Proceedings*, Boston: National Academy of Management Conference.

——— , 1975. "Determinants of Interorganizational Cooperation," *Academy of Management Journal.* 18:846–956.

——— , 1976. "Openness to Interorganizational Cooperation: A Study of Hospital Administrators," *Academy of Management Journal.* 19:225–236.

——— , 1977. "Information Sharing as an Interorganizational Activity," *Academy of Management Journal.* 20:148–153.

——— , 1979. "Interorganizational Development," *Journal of Management.* 5:21–38.

——— , 1980. "Inter-Firm Cooperation as a Resource for Small Business Development," *Journal of Small Business Management.* 18:48–54.

——— , 1981. "Open Questions Limiting the Practice of Interorganizational Development," *Group and Organization Studies.* 6:83–95.

Schermerhorn, John R., Jr., Fottler, Myron, Wong, John, and Money, William H., 1982. "Multi-Institutional Arrangements in Health Care: Review, Analysis and a Proposal," *Academy of Management Review.* 7:67–79.

Schwartz, David S., 1975. "Comments on Market-Structure and Interfirm Integration," *Journal of Economic Issues.* 9(2):337–340.

Sczudlo, Raymond S., 1981. "Antitrust Aspects of Shared EFT Systems," *Journal of Retail Banking.* 3(3):2–30.

Seki, Hoken S., 1977. "The Justice Department's New Antitrust Guide for International Operations," *Business Lawyer.* 32(4):1633–1656.

Shaw, R., 1975. "Joint Venturing a Service: How and Why Dow Jones and Bunker Ramo Combined," *Proceedings*, American Marketing Association. 37:20–22.

Shepherd, William G., 1979. *Economics of Industrial Organization.* Englewood Cliffs, N.J.: Prentice-Hall.

Sheridan, J.H., 1975. "Is Antitrust Sinking U.S. Trade Effort," *Industry Week.* 185(8):23–26.

Shetty, Y.K., 1979. "Managing the Multinational Corporation: European and American Styles," *Management International Review.* 19(3):39–48.

Siegal, Sidney, and Fouraker, Lawrence E., 1960. *Bargaining and Group Decision Making.* New York: McGraw-Hill.

"Siemens Buys Its Way into U.S. Expertise," 1977. *Business Week.* October 17: 42.

Solo, N., 1951. "Innovation in the Capitalist Process: A Critique of the Schumpeterian Theory," *Quarterly Journal of Economics.* 65: 417.

Spence, A. Michael, 1978. "Tacit Collusion and Imperfect Information," *Canadian Journal of Economics.* 11:490–505.

———, 1979. "Investment Strategy and Growth in a New Market," *Bell Journal of Economics.* 10(1):1–19.

———, 1981. "The Learning Curve and Competition," *Bell Journal of Economics.* 12(1):49–70.

Starkweather, David B., 1972. "Beyond the Semantics of Multihospital Aggregations," *Health Services Research.* 7:58–61.

Stigler, George J., 1974. "Free Riders and Collective Action—An Appendix to Theories of Economic Regulation," *Bell Journal of Economics.* 5(2):359–365.

Stockton, William, 1981. "The Technology Race," *New York Times.* June 28: 14–19, 49–54.

Stopford, J.M., and Haberich, K.O., 1976. "Ownership and Control of Foreign Operations," *Journal of General Management.* 3(3):3–20.

"Structure Joint Ventures Carefully to Avoid Future Problems," 1980. *Mergers and Acquisitions.* 14(1):4–14.

Stuckey, John Alan, 1982. "Vertical Integration and Joint Ventures in the International Aluminum Industry," Ph.D. diss. Harvard Business School.

"Suddenly U.S. Companies Are Teaming Up," 1983. *Business Week,* July 11: 71–74.

Sullivan, Jeremiah, Peterson, Richard B., Kameda, Kaoki, and Shimada, Justine, 1981. "The Relationship between Conflict Resolution Approaches and Trust," *Academy of Management Journal.* 24(4):803–815.

"Surprise Get-Together for Two Old Rivals," 1977. "Business Week. June 6: 41–42.

"Sweden: Why a Joint Venture Came Unstuck," 1977. *Business Week.* April 28: 36.

Tagliabue, John, 1984. "The New Phillips Strategy," *New York Times.* January 15: B1, B5.

Taubman, Joseph, 1959. "Pools, Combinations, Conspiracies and Joint Ventures," *Antitrust Bulletin.* 4: 341, 372.

———, 1964. "Pensalt and Entertainment Pepper," *Antitrust Bulletin.* 9(5&6): 813–819.

Taylor, Robert E., 1983. "White House Offers Bill to Spur Investment in Research by Lowering Antitrust Risks," *Wall Street Journal.* September 9: 8.

———, 1984. "Joint Ventures Likely to Be Encouraged by Friendlier Attitude of U.S. Officials," *Wall Street Journal,* Nov. 5: 8.

"Technology Acquisition: License Agreement or Joint Venture?" 1980. *Columbia Journal of World Business.* 15(3).

Telser, L.G., 1972. *Competition Collusion and Game Theory.* New York: Aldine-Atherton.

Tennant, R.B., 1950. *The American Cigarette Industry.* New Haven: Yale University Press.

Thompson, James D., and McEwen, William J., 1958. "Organizational Goals and Environment: Goal-Setting as an Interaction Process," *American Sociological Review*. 23:2–31.

Thompson, Richard J., 1970. "Competitive Effects of Joint Ventures in the Chemical Industry," Ph.D. diss., Amherst, University of Massachusetts.

Tractenberg, Paul, 1963. "Joint Ventures on the Domestic Front: A Study in Uncertainty," *Antitrust Bulletin*. 9(3):797–841.

Treeck, Joachim, 1970. "Joint Research Ventures and Antitrust Law in the U.S., Germany and the European Common Market," *Journal of Law and Politics*. 3(1):18–55.

"TRW: Fujitsu's Key to the U.S.," 1980. *Business Week*. May 19: 118–123.

"TRW-Fujitsu's Plan to Blitz the U.S.," 1981. *Business Week*. March 16: 124D, 124I.

Turner, Donald F., 1965. "Conglomerate Mergers and Section 7 of the Clayton Act," *Harvard Law Review*. 78:1125–1300.

———, 1980. "An Antitrust Analysis of Joint Ventures," unpublished manuscript of Counsel Wilmer & Pickering, Washington, D.C.

Tushman, Michael, and Romanelli, Elaine, 1985. "Organizational Evolution: A Metamorphosis Model of Convergence and Reorientation," *Research in Organizational Behavior*, vol. 7. Greenwich, Conn.: JAI.

Twiss, Brian, 1974. *Managing Technological Innovation*. London: Longman.

U.S. Department of Justice, Antitrust Division, 1981. "Antitrust Guide for Joint Research Programs," *Research Management*. 24(2):30–37.

Uyterhoeven, Hugo, 1963. "Foreign Entry and Joint Ventures," Ph.D. diss., Harvard University.

Van Dam, Andre, 1975. "Joint Planning for an Interdependent World," *Optimum*. 6(4):51–59.

Vanderman, George A., 1968. "The Joint Venture Meets Section 7 of the Clayton Act," *Southern California Law Review*. 38:104–124.

Van de Ven, A.H., 1976. "On the Nature, Formation and Maintenance of Relations among Organizations," *Academy of Management Review*. 1:24–36.

"Venturing Abroad," 1979. *The Banker*. 129(640):23–24.

Verespe, Michael A., 1977. "Joint-Ventures—Marriages of Necessity," *Industry Week*. 194(3):P34–P37.

Vernon, Raymond, 1966. "International Investment and International Trade in the Product Cycle," *Quarterly Journal of Economics*. 53(2):191–207.

———, 1971. *Sovereignty at Bay: The Multinational Spread of U.S. Enterprise*. New York: Basic.

———, 1972. *The Economic Environment of International Business*. Englewood Cliffs, N.J.: Prentice-Hall.

———, 1977. *Storm over the Multinationals*. Cambridge, Mass.: Harvard University Press.

Vernon, Raymond, and Wells, Louis T., Jr., 1976. *Manager in the International Economy*. Englewood Cliffs, N.J.: Prentice-Hall.

Vesper, Karl H., 1980. *New Venture Strategies*. Englewood Cliffs, N.J.: Prentice-Hall.

Vitrovich, Nicholas, 1983. "How Companies Learn to Love Their Competitors," *Wall Street Journal* (Europe). March 15: 23.

Walton, R., 1972. "Interorganizational Decision Making and Identity Conflict," in Tuite, M., Chisholm, R., and Radnor, M., *Interorganizational Decision Making*. Chicago: Aldine, 9–19.

Warren, Roland L., 1967. "The Interorganizational Field as a Focus for Investigation," *Administrative Science Quarterly*. 12:396–419.

———, 1972. *The Concerting of Decisions as a Variable in Organizational Interaction*. Chicago: Aldine-Atherton.

Wasson, Chester R., 1974. *Dynamic Competitive Strategy and Product Life Cycles*. St. Charles, Ill.: Challenge Books.

Weinstein, Arnold K., 1977. "Foreign Investments by Service Firms," *Journal of International Business Studies*. 8(1):83–91.

Weiss, Leonard W., 1963. "Factors in Changing Concentration," *Review of Economics and Statistics*. 45:70–77.

Wells, John R., 1984. "In Search of Synergy: Strategies for Related Diversification," Ph.D. diss., Harvard University.

"West Germany—A Rush to Ensure Access to U.S. Coal," 1981. *Business Week*. July 20: 10.

West, Malcolm W., Jr., 1959. "The Jointly-Owned Subsidiary," *Harvard Business Review* 37(3):32.

"When Joint Ventures Come Unglued," 1982. *Business Week*. April 26: 100.

Whetten, D.A., 1977. "Toward a Contingency Model for Designing Interorganizational Service Delivery," *Organization and Administrative Sciences*. 8:77–96.

Whitt, John D., 1974. "Planning Joint-Venture of the Multi-National Firm," *Managerial Planning*. 23(1):22–36.

Who Owns Whom: North American, 16th ed., 1984. London: Dun & Bradstreet.

Wilcox, Susan M., 1975. "Joint Venture Bidding and Entry in the Market for Offshore Petroleum Leases," Ph.D. diss., University of California, Santa Barbara.

Williams, Winston, 1984. "Japanese Investment, A New Worry," *New York Times*. May 6: 1, 23.

Williamson, Oliver E., 1975. *Markets and Hierarchies: Analysis and Antitrust Implications*. New York: Free Press.

Will the Leading Engine Makers Team Up for the Midsize Jet," *World Business Weekly* (United Kingdom). 4(37):22–23.

Wilson, Howard M., 1965. "Smaller Oil Firms Pool Efforts to Gain Bigger Role in the Gulf," *Oil and Gas Journal*. 63:81.

Wilson, John W., 1975. "Market Structure and Interfirm Integration in the Petroleum Industry," *Journal of Economic Issues*. 9(2):319–336.

Wilson, T.A., 1975. "To Maintain the Aerospace Industry's Economic Health," *Vital Speeches of the Day*. 41(22):685–689.

Winter, S.G., 1971. "Satisficing Selection and the Innovating Remnant," *Quarterly Journal of Economics*. 85:237–261.

Wiseman, Charles, 1984. "Gaining Competitive Advantage: How to Use Joint Ventures to Leverage Information System Assets," New York: Competitive Applications.

Worenklein, Jacob J., 1981. "Profect Financing of Joint Ventures," *Public Utilities Fortnightly*. 108(1 & 2):39–46.

"World Roundup. A Rolls-Royce and Pratt & Whitney Joint Venture," 1976. *Business Week*. May 24: 49.

Wren, D.A., 1967. "Interface and Interorganizational Coordination," *Academy of Management Journal.* 10:6981.

Wright, R.W., 1979a. "Canadian Joint Ventures in Japan," *Business Quarterly.* 42(3):42–53.

———, 1979b. "Joint Ventures Problems in Japan," *Columbia Journal of World Business.* 14(1):25–31.

Wright, Richard W., and Russel, Colin S., 1975. "Joint-Ventures in Developing Countries—Realities and Responses," *Columbia Journal of World Business.* 10(3):74–80.

Young, G., and Bradford, Standish, Jr., 1976. "Joint Ventures in Europe—Determinants of Entry," *International Studies of Management & Organizations.* 6(1 & 2):85–111.

———, 1977. *Joint Ventures: Planning and Action.* New York: Arthur D. Little and the Financial Executives Research Foundation.

Company Index

General Index

About the Author

Kathryn Rudie Harrigan (D.B.A., Harvard; M.B.A., Texas; B.A., Macalester) is an associate professor of strategic management at the Columbia Business School in New York City. Her research interests include industry and competitor analysis, strategic management, turnaround management, competitive dynamics, global strategies, and business-government relationships. Her books, *Strategies for Declining Businesses* (1980), *Strategies for Vertical Integration* (1983), *Strategies for Joint Ventures*, *Strategic Flexibility: A Management Guide for Changing Times* (1985), and *Managing for Joint Venture Success* (1986), are published by Lexington Books.

Professor Harrigan received the General Electric Award for Outstanding Research in Strategic Management, presented by the Business Policy and Planning Division of the National Academy of Management, for her research on declining businesses, and their Best Paper Award in 1983 for her research on vertical integration (or make-or-buy decisions). She also won an IBM Research Fellowship in Business Administration and a Division of Research Fellowship at Harvard Business School, during her doctoral studies.

Professor Harrigan's consulting experience includes work on competitive strategy and strategic management for both private and public organizations. She has acted as consultant to strategic consulting firms, as well. She is a founding member of the Strategic Management Society and appears each autumn on their international programs.

Professor Harrigan writes for and serves on the board of editors of the *Academy of Management Journal*, the *Strategic Management Journal*, and the *Journal of Business Strategy*. She is an ad hoc reviewer for and frequent contributor to the *Academy of Management Review*. Her articles have also appeared in the *Harvard Business Review, Long Range Planning, Boardroom Reports, Executive Woman,* and the *Proceedings* of the National and Regional Meetings of the Academy of Management.